FORENSIC ARTS
THERAPIES

ANTHOLOGY OF PRACTICE AND RESEARCH

EDITED BY
KATE ROTHWELL

FREE ASSOCIATION BOOKS

First published in 2016 by
Free Publishing Limited

English language Copyright © 2016 Kate Rothwell

A CIP Catalogue of this book is available from
the British Library

ISBN: 978-1-8534321-9-4

Typeset in Fairfield 10½pt by
www.chandlerbookdesign.co.uk

Printed and bound in Great Britain by
4edge Limited

CONTENTS

ENDORSEMENTS

'Forensic Arts Therapies is a comprehensive and much needed book for the arts therapies and the forensic services. It documents a range of approaches, which are beneficial to these populations'.

Professor Helen Payne, PhD; Fellow ADMP UK; UKCP Reg.

This anthology provides an excellent practice and research-based insight into the work arts therapists undertake in their everyday practice with some of the most complex offender patients in the UK. As a senior manager within the forensic directorate of the East London Foundation Trust, where Art, Drama and Music therapists are an integral part of clinical provision, I am aware of the benefits that arts therapies has for inpatients with enduring mental health needs and personality disorders; particularly for those service users who are unable to make use of talking therapies, who routinely engage in behaviours that are destructive of themselves and others and who therefore tend to have the longest lengths of stay in secure services. For a significant group of inpatients Arts Therapies is the most effective form of intervention, providing service users with the knowledge, tools and creative insight to map a route to recovery. This anthology makes a clear and coherent case for the quality, value and effectiveness of arts therapies, and the importance of embedding these modalities in service design and delivery through well-considered interventions from acute admissions through to recovery.

John Wilson. Associate Director. Head of Therapy Services, Clinical Performance & Quality. East London NHS Foundation Trust | Forensic Directorate

'this is an interesting and thoughtful book written by highly skilled, creative therapists working with a complex group of people. It is a timely and valuable contribution to the literature.'

Tessa Dalley. Art psychotherapist, Consultant Child and Adolescent Psychotherapist

This book is well overdue but the chapters evidence an authority in sensitive, creative and adaptive arts and psychotherapeutic approaches to the needs of an extremely complex patient group unable to access talking therapies. In this era in which CRES drives austerity in the NHS and prison service, the rigorous and in-depth thinking in this volume will enable practitioners to get creative and achieve clinical progression in offenders patients who would otherwise be stuck in the system.

Estela Welldon. MD DSc (Hon) F.R.C.Psych.BPCHon. Memb. A.Psa.A.

Founder & Honorary Life President. International Association for Forensic Psychotherapy Author of : Playing with Dynamite and 'Mother, Madonna, Whore'.

Emerging out of the collaborative and collective work undertaken by members of Forensic Arts Therapies Advisory Group (FATAG) over many years, this anthology marks a welcome and important addition to the relatively sparse literature on the contribution made by the arts therapies to forensic psychiatry and psychotherapy.

Written with compassion, commitment and honesty, and with a clear focus on client work, *Forensic Arts Therapies* offers unique insights into this specialist area of arts therapy practice and is a must read for anyone interested in the therapeutic potential of the arts in forensic settings such as prisons, young offender institutions and secure hospitals.

As a clinician and a reader, I particularly appreciated the emphasis placed on the story-telling nature of the therapeutic encounter, be this visually, verbally, through play, dance or other forms of enactment, in so many of the chapters in the is book.

David Edwards, Clinical Manager, Share Psychotherapy, Sheffield.

Every change of mind is a creative act. It is for this reason, among many others, that the arts therapies are crucial for the practice of forensic psychiatry. This book is a rich and thought provoking collection of papers that lucidly and cogently set out how arts therapies can bring about change in disabled and dangerous people. It was a pleasure to read this book which, in addition to clear prose, contains powerful images of artworks generated in therapy.

Dr Gwen Adshead. Consultant Forensic Psychiatrist and Psychotherapist. Southern Health Foundation Trust

"This collection of clinical and research-based stories from the front line of forensic art therapy is testament to the rigour and bravery of its authors. It is essential reading for all who are interested in creativity, the challenges of forensic work and the human condition."

Dr Alan Corbett. Author, "Disabling Perversions: Forensic Psychotherapy with People with Intellectual Disabilities"

This anthology brings together the evidence base ,therapeutic skills and creativity of the Arts Therapies as applied to the challenging arena of forensic practice . So often the Arts Therapies are the key that unlocks an understanding of troubled minds enabling individuals to find a new way of seeing and being in their lives. A fascinating read for all those working in forensics services

Professor Dame Sue Bailey

This Anthology shares a rich variety of work within a range of forensic services, and conveys the vitality and importance of the arts therapies within both mental health and prison settings. It provides a rich opportunity to gain insights into the work of practitioners who make up the FATAG community, where experienced practitioner accounts are offered alongside a number of chapters featuring emerging work with newly developed services. The Anthology is particularly pertinent at this time of extreme pressure to many of these services, which are threatened by funding and staffing cuts. The Anthology evidences the value of the arts therapies work in supporting client's well-being and working towards recovery and healthy future living.

This unprecedented Anthology is a vital read to practitioners and trainees across the Arts Therapies, as well as to members of multi-disciplinary teams and commissioners of services.

The accounts of practice in this Anthology illuminate a wealth of experience of cross discipline co-working alliances within teams of Arts Therapists in various settings. The interventions described in this collection of chapters demonstrates how people held in secure settings can engage in forms of therapy other than talking therapies, which enables self-expression in a meaningful way, through engagement with the arts process.

The accounts in this Anthology present the journeys of patients, inmates and service users with sensitivity and humanness, often acknowledging the experiences of mental distress and illness within the client population. The practitioners' capacity to engage with their clients through the container of creative expression enables distressing stories of perpetration to be explored with trust and openness. At the same time the work holds in mind with sensitivity, the ripple effect of primary victims and all those impacted by the actions of these real life narratives. The strength of the 'life-drama' connections is a key aspect in many of these chapters. These connections support clients in transforming their lives towards a safer and healthier future.

This Anthology of work highlights what is needed for practitioners to keep safe and exercise self-care in their practice, through their connectedness as a community of peers of co-therapists and multi-disciplinary-team colleagues.

Dr Emma Ramsden (former Head of Arts Therapies at Broadmoor Hospital)

This book demonstrates the extraordinary resilience, skill and compassion of arts therapists working in forensic setting. It provides rigorous evidence of the effectivity of arts therapies interventions and is a significant contribution to the literature in the field.

Anna Seymour PhD PFHEA, University of Roehampton , London, Editor Dramatherapy, Journal of the British Association of Dramatherapists

The word Anthology denotes both a collection and a selection of literary 'flowers': this fascinating album gathers and weaves and displays a diverse and many-coloured tapestry of narrative and testimony from the myriad multi-disciplinary practices that have developed or are emerging within the field of arts therapies, as it intersects and cross-pollinates with other modalities for the treatment of forensic patients in secure settings.

The reader is invited into a kaleidoscopic, kinetic, multi-modal experience - here is music, images, sculpture, architecture, choreography, theatre and film, as well as speech and prose and poetry - here are individual and group therapies and interventions in the therapeutic milieu - here is humour and fear; suffering and resilience; chaos and mastery. Throughout this anthology, the reader will encounter the distinctive voices of both patients and clinicians as they dance back and forth across the contested, often terrifying, liminal territories of the imagination that lie between playing and reality.

John Adlam

- Consultant Adult Forensic Psychotherapist, Bethlem Royal Hospital

- Formerly Vice-President of the International Association for Forensic Psychotherapy

- Co-editor of The Therapeutic Milieu Under Fire: Security and Insecurity in Forensic Mental Health and Forensic Music Therapy, both published in 2012 by Jessica Kingsley Publishers

I am delighted to read and endorse this welcome and timely anthology of the varied and consolidated contributions that the Arts Therapies have made in the field of forensic services over the years. It presents us with a rich and valuable testimony to the dynamic and diverse treatments offered by the Arts Therapies in what can be experienced as traumatic and painful processes of healing for patients and practitioners.

Celebrating the uniqueness of each of the Arts Therapies, as well as the potency and strengths of different Arts Therapies when brought together, each chapter in this anthology clearly demonstrates the effectiveness of clinical practice while also giving valuable insight into the theories underpinning the work undertaken – from Dance Movement to Story Telling in recovering personal stories; the use of poetry; Symbolic Crime Sandplay Therapy to the use of Masks and the visibility of invisible characters; the efficacy of Art Therapy images in Anger Management; Lacan's Mirror Stage and the use of film and camera in clinical Dramatherapy practice – to name but a few.

I believe this anthology will be a valuable and significant contribution to practitioners and will have an important place in any library.

Bruce Howard Bayley, Ph.D.

"In creating a book that demonstrates the expertise of all of the arts therapies (Art, Music, Drama and Dance Movement), Rothwell and the FATAG show how their service users and teams have benefitted from their sustained commitment to collaborative working and careful thinking across modalities. This integrated text is timely, it models to arts therapists the strength created and benefits from working together, and writing together more."

Stephen Sandford, Music Therapist
Strategic Lead & Professional Head of Arts Therapies
East London NHS Foundation Trust

This book makes engaging and vital reading for anyone who aspires to work in forensic treatment. It is about real clinical work by experienced clinicians who wholly embrace their specialism of working in secure treatment settings with men and women who have committed serious offences.

The authors explain how underlying psychological theories and concepts make sense of clinical presentation, with important reference to the great names in the field of forensic psychotherapy, in particular Dr Estela Welldon.

The range of treatment choices covers inter- disciplinary work between arts therapists of different modalities:(e.g chapter 1 drama and art therapy, chapter 19 music and art therapy.

A broad range of topics are covered throughout this book, including anger management in art therapy, gender specific aspects, marginal gains philosophy and story making structures in art therapy,

Notable are Emma Allen's interesting and thoughtful chapter on the importance of symbolism in Sandplay as part of an arson treatment programme. This describes how the patient gained understanding of himself with reference to his index offence.

This chapter is followed by Dr Hackett's fascinating art therapy research project on the treatment of autism, exploring components that created therapeutic change with a reduction of perverse nightmares. The author helpfully links this to specific art psychotherapy processes.

The book continues with chapters in the use of animation as a medium, followed by Kate Rothwell's thoughtful chapter on the value of understanding the patient's experiences in group art therapy for those suffering with learning disability.

Other aspects covered include Dance therapy and an illuminating description of the trainee's experience. The penultimate chapter by the arts therapies team at Broadmoor hospital describes a live multi- media project which was a hugely creative, collaborative and interactive project using all the arts therapies mediums to demonstrate what we as arts therapists actually do in helping patients to diffuse potentially explosive internal material.

The final chapter is a welcome chapter from the Netherlands, which highlights how previously hidden aspects of the patient are revealed in art therapy. This balances the United Kingdom contributions with a European perspective.

All in all, this book is a testimony to the immense value of the Forensic Arts Therapies Advisory Group (FATAG) and the support and continuous professional development that thus organisation continues to provide for practising clinicians.

Dr Stella Compton Dickinson,
Fellow and Member of The Institute of Mental health, Nottingham.
Affiliate of the Healthcare Economics Department, Institute of
Psychiatry, Psychology and Neuroscience.

Head of Arts Therapies, Clinical Research Lead 2001 to 2013:
Nottinghamshire healthcare NHS Trust forensic services.

This exciting body of work reveals the intense, rich and crucial work of the arts therapies in forensic populations. This rich anthology, skilfully edited by Kate Rothwell celebrates the achievements of arts therapists in engaging with some of the most violent, disturbed and traumatised individuals in society. This is a remarkable collection, carefully and vividly describing a range of arts therapies, from dance movement therapy with violent women, to drama therapy with a mixed sex group, music and art therapy with deeply disturbed and frightening patients. All the authors are highly skilled arts therapists, well aware of their own emotional responses in these intimate and intense encounters with offender patients, both male and female in mental health settings and prisons. Most significantly this book describes the possibilities for change in these patients through their engagement with arts therapies. The courage of those practitioners, and of the patients, in their exploration of their offences, their traumatic histories and their fears of being with one another, is beautifully described throughout. The authors demonstrate the power of their work, and persistence of their engagement with this most damaging and damaged population, bringing theory alive with their vivid and moving clinical illustrations. The power of creativity, within the safe space of an arts therapy encounter, to transform even the most brutal experiences, and to contain primitive emotional states is repeatedly shown through these closely observed descriptions of the work. This valuable text will offer hope to all practitioners working within forensic settings when faced with patients whose pain is too raw and brutal to put into words.

> **Dr.Anna Motz. Consultant Forensic and Clinical Psychologist and Forensic Psychotherapist, Past President of the International Association for Forensic Psychotherapy.**

"While the art therapies in the forensic arenas is still relatively new in the United States, with intermittent publications and presentations covering this wide and vast focus, the United Kingdom has been more proactive and forward thinking in its work for forensic clients, for far longer. Rothwell's text is a clear reflection of this. *Forensic Arts Therapies: Anthology of Practice and Research* is an extensive and impressive collection of conference presentations from--and inspired by-- the Forensic Art Therapies Advisory Group. It marvelously removes all territoriality of professional identities and theoretical orientations to explore the many contributors' work with some of the most difficult, disenfranchised and marginalized populations.

This book is simultaneously wide and deep in its scope, lyrical and clinical in its presentation. Through its combination of illustrative narratives and deeply explored theoretical and research positions, it provides an extremely valuable reference for those new to the arena and those immersed in it for decades, on both sides of the pond."

David E. Gussak, PhD, ATR-BC, Department Chair/Professor, Florida State University; author of *Art on Trial: Art Therapy in Capital Murder Cases*, and co-editor for *Drawing Time: Art Therapy in Prisons and other Correctional Settings* and *The Wiley Handbook of Art Therapy*

This far-reaching book is a timely and important reminder of the powerful role of arts therapies in addressing serious offending. The inner worlds of those who have committed harrowing crimes can be inaccessible, even – perhaps especially – to themselves, repressed and disavowed as too painful and too terrifying to be encountered directly. Through a series of in-depth case studies the authors illustrate how such anxieties can be processed and explored, by engaging with a safe and creative medium. A broad range of chapters allows the therapeutic application of the visual image – including film – drama, dance and music to be chronicled in depth. Again and again, I was struck by the courage showed by both patient and therapist in confronting disturbing and dangerous material of the mind. Arts therapists often work in relative isolation, within secure settings whose culture can be inherently oppositional to the therapeutic task. Both they and other practitioners in the field will find in this book a rewarding source of professional learning, wisdom and community.

Dr. Celia Taylor. Lead Clinician, Millfields medium secure personality disorder unit.

FOREWORD

Forensic Arts Therapies: Anthology of practice and research

COLIN TEASDALE[1]

t is a privilege for me to be able to recommend this timely publication to readers, practitioners and researchers. The arts therapies have pioneered and consolidated treatment, rehabilitation and relapse prevention inputs to United Kingdom (UK) forensic services for more than four decades, since UK Health & Care Professions Council (HCPC) regulated postgraduate training and placements, and nationally registered by law employment opportunities were introduced.

Whilst my forensic work experience is not contemporary, I am well placed to set this book in a historical context:

The field of forensic arts therapies practice and research is dynamic and diverse, as the enclosed chapters testify. Time-limited and longer-term inputs focus on work with: both male and female and young and adult offenders detained in prisons; patients detained in secure health care units for their own and public protection; probation and counselling services as alternatives to or following detention; mediation and victim support; and other areas of advice and liaison connected with understanding the causes and effects of crime, improving wellbeing and reducing risk and recidivism.

The therapies described are, by associating with matters that are malevolent and disturbing, not easy or comfortable interventions.

---

1 Editor, *Guidelines for Arts Therapists Working in Prisons* (First Edition 1997, Revised Edition 2002)

Nonetheless, they are often rewarding for all. With respect to creating more benign outcomes, groundbreaking developments in art therapy, dance movement therapy, dramatherapy and music therapy have run parallel to pioneering work in the fields of forensic psychology and psychotherapy (Cordess & Cox (eds) 1996) which have been influential.

The chapters in this anthology examine why the work has not been without huge hurdles to overcome at empirical, theoretical, financial and professionally resourceful levels. But to their credit, the arts therapies have always been flexible, reflective and passionately committed to harnessing and learning from such material that by nature is controversial, questioning and never easily resolvable - providing useful additions rather than alternatives to forensic treatment programmes.

Forensic arts therapists are either full or part-time employed on fixed-term or permanent contracts as lone specialists, although teamwork has been possible in larger institutions. Crime isolates and often has toxic impacts, and understanding and managing primary and secondary effects can also be isolating but inherent in improving wellbeing and damage limitation. Cordess (1996) for example, spoke about the value of "distributive transference" (p.97) (see Teasdale 1997) in changing offending attitudes and behaviour through treatment whilst supporting the practitioner. He defined this as promoting "… a sharing of the transferential burden, which allows a team - when it works well – to be a greater support and help to some patients than any one individual therapist".

Appreciating the benefits of the collective approaches as outlined above, a way of countering the overt and covert effects of working in isolation was harnessed early on in the development of forensic arts therapies in the UK (Teasdale 1999). In the late 1980s, a national colleague support group was founded by the Association of Dance Movement Therapy (ADMT), the Association of Professional Music Therapists (APMT), the British Association of Arts Therapists (BAAT) and British Association for Dramatherapists (BADTh), in association with HM Prison Service, and then the National Health Service (NHS). This became the Forensic Arts Therapies Advisory Group, (FATAG) that has sustained the test of time to annually organise the dissemination and examination of connected material through seminars, literature and peer dialogue that has been crucial to the conception of this publication. There appears to be no comparable collective service development to date internationally, although this may change in due course.

Many thanks must go to all the colleagues and sponsors, too numerous to mention, without whom forensic arts therapies service development, delivery and networking would not have been possible. Additionally, many thanks must go to the service users, their families and their carers, who have committed themselves to engaging with treatment towards encouraging the pooling knowledge to make this anthology comprehensive.

REFERENCES

Cordess, C. & Cox, M. (eds), (1996) **Forensic Psychotherapy: Crime, Psychodynamics and the Offender Patient,** Vol. 1: Mainly Theory and Vol. 2: Mainly Practice, Jessica Kingsley Publishers: London, Bristol, Pennsylvania.

Cordess, C. (1996), **Introduction: The Multidisciplinary Team**, In **Forensic Psychotherapy: Crime, Psychodynamics and the Offender Patient**, Vol. 2: Mainly Practice, Jessica Kingsley Publishers: London, Bristol, Pennsylvania, pp 97 – 99.

Teasdale. C. (1997), **Art Therapy as a Shared Forensic Investigation,** *Inscape: Journal of the British Association of Art Therapists,* Vol. 2, No. 2, pp. 32 - 40.

Teasdale. C. (ed), (1997), **Guidelines for Art Therapists working in Prisons**, *Home Office: HM Prison Service for England & Wales,* first edition.

Teasdale, C. (1999), **Developing Principles and Policies for Arts Therapists working in United Kingdom Prisons**, *International Arts in Psychotherapy Journal*, Pergamon Press: Elsevier Science Ltd, Volume 26, No. 4, pp. 265 - 270.

Teasdale. C. (ed), (2002), **Guidelines for Art Therapists working in Prisons**, *Home Office: HM Prison Service for England & Wales,* revised edition.

INTRODUCTION

Forensic Arts Therapies: An anthology of practice and research

t is now over thirteen years since the establishment of the Forensic Arts Therapies Advisory Group (and its earlier form: The Arts Therapies Advisory Group to the Standing Committee to the Arts in Prisons). FATAG's 34th conference was held this year at The House of Lords.

The idea of this book started as a collection of presentations from FATAG conferences but has grown to include case studies, research, new developments in theory and explorations into the practice of forensic arts therapies, namely art, drama, music and dance. This book brings together a collection of chapters from FATAG conferences and miscellaneous papers inspired by arts therapists who have attended the conferences and want to share their work and experiences as if 'amongst friends'. FATAG conferences provide a supportive space to share very difficult, complex and, at times, painful work not easily shared amongst a non-forensic audience. FATAG provides that thoughtful, nurturing and enquiring platform.

Its necessary to recognise what is different about forensic arts therapies work and that in many cases the work inherently feels unsafe and sometimes is unsafe, emotionally and physically, for service users and staff. The fact that forensic arts therapists work in unsafe environments, with people who act out through dangerous behaviour, itself suggests the work is not safe. This alone shapes the work of a forensic clinician. By recognising this though, Trades Descriptions expectations and HCPC guidance professionals would be protected from making potentially misleading efficacy claims that cannot be validated unless clearly researched.

Forensic arts therapists all have the aim and objective of trying to provide 'safer' space in terms of therapy i.e. safer than what may have been experienced previously, and 'supportive' space, in terms of supervision and professional development. Inevitably we can only judge that it felt safe, and was safe, in hindsight bearing in mind that many do feel terrified and / or let down by therapy and supervision that did not feel safe, despite best intentions. It's necessary to encourage all to consider this can happen and is possibly where the FATAG conferences have their most significance in learning from hindsight and remaining connected to the ever-present dangers of the work.

The impact that these conferences have on the working lives of arts therapists practicing in prisons and other secure settings is important to acknowledge. Without this, many arts therapists would lack what has become a vital and creative arena for sharing skills and ideas about best practice and for gaining support. With the focus on the extensive range of clinical initiatives used when working with offender patients and prisoners, qualified clinicians and trainees have come together over the years to hear about each other's triumphs and tribulations, inviting presentations from arts therapists in all four modalities as well as speakers from other related professions such as psychoanalysis, psychology and psychotherapy.

The history of FATAG began in the early 1990s. A number of arts therapists had become concerned at the problems faced by their colleagues who worked in prisons and, in particular, experienced incidents of stress-related illness. At the same time, several initiatives to promote the use of the arts within prisons led to the establishment of the Arts in Prisons Working Party set up under the auspices of the Home Office. From 1993, an arts therapies subgroup of this working party met regularly with representatives from our professional associations. Its aims were to promote the safe and effective use of the arts therapies in prisons; to develop a dialogue with the prison education and healthcare services; to provide guidelines and information on the arts therapies; and to seek recognition for our professional status and qualifications. The driving force behind this was an art therapist called Colin Teasdale who was secretary to this group and to its successor, the Art Therapies Advisory Group to the Standing Committee on the Arts in Prisons. (See Foreword)

The work of this group culminated in three main achievements, all of which were aimed at protecting and providing for prisoners and the arts therapists employed to work with them. Firstly, the provision of seminar days or conferences; secondly, the production of the Guidelines for Arts Therapists Working in Prisons (edited by Colin Teasdale 1997); and thirdly, the endorsement of our recommendations about employment conditions as set out in the Prison Service Instruction' to Governors (No. 43/1998). For a more detailed account of the history of the group see: Teasdale, C. 1999 *'Developing Principles and Policies for Arts Therapists Working in United Kingdom Prisons'*. The Arts in Psychotherapy, Vol.26, No. 4 pp265-270.

The Arts Therapies Advisory Group (to the Committee) was superseded by FATAG in 1998 to more broadly incorporate, represent, and support forensic work within the NHS and other areas of service provision as well as through the Home Office.

In its new form, FATAG now caters more directly for people who work in Secure Hospitals; mental health and challenging behaviour secure units in the NHS and in the independent sector; in probation settings as well as prisons. FATAG is a non-profit making charity with funding received solely from conference fees. FATAG remains the only group of special interest not supported by the four professional bodies, yet incorporates all four modalities, seeing this as a strength and representative of arts therapies team working in secure settings. This emphasises the importance of collaborative teamwork rather than separate entities vying to establish an identity, and accurately mirrors the multidisciplinary element of the combined agencies in forensic teamwork.

The consistent high quality of the conference presentations and discussions is evidenced by substantial delegate attendance and in the content of these chapters, however it is necessary that the support continues and grows given the devastation of many London and regional based arts therapies departments over recent years.

The future of FATAG over the next ten years is uncertain given ongoing NHS cuts under the recession and impending privatisation, but it is hoped that therapists are encouraged to take up research in this specialist area to explore their practice in other creative ways. It is also hoped this book will clarify the role of arts therapists who work in forensic settings and thereby create a more formal network in order to disseminate ideas and developments in practice to a wider audience.

In these chapters there is a clear voice of authority and experience within the writing that confirms the confidence now evident in the work. There is a maturity in practice that has grown since FATAG started, and an identity formed over the years that has given shape to a group of arts therapists who work in the field of forensic psychological therapies.

Kate Rothwell
Current FATAG Convener

BIOGRAPHIES

Our contributors

Mario Guarnieri is a dramatherapist, psychoanalytic psychotherapist and clinical supervisor. His work settings have included Broadmoor Hospital, Ealing Forensic Services and Croydon Personality Disorder Services. He is currently in full-time freelance and private practice.

Sydney Klugman trained as an Art Psychotherapist at Goldsmith. His interests have largely been in forensic settings, which have included Broadmoor High Security and The Priory Medium and low Secure Unit. He also runs a private practice offering clinical and supervisory work.

Sydney also works as an artist having had many exhibitions over the years.

Emma Allen is a HCPC Registered Art Psychotherapist and a Sandplay Therapist in Advanced Training. Emma has been training with the British and Irish Sandplay Society (BISS) in London for the last five years and is currently working towards international registration with ISST (the International Society for Sandplay).Emma has over ten years' experience of working in a variety of NHS settings, and has been working at Rampton Hospital, one of the three high secure hospitals in the UK since 2009. Emma is the 'Therapies and Education Arson Representative' as part of an Arson Treatment Expert Group at Rampton Hospital and has designed a formalised arts therapies arson assessment and treatment programme that has been offered in both Rampton Hospital and The Wells Road Centre, a low secure unit in Nottinghamshire. Emma has presented her arson and sandplay work and ideas at the IAFP (International Association of Forensic Psychotherapy) Conference in Utrecht, the Netherlands, in 2014, and at a FATAG Conference in 2015 entitled; *"Opening Up to Emotionality: Symbolic Exploration of Archetypal Defences in Forensic Sandplay Therapy"*. Emma's work aims to highlight the differences between Art Therapy and Sandplay Therapy and assist other arts therapists in utilising a symbolic approach to forensic psychotherapy.

Diane Parker is a therapeutic coach practitioner and dance movement psychotherapist currently working in private practice, community mental health and forensic settings. She was awarded her master's degree in Dance Movement Psychotherapy from Goldsmith's University in London in 2014. She is a member of the Association for Dance Movement Psychotherapy and the Forensic Arts Therapies Advisory Group.

Martina Mindang is an Art Psychotherapist, BAAT and HCPC registered, and clinical supervisor. She has practiced within adult mental health (NHS) services since 1996 in areas of community care, acute admissions as well as high secure hospital care. Martina has a clinical interest in forensic art psychotherapy and recovery from violence using creative approaches. She is also a part- time lecturer on the MA Art Psychotherapy Programme at Roehampton University, London.

Marian Liebmann has worked in art therapy with offenders, women's groups, community groups, and most recently in the Inner City Mental Health Team in Bristol , UK , where she developed work on anger issues, and work with asylum seekers and refugees. She lectures on art therapy at several universities in the UK and Europe . She also works in restorative justice, mediation and conflict resolution, and has run workshops on art, conflict and anger in many countries. She has written/edited ten books, most recently *Art Therapy and Anger* (2008). In 2010 she was awarded her PhD by publications from Bristol University , and in 2013 she was awarded an OBE for services to art therapy and mediation.

Alex Maguire is a Forensic Music Therapist in the NHS, specialising in working with Intensive Care and medication-resistant patients. He is additionally an improvising jazz musician composing, recording and performing worldwide. He has presented his work at numerous conferences and has written for a range of journals and publications.

Angeles Fiallo Montero is registered Dance Movement Psychotherapist, private practitioner and creative dance facilitator. Born in Buenos Aires, Argentina and then move to the UK in 2004. Angeles trained and undertook her Master's studies on Dance Movement Psychotherapy at Dance Voice (Bristol) and Canterbury Christ Church University. Her MA dissertation looked into how Dance Movement psychotherapy can benefit young people in prison. This study was presented FATAG Conference 2011 and International IAFP Conference (International Association for Forensic Psychotherapy), Venice 2012.

Angeles has been practising as a DMP since 2009. She has a wide range of experience working with children, adolescents and adults, including learning and physical disabilities, mental health issues, youth offending and challenging behaviour. Angeles is currently employed as a Dance Movement Psychotherapist at CAMHS (Weston Area Health Trust), Dance Voice and a residential school, facilitating both group and individual sessions. She specialised mainly in children and young people.

Originally trained in ballet, but then discovered there was world outside the stylised movement. Throughout the years Angeles has learnt and perform different dance forms, she is particularly drawn to Afro and Brazilian and dance styles. Angeles believes everyone can dance, regardless of their abilities or experience and as part of her profession, she enables others to express themselves through dance.

Eleonora Rudolf Orlowska is a Registered Dance Movement Psychotherapist with experience of working with trauma in adults and young people . She has provided dance movement psychotherapy in adult mental health and forensic settings in the NHS and in schools. Eleonora has an interest in research regarding creativity and embodiment in relationships, and in group processes pertaining to organizations.

Kate Rothwell, Head of Arts Therapies (ELFT) and Art Psychotherapist at H.M.P Grendon, Kate is HCPC/UKCP State Registered with over 25 years experience working in forensic settings. Currently FATAG convener and previous senior lecturer on the MA Art Therapy training at the University of Hertfordshire, she now has tenure with Derby University on the MA Art Therapy course and a private practice working clinically with children, adolescents and adults. Kate supervises arts therapists across a range of services and is a published author.

Jessica Collier works for East London NHS Foundation Trust as an art psychotherapist and small group facilitator at an adapted therapeutic community for male offenders with severe personality disorder. She also works for Central and North West London NHS Foundation Trust as an art psychotherapist and clinical supervisor working with female offenders in prison. She is a visiting lecturer on the Art Therapy MA at the University of Hertfordshire.

Dr Simon Hackett is an Art Psychotherapist working at Northumberland Tyne and Wear NHS Foundation Trust and Associate Clinical Researcher in arts therapies at the Institute of Health and Society, Newcastle University.

Deryk Thomas is a BAAT/HCPC registered Art Psychotherapist working at Broadmoor High Security Hospital (West London Mental Health NHS Trust) and HMP Grendon, Therapeutic Community Prison. He has for a long time worked with forensic populations in high, medium and low secure settings, and with adults in community rehabilitation and resettlement. Since its start-date, in April 2014, Deryk has worked as art psychotherapist on the adapted TC+ programme, offered to male prisoners with intellectual disabilities, at HMP Grendon in Buckinghamshire UK.

Rose Hall is an art therapist and works in forensic mental health and in schools. She runs creative workshops for arts therapists and is developing work in art schools, which look to explore the artist's drive to make.

Tony Gammidge is a freelance artist, filmmaker, art therapist, lecturer and arts in health practitioner. He has has been running video and animation projects in secure and psychiatric settings for the past eight years. In that time he has been involved in the making of thirty short films, eleven of which have won Koestler arts awards. These films have been screened in galleries and arts centres and international conferences including in London, USA, Brighton and Edinburgh. His own films have been screened in the USA, UK, and Europe in film festivals and galleries. www.tonygammidge.com

Thijs de Moor is a Senior Registered Art Therapist holding a degree in Art Therapy (HAN CTO, 1997, Nijmegen), Professional Education (HAN VO, 2005, Nijmegen) and an MSc Art Psychotherapy (Queen Margaret University Edinburgh, 2015, UK). For nineteen years he has worked in mental health care and forensic psychiatry offering art therapeutic treatment for patients suffering from schizophrenia, eating-, and personality disorders both in the Netherlands and Belgium.

Since 2001 he has worked as a senior lecturer and coordinator at the Institute of Arts Therapies and Applied Psychology, HAN University of Applied Sciences, Netherlands.

On a frequent basis he lectures as an Invited Lecturer in Art Psychotherapy at Queen Margaret University in Edinburgh and at several Art Therapy Education Institutions throughout Europe.

Trisha Montague qualified as a music therapist in 2003. Since then she has worked in various settings including adult mental health, adult and child learning disabilities and palliative care. She has been employed by the North London Forensic Service for the past 12 years as a music therapist and psychotherapist in a medium secure NHS hospital. She has also been working as a psychotherapist in the Camden Psychotherapy Unit (CPU) for the last 5 years since completing an MSc in Psychodynamic Counselling at Birkbeck College, University of London.

James O'Connell has worked as an art psychotherapist in adult mental health and learning disability services, and in neurological rehabilitation since 2003. He is currently working in the North London

Forensic Service where he started in 2005 and also works in the Community Learning Disabilities Service in Enfield.

Lorna Downing is a Sesame trained Drama and Movement Therapist working in an NHS medium secure unit in East London, and a CAST supervisor and a filmmaker. As well as making films including 'Inside Out', 'Kicking Off' and 'Friday Night Fever', Lorna's work has been published in the Sesame Journal and presented at FATAG, IAFP and Badth conferences.

Lisa Shepherd is a creative practitioner, dramatherapist and writer who works with children, young people and adults in a variety of educational and community settings delivering creative and therapeutic interventions with a range of social, emotional and developmental outcomes. Alongside her freelance practice she lectures in creative and therapeutic approaches and youth offending at University of Northampton.

Lynn Aulich has worked for the adolescent forensic services based at Greater Manchester West Mental Health NHS Trust since 1987.

Karl Tamminen has worked as a clinical specialist and clinical lead in low, medium and high secure settings for over 26 years and is currently the professional lead for Art Therapy within the Humber NHS Foundation Trust.

Roanna Bond is a Dramatherapist who specialises in working with Dramatherapy with patients with Borderline Personality Disorder. Roanna currently works in a medium secure unit as well as in a therapeutic community for patients diagnosed with personality disorder. Roanna trained at Central School of Speech and Drama and qualified in 2013.

Laura Scott completed an enriching placement at the John Howard Centre as part of her MA in Drama and Movement Therapy. Laura qualified in April and is currently working with child and adolescent victims of trauma who have complex learning needs and associated social, emotional and behavioural difficulties.

May Maung is an art psychotherapist, who qualified from Hertfordshire University in 2014. She has also acquired an Advanced Diploma from the Institute of Arts Therapies and Education. May has experience working with acute mental health, learning disabilities and substance misuse. Having worked in an acute adolescent inpatient unit and forensic secure unit, she is currently employed as an art therapist in a SEN school for children with behavioural, emotional and social difficulties.

Jenny Wood qualified as an Art Therapist in 1997 (University of Hertfordshire) and has worked primarily in mental health and learning disabilities services (community, inpatient assessment and treatment, and low and medium secure units) in the NHS and private sector. She has also developed her clinical practice in recent years and attained Systemic Practitioner intermediate level qualification in Systemic Family Therapy with Couples and Families (Institute of Family Therapy). Jenny currently has a private practice and also is Clinical Lead for an independent special needs residential school. She has a particular interest in facilitating reflective thinking among multi-professional staff groups; drawing upon multi-theoretical approaches to understand the dynamic, patterns of behaviour and non-verbal communication that occurs between staff and service users, and importantly, acknowledging the emotional impact upon staff working with complex individuals.

Rebecca Johns qualified as an Art Psychotherapist in 2003 from Goldsmiths College, London. She has primarily worked in learning disabilities and mental health in the NHS. In recent years she has been privilege to share in the experience of the transitional journey with staff and service users through service redesigns and restructures, with commissioning led closure of the low secure unit in which she worked and the reinvention as a recovery oriented unit. Working within the dynamic of uncertainty and altered boundaries has sparked a particular interest in attachment theory and narrative work through the use of sandtray. Personal reflection and analysis has brought about a way of retaining resilience and hope for the future.

Ruth Goodman has been a practising dramatherapist and supervisor for over twenty years.

Her work has spanned Education, Social Services and Health; as a lecturer in drama in Further and Higher Education, a senior lecturer in Special Educational Needs and as a trainer for staff working in the mental health sector. She has been employed by North London Forensic Service as a dramatherapist since 1994 and has her own private practice. She was Convener for FATAG and for many years was the forensic lead for BADTH.

Liz Brown qualified in 1993 as an art therapist, and has the PG Certificate in Forensic Psychotherapeutic Theory from The Portman Clinic. Liz was a member of the FATAG committee for about eight years from 2002. Since 1994 she has worked at North London Forensic Service, part of Barnet, Enfield and Haringey Mental Health Trust, running groups and seeing individuals, women and men in acute and rehabilitation wards.

Shaun Wassall is currently the Art Therapy Clinical Lead within an NHS Trust. Shaun facilitates the provision of Art Therapy to both a forensic hospital setting, as well as working within a specialist service for female offenders whom are currently on the personality disorder pathway. Shaun has had 23 years' experience of working within various care settings and as an Art Therapist, believing that reflective art making is essential for the therapists emotional wellbeing when undertaking such difficult and often complex work.

Grahame Greener has been a prison officer for 24 years, predominantly working within the female prison population. For the last 8 years, Grahame has been involved within a specialist service, which offers assessment and treatment for female offenders who are diagnosed with a Personality Disorder, which is linked to their offending.

CHAPTER 1

Trust in a forensic setting
MARIO GUARNIERI[2] AND SYDNEY KLUGMAN[3]

Overview

This chapter is based on and developed from our presentation at the Forensic Arts Therapies Advisory Group conference in November 2002.

We will discuss our work with a group in a high-secure hospital for offenders compulsorily detained under the Mental Health Act for England and Wales. Specifically, we will discuss the dynamics of trust in the group: how it emerged as a theme and then dramatically forced its way in; the way it was struggled with; and finally the way in which the patients found meaning in their own feelings, thoughts and behaviours in relationship to their trust and mistrust dynamics.

We will address our co-working relationship and how we approached this work at the time, as the process also raised in our own minds the question of trusting each other, especially in the face of the dynamic of 'splitting' in the group. As well as the counter-transferences to the patients, we also had to think about our counter-transference between us as co-therapists, and how to manage our similarities and differences.

2 Dramatherapist

3 Art Therapist

Introduction

The subject matter is of a combined art therapy and dramatherapy group with male and female patients in a high-secure forensic mental health setting. As it turned out, this was significant also in the fact that it was one of the last known mixed-gendered therapy groups to run at the hospital before becoming an all-male environment.

Trust was the significant theme of the group. It emerged powerfully from the patients, almost imploring to be worked with directly, rather than be an accepted background issue of all forensic work. In supervision, the question was asked: what would it be like to spend most of one's life not being able to trust, and not to be trusted? It was a rhetorical question and one that generated a deeper sensibility within us as therapists. Operationally, the question was, how might we enable a group, filled with such intense suspicion, to work together in the combined therapies of art and drama?

The dynamic of trust was a question that we, embarking on our first co-therapy relationship and cross-disciplined approach, were inevitably faced with.

Co-working

As therapists in forensics we try and enter into a therapeutic alliance with patients who mistrust trusting. Therefore, risking failure is a therapeutic constant. This thought gave rise to reflections about us working together and combining our two disciplines. What was the potential risk of our alliance? How would we manage splits? How supportive or competitive would we be? Could we recognise and notify each other on our 'blind spots'? And, more simply but importantly, would we *get on* with each other?

We discussed thoroughly our thoughts about approaches to co-therapy well in advance of our beginning the group. A number of papers drew our attention to the difficulties that can arise if the therapeutic coupling had not been thought through seriously.

Dick, Lessler and Whiteside[4] (1980:276-280) identify four stages

---

4 Reflecting on this now, we used this theory as an underpinning to a process that was far more organic.

of growth in a co-therapy relationship: formation, development, stabilisation and refreshment. In the formation stage the focus is on the therapist's own intrapsychic issues about competency, adequacy, identity struggles and performance anxiety. Also, some basic interpersonal issues must be addressed, including theoretical beliefs and treatment philosophies. In the development stage, the focus is primarily on interpersonal issues within which there is mutual support in "making up for each other's perceived deficits or utilising each other's special strengths. One may be more willing to confront, the other more nurturing; one more creative, the other tending to provide structure; one more cognitive, the other more attuned to feelings; one more focused on intrapsychic processes, the other in on group processes." During the stabilisation stage the focus is on the honed tools of co-therapy being used positively: "the therapists function harmoniously, each flowing smoothly into and out of the therapeutic process, and each knowing self and the other well enough to anticipate mutual strategy and tactics." The refreshment stage is the stage of effortless co-therapy, moving beyond technique and into fluidity, innovation and play.

Yalom (1985) says that most co-therapists unintentionally split roles. One therapist may be more supportive and the other more confrontative of group members; one may focus on the group as a whole while the other may focus more on individual members. Although he celebrates the differences in co-therapists, he cautions that group members frequently drive a wedge into the co-therapy relationship and exploit any existing tensions.

Courtois (1988:266) suggests that co-therapists should "function as a team to guard against being split into good and bad parents but their individuality should come through as they engage with the group and its members".

We shaped a model of co-therapy that was safely transparent, allowing the possibility to openly discuss different perspectives so that we could disagree with each other, change our minds and adapt. We thought that it was crucially important for the group to witness the process of negotiating with each other, recognising that differing perspectives and even disagreement need not mean hostility and conflict. One can guess the ways in which contradictions and disagreements were negotiated upon in their own families.

Murray Cox (1974) speaks of the therapeutic process as a continuous process of self-disclosure. He guards against the dangers of co-therapists 'showing off' to each other at the patient's expense. Our role is to enable the patient "...to do for himself what he cannot do alone".

Working with forensic patients requires openness and involves a dynamic process of trust. Coming back to the *simple* reason for coming together as co-therapists: the starting point was that we were interested and curious about each other's thinking, ideas, art and skills. We had the sense that we could argue without causing offence; open to question each other, and ourselves, as we grappled with the uncertainty of holding and containing explosive material. What we had to encounter was our capacity to cope with the *murderousness* of our patients and to trust in their humanity, without losing our way and being led into a state of blind trust.

Setting up

A therapeutic characteristic both in forensic settings and in working with forensic patients is that trust is an ever-present theme. In particular to high-secure hospitals, a constant reminder of this factor is the surrounding high wall, which is meant to contain in order to protect the public from the offender patient, and each patient from each other - as well as from him or herself. In our experience many forensic patients have an extremely confused concept of the trust-mistrust dynamic, having grown up in unsafe, uncontained and unboundaried environments and been badly let down by adult figures. *I MUST NOT TRUST* therefore becomes a necessarily protective, powerful internal script. It refers particularly to authority figures, but includes everyone, even themselves.

The group ran once-weekly for 18 months, starting in May 2000 and ending in October 2001. There was a total of 70 sessions.

Our named objectives were to provide a contained environment to facilitate the combined processes of art therapy, dramatherapy and talking therapy, and to challenge dysfunctional beliefs. The objectives were deliberately kept basic, as we did not want to dictate the direction of sessions. Any theme that emerged would do so by what resonated within the group. We worked on the understanding that the art and drama symbolically created a frame for intrapsychic and interpersonal conflicts to emerge and begin the process of *working through*. We took a gestalt point of view where art, drama and discussion were interchangeable, moving between foreground and background. We worked mainly on an intuitive process, being guided by the *feel* of the group. It was essentially a psychodynamic arts therapy group.

We assessed patients on their preparedness to: engage in art, drama and reflective discussion to work with and explore difficult issues; reflect on present and past experiences; work in a mixed gender group. It was participants who we thought expressed some degree of curiosity about being in the group rather than having been told to. "I'm only here because my doctor said I should", for example, is a line familiar to many therapists in forensics.

Clinical material[5]

There were six patients in the group: four females and two males. In terms of the particular scenes presented in this paper, three patients step into the foreground and three remain in the background.

Beth was in her mid-thirties and had been at the hospital for eight years. She had a dual diagnosis of mental illness and personality disorder. Beth was lively but unpredictable. She was often playful but extremely anxious, with a strong desire to unburden. Beth was supportive of others but also held a rage inside of her that was potentially dangerous. When interviewed for the group, Beth was curious about art and drama and keen to attend, but she drew our attention to a previous group experience in which confidentiality had been broken by other patients, and she was therefore acutely sensitive about discussing personal issues.

Matt was in his late-twenties and had been at the hospital for two years. He had a diagnosis of personality disorder. A popular figure amongst patients; Matt had a charming personality. He came out of a background of drugs, theft and arson. When interviewed for the group

---

5 In order to respect confidentiality and protect anonymity the names of patients have been changed and the clinical material disguised.

he said he would "give it a try" because he was interested in "doing art", though not at all certain about "doing drama".

Treasure was in her mid-thirties and had been at the hospital for four years. She had a diagnosis of mental illness. She was shy and withdrawn but nevertheless cooperative, always polite. Treasure was a contradiction; she was both a hidden figure yet she also stood out. When we interviewed Treasure for the group she said that she was curious about how it would work.

The remaining three patients in the group who inhabit in the background of this chapter are Tony, Angie and Joanne. Tony was in his mid-twenties, diagnosed with mental illness. He struggled with his sense of self and with finding a place where he could feel comfortable. Angie was in her mid-twenties, with a diagnosis of personality disorder. She was petite, timid and passive-aggressive. Finally, Joanne was in her mid-thirties, with a diagnosis of personality disorder. She struggled with feelings of anticipated rejection and a non-verbal communication of 'keep your distance'.

The sessions

Inevitably in a forensic setting, it was suspicion that permeated the initial stage. The patients had entered into an unknown scenario (so had we to some degree). Their fixed perception of what therapy involved was being challenged by the use of art and drama. There were moments of both passive and active resistance, and a perceived attempt at splitting the two mediums, and by implication, the two therapists. In contra, there was curiosity about what the art forms offered, together with non-committed openness toward the session content. They described the sessions, euphemistically perhaps, as: different, weird, playful and interesting.

The atmosphere and dynamics changed a couple of months into the life of the group.

Vignette 1

The hospital's security department was investigating an incident involving Matt, which was felt to compromise the security of the hospital. As a result Matt was moved from being on a lower-risk, lower-dependency ward, onto a ward for high-risk patients requiring higher security. Further to this he was given non-movement status; he was not allowed to attend off-ward activities or therapy.

The story was that Matt was found by ward staff to have been in possession of electrical equipment. Staff suspected him of having recorded, or preparing to record, formal meetings with professionals. News of this incident quickly travelled and inevitably reached the patients on other wards across the hospital.

In the next session, with Matt not allowed to attend, there was great anxiety, particularly from Beth who began to feel paranoid. She vociferous in her concerns, expressing both anger and fear at the possibility that Matt taped the sessions. Her anxiety raised some confusion and suspicion towards what Matt could have done if he had been in possession of any information. Beth had bravely been the first to start to disclose snippets of personal material and was now imagining details of her story being spread all over the tabloids. Beth stated quite categorically that Matt should be "thrown out" of the group and that if we allowed Matt to return, she would leave the group.

We had sympathy for Beth's feelings and need to take this position. We also discussed the importance of managing the situation with us rather than abandoning the group and thereby leaving herself vulnerable to increased paranoia. We suggested she could try and see/ hear what Matt had to say and not deny herself the opportunity to challenge Matt. As well as sympathy, we also were not comfortable with Beth's ultimatum. We clarified that any 'hiring and firing' of group members would be our responsibility. As far as this group was concerned Matt had not broken any rules, and if Matt had acted-out in this way then denying him therapy would be counter-therapeutic. We were secure in our knowledge that Matt could not have secretly planted recording equipment in the therapy room. Underpinning our decision, Yalom (1985:311) suggests "scapegoating of other members is another off-target manifestation, and may reach such proportions that unless the therapist intervenes to direct the attack onto himself the sacrificial patient may be driven from the group."

The other members offered supportive words to Beth; they each expressed their own frustration, anger and suspicion toward Matt. However, they also wanted to hear what Matt had to say. They reasoned over the unlikeliness of him recording our sessions. There was a feeling of confusion.

During this difficult period, both of us came away from sessions feeling somewhat mentally battered. As testing as this was we managed to struggle with the tension creatively by open reflection during debriefs and in consultation with other arts therapists and the psychotherapy department. We managed, just about, to hold onto and trust our own and each other's skills, knowledge, experience and intuition.

Our decision was that not only should Matt return to the sessions, but should do so as soon as possible, and face the group over this issue. To avoid it would only harbour more paranoia. Something important was being played out in the group, yet the antagonist was not present.

Security surrounding Matt was still tight. We needed permission from the security team to allow Matt off the ward and back into therapy. With support from his consultant psychiatrist and care team we voiced our concerns that Matt's absence was having a destructive effect on his and the group's therapy. We raised the important therapeutic benefits of Matt's return. The security team accepted our position.

We visited Matt on the ward. He told us, sheepishly, that indeed he had attempted to sound record clinical team meetings, but was unsuccessful. As for coming back to the group he said that he needed time to consider. He spoke of his own feelings of insecurity. To add to the suspicious dynamic, Matt said that he had disclosed sensitive family information to the clinical team and had been informed that, due to the nature of the disclosure, it had become a safeguarding issue and confidentiality could not be maintained. Matt said: "I can't speak to anyone, I can't trust anyone." He viewed the team's reaction as a betrayal. He also wanted to protect his family himself rather than the agencies, "the authorities", by whom he claimed to have been let down by many times previous.

This anxiety of not being able to trust resonated in the whole group. There seemed to be layers of fear and paranoia that needed containment.

Yalom (1985:310) says that: "The therapist who withstands an attack without being either destroyed or destructive in retaliation, but instead responds by attempting to understand and work through the sources and effects of the attack demonstrates to the group that aggression need not be lethal and that it can be expressed and understood in the group." The fragility of the group was evident, and as co-therapists we knew we had to tread carefully to stop the group from disintegrating. This scenario was, of course, a mirroring of the dynamics experienced by all of the group members in their own family history.

We invited the group to focus on the process of what was happening by first exploring the group's interpersonal relationships through the use of object work. Jones (2007:146) says that: "This area of work within dramatherapy creates a theatre space in miniature." Each person portrayed the group, as they experience it, through choosing objects representing each individual. On an A3 sheet of paper, they placed the objects in relation to each other, as a representation of the relational *space* between them. The sheet of paper represents a stage, and because it has an edge - in other words, a boundary - it also serves to symbolically contain the material being worked on. We then looked at the links with their families and considered what was being played out in the group. The family was symbolised through the use of the art materials and through the metaphor of a painted house. Moving from this, they imaginatively transformed the physical space of the therapy room to represent their respective houses from within. Expanding further, through the methods of monologues and role reversal, thoughts and feelings about family members were explored.

It was during this difficult stage and through this process that Beth was able to reflect on issues of trust in her own history. She was able to explore and reflect on past physical and sexual abuse within the family. Having summoned the courage to tell her parents, they had "swept it under the carpet", leaving her feeling distraught. The group encouraged her to not sweep this issue, with Matt, under the carpet.

Treasure, Angie, Joanne and Tony also explored their own family relationships symbolically and concretely with images, physicality and words through the process of object work, painting and role-play. Some very sensitive personal material was being disclosed and the group was becoming more cohesive. However, we were still without Matt.

Beth felt ready and able to challenge the situation. However, she was still very anxious and could not be certain about whether she could stay in the room when Matt returned.

After seven consecutively missed sessions, Matt returned to the group. He avoided eye contact. The atmosphere was tense. Each patient's physicality signified their deep sense of apprehension about being in the group. There was silence. Beth suddenly stood up, left the circle and walked towards the opposite end of the room. She leaned on the windowsill and stared out of the barred windows. More silence. She was visibly agitated. The physical reactions of the others were to fidget, or stay absolutely still, or to stare into space. As co-therapists, our senses were in a heightened state. We kept our eyes and ears on each patient, as well as making eye contact with each other, trusting our own and each other's intuition as to how to respond. As difficult as it was, it felt more containing to stay within this silence.

Eventually, Matt spoke: "It looks like I'm not wanted here".

Beth turned around, looked directly at Matt and said: "Can I trust you?" There is silence. Then Beth speaks again: "Am I safe with you here?"

Matt looked stunned by the direct question. He stuttered, whilst telling Beth that she was safe with him, that he would not harm her or any other member of the group. He told the group of his own ambivalence at coming back, and that he could understand why they would not want him back. But he wanted to assure them that they were all safe with him. He explained to the group what had and had not happened regarding the recording incident. Matt apologised to the group, and this felt genuine to us. He acknowledged his sabotaging patterns, and particularly those of any kind of emotional contact. Matt said that despite his reservations, he recognised quickly that this group had the potential to make him "feel something" and was finding it more difficult to hide. He did want to feel and did not want to hide anymore. This was not easy.

Another long silence followed Matt's address. Slowly, Beth walked towards the group, re-joining the circle. This was a moving and symbolically defining moment in instigating the change in the relationship dynamics of the group. There was a notable sense of relief both from the group and ourselves. This was a point where the group could either have disintegrated or moved forward, and Beth, by her actions, helped the group reintegrate.

Vignette 2

During the time of this group, making masks and role-play were significant methods used in exploring personal identity. The artwork was further explored through the opportunities that role-play offered, gaining both distance and intimacy, and offering a safe space to explore intensely personal and frightening material.

We invited each member to think of and name roles they perceived to have historically inhabited in their lives, either willingly or willingly, and what associations these roles had for them. The roles included familial, social and psychological, for example: sister, father, student, taxi-driver, survivor, martyr, victim, opportunist etc. (Landy, 1983). Then, one role was chosen that each thought had particular resonance. Next came the designing and making of the masks that represented the chosen roles. Once completed, they used the masks to enact important events in their lives. The masks were also used as bases for story writing. Amongst these stories, we have selected one to illustrate how this worked.

Fig. 1. Clown   Fig. 2. Murderer

Fig. 3. Protector

Treasure chose to include in her story the masks: clown, murderer and protector. (See Fig. 1, 2 and 3)

She called the story 'The Three Masks'.

Treasure had a quiet dignity in the group. She was respectful and supportive. When she did anything creative she came alive, she was 'seen', and her potential was recognised rather than hidden. However, Treasure's learnt habitual way of being was to stay in the shadows. There was a discomfort expressed physically that left her exposed and vulnerable. There was an internal sadness and a feeling that she was crushed by circumstance. Treasure was unable to make the final step from disbelief of herself toward a real sense of herself.

Treasure's story *(as written)*:

'The man walked through the forest, dehydrated and hungry. All of a sudden there was a bright light in front of him. The light was breaking through the trees. The flash of light was different colours. Colours of the rainbow: blue, pink, yellow, green. The man wished it could be real. Suddenly he was back in the forest surrounded by tall dark and menacing trees and plants. How long did he have to walk before he saw any kind of human life? Could anyone hear him? He saw before him a

mask of a clown, a joker's face. He wasn't at the circus. Where did this joker's face come from? It disappeared as quickly as it appeared. The man was alone again, and frightened. What would he see next? There in front of him was a lion, hungry and mean. The animal crept towards its meal tentatively. Out of the blue there appeared a mask. It was mean but it meant protector. As soon as it appeared the lion roared, but was no match for its opponent. The mask circulated the animal and was ferocious and triumphant in all its glory. It won. The man awoke and was startled but felt safe. He had been walking for about 20 minutes when a man jumped out of the trees, he was a murderer. The man cowered hideously.'

There was a silence. Matt said: "I wish I could be as creative as you". Treasure said that the story was unfinished and that she could not think of how the protagonist could get out of the forest.

This story clearly had an impact on the group. This led us to wonder whether this story was a personal story for Treasure, bringing out all three aspects of her psyche: her murderousness, her victim and her sadness, as depicted by the three masks. We also wondered whether the story was an attempt to find a solution for the group and to find some form of reparations as Treasure struggled to get out of the forest into the world outside – from high security to freedom; possibly prompting Matt's comment.

The nonverbal form of art and the physical aspects of drama offered the opportunity for animation.

Kuhns (1983) describes the art experience as surprising because it permits, often unavailable, thoughts to occupy our consciousness. He further postulates that through careful and sustained interpretation, the reality of objects yields the mask of the poet. We, through the art object and the mask of our patients, like Treasure's story, attempted to explore our belief in the poems they possessed.

Discussion

This paper reflects our thoughts on the manner in which trust was observed and worked with in the development of our art and dramatherapy group. Trust, from the group's inception to its culmination, acted as a focus and a guide in the individual and group development of all the members, including ourselves.

Grotjahn (1993:167-175) postulates how the ideal therapist must be reliable and confident in himself and the beliefs of others, as only then will he invite in trust. He further suggests that the therapist must have a degree of spontaneity, as spontaneity is embedded in trust. He suggests that this takes courage and the ability to withstand bad experiences without despair. The good enough therapist he speaks of should be open and should acknowledge mistakes. The therapist must also have the capacity to be a bystander in the interactive process.

Winnicott (1971:91-92) suggests that positive change does not necessarily depend on interpretive work but depends on the analyst's survival of the attacks, "which involves and includes the idea of the absence of a quality change to retaliation. These attacks may be very difficult for the analyst to stand...which makes the analyst do things that are technically bad...Better to wait till after the phase is over, and then discuss with the patient what has been happening."

If Matt had been successful in *killing off* the therapy, imagine how traumatic the *death* of the therapist can be when this kind of work is in progress.

What we were aware of was the aspects of working in a secure environment where relational security and physical security dance to the precariously balanced tune. So much of our work is intuitive, relying on trusting our judgement, but not misplaced trust.

As arts therapists, a great deal of our work is about the senses, and we have to be able to *hear* what our patients are saying and *see* what they are showing us. There is often an intuitive part to self-disclosure, which gives the patient courage and the ability to trust us with material that they find explosive and painful, and which causes fear that they might annihilate us with it. We have to trust each other and ourselves that we can survive that which is almost impossible to hear.

The patients we worked with had suffered from unmet basic trust needs. Their early emotional worlds were coloured by their early life experiences, which coloured their ability to trust. What we tried to do in this group was to show that trust starts and grows out of a collaborative effort and mutual respect. It means balancing agreed rules with tacit rules of behaviour. One has to start somewhere.

Conclusion

We use a quote from Dick, Lessler and Whiteside (1980:276) to summarise our thoughts on co-therapy partnership, elements of which they liken to a marriage.

"Success… is strongly facilitated by mutual openness, honesty, and directness in the here-and-now about thoughts and feelings, leading to a satisfying productive balance between separateness and togetherness. Each partner's awareness, acceptance and integration of his/her own and the other's talents and their interactive nuances seem to be the primary determinant of positive outcomes."

To expect a complete turnaround from mistrust to trust in eighteen months is, of course, unrealistic. The experience of the individuals in the group, however, was this: by staying with and exploring their complex lives, their personal dynamics as they interacted with each other, the materials we provided and our own engagement, this created a curiously rich tapestry of experience. And, we went some way towards a sense of group affiliation, inter-connectedness and mutual trust.

Finally, a quote from Matt: "The people in this group have shown me that there is humanity."

REFERENCES

Cox, M. & Theilgaard, A. (1997) *Mutative Metaphors in Psychotherapy: The Aeolian Mode.* London: Jessica Kingsley Publishers.

Courtois, C. (1988) *Healing The Incest Wound: Adult Survivors in Therapy.* New York: Norton Professional Books.

Dick, B., Lessler, K., & Whiteside, J. (1980) 'A Developmental Framework for Cotherapy', *International Journal of Group Psychotherapy,* 30 (3): 273-285.

Grotjahn, M. (1993) *The Art and Technique of Analytic Group Therapy.* London: Jason Aronson Inc.

Jones, P. (2007) *Drama as Therapy: Theory, Practice and Research* (Second Edition). London: Routledge.

Kuhns, R. (1983) *Psychoanalytic Theory of Art: A Philosophy of Art on Developmental Principles.* Guildford: Columbia University Press.

Landy, R.J. (1993) *Persona and Performance: The Meaning of Role in Drama, Therapy, and Everyday Life.* London: Jessica Kingsley Publishers.

Winnicott, D.W. (1971) [Reprint: 2002] *Playing and Reality.* Hove: Brunner Routledge.

Yalom, I.D. (1985) *Theory and Practice of Group Psychotherapy,* (3rd edition). New York: Basic Books.

CHAPTER 2

Embodied furies: Perversion, ambivalence and use of the body in dance movement psychotherapy

ELEONORA RUDOLF ORLOWSKA[6] AND DIANE PARKER[7]
SUPERVISED BY DAWN BATCUP[8]

Introduction

"In female perversion not only the whole body but also its mental representations are used to express sadism and hostility. Women express their perverse attitudes not only through but also towards their bodies, very often in a self-destructive way"

(Welldon 1988, p.33).

The concept of female perversion was first introduced and explored by Welldon (1988), who suggested that perversion in women is also a perversion of motherhood. She examines the inter-generational dynamic between mothers and children in the creation of perversion or female deviant behaviour.

Perversion in women is also characterised as "crimes against the body" (Motz 2008) and manifests itself in violence against the self in the form of self-harming behaviours. Where mothers view their children as a narcissistic extension of self (Miller 1987), children are also the victims of this violence, so the cycle of abuse is perpetuated across generations. Perversion in women is primarily a sadistic attack

---

6 RDMP

7 RDMP

8 ADMP private practitioner and supervisor, BPC MBT, UKCC RMN & RGN

against an internalised mother who is both loved and feared, resulting in violent behaviour against self and other. Viewed through the lens of female perversion then, crimes committed by women may be seen as attacks against the internalised mother as a manic defence against loss and annihilation.

Taking the concept of female perversion as our starting point, this chapter describes our work as trainee dance movement psychotherapists with female offenders in both a prison and a NHS medium-secure forensic clinic. We suggest that the creative, symbolic and non-verbal aspect of Dance Movement Psychotherapy (DMP) can help these women access some of the feelings linked to their offences, offering a means to help them begin to understand their mental and emotional states that lead to offending behaviour. We also suggest that the body-oriented aspect of DMP offers a direct route into the embodied nature of female perversion, and so provides a powerful therapeutic model for working specifically with perverse and/or violent women.

Welldon (2009a) suggests that our inexperience as trainee therapists can make us more "available" to examining our own motivations for working with this particular population. The reflective space provided by regular supervision proved to be crucial for both of us throughout our work with these women – indeed, most of the insights and reflections offered here were gleaned through group supervision and personal therapy. In addition, using the body as a medium for communication makes an exploration and focus on countertransference, experienced somatically, especially pertinent. We suggest that our somatic experience of being and moving alongside our clients gave us access to a wealth of information of what it may have felt like to be them in a bodily sense – and by extension, their world.

In our explorations of both individual and group work, we also suggest here a working model for DMP in forensic settings for the future.

The relational needs of female offenders

The relational needs of female offenders and the values society places on the meaning of femininity and motherhood (Parker 1995, 1996; Welldon 2009b) require psychotherapists to pay attention to the meanings of gender and gender-specific dynamics in their work with offending women. The specific needs of female offenders are increasingly recognised by professionals and researchers working in the criminal justice system. Many women have been abused and often struggle to manage deep feelings of shame by acting on destructive or maladaptive impulses. Women with the most complex needs experience persistent difficulties in their relationships. They are often regarded as "difficult to place" (Gorscuh 1998) and demanding, and may be offered limited support. Extreme fears of dependency and abandonment can give rise to feelings so overwhelming they are acted out impulsively. Such women frequently enter into what appears to be a convoluted relational choreography with others, which is often perceived to be controlling and functions as a defence against unbearable mental states.

Our early experiences are formative and help to lay down the blueprints for the basis of our later relationships. Many offenders have experienced deprivation or trauma in some capacity, and find that the crimes or anti-social or violent acts they commit are a symbolic enactment of internal conflicts (Cordess & Hyatt Williams 1996).

Violent behaviour in women subverts gender stereotypes, and is therefore often taken as evidence of mental illness (Mezey & Bartlett 1996), which could account for the higher rate of offending women detained in forensic psychiatric units rather than prison (Jeffcote & Travers 2004). A large proportion of people in the criminal justice system and in medium-secure units meet the criteria for personality disorder, as is the case with the women presented in this chapter. Generally such patients have sustained developmental trauma, adversely affecting neurological and emotional development (Schore 2001), including the capacity to modulate emotions and self-soothe, along with deficits in "mind mindedness" (Fonagy et al 2004). From an object relations perspective, these patients could be described as lacking robust ego strength and an internalised soothing maternal object, and must therefore contend with raging primitive impulses (Kernberg 2004). For these patients, small interpretations based on the here-and-now experience of the therapeutic relationship provide containment while providing an appropriate level of challenge to the patients' dysfunctional ideation (Fonagy & Bateman 1996).

Traumatised people often lack an internal space in which to hold onto, play with, and therefore metabolise emotional experiences. When working with forensic patients, remaining curious about the index offence can provide insight into the offender's internal world (Cordess & Hyatt Williams 1996). As these women were able to develop their capacity to understand and tolerate their distress, they were more able to contain ambivalent feelings, enhancing their ability to relate.

DMP seeks to utilise the bodily experience and ability to play as a tool to enhance the offender patients' reflective ability, and therefore, capacity for relationships. DMP can also be applied specifically with personality disordered patients to provide containment and holding (Batcup 2013, Manford 2014, Meekums 2002). The body-mind link is a central tenet of DMP. Movement analysis can be used to gain an understanding of the meaning in patients' movement and postural responses, and can provide a richer perspective into what is being evoked in the therapeutic relationship (Koch et al 2011, Levy & Duke 2003, Stanton Jones 1992).

DMP also offers opportunities for symbolic expression and externalisation through metaphor and imagery elicited by movement, the use of props (Halprin 2003, Novy et al 2005) and the use of voice and verbalisation (Stark & Lohn 1989, Newham 1999). This in turn can be utilised to support cross-modal attunement between therapist and patient (Stern 1985) and can promote kinaesthetic empathy in the therapeutic relationship (Fischman 2009).

Maternal ambivalence and female perversion

Children who experienced a deficit in responsive relationships, where their affective states are mirrored by care-givers, do not have the opportunity to build strong "narcissistic ties" (Lampl de Groot 1975), and therefore lack an internalised mother that is robust enough to withstand fierce emotions. A child whose mother is preoccupied with servicing her own needs through her relationship with the child may experience her as too close, controlling, not allowing the child freedom to explore and may produce feelings of anger or hostility when the child attempts to reassert her developing sense of self. Alternatively, a care-giver who appears too distant, unresponsive or uncaring may cause fears of abandonment. Consequently, women who experience overwhelming fears of abandonment or engulfment must find a way to regulate the experience of intimacy and self-boundaries. Aggression directed towards the self can be seen as an attack on the faulty maternal object, and also serves the function of defending against fears of engulfment. The following vignettes aim to demonstrate this process in DMP:

> Linda, a young woman in her twenties, was in prison for burglary. Linda had an extensive history of inflicting harm against herself, mainly through cutting but also through overeating and purging, drug use and ingesting sharp materials. The staff who worked with Linda tended to be polarised in their responses to her, describing her as compliant, or finding her intolerable. In the first DMP session, Linda spoke about her self-abuse, which had resulted in her children being taken into care. In contrast to the violence of the acts that she described, Linda seemed passive and lacking in vitality, and appeared younger than her age. Her narrative contained little sense of agency, which seemed embodied by a lack of muscle tension or directionality in her movements (Davies 2001).
>
> As she explores the bag of movement props, Linda notes that it contained a number of balls of various shapes and sizes. She tells me that she was "scared" of balls and I wondered about removing some of these before her sessions. Inwardly I curse, feeling like the "bad mother". We enter into a movement dialogue, comprising soft, fluid, swaying movements in an oral or "sucking" Tension Flow Rhythm (Kestenberg, Amighi and Loman 1999). Linda would frequently use these rhythms, which are akin to the changes in internal muscle tension that occur when an infant feeds and are then reciprocated by the nursing mother, facilitating a bodily-sense of attunement. However she was unable to sustain them for long and would turn away, or otherwise withdraw from the interaction often causing me to feel frustrated and helpless.
>
> In the following session, Linda is wearing her hair in the same style as me, and talks about her romantic relationships. This signals the beginning of a period of identification with

me, where Linda expresses a less conscious desire to become overly close. She brings in stories of boundary-less relating and stormy arguments with her cellmate. Throughout this time I felt loving and protective countertransference feelings towards her, often accompanied by a feeling of fullness and satiation.

The polarisation of staff perspectives around Linda suggested that she maintained her apparent passivity by rejecting the more active or hostile parts of herself, and projected them outwards, where they were received and felt by others. Her disavowal of these parts may have been an attempt to avoid bringing them into the therapy sessions and in doing so to preserve the nature of her relationship with me as her therapist. Although Linda's use of a sucking Tension Flow Rhythm (Kestenberg et al., ibid.) suggested her need to enter into an attuned psychotherapeutic relationship, her rejection of it hinted at ambivalent feelings. Linda externalised her frightening experiences by projecting them outward, onto the props. My concern with the balls was that I had re-enacted something of her experience of her early relationships, becoming the neglectful parent in the countertransference (Russell and Marsden 2006). The loving countertransference feelings and sensations of fullness I experienced were perhaps a response to Linda's hope of obtaining "nourishment" from the psychotherapeutic relationship.

The concept of love and hate within the maternal relationship is a key characteristic of female perversion (Welldon 1988, Motz 2008). In understanding violent or perverse behaviour in women then, it is helpful to recognise the concept of maternal ambivalence: the experience shared by all mothers in which both loving and sadistic feelings for their children exist simultaneously (Parker ibid., Hollway & Featherstone 1997). The difficulty of acknowledging this experience is exacerbated by cultural ideals and expectations around motherhood. Historically, the psychoanalytic focus has been primarily on the negative impact of maternal ambivalence on the child, rather than on its contribution to discourse about understanding maternal development and female perversion (Parker ibid.). As Hollway and Featherstone (1997) assert: "The idea of mothering ...... arouses anxieties managed through defences which, reproduced at a cultural level, are manifested in the

idealisation and denigration of mothers – neither set of images faithful
to reality" (p.1). It is hard for us to bear the thought that mothers can
abuse or fail to protect their children. The societal assumption is that
"women do not do these things" (Lloyd-Owen 2003).

Therefore, in a society where motherhood in general is both
idealised and denigrated, this sets the scene for a lack of understanding
of the difficulties facing women, the inter-generational dynamic of
mothers and daughters, and consequently the link between maternal
ambivalence and female perversion (Welldon 1988, 2009a, 2009b).
The following vignette of a DMP group demonstrates how maternal
ambivalence can be expressed through movement and creative
symbolism in relationship with others.

> Kim and Maria are inpatients of a medium secure women's
> ward of a forensic unit and are participating in a co-facilitated
> dance therapy group. Both women are in their forties and
> have children. Kim and Maria were hospitalised within weeks
> of each other and have formed a strong bond on the ward.
> They each committed arson in their own homes, directly
> endangering the lives of their children. In the second group
> session, Maria cradles a large blue ball and begins to cry,
> saying that she is holding her "children", her "family"... "I'm
> holding the whole world". She expresses reluctance to pass the
> ball around to other members of the group, wanting to "keep
> it to myself". Kim, on the other hand, seems at a loss to know
> what to do with the ball when it is passed to her and wants to
> give it away immediately, seemingly unable to make use of it.
>
> In the following session, Maria expresses her love for the
> group and says she wishes it could "go on forever". She is curious
> about whether my female co-therapist and I are mothers,
> "blessed with children". I ask her if she considers children to
> be a blessing, and she agrees wholeheartedly. However, later
> in the session, as the group are moving together, she suddenly
> drops the cloth we are holding and goes to lie down in the
> corner, turning her face away to the wall, embodying her
> "rejection" of the group maybe. As my co-therapist leads the
> movement, she is interrupted by Kim who suddenly asks if I

will "do her hair" and make her "look pretty". I am annoyed,
confused and feel guilty for the interruption, and later wonder
if I have been placed in the role of "good mother" (idealised,
nurturing), while my co-therapist has been placed in that of
"bad mother" (punishing, abusive, withholding).

The use of props in these sessions enabled the women to externalise
and express their feelings, and provided symbolic representation of
significant relationships, in this case, their children and families (their
"whole world") (Winnicott 1971). However, their body movement
in relationship to the group also suggested their ambivalent feelings
towards the idealised "mother", represented by the group, as when
Maria literally turned away, demonstrating a desire for intimacy, but
an equal hostility towards the group. It was significant too, that her
idealisation of the group took place during a session in which they were
the only two present, suggesting either a female solidarity or difficulty
with being in a group. My countertransference feelings of shame and
guilt at Kim's interruption later in the session, and her rejection of
my colleague's interventions, may have also been an indication of the
women's ambivalent feelings towards getting on with the work of the
group, mothering and being mothered.

Perverse pleasure

"A woman uses her body as her most powerful means of
communication and her greatest weapon"

(Motz 2008, p.1).

In Welldon's view, women's violence against their own bodies can be
seen as a response to annihilation anxieties. The violent act can be an
attempt to ward off a fear of not being allowed to exist as a complete
person, separate and distinct from the maternal object (Verhaeghe
2009). Aggression for self-preservation may also be sexualised, become
tinged with pleasurable impulses and develop into sadistic behaviour
which, according to Glasser (1979), serves the function of controlling
the maternal object to avoid overwhelming painful feelings.

*Linda had been displaying increasingly covert hostility in our
sessions. She had recently spoken to a colleague about joining
another therapy group, and had been engaging in crude, home-
made tattoos, which she saw as an improvement on cutting.
Today Linda enters the room and chooses to position herself
on a chair as far from me as possible. She begins to tell me
about the scabs on her back and shows me a new tattoo that
she has inscribed on her leg. Linda goes on to talk about her
sexual relationships and previous offending history, in both
instances describing herself in predatory roles. The tension
in the room feels 'live' and unpredictable. As Linda recounts
these stories, she scratches the skin where she has tattooed the
names of significant people in her life.*

Linda's communication of hostility by "threatening" to leave her sessions
and find a new therapist suggested that she was seeking to control her
experience of intimacy in the psychotherapeutic relationship, and may
have begun to feel overwhelmed in response to persecutory feelings.
Linda's use of tattooing can be seen as a reaction to a fear of losing
her sense of self. The act of delineating her body boundaries perhaps
facilitated some recognition of her skin as a physical boundary between
self and other, and may have been an attempt to ward off an increasing
sense of fragmentation in her internal world (Bick 1968).

Linda seemed to be struggling with conflicting needs and wishes,
simultaneously communicating her feelings of vulnerability alongside
her potential for aggressive acts. The tension that I felt as Linda spoke
filled the liminal space with something that felt erotically-charged and
dangerous. Linda's frequent self-touch had an auto-erotic quality to
it, as if I was witnessing the outpouring of a tension that had slowly
been building, and I alternated between feeling as if I was witnessing
a peepshow and a crime. She prevented herself from feeling seduced
or abused in the transference by taking on these roles in a sadistic
attack. This functioned as a sexualised defence against the terrors of
engulfment and ceasing to exist (Wood 2014).

Sadism, anger and hidden hostility

An inability to recognise, access or express feelings of anger and hatred can mean that these feelings are often pushed down, projected, masked by other feelings or by feelings of "nothingness" or numbness. Welldon describes this as "a disavowal of destructive annihilation" (Welldon 1988). Our countertransference feelings that emerged when working with these women indicated the true, authentic feelings that lay below the surface, and were indicative of the women's inability to express anger or hostility honestly.

> While Maria's children are in care, she is still in contact with them, whereas Kim is estranged from hers. Following a visit to the ward from Maria's daughter, in our next group session Maria is keen to share with the group the details of her daughter's visit. I notice as she is speaking that Kim is becoming increasingly quiet, and I feel ashamed that I am unable to protect her from the unbearable pain of losing her children. At the same time, I experience an overwhelming urge to tell Maria to "shut up" and I am angry at her insensitivity to Kim's pain.
>
> I lead the group in a "turn-taking" exercise, where each participant shares a movement or gesture for the other group members to follow. Despite initial claims that she wouldn't "be doing any dancing today", Kim is an active participant, sharing a rhythmic and sensual rolling of the shoulders in an indulgent sucking Tension Flow Rhythm (Kestenberg et al. ibid.). Her earlier pain and sadness has seemingly dropped, and I feel confused and disorientated. When it reaches her turn, Maria leans back in her chair, raises her arms high and mimes yawning, and I am horrified at the violent rage that suddenly arises in me as I want to hit her. I immediately push this thought away and go blank. Later in the session, both Maria and Kim begin giggling and my co-therapist joins in with their laughter. I see the laughter as a defence mechanism and feel angry, with both the women and my colleague for, in my mind, colluding with their defences.

*I attempt to introduce focus and concentration in the
group by suggesting that we continue to share movement but
without obviously passing our movement on: "...so we have
to really watch each other, and notice when the movement is
changing, because we don't know who is leading, or who is
following..." I introduce a movement that is strong, sustained
and direct. This seems to help the women regain focus,
their laughter ceases and they diligently apply themselves to
the task.*

*The following week, while visiting another patient on the
ward, I am confronted by Maria who says she has something
"urgent" to tell me. She says she will be unable to attend group
therapy this week, as she and Kim had a fight on the ward
during which Kim physically attacked her. I feel panic rising
in me and feel my face flush as I try to remain present with
my other patient and at the same time, process what Maria is
telling me. I realise I knew instinctively that something like
this was going to happen, and I feel helpless and ashamed that
I wasn't able to address the underlying hatred and hostility that
I felt surface in our session the previous week.*

Welldon has written of the danger of the therapist's "perverse
collusion" (2009a p.155) and how inexperienced or trainee therapists
are particularly at risk of being "seduced" into colluding with such
defences. The incident in which I was confronted with Maria's
"urgency" on the ward was a significant example of the challenge this
could present in impairing my own ability to think and act "under
fire". As my countertransference feelings of shame and guilt with
Kim and Maria possibly represented a projection of the women's
ambivalent feelings around mothering, so my anger could also have
been a projection of hostility and sadism that the women were unable
to express towards me and my colleague, for fear of destroying the
group and what it represented – "mother". My anger could also have
been a reflection of both the love and hatred the women felt for their
own mothers – hatred felt even more strongly towards their mothers
than their abusive fathers.

The denial or "disavowal" of destructive or violent impulses in women can mean that these feelings are projected powerfully into others, and then, as in the case of women who kill their abusive partners, the victim suddenly becomes the aggressor, with explosive results (Motz 2014). My countertransference feelings of impotent rage at the women's laughter suggested I was holding all of the anger in the group – Kim's attack on Maria the following week was an inevitable consequence of this disavowal. Our cultural denial of violence in women persists, but we ignore it at our peril (Motz 2008).

Conclusion: A model for DMP with female offenders?

The painful and overwhelming feelings that lead women to perverse and violent behaviour are often strongly defended against (Welldon 1988). Engaging in DMP offered these female prisoner/patients an opportunity to explore their emotions in a creative, symbolic way. The synchronous movement of shared leadership and turn-taking provided opportunity for the women to see themselves in relation to others and support their ability to think about their own and others' emotional states (Bateman & Fonagy 2004, 2006) through non-verbal means. The use of props also enabled the women to externalise their feelings through symbolic representation of reality (Winnicott 1971). The introduction of imagery and metaphor evoked by movement and facilitated by props, provided an "anchor" for the emotional content. As Seligman (2008) describes: "The use of a metaphor provided the opportunity for us to talk about a [patient-like] character as a third person, in a transitional space that supported symbolization and self-reflection [...] the developing sense of having one's own mind in a field of others is supported when two people share attention to a third object" (pp. 364-5).

The use of props also enabled symbolic externalisation of feelings for the women, particularly around their own roles as mothers, and the props came to significantly represent transitional objects in the absence of their children (Winnicott 1971). The women were able to use the work to experience being held and supported by a container provided by the therapeutic space (Meekums 2002, Manford 2014) and to use

DMP as a way of seeing and being seen subjectively (Stern 1985). Our varied countertransference feelings of maternal love contrasted with feelings of hatred (Winnicott 1949) created an experience of maternal ambivalence (Parker 1995, 1996), suggesting we had each been drawn into playing a maternal role for the women, and our love/hate responses mirrored the complex and conflicting relationships with their own internalised maternal objects (Klein 1932).

Furthermore, our findings have prompted an evaluation of the current model of DMP in the forensic setting. A core symptom of the borderline personality is an impaired capacity to regulate emotional states, making group work challenging for both patients and therapist(s) (Bateman & Fonagy 2004). The feelings experienced by individuals within the group must be differentiated from the general feeling within the group, so that patients are able to recognise the feelings of others and differentiate them from their own. In retrospect, perhaps we each would have benefited from working closer to the mentalisation-based therapy (MBT) model, whereby group therapy is conducted in conjunction with one-to-one therapy. This would have served to address Kim and Maria's individual needs and given them the opportunity to explore their emotional effects in the contained structure of a one-to-one relationship. Similarly, the structure of a group may have provided Linda with a sense of containment and helped regulate the intensity of a one-to-one relationship (Bateman and Fonagy 2004, 2006; Welldon 1993).

Bateman and Fonagy (2004) argue that "the simultaneous provision of group and individual therapy is an ideal arrangement within which to encourage mentalisation" (p.200). Patients who are excessively anxious in a group context are able to use individual therapy sessions to reflect critically about themselves in the group. The therapist however, uses his/her knowledge of the patient's problems to concentrate on the interpersonal context in the group that may be the cause of the patient's anxiety, and how this may relate to aspects of the patient's life. This requires "careful coordination between the individual and group therapists to minimise adverse consequences of splitting of the transference and to make certain the patient moves toward mental balance rather than continuing to manage anxiety through splitting, idealisation, denigration and withdrawal" (ibid. p.200).

As Welldon asserts: "a crucial point about forensic psychotherapy is that it is a team effort, not an heroic action by the psychotherapist alone" (1993, p.488). Lloyd-Owen (2003) considers the "triangulation" of supervision especially important when working with clients who have rarely experienced the layers of containment in relationship with their primary care-giver. Furthermore, through open dialogue and consultation among the wider multi-disciplinary team, DMP therapists have the opportunity to raise awareness of creative and somatic responses among their colleagues, particularly in relation to difficult countertransference feelings.

When applied as part of a wider treatment programme, DMP can be of benefit to female offenders in providing a means to explore painful and overwhelming feelings that lead to perverse behaviour and are strongly defended against. The non-verbal and creative aspect of DMP helps bypass these defences and helps the women communicate feelings that may be hard to put into words, particularly those around their complex relationships with their mothers, their children and their own bodies. The embodied nature of DMP can be of particular benefit in helping these women develop a separate sense of self, and to think about their own emotional states in relation to those of others.

In this way, DMP can help support the work of other professionals in the forensic environment, in providing a therapeutic intervention that meets the women's emotional and relational needs. At the same time, through ongoing communication and open dialogue, DMP therapists can find a level of containment within the team to support them in their work with this complex and challenging population.

BIBLIOGRAPHY

Batcup, D.C. (2013). A Discussion of the Dance Movement Psychotherapy Literature Relative to Prisons and Medium Secure Units. *Body, Movement and Dance in Psychotherapy*. Vol 8 (1): 5-16. DOI: 10.1080/17432979.2012.693895.

Bateman, A. and Fonagy, P. (2004). *Psychotherapy for Borderline Personality Disorder: Mentalization Based Treatment*. Oxford University Press, Oxford.

Bateman, A. and Fonagy, P. (2006). *Mentalization-Based Treatment for Borderline Personality Disorder*. Oxford University Press, Oxford.

Bick, E. (1968). The Experience of Skin in Early Object Relations. *International Journal of Psycho-Analysis,* 49, pp.484-486.

Cordess, C. and Hyatt Williams, A. (1996). The Criminal Act and Acting out. In: C. Cordess and M. Cox (Eds.) *Forensic Psychotherapy: Crime, Psychodynamics and the Offender Patient.* London: Jessica Kingsley.

Davies, E. 2001. *Beyond Dance: Laban's Legacy of Movement Analysis.* London and New York: Routledge.

Fischman, D. (2009). Therapeutic Relationships and Kinesthetic Empathy. In Chaiklin, S. and Wengrower, H. (eds). *The Art and Science of Dance/Movement Therapy: Life is Dance.* Routledge, New York.

Fonagy, P., Gergely, G., Jurist, E.L., Target, M. (2004). *Affect Regulation, Mentalization and the Development of the Self.* Karnac, London.

Fonagy, P. and Bateman, A.W. (2006) Mechanisms of change in mentalization-based treatment of BPD. *Journal of Clinical Psychology,* 62 (4), pp. 411-430.

Gorsuch, N. (1998). Unmet Need Among Disturbed Female Offenders. *The Journal of Forensic Psychiatry,* 9(3), pp. 556-570.

Halprin, D. (2003). *The Expressive Body in Life, Art and Therapy: Working with Movement, Metaphor and Meaning.* Jessica Kingsley Publishers, London.

Hollway, W. and Featherstone, B. (1997). *Mothering and Ambivalence.* Routledge, London.

Jeffcote, N. and Watson, T. (eds) (2004). *Working Therapeutically with Women in Secure Mental Health Settings (Forensic Focus 27).* Jessica Kingsley Publishers, London & Philadelphia.

Kernberg, O.F. (2004). In: J.J. Magnavita (Ed.) *Handbook of Personality Disorders: Theory and Practice.* John Wiley and Sons, New Jersey.

Kestenberg, J. Amighi, S. and Loman, S. (1999). Tension Flow Rhythms. In (Eds.) J. Kestenberg Amighi, S. Loman, P. Lewis and K.M. Sossin. *The Meaning Of Movement*. Gordon and Breach, Amsterdam.

Klein, M. (1932). *The Psychoanalysis of Children*. Hogarth Press, London.

Koch, S.C., Glawe, S. and Holt, D.V. (2011). Up and Down, Front and Back. Movement and Meaning in the Vertical and Sagittal Axes. *Social Psychology*, 42(3), pp. 214-224.

Levy, J.A. and Duke, M.P. (2003). The Use of Laban Movement Analysis in the Study of Personality, Emotional State and Movement Style: An Exploratory Investigation of the Veridicality of "Body Language". *Individual Differences Research*, 1 (1), pp. 39-63.

Lloyd-Owen, D. (2003). Perverse Females: Their Unique Psychopathology. *British Journal of Psychotherapy*. 19 (3): 285-296.

Manford, B. (2014). Insecure Attachment and Borderline Personality Disorder: Working With Dissociation and the 'Capacity to Think'. *Body, Movement and Dance in Psychotherapy*, 9(2), pp. 93-105.

Meekums, B. (2002) *Dance Movement Therapy*. Sage, London.

Mezey, G. and Bartlett, A. (1996). An Exploration of Gender Issues in Forensic Psychiatry. In Hemingway, C. (ed). *Special Women? The Experience of Women in the Special Hospital System*. Avebury Publishing, Aldershot.

Miller, A. (1987). *The Drama of Being a Child*. Virago, London.

Motz, A. (2008). *The Psychology of Female Violence: Crimes Against the Body*. Routledge, London.

Motz, A. (2014). *Toxic Couples: The Psychology of Domestic Violence*. Routledge, London.

Newham, P. (1999). *Using Voice and Movement in Therapy: The Practical Application of Voice Movement Therapy*. Jessica Kingsley Publishers, London.

Novy, C., Ward, S., Thomas, A., Bulmer, L. and Gauthier, M-F. (2005). Introducing Movement and Prop as Additional Metaphors in Narrative Therapy. *Journal of Systemic Therapies.* Vol 24 (2): 60-74.

Parker, R. (1995). *Torn in Two: The Experience of Maternal Ambivalence.* Virago, London.

Parker, R. (1996). *Mother Love/Mother Hate: The Power of Maternal Ambivalence.* Basic Books, London.

Russell, G. and Marsden, P.(2006). What does the Therapist Feel? Countertransference with Bulimic Women with Borderline Personality Disorder. *British Journal of Psychotherapy,* 15(1), pp. 31-42.

Schore, A.N. (2001). The Effects of Early Relational Trauma on Right Brain Development, Affect Regulation, and Infant Mental Health. *Infant Mental Health Journal,* 22 (1,2), pp. 201-269.

Seligman, S. (2008). Metaphor, Activity, Acknowledgement, Grief: Mentalization and Related Transformations in the Psychoanalytic Process. In Jurist, E.L., Slade, A. and Bergner, S. *Mind to Mind: Infant Research, Neuroscience and Psychoanalysis.* Other Press, New York.

Stanton Jones, K. (1992). *An Introduction to Dance Movement Psychotherapy in Psychiatry.* Routledge, London.

Stark, A. and Lohn, A.F. (1989). The Use of Verbalization in Dance/Movement Therapy. *The Arts in Psychotherapy.* Vol 16: 105-113.

Stern, D.N. (1985). The Sense of a Subjective Self: II Affect Attunement. In *The Interpersonal World of the Infant: A View from Psychoanalysis and Developmental Psychology.* Basic Books, New York.

Verhaeghe, P. (2009). Perversion: 'Your Balls or Your Life'- Lessons by Estela Welldon. *British Journal of Psychotherapy,* 25(2), pp. 183-189.

Welldon E.V. (1988). *Mother, Madonna, Whore: the Idealization and Denigration of Motherhood.* Karnac, London.

Welldon E.V. (1993). Forensic Psychotherapy and Group Analysis. *Group Analysis* Vol 26: 487-502

Welldon, E.V. (2009a). Dancing with Death. *British Journal of Psychotherapy* Vol 25 (2): 149-182.

Welldon E.V. (2009b). *Playing with Dynamite: a Personal Approach to the Psychoanalytic Understanding of Perversions, Violence and Criminality.* Karnac, London.

Winnicott, D.W. (1949). Hate in the Countertransference. In Winnicott, D.W. (1979). *The Maturational Processes and the Facilitating Environment.* Hogarth Press, London.

Winnicott, D.W. (1971). *Playing and Reality.* Routledge, London.

Wood, H. (2014). Working with Problems of Perverse Patients. *British Journal of Psychotherapy*, 30 (4), pp. 422-437.

An earlier version of this paper was presented at the 24th Annual Conference of the International Association of Forensic Psychotherapists, *Recovering From Violence: Victims, Perpetrators & Communities at Yale University*, March 2015

CHAPTER 3

Which road do you take?
Art psychotherapy within a modified therapeutic community

JESSICA COLLIER

"You road I enter upon and look around, I believe you are not all that is here, I believe that much unsaid is also here."

(Song of the Open Road, Walt Whitman)

Introduction

This chapter explores the difficult journey of a forensic patient in a modified therapeutic community back to prison to complete his sentence before release.

This man was initially referred for individual art psychotherapy to support him in finding his voice in the wider therapeutic community, where he slowly progressed from individual to group work. Using case material from both these pathways, I will detail the development in his understanding of his index offence as a re-enactment of the violence he witnessed as a powerless child, and his acknowledgment of the excitement and escape violence offered him as an independent adult. Through the making and sharing of art objects, this young man began to recognise the effect his violence had on his own internal world and the external world around him. His artwork appeared to shift from an impenetrable and solitary evocation to a more chaotic but shared expression. This seemed to further his ability to make connections in the therapeutic community, allowing him to form relationships that felt safe enough for him to finally speak openly about his overwhelming feelings of rage. He seemed tenacious and motivated to understand the violent path he had chosen. During his final session, he made an image for the group and asked the question: "Which road do you take?"

This modified therapeutic community is for men with severe personality disorders, and is located within the grounds of a medium-secure hospital. It was originally conceived as part of the Dangerous and Severe Personality Disorder (DSPD) programme (Department of Health 1999), and was one of a number of specialised intensive units in selected prisons and forensic hospitals for the treatment of patients assessed as posing a significant risk of serious offending or harm to others and whose risk was linked to their personality disorder. DSPD was seen as contentious as it had no legal or medical basis and was interpreted as a political definition deriving from the government consultation paper 'Managing dangerous people with severe personality disorder' (Department of Health 1999). This has now been reorganised as a national Personality Disorder Pathway (Joseph, N & Benefield, N 2012). The men resident here are immersed in a full programme including group art psychotherapy, psychodynamically informed small group psychotherapy, community meetings, cognitive therapy programs and occupational therapy. The timeframe for treatment before release or transfer back to prison is approximately two years.

Within this highly structured environment, my job as a community member and art psychotherapist is to support the men in seeking to look at their world from new and different perspectives. Paradoxically, having chosen to write about this I found it difficult to decide which perspective or which pathway to choose in presenting the work. When working with and thinking about these men's emotions and experiences which are so complex, so nuanced and so filled with subjectivity and personal resonance, which road *do* you take? How do these men find a way to recover from violence?

I would like to think about how change can happen through encouraging creativity and recognising patterns that may link current feelings and future possibilities with the buried trauma of past experiences, trauma that with these men has too often resurfaced as violence. Bracha Ettinger suggests that the making of art signifies "… the threshold between the human pain of the past and the human compassion of the present" (Pollock 2010). I would like to explore this

idea of the "borderspace" (Pollock 2012), the place between trauma
and recovery that exists in the act of creativity, and the resulting
possibility of these men seeing the world differently, alongside peers
and professionals who feel compassion, exhibit personal curiosity and
offer a supportive environment for growth and change. All of which are
considered fundamental to the therapeutic community ethos. (Royal
College of Psychiatrists 2008)

Despite these explicit objectives, the therapeutic community
itself and the position art psychotherapy has within it, is complex. I will
focus on a case study to illuminate the contribution art psychotherapy
can make to greater self-awareness and the progress men here can
make back into the community outside. I hope to demonstrate that art
psychotherapy can help change the rigid perception of environment
and relationships that may be inherent in individuals with a severe
personality disorder, and also an institution whose priority has to be
physical rather than psychological security. These two aims may not
be mutually exclusive.

The therapeutic community and the position of art psychotherapy

Currently the therapeutic community accommodates 16 residents, thus
housing 16 different individual's perspectives. There are many more
staff of course; all of whom inevitably bring their own perspectives into
the environment. This is important to keep in mind, to allow space for
thoughts, views and observations to meet, to touch and to intersect.
John Berger suggests that "perspective is not a science, but a hope"
(Berger 2002). I think it is the meeting of different lines of perspective,
of new paths of enquiry, that offer the patients an opportunity to choose
a different road and an opportunity to hold some hope for the future.
When a violent act has been committed, the trauma of committing the
act itself may produce a feeling of internal chaos that is impossible to
see through or past, or to imagine escaping from. It is for patients and
staff to collectively establish an environment that feels safe enough to
discover roads through or out of this chaos.

There are residents who have been incarcerated for up to 25 years
or more, and others who may have many years left on their sentence.

This may seem like a never-ending road, as members of the art therapy group often articulate in their drawings of isolated and harsh environments. Others are nearing the end of their time in custody and are using community leave or awaiting release, but this too may be a frightening prospect. However far away or imminent release back into the community may be, if outside has been experienced previously as violent, isolating or deprived and the individual has been left feeling paranoid or abandoned, then the world waiting through the gate may be a lonely place indeed. This mutable dynamic in the patient cohort is also reflected in the staff group; some of whom have been part of the therapeutic community since its inception and are deeply invested, and others who have just arrived and have yet to find their place or voice.

The intimacy in such a small community highlights the division between the patients and staff and within the hierarchy of the staff team itself, which is often parodied by the men as Upstairs Downstairs, a reference to the classic British costume drama. Hyatt Williams suggests that attacks on the process are inevitable and may be institutional. He states that "caricature is a common way of ridiculing one or more staff members, and sometimes the recognition of what is happening gives the staff members themselves opportunities to change" (Hyatt Williams 1998, p262). It is important that we recognise the difficulties posed by professional egos and rivalry within the staff team, and there is some accuracy to the Upstairs Downstairs parody. Of course positions and roles are allocated, each with a particular status, and the men obviously examine and note any discord or allegiances, which in any group are inevitable. The concept of a staircase also illustrates well the complexity of a system that seems easy to navigate but is multi-layered, highly intricate in design and may be essential for egress. In addition, positions above and below of power and powerlessness cannot be avoided in a secure setting where some members of the community have keys and others do not. However, while there is fertile ground for vigorous splitting, projection and parallel processes there is also an opportunity to acknowledge group dynamics, offence paralleling and re-enactments of past relationships and behaviours.

I spend two days a week in the therapeutic community as part of a community meeting, facilitating an art psychotherapy group, a clay group and co-facilitating a small group, all with the patients who live on the ward. I try to be imaginative and demonstrate creativity in my thinking but this, particularly as presented in the art psychotherapy group, is often attacked. It is done both overtly, by the men missing or leaving sessions or diminishing their experience in the group feedback, or unconsciously by the wider community, most commonly through omission and neglect or through attacks on the space itself. I think of this communal neglect perhaps as a paralleling of the men's early interpersonal experiences where creative and imaginative processes might have been overlooked by the necessity of merely surviving invariably traumatic, violent or neglectful childhoods. A similar parallel process happens in the inevitable idealisation and denigration of the art psychotherapy. Patients who have been eager to join are disappointed or unsatisfied with the reality of the experience they are offered, an experience of their own making which can feel exposing or infantilising.

Despite daily meetings, communal meals and frequent feedback, often the overwhelming anxiety for staff and patients is not knowing what is happening or what is about to happen in the community, the anxiety of holding onto and bearing uncertainty. As Bion reminds us, we must be able to tolerate mystery and our own ignorance to allow a new way of thinking and seeing to emerge (Bion 2014). Responding to this perpetual anxiety in a concrete and tangible way, the daily routine in the community is full of structured activity. This is clinically important so the simple concept of boundaries can be demonstrated and applied to support the men in feeling safe enough to learn to trust the intentions of staff and peers and have some confidence in the process. But my experience is that the order and boundaries are also personally important because it feels so easy for my mind to become clouded, confused and separated. In an environment characterised by emotional fragility and suspicion, it is essential to avoid emotional detachment or emotional over-involvement and to work in a boundaried manner (Norton 2012).

Simultaneously, emotional resilience is fundamental to being able to sit with the mess. There are regular times set aside for supervision and support during which staff can reflect and discuss their emotional responses to the men and to each other. This processing through supervision is vital (Rothwell 2008); though it too has its own complexities and is not always the panacea we might hope for. Metaphorically, a framework that is robust and can hold weight, while also accommodating movement and space, is as fundamental to building relationships and a successful therapeutic community as it is to any ambitious and creative architectural structure (Kolarevic & Parlac 2015).

Nevertheless, the routine and activities of any institution give rise to patients feeling both infantilised and dependent, and in this respect the therapeutic community is no different. Where there is a distinction, which is especially marked in a cohort with severe personality disorder, it is in the simultaneous sense of entitlement and "specialness". There is often a perception that the men are doing the staff a favour by taking part in their own treatment, and this sense of entitlement has to be kept in mind to prevent the therapist and the community itself feeling special (Gutheil 2015). I have been told by more than one patient that if they choose not to come to therapy I would be out of a job, and they attend only so that I will not be upset. While there is a kernel of truth to this, including my perpetual professional anxiety that I am ineffectual, there may also be a projection of their own sense of inadequacy, and this is important to concede.

Case study

To better understand how art psychotherapy in a therapeutic community can foster the ability for these men to create, develop and widen their own new perspectives, whilst simultaneously encouraging a mentalising capacity to imagine each other's different points of view, I will write about the creative process of one young man I will call Ivan.

I would like to thank Ivan for giving his consent to use the images he made during art psychotherapy.

Beginning and being together

Ivan engaged in individual sessions for twenty-six weeks before joining the group for a further thirty weeks. He was referred because he was struggling to speak in the community meetings and small groups. It was hoped by the team and his peers that art psychotherapy would help him articulate *his* perspective. Ivan said he would like to use art psychotherapy to help him express himself and to gain confidence in speaking about his feelings.

Ivan was a young man in his early twenties. He was a prison transfer serving an indeterminate sentence for public protection (IPP) for robbery with violence. The giving of these sentences has been abolished after some controversy, but this is not retrospective and prisoners already serving IPPs have no automatic right to release (www.justice.gov.uk 2012).

Ivan had viciously attacked three different men on three separate occasions late at night, all of whom he met at railway stations. On all three occasions he had hit his victim on the back of the head with a weapon, once with a house brick, resulting in the victim falling unconscious onto live railway track. All three of his victims were vulnerable at the time of the attacks. They had all been drinking and one of them had a serious physical disability.

During our first meeting, Ivan spoke initially about the thrill he experienced thinking about the violence he had committed and the excitement of feeling in danger himself. He was from a home where he witnessed extreme domestic violence as a child, on one occasion witnessing an attack where his mother was hospitalised. Ivan described a raw and powerful hatred of his father, whom he said he would kill if he ever saw, and he idealised his mother, who despite being supportive since her son had been incarcerated, had been unable to protect Ivan, his younger brother or herself from his father's violent attacks. This experience may have left Ivan feeling that he too had been unable to protect his family, leaving him feeling ashamed and leading to further acts of aggression (Mills & Kellington 2012, Target & Fonagy 2000, Gilligan 1999).

In the first few sessions Ivan's communication mirrored his behaviour in the community. He said almost nothing, gave very limited eye contact and made an image which he labelled, perhaps in an attempt to help clarify its meaning. Ivan continued adding to this image over several weeks, appearing to delay taking any creative risk that might expose his vulnerability. Ivan became lively talking about the violence the image depicted, and he drew lines connecting the various illicit objects and symbols in his image together. Looking at these lines,

I was reminded of "desire lines", the short cuts made by footfall taking the quickest or most desirable route from A-B. I imagined how Ivan might use the drugs, alcohol and money depicted in his montage as the quickest route away from his emotional pain; "desire lines" leading away from the emotional trauma of his past (see figure 1).

Fig. 1. Desire lines

After a few weeks sitting together with this picture, Ivan was able to identify gaps and spaces that seemed to highlight emptiness, isolation and a lack of intimate relationships. Ivan explored loss in relation to his family, including a deep sense of loss and fragility emphasised by his grandmother's grave and a heart that remained separate from the other symbols in the image. This poignant separated place brought to mind the impossibility for Ivan of assimilating sadness, loss and grief alongside his unassailable defences. Bowlby reminds us that the loss of a loved person is one of the most intensely painful experiences any human being can suffer (Bowlby 1998). We said little in the sessions together, but Ivan's artwork slowly progressed and developed. He attended every week and appeared to be making an attachment to the sessions. During this period he mixed his own strong adhesive from all the different bottles of glue in the cupboard and began to build a matchstick sculpture. Ivan began cautiously attaching the small pieces of wood together using the adhesive he had made. As he worked he began to speak tentatively about the feelings of powerlessness he had felt as a child, unable to protect his mother or brother from his father's violence. He linked these early experiences of aggression with his own desire for control, which he felt he achieved as a violent adult whom people feared and which is a common response to childhood trauma in this population (Renn 2004).

Following these reflections about the fear he instilled in people, Ivan put the sculptural work aside for some weeks and began working with clay. This seemed to reflect an uncertain period in the therapy as he made and recycled several small pots. Ivan seemed to demonstrate some ambivalence, which manifested in him working on several images at once and finishing none of the work he began. The pots were badly made and he seemed unable to continue working with the clay, perhaps feeling overwhelmed by the intense emotions clay work can evoke (Scholt & Gavron 2010). During this time I too felt cautious and was aware of feeling scared of Ivan's potential for violence. This was particularly apparent when he reached into the cupboard directly behind my head to retrieve a rolling pin, a weapon that might symbolise domestic violence. It was at this point in the therapy that Ivan missed a session, perhaps sensing my own fear and ambivalence.

When he returned the following week he went back to his wooden box. Ivan continued to build up the layers of his matchstick sculpture and he began to talk about value and worth. He came to see his artwork as a container. Initially we thought together about the space inside the box being dark, empty, unseen and protected by very strong fortified walls. Ivan decided it was a container for his emotions and described it as a strong box, a safe, which appeared flawless, unbreakable and impenetrable. His description appeared to define a symbolic "psychic retreat", a state of mind Ivan could occupy to escape anxiety and mental pain, but where he might remain stuck, unable to progress emotionally (Steiner 1993). However, Ivan may also have seen the box as a symbolic container in which he could feel safe enough to begin reflecting. He began to show some pride in his artwork, especially in relation to how his mother and his late grandmother might feel about his progress. He spoke with regret that his grandmother could not see how well he was doing and he said, "She would have been proud of me and seen the grandson she would have wanted".

Ivan worked continuously on his box, sanding it down and making it perfect (see figure 2).

Fig. 2. Ivan's Box

During these sessions I would sit with feelings of enormous frustration at how long the process was taking him and how amateurishly he was doing the work. While I might need to understand this counter-transference as my own feeling of inadequacy and desire for tangible progress, it also needs to be noted that the institution has to comply with a wider organisational objective to "fix" these highly dangerous men in their two year stay. It can be difficult *not* to collude with the idea that patience and perseverance and psychological "holding" can be put aside and disregarded.

Ivan finally completed his matchstick sculpture and he saw it both as an illustration of his current experience, safe inside a secure building, and as a metaphor for his own emotional defences, an internal prison of his own construction that would protect him and help him to survive. Ivan stated that things of value, important things, must be kept hidden away, out of sight.

Separation and maturation

Meanwhile, outside of the sessions in the therapeutic community, Ivan was beginning to speak a little more. We agreed it was time for him to transition to the group, and Ivan initially seemed to fit in and appeared to enjoy looking at the artwork collectively and creatively exploring different layers of possible meaning. Shortly after he joined Ivan spoke to the group movingly about his feelings of loss around his grandmother and the complicated dynamics within his family. He thought about the motivations for his violence and his understanding of feeling powerless as a child and his experience of feeling abandoned and unsupported. He directly connected the closed and impenetrable emotional defences reflected in his artworks with the losses he had experienced. It did not seem possible at this time to think about the loss of his individual sessions with me and the feelings of abandonment this might have provoked. It felt like this would be too exposing in front of the group and perhaps unconsciously, I did not want to acknowledge my own responsibility for ending our sessions and concede the uncomfortable feeling that I had abandoned Ivan and was not a "good enough mother" (Winnicott 1958).

Ivan remained confused about the excitement he experienced when he talked about violence, but thought more about the feelings of loneliness and abandonment he felt prior to committing the offences, his desire for comfort and care at this time, and how his failure to find emotional shelter might link with his violence. He seemed to begin to appreciate just how vulnerable *he* had felt when he attacked these vulnerable men. His identification with such defenceless individuals at a time when he felt totally alone and unsupported was perhaps intolerable and he may have divested his own unwanted vulnerability and feelings of abandonment and deposited them in his victims whom he then despised. In attacking his victims and in seeing his own fear and shame in them, Ivan may have found a way to do actively what he had previously been forced to suffer passively. At a time when he felt abandoned, he could be frightening instead of feeling frightened (Ogden 1979, Sandler 1989, Gilligan 1999).

Ivan could see the emptiness of his internal world in his artwork, and he began thinking about his relationships in the group and in his life. He thought about his relationship with his younger brother and drew two boats seemingly reaching out and keeping one another afloat, perhaps through the violence of their childhood. He thought about friendships he had made as a young boy when he was on holiday, and made a drawing of the places they explored together. It showed buildings and roads seen from an unusual and different perspective.

However, following his move from individual to group work, Ivan's relationship with me had become hostile in the sessions as it had never been in one to ones. This animosity seemed to surface once he had spoken about the loss of his grandmother to the group, and as he began making work about his mother and father and his place in the family. He was sarcastic and rude to me, behaviour that was unseen in any other forum, and this was exacerbated further when I became the co-therapist for his small group. The merging of my role seemed to unsettle Ivan and he appeared verbally aggressive.

From the beginning of our work together I had been conscious of a protective maternal countertransference, often identifying an impulse to help him with his work or reach out and touch his hair. But this seemed to coexist with a feeling that I was letting Ivan down, and not providing him with enough. Once again in the countertransference I felt inadequate and had to wrestle with feelings of guilt and cruelty that I had abandoned him before he was ready and pushed him into a group. The move had been agreed from the beginning and had been a community decision which I had been part of. Nevertheless, I felt that perhaps my decision had been pressured, and I thought about his mother's inability to stand up for her son as his violent father exerted his control over her and how Ivan had watched, powerless, unable to intervene or express his own needs. I wondered if the anger Ivan might have felt at his mother's failure to protect him was re-enacted in his apparent anger towards me.

For several weeks Ivan railed against any remark I made and appeared intensely angry with me and belligerent towards the group itself. His responses to any comments or observations I made remained abrupt and sarcastic. This behaviour also appeared to coincide with the timing of a difficult anniversary connected with a particularly violent assault on his mother Ivan had witnessed as a child. Over the next few weeks he worked on several images overtly about his mother. He struggled meanwhile to address me directly, as he had been unable to ask his mother for help prior to the offences. He told the group that he felt like a child doing art psychotherapy with me. When I suggested this parallel between his communication with his mother and with me, Ivan shouted angrily, "You could never be my mum, you'll never be anything like my mum". However, he seemed open to the group suggesting that talking about violence might be difficult with a woman, just as he had never spoken with his mother about his violence.

Ivan seemed to be using these live feelings, alongside his image making, to begin to process his anger around feeling powerless. Perhaps in his attitude towards me Ivan was now identifying with the aggressor, behaving as his father had towards his mother in an attempt to feel some control (Freud 1936). His work around this time was messy, repetitive and difficult to make sense of. He seemed to be addressing the familial conflicts from his past, and as he tried to print his artworks perfectly over and over again the unformed images reappeared liked ghosts. (Fraiberg, Adelson & Shapiro 1975). Finally, frustrated with the process and unable to express what he wanted to, Ivan asked me for help.

Ettinger succinctly sums up the making of art "...as a means to effect the passage to a future that accepts the burden of sharing the trauma while processing and transforming it" (Pollock 2010, p830). Following this request for help, Ivan worked collaboratively with me and the group. He took ownership of the space, assisting other members with choosing materials and making use of a range of resources, often asking for help and advice and offering ideas. He seemed to have matured in the group and he developed an ongoing piece of work making a montage of his images, processing them perhaps and transforming them, assimilating them into one. He took time to make it, exploring his family and his feelings about them. It was this work Ivan chose to take with him when he left.

However, in the approach to him leaving the group in readiness to move on, Ivan continued to make work reflecting on his complicated experiences, his future and what it might hold. Where his images had initially suggested closed and impenetrable emotional defences, he slowly moved into a way of working which appeared more open and in which he directly exposed his feelings of vulnerability and conflict. He worked up images of pathways and roads showing perspective, direction and dimension that seemed almost architectural in form. One particular image Ivan drew appeared to encapsulate some of Daniel Libeskind's ideas of architecture. The image itself looked visually very similar to Libeskind's architectural drawings, but it also seemed to be expressing something inexplicable about memory, risk, space and optimism while addressing real concerns (Libeskind 2009). Libeskind imagines successful architecture to be democratic, and for democracy to succeed we must rely on others.

Ending

Ivan found a voice in the wider community. He came to see his index offence from a different viewpoint, perhaps as the re-enactment of the violence he had witnessed as a powerless child. This had offered him escape as an adult, but no longer seemed to excite him as he identified his own vulnerability and need for care and support. Ivan's art making and his relationship with his creativity and the group helped him to recognise the effect his violence had on his own internal world and the external world around him. He was able to make connections and form relationships that seemed safe enough for him to finally speak openly about his fear, confusion, pain, loss and anger. During his last session, Ivan completed an image for all the members of the group asking us: "Which road do you take?" This artwork appeared to reflect the complexity of pathways, layers and different intricate perspectives he had come to see as he emerged from the fortified walls of his defences. But perhaps more importantly, his image evokes possibilities; roads and pathways he can choose to take in the future (see figure 3).

Fig. 3. Roads

John Berger observes that: "A line, an area of tone, is not really important because it records what you have seen, but because of what it will lead you on to see" (Berger 2013). Ivan remained a quiet member of the community, but he seemed to discover different aspects of himself; curious, asking questions and secure enough to share something of his complex and multi-layered internal world. Many young men in the criminal justice system have experienced life as a series of traumas from which they have been unsupported in recovering (Harris 2015). When an individual's emotional defences are so impenetrable, which road *do* you take? Ivan's final image appeared to hold multiple meanings; the acknowledgement of different viewpoints, the possibility of opportunity, of lines meeting, of making choices and even the risk and fear of falling. In his early artwork Ivan had described the concealment and locking away of fear and abandonment, feelings of inadequacy and loss, even his valuable memories of care and love. Yet as his work progressed and he came to better understand his internal world, Ivan's images offered the group a new perspective; one of uncertainty, possibility and perhaps, of hope.

BIBLIOGRAPHY

Berger, J. (2002) *Past present* The Guardian. On-line, 12th October

Berger, J. (2013) *Drawing is discovery* The New Statesman. On-line, 1st May

Bion, W. (2014) *The complete works of W.R Bion Volume 1*. London: Karnac

Bowlby, J. (1998) *Loss - Sadness and Depression: Attachment and Loss, Volume 3*. London: Pimlico

Department of Health (1999). *Managing dangerous people with severe personality disorder* www. homeoffice.gov.uk

Fraiberg, S., Adelson, E. & Shapiro, V. (1975) *Ghosts in the nursery,* Journal of American Academy of Child Psychiatry. Summer, 14(3): 387-421

Freud, A (1936) *The ego and the mechanism of defence* London: Hogarth Press

Gilligan, J. (1999) *Violence: Reflections on our deadliest epidemic.* London: JKP

Guthiel, T, G. (2014) Boundary Issues. In Oldham, J., Skodol, A. & Bender, D. (Eds) *The American psychiatric publishing textbook of personality disorders: Second edition.* Arlington: American Psychiatric Association

Harris, T. (2015) *The Harris Review: Changing Prisons, Saving Lives: Report of the Independent Review into Self-inflicted Deaths in Custody of 18-24 year olds.* Crown Copyright

Hyatt-Williams, A. (1998) *Cruelty, Violence and murder* New Jersey: Jason Aronson

Joseph, N. & Benefield, N. (2012) *A joint offender personality disorder pathway strategy: An outline summary.* Criminal Behaviour and Mental Health, 22, 210-217

Kolarevic, B. & Parlac, V. Eds (2015) *Building dynamics: exploring architecture of change.* New York: Routledge

Libeskind, D. (2009) *17 Words of architectural inspiration. www. ted.comhttp://www.ted.com/*

Mills, E & Kellington, S. (2012) *Using group art therapy to address the shame and silencing surrounding children's experiences of witnessing domestic violence.*

International Journal of Art Therapy: Formerly Inscape, 17:1, 3-12

Ministry of Justice (2012) *Life sentences prisoners. https://www.justice.gov.uk/offenders/types-of-offender/life*

Norton, K. (2012) Forward in Adlam, J., Aiyegbusi, A. Kleinot, P. Motz, A & Scanlon, C (Eds) *The therapeutic milieu under fire* London: JKP

Ogden, T. (1979) *On projective identification.* International Journal of Psycho-Analysis, 60:357-373

Pollock, G. (2010) *Aesthetic wit(h)nessing in the era of trauma.* EurAmerica Vol.40, p860

Pollock, G. (2012) *After-affect? After Image – trauma and aesthetic transformations.* AHRC Research Fellowship Symposium, Anna Freud Centre

Renn, P. (2004) The link between childhood trauma and later offending. In Plafflin, F. & Adshead, G. (Eds) *A matter of security* London: JKP

Rothwell, K. (2008) *Lost in translation: Art psychotherapy with patients presenting suicidal states.* In International Journal of Art Therapy: Inscape 13(1): 2-12

Royal College of Psychiatrists' Centre for Quality Improvement (2008) *Briefing Paper: The Development of Core Standards and Core Values for Therapeutic Communities.* http://www.rcpsych.ac.uk/workinpsychiatry/ qualityimprovement/publications/2008.aspx

Sandler, J. (1989) *Projection, identification, projective identification.* London: Karnac

Scholt, M., & Gavron, T. (2006) *Therapeutic qualities of clay-work in art therapy and psychotherapy: A review.* Journal of American Art therapy Association, 23(6), 66-72

Steiner, J. (1993) *Psychic retreats: Pathological organizations in psychotic, neurotic and borderline patients.* London: Routledge

Target, M & Fonagy, P (2000) *Attachment and reflective function: Their role in self-organisation* Developmental Psychopathology 9, 679-700

Winnicott,D.W. (1958) *Collected papers.* London Tavistock Publications

CHAPTER 4

Art therapy for anger management
MARIAN LIEBMANN

Introduction

first became involved in anger work as a probation officer, helping to run Anger Management groups for adult male violent offenders. Attendance at these groups was usually by court order, and they were often heavy going, but I gained considerable satisfaction – I enjoyed the psychological challenge and there were quite a few 'success stories'.

Until then I had subscribed to the prevalent therapy philosophy that it was useful to express anger and 'let it all hang out'. This helped me with my own anger, but coming face to face with violent offenders and their actions, challenged this whole idea. Here were people who had no problem expressing their anger – often causing severe injuries and other damage. I needed to radically rethink the model.

The probation Anger Management groups used Cognitive Behavioural Therapy (CBT) principles, helping offenders think differently about their offences and develop new strategies (Novaco, Ramm and Black 2000).

When I moved to an inner city community mental health team, many workers had angry clients on their caseload. Often there would be a distressed and angry service user in the waiting room banging on the glass window because his or her needs were not met. There was a need for Anger Management groups here too. Now working as an art therapist, I had extra tools in the form of art materials and art therapy techniques, which I hoped might side-step the wordiness of the verbal programmes and give service users a deeper experience.

Following a request from the consultant psychiatrist, I developed a group work model for inner city clients with anger problems. The approach was derived initially from the CBT-based course for probation clients, translated into art therapy themes. I added relaxation and guided imagery; awareness of physical symptoms; and layers of anger. As anger involves thoughts, emotions and behaviour, any programme must also contain these three elements (Tavris 1989).

Involvement in art therapy provides these elements and offers another way to communicate for people who find it hard to verbalise why they get angry. The process of doing artwork slows clients down and helps them reflect on what is happening. Group work helps people feel less isolated, when they realise that others too have anger issues.

I will reflect on work in both settings, and include group and individual work. Many clients with mental health issues were also offenders, or exhibited attitudes closely connected with offending behaviour. I will refer to work in four art therapy anger management groups: two mixed-gender, one women's and one men's group. Some of these groups have been described before (Liebmann 2004, 2007, 2008) but the focus here is on how such groups can offer ways forward for those with offending behaviour.

Anger issues are not always identified by clients themselves. Often it is people around them who experience the problem. I spent an assessment session discussing anger work with a woman referred to me for angry behaviour which included pulling a therapist's hair, damaging her neighbour's car and spray-painting her house. We seemed to be talking at cross-purposes. I asked her, "I thought you came here because of problems with anger?" She retorted, "I don't have any problems with anger, it's just the mental health service keeps winding me up." It may take a court case to bring people to face up to their anger and its destructive results. In the mental health service, anger management work is only successful if clients are motivated.

The group programme

I developed a theme-based art therapy group as outlined in the introduction. I wrote handouts linked to each session, for those who found them useful. Each session was two hours long, with a refreshment break in the middle. The programme covered the following:

1. Introductions and ground rules

Helping the group to formulate ground rules was very important in making the group a safe place to work on a subject often seen as frightening. This was followed by a simple art exercise for people to introduce themselves to the group.

2. Relaxation and guided imagery

This session helped service users identify a peaceful place to return to at any time. It also paved the way for short relaxations at the end of every session, both as a practice to develop and as a way of leaving behind any upsetting feelings from the session.

3. What is anger?

It was interesting for clients to see how everyone thought of anger in different ways.

4. Physical symptoms of anger

These can often arise before we are conscious of our anger, so awareness of them can provide time to take avoiding action. Marking these on a large body outline as a group can also be fun.

Anger – good or bad?

Most people referred to an anger group think of anger as purely negative, so it is instructive to look at its positive aspects.

5. What's underneath the anger?

This important exercise helps participants identify underlying hurts, unmet needs and fears – which can often be worked with more easily than the resultant anger.

6. Early family patterns

This session can help clients recognise learned dysfunctional ways of handling anger. It may also uncover physical, emotional and sexual abuse, so needs to be handled carefully.

7. Anger and conflict

Sometimes conflict leads to anger, sometimes anger leads to conflict. Reflecting on these can help participants to react more constructively to both.

8. Feelings and assertiveness, I-messages

Assertiveness and speaking for oneself is an important tool in anger management, and the visual theme I use is 'a picture of the real you'.

9. Picture review

In this session participants can notice themes in their work and often see progress.

10. Group picture/activity and ending

It is important to round off a group, using an ending ritual such as a group picture or metaphorical gifts from participants to each other.

Mixed-gender groups

I ran two such groups. Ten clients were accepted for the first one, six men and four women. Two of the women dropped out before the group started, leaving the other two feeling 'outnumbered' – one attended twice and the other only once. This left five male clients. My co-facilitator was a male community psychiatric nurse; a female student also joined the group, making six men and two women. Clients' anger issues, identified in their pre-group self-assessments, are shown in Table 1.

Table 1 – Number of people expressing each issue	
Aggressive outbursts	5
Bottling it up	4
Angry with life and discrimination	3
Triggers events from the past	3
Inability to identify feelings	3
Provoke confrontation	3
Feeling unsafe around anger	3
Blaming myself	2
Physical tension	2
Self harm	1

Clients were also asked to rate their problems with anger on a five-point scale, and repeat this at the end of the group - all felt they had made progress with their issues.

One member of the group, Paul, expressed a problem with anger turning into violence. His life was fairly chaotic – he moved house, lost his girlfriend and broke his leg during the course of the group. He was sometimes too stressed to draw or paint, but attended very regularly and contributed well to the group. In most sessions he used felt tips to create very graphic images of his life, but felt the guided imagery painting from Session 2 was the most important. Paul had painted a lake with bulrushes and said he imagined his lake whenever he felt stressed. He said, "I can relax if I make a conscious effort, I don't get so angry with people now."

The second mixed group started with eight clients (from 17 referrals), four men and four women, but finished with three men and one woman. My co-facilitator was again a male CPN.

One member of the group, Steve[9], aged 32, was a 'heavy-end' offender as well as suffering from depression. He had been seeing a psychiatrist for depression following the breakdown of an 11-year relationship (including a son) three years previously. He had also been attacked by his ex-partner's new partner, and needed 120 stitches. He was on regular medication for depression.

Steve also had long-standing problems with alcohol and anger from early teenage years, and had left school without any qualifications. He had been in prison four times, and had numerous convictions for drink-driving, robbery and violence. Sometimes Steve could not remember what happened when he 'lost it', and he admitted that he had sometimes been very violent, using knives. He knew he had a problem with anger and had tried a course in prison, but it made him even angrier. So he was quite wary of the group, and very sceptical about art therapy.

He attended the pre-group interview and listed his problems with anger, rating them from 1 to 5 in terms of severity (5 being the highest):

1. I do violent things and afterwards can't remember why or even what happened. It can be for no reason. Prozac has helped me with this. (4)

2. My relationships with girls – I would like not to hit them. It doesn't happen often, but it's worse than hitting blokes. (3)

3. I totally over-react and flip most of the time. (4.5)

4. I'm verbally violent – swearing, etc. (5)

5. I'm on my guard all the time (5)

---

9 This case study and its accompanying picture were originally published in 'Art Therapy and Social Action' (Jessica Kingsley Publishers 2007) and are included here with permission from the publishers.

The assessment form also asked him to list the ways in which he wanted to change:

1. I'd like to be calmer.

2. I'd like to be able to argue and put my point across without being aggressive and violent.

3. I'd like to be able to handle wrong looks, bad-mouthing, etc, with different strategies.

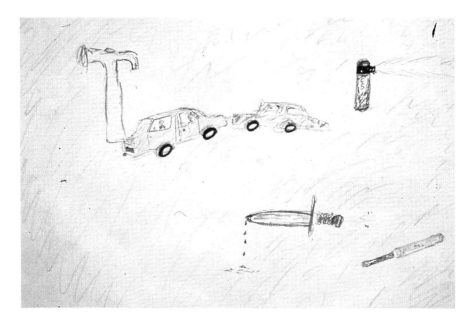

Fig. 1. Anger equals Violence

His main goal for attending the group was to 'become a calmer person'.

His introductory picture showed him on a good day and a bad day. His guided imagery picture in Session 2 was of a cemetery, the only place he could feel relaxed and off-guard. In the session on 'What is anger?', he drew a picture (see figure 1) of tools of violence, some of them being used: a big hammer; a car he used intentionally to ram another one belonging to someone he hated; a CS canister spraying gas; a dagger dripping blood; and a baseball bat. He added a title

'ANGER = VIOLENCE'. He related an incident in which someone in a pub had made a putting-down remark to him. He left the pub, went home and thought about it, then went back to the pub with a knife, as he felt he couldn't let an incident like that pass.

Anger equals violence

Before the next session Steve had a court appearance for an assault committed prior to starting the group. Very relieved to escape another prison sentence, he was given a two-year probation order, on the understanding that he would continue to attend psychiatric appointments, including the group. The next art therapy theme was 'Anger – good or bad?' and his picture showed Steve's partner and son divided from Steve, who was behind bars. He entitled it 'ANGER=CRIME'.

Both pictures showed close connections in Steve's mind between anger, violence and crime. With that thinking frame, anger would always lead to violence and crime, as it had done for most of Steve's life. He needed to find a different path for his anger that did not have such dire consequences.

Steve completed the group, with some challenges from others about his sexist attitudes, and experimented more with different media, completing a pastel picture of himself playing with his son in an atmosphere of 'peace, harmony and happiness'. He felt that anger, stress and hurt were being lifted off him. He found the relaxation and the artwork unexpectedly useful, and was pleased and surprised that he stayed out of trouble for the duration of the group. He had thought the group would be a waste of time, but it was not. He felt he had come quite a long way towards his goal of becoming a calmer person, and said, "I enjoyed the group but it would have been good to get help quicker, before all the trouble I've been in."

Gender issues

In both these groups a roughly equal number of men and women were due to start. But in both cases, the women's attendance dwindled to nothing. With the first group, I did not think it was significant – women still have a much larger role in childcare than men, especially in areas of deprivation. The reasons given seemed to make sense – children's illness, own illness, moving house or flat, family problems, etc. But when it happened the second time, I suspected there was more to it. I contacted the one woman who had attended five sessions before leaving, and she wrote a letter to the group:

"I have been wondering anyway if this is the right group for me as some of the group dynamics I found to be a bit too male-orientated, which I understand cannot be helped as people are the way they are. I cannot expect to change that, but even so, I don't want to attend an anger management course to be around the kind of negativity I found there."

We read this letter to the group and then wrote to her inviting her back. She did come back and was able to say how she felt, and suggested stricter boundaries around 'air time', i.e. equal time for each person to speak. We did this and she completed the group.

Women's group

Following on from the experience with the mixed groups, I ran a 'women-only' anger management art therapy group. This group ran for eight weeks (keeping to term times) and comprised four women (from eight referrals), with an age range from 18 to early thirties and of mixed ethnic backgrounds. Attendance was consistent throughout the group. The problems expressed by the four participants in their pre-group interviews are shown in Table 2:

Table 2 – Number of women expressing each issue	
When things go wrong, I get angry and lose my temper	4
Getting stressed/ wound up in situations, leading to anger	4
Can't handle family situations past/ present	4
Express my anger in a negative way	4
Internalising anger, unable to express it directly	2
Violent to other people	2
Can't control my anger	2
Anger with men past and present	1
Fear, guilt and shame of anger	1
Fear of hurting others	1
Verbally abusive	1

These are fairly similar to the issues of the mixed-gender group.

The first two sessions took place in the usual way – introductions and ground rules, then relaxation and guided imagery. The third session combined 'What is anger?' and 'Is it good or bad?' and led to the depiction of situations of anger, such as incidents with family members, conflicts at school, arguments with authority figures, work situations and relationships. During this session it emerged that all the women had been raped or sexually abused during childhood, and this had been the starting point for their anger, which they needed as a defence. However, they realised they were now taking their anger out on the wrong people – children or work colleagues, for example. I asked the women if they would have attended a mixed group on anger, and they all replied 'No way.'

The youngest member of the group, Joanne, had been physically abused by her mother and sexually abused by a neighbour from the ages of seven to eleven. She had a history of self harm and aggressive behaviour, attacking others including her mother and brother. She had a baby son (whom she loved very much) who had been removed because of her aggressive outbursts, climbing on the table and shouting at people at case conferences, and hitting her ex-partner. Her aim in attending the group was to find another way of dealing with her anger – she hoped this would lead to reclaiming her son.

Joanne found it very difficult to relax initially, but enjoyed the art work, especially painting. Her picture for Session 3 is shown in figure 2. She started with a red border for her anger, then purple bits for vulnerability, then yellow and gold for her rage getting out of control, then a blue background ('cold like ice') with a black heart for the hurt she was experiencing, along with feeling lost and confused as she tried to cope. She related how her anger felt like ice that nothing could touch, so she did not care about anyone. It was a relief for her to put it all into a painting. At the end of the group she painted a similar picture, but with a golden heart in the middle – her positive experience of the group - and less anger around the edge 'although it is still there', she said. She added blue (a different blue from the picture in Session 3) and yellow for calm and hope.

Fig. 2. Anger – good or bad?

Joanne also used the handouts with exercises for anger, and surprised her next case conference with a much more reasonable approach. She enjoyed seeing the amazement on people's faces as she argued her case logically instead of losing her temper and lashing out. Unfortunately it was not enough to get her son back, and she was very disappointed. Nevertheless she felt very positive about the group, and wrote at the end, "It has helped me change as a person and helped a great deal. The art was important as it helped me express myself in a way that I don't have to use words." She also received positive feedback from the group about the changes she had made.

The Anger Management Art Therapy group provided a safe and supportive space for the women to express and examine their feelings of anger. They realised they had a right to be angry with their abusers, and this helped them to stop taking it out on others. They were able to make positive changes in their lives, such as using physical exercise to defuse anger, and feeling more positive about themselves.

Men's group

The corollary of running a women's group was to run an intentional men's group. Eight men were accepted in December to start the group, but four had mental health crises so only four attended in January. One of these soon went into hospital. Scheduled as a ten-session group, absences meant it had to be rearranged to nine sessions. The remaining three attended six or seven sessions out of the nine, and seemed committed to the group. I led the programme and the exercises, while my co-facilitator (a male social worker) was ready to support participants if they needed some time out (which happened on three occasions). My student on placement (a woman) took responsibility for materials, refreshments and client notes. So we were four men and two women.

Our three service users were fairly different from each other. Dan, the oldest at 37, had a long history of persistent anger problems, and a past history of alcohol use (but had stopped drinking two years previously). He had a degree and had worked in IT but had abandoned this. Brought up in Northern Ireland, he had possible PTSD from witnessing a fatal IRA attack. He was unable to trust people, especially women. He felt he was "born angry" and there was little he could do about it, although he wanted to manage it better, recognize the danger signs and prevent himself losing his temper. He also wanted to be able to relax. He liked art and enjoyed the art work, using colour in a sensitive way.

Rob was 25, with some learning difficulties at school. He had a good work record but was suspended and in the process of being disciplined for an incident at work. During the course of the group, he lost his job. He had a baby daughter but was prevented from seeing her by his ex-partner. He had a history of self harm, overdoses and angry outbursts, occasionally physically harming others. He wanted to stop self harming and lashing out and be a respectful person to everyone. He struggled with the art work but always managed to produce something.

Mark, the youngest at 22, grew up in Australia with a violent father, coming to the UK at the age of seven. He came into mental health services at the age of 13 because he was threatening to his family. He had received several diagnoses, none of which seemed to quite fit. He had thoughts of planning violence to others, had provoked fights, and had poor self esteem. While saying he wanted to work on his anger, he espoused a macho self image in which anger was a positive part of his identity. His pictures were difficult to understand, being based on esoteric signs and symbols.

Fig. 3. Early family patterns

In the relaxation and guided imagery session, Dan drew a night-time coastal scene with a lighthouse as a 'beacon of hope'. Although Rob missed this session due to his disciplinary hearing at work, he joined in with subsequent relaxations and visualisations and found them very helpful, continuing on his own at home.

In the session 'Is anger good or bad?', Rob depicted all the ways in which anger got him into trouble, while Mark drew a happy face accompanied by a hammer, knife and gun – he experienced anger as a purely positive feeling which he enjoyed. Dan's picture was balanced with negatives and positives.

In the next session, 'What's underneath the anger', Rob was very upset. He had been to court and had a non-molestation order issued against him. He drew the court scene with officials behind heavy desks, and him on his own, isolated, angry and upset. He was too upset to stay in the session, so left the room for some time out.

The session on 'early family patterns' evoked strong responses. Mark spoke about his father and then had to leave the room. Dan drew the 'inferno' of violent anger from his parents (see figure 3) in orange pastel, with the question 'Why?' underneath and a sad child's face. He was beaten by his parents but did not understand why they were angry with him.

In the 'anger and conflict' session, Dan drew a graphic picture of the IRA blowing up the police barracks next door to their family home; this incident may have led to PTSD, as Dan still imagined it vividly. Meanwhile Rob depicted an incident when he arrived home hungry to find only a tin of soup in the house. This led to a discussion of how lack of money can lead to domestic abuse.

Of the three men in the group, Rob seemed to gain the most benefit. He regarded anger as a destructive response to circumstances, and was ready to engage with alternative ways of dealing with it. Although he had a very stressful personal life during the period of the group, he had no incidents of self harm or angry outbursts since the start of the group. He was able to use the relaxation/ meditation techniques to deal with difficult situations, and was taking steps to find work and to see his daughter through a contact centre. Dan felt the insights he had gained into his relationships with women, and the discussion of PTSD gave him new paths to explore. Mark seemed unable to reflect or consider the ideas and strategies of the group, being still enamoured of anger and violence - but gained a friendship with Rob.

This group highlighted the way participants' beliefs about anger can influence their readiness to consider change, and the benefits they gain from the group. This seems to have little to do with educational ability, and more about an attitude of openness. The group was a good vehicle in which to challenge some of these beliefs, as discussion often arose around these issues. It also increased participants' motivation to take further steps.

In my chapter 'Working with Men' (Liebmann 2003), I concluded that art therapy has something special to offer men, in being 'action-orientated' rather than purely verbal. Group work in particular seems to suit men in providing a safe place where they can – to their surprise - meet others with similar issues and feel less isolated. This may apply particularly to anger work, where there may be shame attached, as their behaviour towards others is being criticized.

Individual work

Many individuals were referred to me when there was no group for them to attend, or group work was not appropriate. I often used similar themes with individuals, but as a menu from which they could choose those most relevant to them. I have written about this in a chapter about a deaf man with anger issues (Liebmann 2008). For him the most important sessions were the ones looking at his underlying needs, and early family patterns. Drawing a picture of his family helped him realise that his isolation from other family members was due to his deafness, not their dislike of him, leading to much increased self esteem.

Working with Alan had a different emphasis. An African-Caribbean man aged 47, in his early twenties he had served a three-year prison sentence for robbery. In his late twenties he was admitted to psychiatric hospital with a diagnosis of schizophrenia. From then on he had a history of making verbal threats to harm others, assaulting others and setting fires in hospital and in his flat. When I met him, he was living in a care home, with the same behaviour causing problems there. He was referred for help managing his anger in a more constructive way. We looked at the list of topics, and started with 'What does anger look like?' This led on to physical symptoms and then ways of calming down, and finally triggers of anger – all using art materials and discussing each picture as he did it.

Comic strips

I have written elsewhere about this technique (Liebmann 1990 and 1994). It is particularly suitable for looking at anger incidents because it slows down the process. Often people with anger issues are overwhelmed by the speed at which their anger overtakes them and feel they have little control over this. They experience anger as 'coming from nowhere'. Exploring events frame by frame can help restore a sense of control, and identify where the person might act or react differently. Some therapists disparage this approach as superficial, but in my experience it is difficult to look at deeper issues until 'first aid' has provided a calmer space in which this can be done.

I have not used this very much in group work, except in a very truncated form (Liebmann 1990, pp.146-150), because many of the issues are very individual, and clients may take varying amounts of time to draw the story of their offence. Often a comic strip for one incident can be done in one session, but sometimes it may take much longer. One probation client, Gary, took three hour-long sessions and 27 frames to explain how his offence arose, and a further two sessions to discuss and draw out pointers for next steps (Liebmann 1994, pp. 256-263).

I have often worked comic strips and anger themes into other individual work. For instance, while working with a woman referred for depression, it came out that she often felt angry with children and had to hold on to her hands to avoid assaulting them. We deviated from the work she was doing on depression, to look at her anger using comic strips and then the 'early family patterns' theme to look at the abuse she had suffered from her mother. This led to her feeling more in control of situations where she felt angry. She also worked out strategies to take herself out of situations she felt she could not control.

Conclusion

Many offenders have issues with anger. This is obvious with violent offences, which often (though not always) stem from anger, but can play a part in other offences too. Art therapy has proved a useful mode to work with the different issues involved in anger, and group work can provide a safe and supportive setting for this. The themes described are not the only way of working with anger, but they have proved useful and welcome for many clients.

Issues may be different for men and women, so it is best to do this work in same-gender groups. Individual work can also use the same themes, in a flexible way to suit individual needs. There is a great need for work with anger, whether with groups or individual. And the aim is not to 'get rid of' anger – it can be useful – but to help clients to manage it constructively.

REFERENCES

Liebmann, M. (1990) ' "It Just Happened": Looking at Crime Events.' In M. Liebmann (ed), *Art Therapy in Practice*. London: Jessica Kingsley Publishers.

Liebmann, M. (1994) 'Art Therapy and Changing Probation Values.' In M. Liebmann (ed), *Art Therapy with Offenders*. London: Jessica Kingsley Publishers.

Liebmann, M. (2003) 'Working with Men.' In S. Hogan (ed), *Gender Issues in Art Therapy*. London: Jessica Kingsley Publishers.

Liebmann, M. (2004) *Art Therapy for Groups*. 2nd edition. Hove: Brunner-Routledge, pp. 112-115.

Liebmann, M. (2007) 'Anger Management Group Art Therapy for Clients in the Mental Health System.' In F. Kaplan (ed), *Art Therapy and Social Action*. London: Jessica Kingsley Publishers.

Liebmann, M. (2008) *Art Therapy and Anger*. London: Jessica Kingsley Publishers, chapter 11, pp. 180-194.

Novaco, R.W., Ramm, M. & Black, L. (2000). 'Anger treatment with offenders'. In C. Hollin (ed) *Handbook of offender assessment and treatment*. London: John Wiley and Sons.

Tavris, C. (1989) *Anger The Misunderstood Emotion*. 2nd edition. New York: Simon & Schuster.

Figures

1. Anger equals violence AM S3

2. Anger – good or bad? WAM G3

3. Early family patterns IMGP 8313

CHAPTER 5

The component parts: The application of the Marginal Gains Philosophy for a successful art therapy group on a psychiatric intensive care unit in a medium-secure hospital

ROSE HALL

Introduction

This chapter discusses The Marginal Gains Philosophy, as epitomised by the Great British Cycling Team, to frame and consider the process of maintaining and developing a successful art therapy group on a Psychiatric Intensive Care Unit (PICU) within a medium-secure hospital.

The Marginal Gains Philosophy is considered in relation to an art therapy group provision in a medium-secure unit. It looks at the patients' attendance and the aims of the group, referring to the philosophy and the process of running an art therapy group in component parts, and describes each in detail with the support of vignettes. Following on from this, it looks at the patients' engagement within the art therapy group, and concludes with a discussion about what this means for the future of the art therapy group, the patients and the idea of "marginal losses".

The Marginal Gains Philosophy outlines a way of improving results by focusing on component parts rather than the combined whole - the main objective of the task. The Great British Cycling Team's performance director Dave Brailsford said, "If you broke down everything you could think of that goes into riding a bike, and then improved it by one per cent, you will get a significant increase when you put them all together". The Great British Cycling team takes this very seriously and has a designated 'Department of Marginal Gains'. Interventions that are incorporated are measured and re-evaluated continuously.

The application of this philosophy to clinical practice is relatively young and continues to be developed. However, this mind-set has already helped in considering what is needed to run an art therapy group in an unpredictable and difficult environment, and offers a way to give value to not only the actual art therapy session, but all the component parts needed to ensure success. Applying the principles constantly and consistently over time gives an opportunity to improve and get nearer to fulfilling the potential.

The ward

The ward in which the group runs is centred round a large high-ceilinged communal space with four sofas. There is an entrance corridor leading to it and beyond is a further corridor that leads to the seclusion room. There is a small courtyard, dining room, sensory room, TV-lounge, activities room and meeting room. The nursing station is like a big fish bowl in the middle of the space, which helps to maintain eyesight of each area of the ward.

The ward atmosphere can range from deathly quiet to manically vibrating. At times, the communal space can be empty of patients, who would rather be in their own room, or it can be buzzing with activity with patients talking, sleeping, reading or walking around. Staff are always available to support patients with their basic needs, such as getting drinks, or to support behavioural and psychological challenges the patients may present.

Sometimes it can feel like a policed ward, with staff having to take on the role of security guards managing violence and aggression. The ward manager explained that staff recruited need to have a "strong presence", with a 70/30 ratio of male to female staff. This does not necessarily mean that staff need to be physically strong, but must have a strong sense of boundaries if they are to survive. However, this can preclude staff from talking about feelings of vulnerability. Reflective practice and daily debriefs continually offer an opportunity for reflection.

The component parts: The application of the Marginal Gains
Philosophy for a successful art therapy group on a psychiatric
intensive care unit in a medium-secure hospital

89

Fig. 1. Art therapy group

Figure 1 shows an image a ward staff member made during an art therapy group. He described the ward as if being on the front line reacting to any threat. The image seems to show the perceived role as a soldier in battle on the ward.

With beds for 11 patients and six staff on day shift, this is a greater staff to patient ratio and fewer total patients than on other wards. The Multidisciplinary team is made up of professionals with years of experience in the field including a ward manager, modern matron, consultant, doctors, occupational therapist, psychologist and social worker dedicated to the PICU. The arts therapists, educational therapists and sports therapists work across site.

The patients

The patients are admitted to the ward via different routes with different mental health diagnoses including schizophrenia, depression, personality disorder and learning disabilities. Some patients develop mental health difficulties while in prison and are transferred for assessment and treatment in hospital. Others come from high-secure hospitals on a step down to medium-secure, or have moved from another ward after an incident or deterioration in their mental health, thus requiring more intensive treatment. Some patients have been on the ward for months, some several years and others stay for only a few weeks.

The complexity of patients' mental health needs can cause unpredictable physically and psychologically aggressive behaviour making it difficult to settle on the ward. This often generates feelings of fear and anxiety in new staff members. I too find myself holding these feelings after a group, which have to be processed in supervision.

High levels of containment are maintained through tight physical and relational boundaries. At times patients require extra medication, restraining and periods in seclusion to ensure safety to self and others. The ward can feel hostile, highly anxious and hard to contain, but at other times it can feel relaxed and playful.

The art therapy

On the PICU it is expected that patients will find it difficult to engage in a sustained and in-depth way. Therefore, the focus is on small but significant moments of engagement and change. Within the arts therapies, The Early Interventions Screening Service (EISS) was designed and developed by Kate Rothwell, Head of Arts Therapies, as a way of capturing these small engagements of patients at the point of admission and beyond. The idea is that there are several stages of engagement from pre-therapy through to treatment that are significant and relevant to each patient's capacity, from acute admissions to recovery and eventual discharge back into the community. This follows a care pathway during each treatment phase as the patient moves through the hospital.

The PICU art therapy group is positioned at the start of this process and has been running for three years since the PICU was opened. There have been different therapists, different ward teams and different types of facilitation, but the group has been consistent and in place all the while when other groups have been and gone. It was passed to me when an art therapist retired after 13 years of service. I previously co-facilitated the group whilst on an honorary art therapist contract. I learned a lot through this experience and although I had a lot to live up to, there was also room for improvement and change.

The component parts: The application of the Marginal Gains
Philosophy for a successful art therapy group on a psychiatric
intensive care unit in a medium-secure hospital | 91

Co-facilitated by an art therapist and a dramatherapist, this group offers an approach whereby patients are invited to 'drop in' for as long as they want to during the hour and to use art materials if they want. There are art books available to browse through and patients are encouraged to exercise their curiosity to see what has been happening in the group, even if they don't want to sit at the table. Likewise, ward staff are encouraged to work alongside patients whilst both co-facilitators also make use of the art materials.

The duration of the group ensures physical and psychological safety. Rigorous attention to tight boundaries allows freedom within the group. We provide a consistent space mid-week, in the centre of the ward, where we reflect on the experiences everyone faces through visual and/or verbal communication. This gives an opportunity for the whole ward to work together and experience themselves and others in a different way.

Art therapy is well positioned here for two main reasons. Firstly, art therapy has a reputation within the hospital for engaging hard to reach highly resistant patients. In this group we attempt to enable patients to move to a position of reassuring safety, where they can start to just sit with themselves and others with no demands made of them.

This stage of the EISS is also effective in assessing patients' needs and enabling them to engage in other psychological treatments and group programmes. Here we are able to make contact with patients early on in their admission and can start the process of building relationships that will continue throughout their stay in the hospital, in effect staying with them as we move them through.

Initially we found engagement overwhelming, and wondered whether we were doing it right, unsure if any of our interventions were making sense. We now feel able to tolerate and work with the intense dynamic projections that are particular to this ward. The art therapy group initially felt too impossible and painful. We frequently cancelled the group due to the powerful unconscious projections that made running it intolerable.

Now not only is it possible, but also thriving, alive and full of opportunity for patient engagement, with facilitators embedded within a team who feel safe and supported. It is one of the most solid parts of the week for the arts therapists, which is surprising as it's on what is considered the most dangerous and volatile ward in the hospital with the most number of violent incidents recorded.

Looking at the component parts within the Marginal Gains Philosophy has certainly been the major factor in this and could be the major factor in its continued development.

The component parts

The Marginal Gains Philosophy gives value to the component parts of the whole. Applying this philosophy has contained the arts therapists in their thinking and preparation in offering the opportunity for therapeutic engagement with emotionally distressed patients.

A united mind-set is vital, where everyone in the team is clear about the foundations in place and why we are doing this work together, to identify areas that can be improved no matter how peripheral they might seem at the outset. There is much that we don't know, so we must be prepared to learn from others but also to bring everyone on board to share a common desire to improve.

When cycling, the bike needs each component part to be functioning well. It may be possible to cycle with a wonky saddle, but if it is missing completely or if there is also a wonky wheel then it will probably be impossible to travel for any distance. Here, I will describe the key component parts identified to run the art therapy group on the PICU. These parts were optimised through careful consideration. As with the bike, if one 'part' of the group is not working so well then it may be possible to run the group, but if several 'parts' are hampered it could be dangerous to continue. As in the case of the Great British Cycling Team, the analysis of the marginal gains of the component parts is constant and active, and ensures a relevant and successful group is maintained.

The component parts covered are:

- The co-facilitation partnership,
- Embedding within the community,
- Entering the ward, handover and debrief,
- Ward staff,
- Setting up for the hour long group and art materials.

The component parts: The application of the Marginal Gains
Philosophy for a successful art therapy group on a psychiatric
intensive care unit in a medium-secure hospital | 93

The final section looks more in depth at the patients and the idea of "marginal losses".

Co-facilitation partnership

For a successful co-facilitator partnership, it's important both partners are united in tandem and can turn to each other for support when running the group. This includes opportunities to develop this working relationship and also includes an understanding of what support each facilitator needs to give or take from the other. Ideally both parties have to be in good physical and psychological health. If not, an open discussion is needed to ensure there is enough energy collectively to make it possible to run a safe and effective session. Simply saying: "How are you today?" starts this checking in process and turns the focus from working separately to working together. Peer supervision and team meetings are used to not only look at the content of the group but also at what might be held within the relationships.

This shows a marginal shift from a time where it was not uncommon to cancel the group to now, where cancellation is a rarity due to a strong co-facilitation partnership and support from the ward. Developing the co-facilitator relationship has been an interesting challenge that both therapists have been open to exploring. The different skills and ways of working have been considered, but the most important aspects are to develop a rhythm of working through familiarity with each other and the time and space to reflect on the group together.

Embedding within the community

The arts therapies co-facilitators must first be embedded within the whole ward community, and need to be considered as part of the team so that the art therapy group becomes a shared responsibility and is jointly looked after and owned. Attending ward round, service development groups and community meetings are integral to this process.

The community meeting is held at the beginning of the week and the art therapy group is midweek. By attending the community meeting we are able to begin the process of building relationships with everyone associated with the ward and are able to keep track of current events and patients' mental health. This makes it easier for patients and staff to attend the art therapy group as they already have a sense of who we are and what the group is about. This is essential given the potential high turnover of new staff and patients.

It also gives the co-facilitators a chance to gauge the emotional temperature of the ward. Building on human contact takes us beyond the fear of the unknown and helps us better understand what we may be initially holding prior to the group. This also helps develop weekly containment of the co-facilitators, the patients and the group as a whole.

Interestingly, now that the group is embedded within the community, it almost runs without the arts therapists. Generally the group needs two arts therapists to run successfully. However, during an unavoidable break of five weeks, when one of the facilitators was on leave, the ward staff recognised the importance of keeping the group going and spontaneously offered their support to ensure it continued during this period when one 'part' of the component whole was absent. As a team, we have identified that when arts therapies is positioned externally to the main body of the team, the discipline loses out on vital support. The practitioners are in danger of being split off and are therefore more vulnerable to attack of one sort or another, or to being seen as irrelevant or superfluous.

One particular incident highlights this issue, when a micro-system is not well embedded within the community both physically and relationally. On this occasion the group was held in the activities room, which reduced opportunities to develop relationships with the team and patients outside of the group, understandably increasing a feeling of separateness. A patient had auditory hallucinations telling him to attack one of the facilitators and responded to these commands. It was difficult to exit the room safely, and as the therapist had not had a chance to benefit from the team's knowledge of this patient, they did not know how to respond. More information on the patient and a less isolative environment would have been safer in containing this incident.

After the incident, the team agreed that moving the group to the communal area would make it safer to run, and opportunities were made for patient and facilitator to reflect on the incident and hear

The component parts: The application of the Marginal Gains
Philosophy for a successful art therapy group on a psychiatric
intensive care unit in a medium-secure hospital   95

from each other. Both parties survived the attack and continue to work together two years later in an off ward art therapy group.

Entering the ward

As the arts therapists are not on this ward all the time, how we enter this space needs to be consistent and in line with procedure. Partly we are stepping onto 'our' ward, but we are also entering someone else's home. There is a sign on the door asking staff to press a buzzer before entering; this is taken seriously. If, having pressed the buzzer, it is safe to enter then the arts therapists are welcomed in, but there have been times when waiting until the right moment has been imperative. This shows respect to the ward staff and acknowledges the difficult job they have keeping everyone safe. Just as the co-facilitators turn their attention to each other, this is an important moment when the arts therapists and ward staff do the same and become united in partnership ready to run the group. This could be comparable to new cyclists joining the race and filtering into the team, rather than colliding into each other and causing accidents.

Handover and debrief

Each day begins with a whole ward handover, whereby an overview of patients over the week is provided to highlight any risk issues. The arts therapists attend on the morning that the group runs. By being on the ward early, they show the ward staff that they are present and in attendance, that the group will be run later and that the ward is being thought about. This is a change from previously when handover would be 20 minutes before the session was due to run, leaving too much time for a build-up of anxiety.

Interacting with the rest of the team to gain a picture of the patients and the ward dynamics helps prepare for the kind of group that might run later. This is an opportunity to consider if there needs to be extra support to contain patients or to prepare for the likelihood that no one will attend. A post group debrief is important to reflect on the group that day and what, if any, actions might be needed. This used to be called "handover", where the arts therapists would give feedback from the group to ward staff rather than a joint discussion. The former process positioned the arts therapists separately from the team and was detrimental to maintain a sense of 'group as a shared responsibility' leaving other important professional voices lost. Hearing from all members of the team gives the opportunity to strengthen working relationships and to look to areas of future potential marginal gains.

Setting up for the hour long group

When arriving back onto the ward to start the group, we let ward staff know we are there before setting up. This ensures we have an opportunity to hear of any risk issues that may have surfaced since handover earlier that day. It also announces the combined effort to get the tables, chairs, art materials and patients ready for the group.

The tables and chairs are always arranged in the same way. There are two tables, one slightly bigger than the other, four chairs that come from the dining room and two squishy chairs that come from the communal space. Not everyone holds onto this, but it is important to arrange everything to the usual places if they have not been set right. This can be handled in a playful way as not everyone sees the importance of this.

One of the sofas is turned around to face the tables but at a distance, so patients and staff can be involved if they find it uncomfortable to be at the table. Art books are arranged on the sofa, and more recently a marginal gain of proximity is negotiated with art books put even further away with the other sofas for patients and staff who would rather sit at a distance. This means as many people as possible can be reached during the group's one hour session.

Once the tables and chairs are in place, it is important to check the exit routes every session. If someone comes too close there needs to be space to move away safely. This includes moving away from physical attack but also includes safety from powerful projections that may overwhelm both patients and ward staff. Keeping the consistency of the space is necessary at a basic level to maintain the rhythm of setting up the group. For patients and staff who come consistently, any change will be noticed, unconsciously at least and this change could have a negative impact.

The component parts: The application of the Marginal Gains
Philosophy for a successful art therapy group on a psychiatric
intensive care unit in a medium-secure hospital | 97

Ward staff

Although the arts therapists lead the group, it can't run without extra support from the ward staff. There is always at least one member of ward staff at the table and another further away to support from a distance. This provides layers of containment for the duration of the session.

This set up of staff is not dissimilar to flying buttresses seen in gothic architecture. This arrangement derives strength though reinforced support. Ward staff supporting from a distance are able to see moments of engagement that are hard to pick out at close range, whilst ward staff sitting closer can immediately offer their expertise in containing the group.

Staff have described their purpose as being role models to encourage patients to express themselves. It has also become evident that staff want to drop their macho guard image by getting involved in an activity that may often be understood as more feminine and weak. Another member talked about his need to keep himself available rather than get absorbed in his own art making to ensure he can be responsive and look out for the group. Each position has its own benefits and necessities.

Without this support, the group has the potential to be an unsafe space on many levels both externally and internally. For example, on one occasion the therapists considered ending early as these important buttresses of support had wandered off. The ward was feeling particularly tense that day. As a result from what seemed to be an unconscious need to get away from unbearable feelings, tasks such as organising patient property from a new admission and activities in the courtyard were prioritised as a diversion. The arts therapists have to be responsive to the needs of the whole ward and were prepared to end in support of working with what was tolerable for all. Fortunately one ward staff member highlighted what was going on, thus sending attention back to the art therapy group, and play was resumed. When it is tense on the ward it's perhaps too easy to cancel the group. On another occasion, ward staff were unsure whether they had enough people on shift to run the group. It appeared that they were feeling vulnerable and tired that day. Someone had just returned from sick leave after being physically attacked, emphasising the reality of the potential for violence and the need for safety. The arts therapists were prepared not to run the group. However, with the aid of support from the ward manager, a solution for staffing was found and the group went ahead.

Art materials

The art therapy materials trolley is an old medicine cabinet. The materials are checked in and out. It contains chalk pastels, oil pastels, pencils, coloured pencils, felt-tips and charcoal. There are bottles of liquid paint that do not always get put out, but are in there in case it feels safe enough to do so. Paint can be messy and unpredictable, which can be experienced as overwhelming for patients and staff on this particular ward. We also don't want art materials to be used as weapons; however, there is access to paint in the form of poster paint blocks, which provides the opportunity to explore the material in a more contained way. Art postcards are placed on the table and by the sofas for when ideas for an image are needed but hard to find.

An incident occurred during the group where a patient attacked a member of staff. The therapists pulled their alarms and quickly gathered up all the most dangerous materials such as paintbrushes and pencils, which could be used as weapons. Before that point, it had not been considered an area for marginal gains, but now we understand how we can continue to engage when there's a heightened risk of attack. The group on that occasion continued without said materials and offered a space for everyone to reflect on what had happened.

During a different group, ward staff made use of the recent addition to images in the sofa area. They spent time looking at an Escher image called "Ascending and Descending" (see figure 2). This discussion from a distance was in line with the aims of the group. They were able to bring their ideas to the table and share with everyone at the end of the session. Important thoughts about roles and the challenge of, what can feel like, relentlessly going round in circles were discussed. Themes of a sense of powerlessness and lack of autonomy over one's life on the ward came up and the group was able to use each other to consider the image and these themes from different angles to make a shift.

The component parts: The application of the Marginal Gains
Philosophy for a successful art therapy group on a psychiatric
intensive care unit in a medium-secure hospital

99

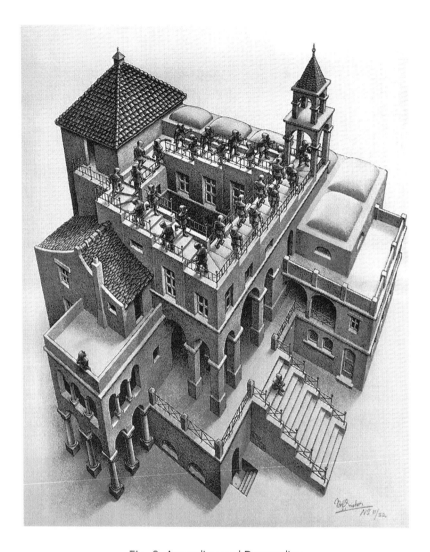

Fig. 2. Ascending and Descending

Final components

Only once the described component parts are firmly in place, can our
attention look to the patients - the overall goal of the task.

Patient engagement

Patient engagement depends on a range of factors. This may be their first week on the ward; they may not have slept well; they may be distressed by mental health problems; they may have had good news; there may have been an incident; their favourite ward staff member may be on shift. These factors, and more, feed into how the patients engage and the quality of their engagement.

Each individual has their own starting point for each day and different pathways through the stages of engagement. It is important to capture the smallest of engagements. The pathway can be unpredictable and changeable. There are patients who don't attend the group; patients who make verbal or visual contact; patients who engage away from the table; patients who engage at the table and patients who move through each of these stages at one time or another.

Figure 3 shows a 10 week sample of patient engagement. You can see that each week the number of patients on the ward changes and there are varying degrees of engagement, which is particular to this ward. Other wards show a more stable and similar level of engagement from week to week.

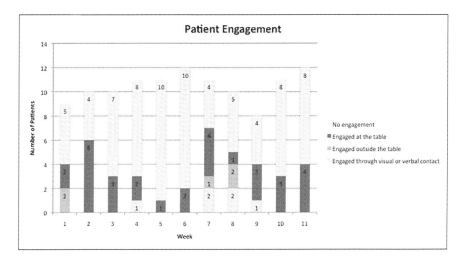

Fig. 3. Patient engagement

The component parts: The application of the Marginal Gains
Philosophy for a successful art therapy group on a psychiatric
intensive care unit in a medium-secure hospital

101

A typical journey of patient engagement will begin with patients spending a few weeks simply saying hello; then over time, they will risk joining us at the table, and will later start to use art materials. The opposite can be equally true; patients may on their first meeting come in so close as to almost sit on the therapist's chair and energetically make images.

Glasser's theory of Core Complexities helps us to understand the clinical material the arts therapists work with. Glasser says, "To envisage closeness and intimacy as annihilating, or separateness and independence as desolate isolation, indicates the persistence of a primitive level of functioning" (Glasser 1979:285.).

Because of the Marginal Gains Philosophy and a focus on maintaining and improving the component parts, the group is able to work with this challenging clinical material. Each week we are able to work with the unpredictability of the different levels of engagement and can accompany patients on their journey.

Conclusion

This chapter refers to The Marginal Gains Philosophy in consideration of the processes involved in maintaining and developing a successful art therapy group on a PICU within a medium-secure hospital. Dividing the main objective (running the art therapy group) into its component parts has led to an improved understanding of what is needed to run a group in this environment and has given space for acknowledging the marginal gains that push its success further.

The art therapy group has shifted from being intolerable to being alive, but we must not lose sight of the hard work, perseverance and attention that got the group to this place. Within a ward where the projections are overpowering, there have been times when each component part has been let slip. In this case, marginal losses can occur and over time the one per cent gain can turn into a one per cent loss, making a big impact on not only the success of the group but on the safety of all. Discipline and stamina are needed to continue to focus on the component parts and to continue to maximise their impact to achieve long-term gains. These are the gains that the arts therapies team see in the patients' progress when they are moved to less intensive wards in the hospital.

As suggested by the philosophy, each component part can be developed to find further marginal gains as well as to discover new peripheral areas for thought. As you can see from figure 3, there are patients who are not being reached each week and this needs to be addressed. Examples of how to make marginal gains to support their engagement could include sound dampening in the large echoing communal space; the ward staff could join peer supervision with the art therapists to reflect on the group and the images they make within it, and staff could also add a third table to make more space when the seats are full.

The Marginal Gains Philosophy is simple and has already made substantial improvements to the art therapy group. One of the key ideas of the philosophy is to use the team and surrounding support to achieve a shared goal, to talk about what the goals are and to look for new areas to find marginal gains. The hope is that this will be the start of a shared development in applying this philosophy to this art therapy group and eventually to others in the future.

BIBLIOGRAPHY

Sir Dave Brailsford at British Cycling - A career retrospective. 2015. *Sir Dave Brailsford at British Cycling - A career retrospective*. [ONLINE] Available at: https://www.britishcycling.org.uk/gbcyclingteam/article/gbr20140411-British-Cycling---The-Brailsford-years-0. [Accessed 18 September 2015].

Glasser, M., 1998. On violence: A preliminary communication. *The International Journal of Psychoanalysis*, 79, 887–902.

CHAPTER 6

Telling the story
RUTH GOODMAN[10] AND LIZ BROWN[11]

How should we be able to forget about those ancient myths that are at the beginning of all peoples,

The myths about dragons that at the last moment turn into princesses; perhaps all the dragons of our

Lives are princesses who are only waiting to see us once beautiful and brave. Perhaps everything

Terrible is in its deepest being something helpless that wants help from us.

So you must not be frightened.... If a sadness rises up before you larger than any you have ever seen;

If a restiveness, like light and cloud shadow, passes over your hands and over all that you do.

You must think that something is taking place in you, that life has not forgotten you,

That it holds you

In its hand; it will not let you fall.

(Rainer Maria Rilke)

10 Dramatherapist

11 Art Therapist

There have been numerous occasions over the past 20 years when someone, after hearing that we work in forensics, asks with incredulity, "How can you work with those people?" The implication is that either 'those people' are more deserving of punishment rather than treatment, or that we, as therapists, are foolishly exposing ourselves to the danger of becoming victims of their violence or abuse. One of the answers to their question must be: "It's the stories". By stories, we don't mean the sensationalist aspects of gruesome crimes, compelling as they may be in tabloid headlines or popular fiction. Many a time the stories we hear are of suffering, trauma and abuse, of early deprivation, displacement, tragic loss, and of course in the hospital setting in which we work, of severe and disabling mental illness.

In over 20 years of working with forensic patients in our shared and separate arts therapists roles, we continue to be both humbled and intrigued by the vicissitudes of human nature and the complexities of people's lives. We continually ask ourselves questions about why some people behave in the way that they do, why some act out in violent ways, against themselves or others. Our work, however, is not primarily to make sense of somebody else's life but, most importantly, to enable them to make sense of it for themselves. Until a person can begin to find a coherent narrative for their lives, they may be subject to repeating destructive patterns of behaviour in a vain attempt to manage pain and difficulty.

In the medium secure unit in which we work, co-working is often recommended due to the practicalities of minimising risk in group work. It gave us the advantage of working with one another, combining our individual skills in art therapy and dramatherapy to offer a wider scope for creative self-expression. We have found that as well as the mutual support, we are also able to provide our patients with the security of consistent co-facilitators. It also has the added benefit of dual witnessing and shared thinking that enables us to reflect on some of the more complex projections and transference issues as we experience them. The stimulation and creative energy that we have found in working together and when combining the arts has helped to prevent us from 'burn out' over the many years of our work in forensics. We have also been fortunate to have the continuing support of our managers and clinical teams over the years, which have encouraged the development of ideas and new initiatives.

When we first started working together at the hospital, men and women shared wards. We started by offering closed groups for these patients and later, when women's wards were established, we began a slow open women's group that is still running. One of the advantages of a forensic setting is that we have the opportunity to develop long-term relationships with our patients. Not being ward or team based, we often accompany them through their journey of recovery from acute wards to rehabilitation, even continuing to work with them after they are discharged into the community, when they return as outpatients.

> 'To be ourselves, we must have ourselves – possess, if need be re-possess, our life stories'
>
> **(Sacks 1986 pp. 105).**

In common with many forms of psychotherapy, our work is primarily aimed at helping our patients tell, 'possess' and find expression for their personal life stories. The need to be heard and to relate personal experiences is fundamental to our sense of wellbeing, our sense of self and our relationship to the world. Personal stories, therefore, are at the heart of the work. We are primarily concerned with helping our patients engage with their own story. We also appreciate, that sometimes however, there are many reasons *not* to tell.

Sometimes, through illness and trauma, patients lose their capacity to tell their story. It is not uncommon for some patients to be traumatised and disorientated when they first come into hospital. They are often suffering from acute states of psychosis and paranoia, and may be confused and fearful to find themselves under section in a forensic unit. Some patients will say they have no recollection of their index offence and feel they have been misunderstood, denying illness or feeling wrongly accused of something they have no memory of. It may seem paradoxical, therefore, that there is an expectation, if not a necessity, in forensic psychiatric settings, for patients to tell and 'possess' the story of their illness, and in particular, their index offence, in order, it is thought, to reduce the likelihood of relapse and reoffending.

For some of our patients the *need* to tell may be compelling, as the person "seeks an opportunity to explore, appreciate, and appropriate his story, so that it loses its hold." But the telling can also be painful and difficult, as their story may be "so disturbing that it is repressed and thus banished beyond the possibility of verbal access" (Cox & Theilgaard 1997 pp.: 2 -3, 18). They nevertheless suggest that "however painful the telling may be, it must be attempted".

Some patients find the fear of telling their story too great and it must be suppressed.

Clare's Story

Clare's story, in which she was implicated in a series of deaths, including that of her child, was much too painful, perhaps too shameful for her to acknowledge, even to herself.

In a story-making exercise in the women's group, she chose to tell a fictional tale about a princess in a castle. She developed the story over several weeks, increasingly emphasising the princess's desire to run away from the constraints of her life in the castle. The castle, she said, was occupied by people who were abusing the princess and it was becoming increasingly urgent that she should escape. Try as she might, however, the princess could not find a way to leave, because fierce guard dogs surrounded the castle. She was trapped and paralysed. Clare's story was an evocative indication of the intrapsychic war she was experiencing in her internal world. Her growing realisation that her fictional story closely mirrored her own internal entrapment became overwhelming and she abruptly decided to leave the group. Her festering personal story threatened to erupt and rupture her fragile defences; and her feelings of paranoia increased rather than diminished.

It was a reminder to us of the potency of this work and that, in some cases, the strength of the therapeutic alliance cannot always be sufficiently trusted or feel secure enough to hold unbearable feelings.

For Jane, the story of her early years of deprivation, separation from her family and childhood trauma could not be told for many months. Her sudden illness, index offence and the consequential loss of her children, who were taken into care, left her frozen in shock and grief. She vigilantly hid behind a fixed mask, cautious of revealing any information or feelings about her past history. Instead, she resolutely chose to stay focused on the future, making meticulous practical plans for herself and demanding schedules designed to fully occupy her time.

Using art materials to represent her lifeline, Jane took a black wax crayon and scribbled over a large sheet of paper energetically covering it with vigorous marks so that the white beneath could hardly be discerned. She then put over it a layer of thick black paint. She had literally blacked out and symbolically blocked out her memories and feelings of her early years.

"I remember the only way I could sort of paint it to describe what my feelings were of my childhood was to just put it in black paint and just cover the whole area in darkness because part of me didn't want to realise it, part of me didn't even remember it really but I knew that it had, you know, a big impact on my life and in my future." (Jane, Women's group)

Consultant Forensic Psychologist, Anna Motz, describes the notion of hiding, losing and being found in relation to the experiences of women in secure mental health settings which include a profound sense of shame, in which they have "lost their sense of identity, within their families, peer groups and wider society." She suggests that the banishment of stories is not only confined to the patients themselves, but their histories can also unconsciously be lost or ignored by staff working closely with them, perhaps as a defence against the overwhelming anxiety of so much pain.

"'Losing' the memories of abuse and trauma that the women have experienced, also seems to be designed to block out and cover up the psychic reality these women face now and have borne in their past". Motz. 2009. Pp. 37-41)

Motz suggests that some of the ways these women might begin to give a voice to their hidden experiences and be able to disclose and explore their violent thoughts, feelings and actions, could be found "symbolically through music, dance and art as well as through words". (Motz 2009. pp. 37-41)

And this is the essence of our work.

"The moment that an art therapist 'moves' a picture they are entering into a dramatic domain and, similarly, the moment that a dramatherapist 'freezes' a scene they are entering into the artistic domain" (Jennings and Minde 1993 pp. 48, 12).

Together, using art therapy and dramatherapy, we are able to offer a number of different symbolic pathways that help gain access to hidden material. We often begin with the non-verbal such as sculpts, movement or the use of art materials to release inhibitions, connect to the unconscious and give form to yet unexpressed feelings and ideas. This can develop, organically, to include the use of words, either written, for example in a poem or story, or spoken in a dramatised enactment through improvisation and role play. Integral to the process is time for sharing, reflection and debate.

In our groups we move fluidly and playfully back and forth between our two disciplines, from the more objectifying, distancing techniques of art therapy to the more experiential, interactive elements related to dramatherapy. Usually this happens intuitively depending on the needs of the group, their motivation, mood or their degree of mental distress. In the many years of working together, we have learned to allow ourselves to trust one another's judgement and, most importantly, trust the process. At any time, one of us may be inspired to initiate an exercise spontaneously and the other will support and develop the idea as it unfolds. We cannot always maintain synchronicity and sometimes patients may try to split us. One of us may experience the split off bits of the patient that the other may not feel or miss entirely. It is only on reflection and in shared processing that we can consider its meaning for the patient and how to integrate our understanding into the work.

"The task of the therapist... is the same as that of the examining magistrate. We have to uncover the hidden psychical material; and in order to do this we have invented a number of detective devices" (Freud 1906. pp. 108).

Our work isn't to play detective, although, at times, we can 'sense' a story that is longing to be heard. We have to bear in mind where and perhaps why, the story is blocked and the distress this is causing the person. We can sometimes see this expressed in the symptoms of their illness, in their behaviour and in their ability or inability to relate. One of the 'devices' we use to release these stories is with story itself. What we have found primarily is that when we work with story, that is storytelling and story making, our patients begin to find expression and a language for their own life stories.

It is through the use of story itself that we encourage other stories to be told.

"One story begets another"
(Gersie 1997 pp. 102, 151).

Patients who may be initially resistant to engaging with their own story are often more responsive to more oblique ways of relating experience. The fictional story can act as a 'protective analogy', a container where patients can explore experience with less inhibition and in which emotions can find expression within the secure boundaries of the story structure.

Maya

Maya, a woman from a traditional Moslem family, had been admitted into hospital following a violent attack on her mother. She had struggled for some time to become independent from the constraints of her family but at the same time feared their disapproval and rejection. Remorseful of her actions, she had since re-established a close relationship with her family, but, it seemed, at the expense of her freedom of choice, and freedom of speech. In a similar way she always appeared compliant and polite in the group, keeping any ambivalent thoughts or feelings hidden. Instead, she made attempts to avoid the sessions by arranging other activities at the same time of the group. In one session, Liz asked her: "If you were a colour, what would it be?" "Green", Maya replied, "Calm and peaceful". She thought some more and then said, with a wry smile, "It's also the colour of jealousy". She then looked through the Archetype cards and picked up the 'Seeker' and 'Rebel'. Tell me a story about the 'Seeker', Ruth suggested. She began to talk about a young woman who was constantly seeking 'the truth', but, however hard she tried, it always eluded her. "Tell me a story about the 'Rebel'", we then asked. The Rebel, she suggested, defies her family by having a secret boyfriend. Maya then began to reveal her own history and spoke about her family's disapproval when it was discovered that she had a boyfriend when she a teenager. She talked about the pressure she was under meeting her family's expectations, and the disappointment and suffering she had brought to her mother.

Ruth then told the classical myth of Persephone and Demeter. Demeter suffered grief at the kidnap of her daughter, Persephone, taken to the Underworld. To Demeter's joy, Persephone was returned, but at a price, having to spend one month in Hades for each of the pomegranate seeds she had eaten there. Maya said that she felt the story was "very sad". In a dramatisation of the story, she identified with Demeter's suffering. It opened up a discussion about the often complex relationship between mother and daughter, the pain and difficulty of separation and the importance of being able to let go, to allow for growth and independence. Maya then began to speak about her own ambivalent feelings; her attempts to separate from her mother and live her own life, her feelings of guilt and desire to stay loyal to her family, but also her need to be accepted in her own right.

It was an example of how the analogy of a fictional story can open access to the personal story. Personal themes can also find comfort and containment within the universal themes of a mythological story. Moving backward and forward through this process, pertinent themes and issues can be identified, acknowledged and thought about with more clarity and authenticity.

Art therapy and dramatherapy share a tradition of storytelling. Art therapy offers image-making as a way of relating something about an experience, or symbolising aspects of the inner world as well as portraying, in whole or in part, everyday life situations. Narrative art may relate the story of myth, legend and autobiography. In dramatherapy, story making and storytelling is inherent to the work, whether it is using a given story such as a traditional myth or folktale, a self-authored fictional story or a spontaneous story created through group improvisation. Each story involves the telling and retelling of experience, reliving it and reworking it through symbols, metaphor, play and enactment. Story provides a link between the past and present, present and future, fantasy and reality. It provides opportunities to revisit the past, explore the present as well as rehearse the future. Through exploration of the themes, metaphors and symbolic meanings within story, there is the possibility to help transform the lessons learned from past events into new possibilities for change. In forensic work, the need for change is fundamental if our patients are going to be able to safely reintegrate into society. The long and often painful process of recovery involves recovering the known and unknown stories of the past. Only then can a person begin to make a story for the future.

Usually, by the time we come to meet the patients, we often find a number of different stories attached to them. There is the mental health story, the official index offence story and then there is the patients' personal story seen from their own perspective that may or may not be known and is often untold. Each of these stories may be incomplete, a version of the true story, or be subject to different opinions.

Amongst the many theories of storytelling and story making that we hold in mind in our practice, we are reminded of Barnett Pearce and Vernon Cronen's 'LUUUTT' model (Littlejohn and Fois 2009. Pp 203-3) that categorises different types of stories. According to their theory, there are stories that are 'Lived', some 'Told' and some 'Untold'. Some stories may be 'Unheard', having been told but others have failed to hear. We believe that if a person's story remains untold or unheard it may continue to ferment and fester. A festered story may then be acted out unconsciously in destructive and sometimes violent ways.

There are also 'Unknown' stories that the person themselves may either not understand well enough to communicate, or may not even know exist. Some, as we have heard, such as Jane's childhood story, may have been banished or 'forgotten' through trauma or humiliation. We often find that 'Stories Lived' and 'Stories Told' do not always match up, particularly for those people who have a forensic history. Parts of their story may be hidden, or be psychically split off, sometimes as a defence against shame.

We know that people who perpetrate violence are often themselves victims of traumatic physical or psychological abuse. Many of our patients' personal stories include a victim story as well as a perpetrator story. The victim story as well as the perpetrator story, each need to be told; although both may be equally difficult to relate. In some cases the victim story remains dominant and fixed. We often have to allow the victim story to be heard fully, and with compassion, before the perpetrator story can begin to be explored.

Our work involves listening, hearing and holding the threads of each of these stories in the hope, that in time, the victim story, the perpetrator story and the personal story can be woven together into a coherent relationship. When these stories can be told and met in understanding, they may gradually become the story of recovery.

At the beginning of our work with patients, we often find they are unwilling or unable to begin to tell their stories. Often what we receive are mere hints of stories, a fragment or perhaps a small glimmer of a story. They lack coherence.

We often wonder whether these fragments of stories represent the fragmentation of parts of the self.

In our work we listen out for these hints and fragments of stories, often echoed time and again in their work.

For example: "What is real?", "How can medication change my personal beliefs?", "I'd be better off serving time in prison", and "It wasn't the real me that did that, it was my illness".

Sometimes these fragments may appear as a short phrase or a recurring image, a presenting metaphor or symbol of the full-fledged story that the patient may need to tell. We don't always understand, at first, their meaning for the patient but try to remain attentive to it and gently follow its lead. These hints of the bigger story are sometimes evoked by a ritual, such as the circle at the start of the sessions in which we give time for each individual to speak spontaneously about whatever comes to mind for them. Or we may observe a recurring gesture, statement or movement. They might also be triggered in response to a given image, story or poem. Like pieces of a jigsaw we collect these fragments, and try to imagine the bigger picture.

It can sometimes be a long and frustrating process. At times we may feel bored, angry, exhausted and inadequate. Sometimes we feel despair, muddled, helpless and hopeless, often caught up in their defences. We can even, as Motz suggests, 'forget' the 'official' story we have read in their notes, perhaps distracted, blinded or defended from the pain of knowing. One of the great benefits of working together is being able to consider and reflect on this type of counter-transference. We consider these feelings to be equally integral to the fabric of the bigger picture. So we wait, sometimes for many years, and continue to offer a framework in which these 'fragments of experience' can begin to enter into a more coherent relationship. What we are hoping to do is enable patients to tell a complete story that has a beginning, middle and an end, and to help them find coherence between the fragmented parts of their stories and the fragmented parts of themselves. A complete story, which has a beginning, middle and end, offers a narrative coherence for when patients lack confidence to tell their full story or experience chaotic thought that fractures the internal coherence of their telling and image making.

The Bridge
Yet whenever I cross the river
On its bridge with wooden piers,
Like the odor of brine from the ocean
Comes the thought of other years.

Each story, whether a response to a traditional story, a fictional self-authored tale or a personal memory, presents an aspect of the patient's inner world and life experience. These stories may act as a thread, a connective narrative between the conscious and unconscious, past and future, fantasy and reality.

Cox and Theilgaard use the term the 'Aeolian Mode' to describe the use of the aesthetic in psychotherapy in which "an aesthetic imperative augments the patient's access to his inner world". They suggest "metaphor exerts its mutative effect by energising alternative perspectival aspects of experience". (1987. Pp.2-3.18)

We try and gather the fragments, themes and images we collect from our patients to 're-seed' them as metaphors in the hope that they may germinate and take root. We allow the metaphor to rest within the patient's psyche to do its own work. We cannot know or predict which metaphor will act as a catalyst for a particular patient. Sometimes, it seems to come out of the blue with a sense of mystery and surprise.

One example of this was in the choice of the poem, 'The Bridge' by Longfellow that we brought into the group. The bridge in itself is a metaphor for something being 'carried across'. It followed several weeks in which members of the group were speculating about their future and the difficulty of the transition from hospital to the community. We had used the analogy of a bridge in an enactment of an imagined experience. In a dramatisation, Jane visualised crossing the bridge to connect with friends and family on the other side. The poem was then shared in the group:

I stood on the bridge at midnight
As the clocks were striking the hour
And the moon rose o'er the city,
Behind the dark church –tower

I saw her bright reflection
In the waters under me,
Like a golden goblet falling
And sinking into the sea.....

.... Among the long black rafters
The wavering shadows lay
And the current that came from the ocean
Seemed to lift and bear them away

.......And like those waters rushing
Among the wooden piers,
A flood of thoughts came o'er me
That filled my eyes with tears.....

(The Bridge)

Several weeks later, without prompting...

Jane, who had been unable to release the pain of her personal story for many months, took a blank sheet of paper and painted a bridge with water running beneath. She sat silently staring at the image for a long time and then began to cry, her tears flowing uncontrollably.

Some years later she recalled that moment....

"I think with the bridge it was showing the waters that had passed under the bridge in my life, and some of it had been from say my index offence. When everything happened the water was quite turbulent, you know, it was a storm, and that's what I was going through. But then when I got to a stage in my recovery in fact the waters they'd calmed down but they were still flowing, so much was flowing underneath that bridge for example with my children, my partner, the loss of my partner, all the losses that I had faced in my life.... I was shedding the hurt, shedding the pains of what had happened in terms of the water going under the bridge. But then what I'd come to realise, maybe recently actually, is that even though the waters are calm they're not too turbulent, there's many, many undercurrents that are going on where the waters are so deep, you know, undercurrents. For example, when it comes to holidays or Christmases, birthdays, I think of my children and it is like it will just surface to the top, and it will cause the waters to be unsettled.

Fig. 1. The bridge

... So the bridge definitely done that, you know, just it brings that part of you forward because there's so much sort of hurt, there's so much kind of feelings and hurt and pain that is running through me and it's like well, I want to release it, I want to release it and being here is something to release some of that. Because like I said with the bridge, the bridge is very calm. There's so much water gone underneath it, but underneath when you go right down, down deep inside, there's undercurrents of flowing, there's commotion and sometimes art and drama therapy can bring that to the top safely, without it affecting the top too much. It can bring it to the top and it will be acknowledged, it will be noticed, it will be thought about. Then you can kind of move on and I think that's what its looking for, acknowledgement, so definitely."

Jane's ability to mobilise the metaphor and use it, symbolically, to "make a bridge between the inner and outer reality" (Jennings and Minde 1993. Pp. 48, 12), seemed to indicate a significant stage in her recovery.

One method we frequently use to help our patients build a framework for story making is a 6/7 piece, a step-by-step story making technique based on Lahad's model of assessment and the inspiration of the Therapeutic Story Making Structure (Gersie 1997). We often use this exercise in the early stages of a group. It provides a formal framework in which patients can begin to use the elements and tools of story making. It also begins to offer us insights into the patient's internal world. The method will usually involve making images as well as words.

The step-by-step story-making structure

- Based on sequenced questions:
- The landscape
- The dwelling place
- The person/creature who lives in the dwelling place
- The character's problem/difficulty/aspiration
- The help offered
- The obstacle
- The resolution

The method invites answers to the questions (amongst others)

- Where? Orientating a sense of place. A starting point.
- Who? That is the protagonist.
- What? Is the problem and how does it affect the character?
- What if? Can help or a resolution be found?

The initial story begins to illustrate the person's current concerns, as well as their imaginative ability or inability to overcome obstacles and difficulties. Some patients, particularly in the early stages of the group, cannot find a resolution to their story, or perhaps cannot even identify the help that could be found.

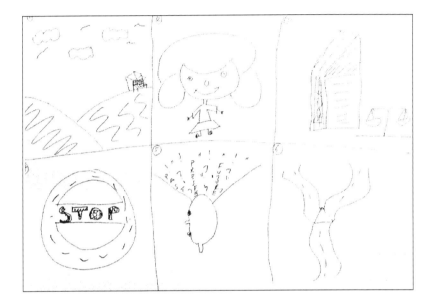

Fig. 2. Making a structure

Example of the step-by-step story-making structure:

The protagonist is a young girl who is superficially 'happy go lucky'. She lives in a nice house overlooking a park. Her problem is that she is trapped by her criminal past dealing in drugs. She is helped by an old woman who encourages her to stop her drug habit. But she is unable to escape the past and her addiction. In this case, the outcome of the story was unresolved as her dilemma of which path to take remained unclear and uncertain.

The story-making structure is also very useful in ongoing work, particularly if we feel the group has become stuck. The patients' stories are shared and developed in the group through 'response tasks', in which each person can contribute to the other's story with statements, images, poems or letters to offer their own perspective and ideas (see Gersie). In shared story telling there is a recognition of the uniqueness of each individual's story and experience and this can be affirmed by others, offering support and empathy.

The stories can then be further explored through dramatic enactment in which each person becomes dramatically involved in each other's story. It is through this process that we may then begin to pose the question "How come?" that is "Why?" the protagonist found themselves in their current dilemma, inviting the consideration of historical cause and effect. It encourages the individual to make links between past and present events through which lessons may be learned and personal judgements can be made.

For many of our patients, the losses they have suffered in the past are severe and significant, be it through illness or personal circumstances. In addition they may also carry a sense of the loss of the future, of opportunities, dreams and aspirations of what might have been or could be. They may have lost trust in their own inner resources to change their life for the better. Through story we can begin to help instil renewed hope by inviting them to imagine different possibilities and future outcomes.

For example, at the conclusion of one story we may invite another, by asking the question: "What might the situation be in the future?" and "What could be?" This exploration can dynamically activate new ideas of how change can come about.

Working in a group in this way allows each person to become a witness and activist to the other's story, offering ideas and the wisdom of their own experience. The group becomes a circle of engagement in which the individual no longer feels isolated in their own story but connected, in a useful and meaningful way, to the other. Most importantly this work also offers opportunities for the person to take on the role of 'helper' instead of victim, mobilising their own imaginative inner resources.

Having found confidence in creating and working with their individual fictional stories, we may then further encourage interpersonal cooperation through the creation of a group story, using similar principles to the step by step story structure. It helps to affirm, strengthen and develop their story making capacity, offering further opportunities for interaction and negotiation.

This is an example of a story making project that took place in a mixed group of male and female patients in which each member of the group created their own imaginary journey. The other members of the group were assigned roles to assist them over the course of their journey to overcome obstacles they met on the way.

- A mixed group worked together on a painting that became an island landscape, the central part made spontaneously into a mountain. Using paint allowed the potential for less control and more unconscious material to find expression.

- Each found a starting place, which symbolically represented the dwelling place, on the island they had created together. We then invited each person to describe the circumstances of their arrival on the island. We felt that the island seemed to represent the shared metaphor of their sense of isolation and detention.

- We posed the question: "How did you get here?" so that each person, metaphorically, would need to reference their personal history and its links to the present.

- Each was asked to identify the destination of the next part of their journey and why they wanted to go there.

- Then each one identified the obstacles they would need to overcome along the way.

- They also needed to identify the help they would need at each stage of their journey.

- Every stage was explored through one or more ways of working such as image making, written story, poems, sculpts and dramatisations. Each person in the group involved themselves in the others' stories as well as their own, offering improvised suggestions on how to overcome the difficulties they met on the way.

- In a later stage the stories were moved into an imagined future with the question: "What is the situation a year later?"

- Each person writes a sequel to their story, "What has changed?" "What has been learned?"
- A group collage to reflect memories of the project and how their stories were interwoven.

For Jonathan, his destination was a cave full of treasure:

"When we arrived, the cave was covered up with branches and rocks so we moved the branches and then some of the rocks, we entered the cave which was quite dark except for a ray of light which shone on the other side of the cave."

In the dramatisation of this story, Jonathan asked help from others to remove the branches and the rock, which blocked the entrance to the cave. Bella took the role of the light at the end of the tunnel. She warned him not to venture too far or too quickly in search of treasure as "curiosity killed the cat".

Gabriel fell from a hot air balloon on his voyage across the sea. The group took the parts of the rescuers arriving in their lifeboat to haul him on board and back to shore. Gabriel used the story to find expression for his underlying fears about relapse, in the form of an SOS. It seemed important that he was able to articulate his distress within the dramatised scene and his need to accept help from others.

In another dramatised scene, Jonathan helped Bella to cross the mountain, but whenever he suggested stopping to explore, she said she needed to continue on. She had no sense of where her destination was but she was compelled to keep moving. Gabriel remarked on her lack of provisions and equipment to sustain her. When Jonathan asked why she had chosen to climb the mountain rather than find a path around it, she said that she "didn't have enough time". Perhaps here was a message to us about her awareness of time passing and her fears that she may never leave hospital. At one stage she said she feared the mountain was

"a volcano which might erupt at any minute".

In the course of her journey, Bella encapsulated her feelings in a poem:

I want to be the little girl
Who held it back so well
I want to find the door once more
And leave my living hell
I want to find a friend
Someone I can tell
About the pain
I'd like to move along in life
And not be anchored here

In the course of this work, patients were able to use the analogy of an imagined story as a creative tool for personal development and progression. In this case, however, it was not only used as pure analogy, it placed the real self as the protagonist within an imagined scenario.

The concept of a journey can itself be a metaphor for progression. It can encourage the belief in being capable of moving on when there is an overwhelming feeling of being trapped or imprisoned in a blocked or locked in story. The group had learned to engage in a variety of story making methods using image making, drama, role play, sculpts, writing and discussion. By combining art therapy and dramatherapy, we were able to broaden and deepen their potential for self-expression using story, by dynamically mobilising the image from paper to dramatic action and back again. The story structure invites a consideration of 'what if?', which prompted the group to explore and test out future possibilities. They were also able to try out unfamiliar roles, from victim to helper, each finding a capacity to support one another along their journey. Each of the group had managed to find a way to develop and enhance their story making capacity to create full-fledged stories. It seemed that their internalised story making capacity was then strong enough to build on.

From story analogy, we then felt the group were able to risk working more directly with personal story. We invited them to make an image of a significant event in their life.

- Jonathan's painting was of a landscape featuring a small figure and a very large red sun. He then was able to tell the story of his relationship with his father and his childhood feelings of powerlessness which he had never learned to resolve.

- Gabriel used image making to describe his feelings about being detained and his frustration about being in hospital, shown as ball and chain around his ankle. It gave him the opportunity to talk about the story of his illness, his drug abuse and the factors, which led up to his index offence.

- Bella made a drawing to show herself still tied up in knots and unable to look backward or forward.

These visual stories were connected to the essence of each of their own situations and were linked inevitably to their offending behaviour, whether it was the cause or the effect. Jonathan had attacked his father; Gabriel addressed the way that his drug-taking lifestyle was linked to his offence; Bella conveyed something of the state of mind that had trapped her into offending. Each piece of artwork enabled them to stand back and view their inner world and their personal self from a distance, allowing it to be seen by others who were able to hold in mind the parts of the stories already told in earlier work and make connections.

> *How often, O how often,*
> *I had wished that the ebbing tide*
> *Would bear me away on its bosom*
> *O'er the ocean wild and wide!*
>
> *For my heart was hot and restless,*
> *And my life was full of care,*
> *And the burden laid upon me*
> *Seemed greater than I could bear.*
>
> *(The Bridge)*

One of the most difficult, but most significant stories that are told in the group are those of a person's index offence. The purpose of the group is to provide a confidential space that feels safe enough to speak of the unspeakable. Although we don't direct people to tell their index offence story, in time, it is inevitable that it will be told in one way or another. Finding a language to express these stories is hard, and it requires strength of trust in themselves, the other patients in the group and in us. Working with personal story, quite often, evokes the telling of the index offence story. It is no longer split off or banished but can gradually begin to be incorporated into the whole story.

When a person decides to take the risk of telling and survives, it can indicate to us a significant therapeutic advance, an unburdening as well as a readiness to change. The trigger may come obliquely through metaphor, such as this poem we shared in one session of the women's group:

Angelic Water Carrier

> *Can you gather water through the cracks of time?*
> *Use secret avenues deep within your mind?*
> *There is a pool of knowledge where you must go.*
> *Will you partake only or let water flow?*
> *.......So bring your earthen vessel fill to the brim.....*

> **(Anon)**

Mary, in response, made a drawing of a container. She spoke about it:

"When I committed my crime, my index offence, it's like I had opened a box that had a seal, and it was all coming out now. I had gone beyond what should be just every day sort of human nature towards each other. Over a long time what I felt is that even though I could see that the box was managing to close itself back down and was attempting to reseal itself, the fact of the matter is, is that that seal had already been tampered with .... you get the seal, the plastic seal that you rip open and then once you've done that, you've opened it up, you can reseal it and it can reseal itself but you've opened it. So that's what I meant in terms of my index offence, it basically just opened up Pandora's box and I'm still having to live with the consequences of that till this day and I don't think it's something that will ever actually go away."

Fig. 3. Water carrier

In the mixed group, Raj picked up a postcard of a painting by Chagall that he described as representing a dream.

He said he was struggling to make a distinction between reality and unreality, piecing together the facts surrounding his index offence to make sense of what he had believed to be a dream and what he had been told was reality. He then painted a memory of himself at the time of his arrest, becoming both the teller and observer of his own story. In the telling, the group, as active listeners and witnesses were able to reflect it back to him so that he could begin to make sense of it.

> *But now it has fallen from me,*
> *It is buried in the sea;*
> *And only the sorrow of others*
> *Throws its shadow over me.*
>
> *(The Bridge)*

Each story can act as a building block, 'storeyed' one over another, to create an internal framework of meaning. The hope is that this structure can become strong and resilient enough to sustain them in the future. For some of our patients it may never be sufficiently repaired, stable or robust enough to withstand the challenges of sustaining a fertile life in the community. Some suffer relapse and return. For some, the 'concrete mother' of the institution provides the only sense of containment in which they can feel safe. Some patients come back to the group, and we need to pick up the threads once again. Some continue to attend after discharge, bringing new stories with them.

So once again we continue to weave stories, from the inner world to the outside world, from the personal to the universal, from make believe to reality, from my stories to our stories. We continue to cross the bridge back and forth from past to present, present to future; from what was, to what could be.

This story of our work is not intended to give a definitive account of over two decades of running groups. So many people have passed through our lives in that time. We have been confidants of their stories and have shared their laughter and sorrows, hopes and struggles. We have tried to help them through the difficult process of change and they, in turn, have changed us. That is the hazard and privilege of this work. We hope that in these few pages we have provided a glimpse of the richness of the work and some of its complexities and mysteries. It is one story. There are, of course, many more.

REFERENCES

Cox M and Theilgaard (1997) A Mutative Metaphors in Psychotherapy. Jessica Kingsley Publishers. London and Philadelphia.

Freud .S. (2001) The Standard Edition of the Complete Psychological Works of Sigmund Freud Volume IX Jensen's Gradiva and Other Works. Vintage Books. London.

Gersie A. (1997) Reflections on Therapeutic Storymaking: The use of stories in groups Jessica Kingsley. London and Philadelphia.

Gersie A, Nanson A, and Schieffelin E, Eds. (2014) Story Telling from a Greener World: Environment, Community and Story Based Learning. Hawthorn Press. Stroud.

Jennings .S. (1992) Dramatherapy: Theory and Practice. Tavistock. Routledge . London and New York.

Jennings, S. and Minde .A. (1993) Art Therapy and Dramatherapy: Masks of the Soul.

Jessica Kingsley Publishers. London and Philadelphia.

Littlejohn S and Fois K., (2009) Eds. Encyclopaedia of Communications Theory Sage Publications Inc. Los Angeles and London.

Motz A. (2011) The Psychology of Female Violence Brunner Routledge. Hove and New York.

Motz .A. (2009) Hiding and Being Lost: the experience of female patients & staff on a mixed sex secure ward. International Forum of Psychoanalysis. Vol. 18 Issue 1.

Myss .C. (2003) Archetype Cards Hay House. UK.

Sacks .O. (1986) The Man Who Mistook His Wife for a Hat and Other Clinical Tales Picador London.

CHAPTER 7

"Lighting Up" The symbolic crime: New approaches in sandplay therapy & fire-setting analysis

EMMA ALLEN

Sandplay Therapy is in itself, unfamiliar territory in the current arts therapies forensic field, and even less familiar is its relationship with fire-setters. A spark ignited from offering a three dimensional approach in Sandplay with fire-setters where fire emerged as a symbolic subject; demanding further attention. Sand has the ability to extinguish fire and Sandplay through its use of symbolic miniatures, has the ability to create scenes that explore the symbolic significance of fire to the offender's internal and external world. Developed by Dora Kalff from Lowenfeld's 'World Technique' (1929, 1960), based on Jungian archetypal psychological theory, sand trays are thought to contain contents of the psyche, where movement of symbols represent psychic conflict and development towards a sense of self, the individuation process (discovering one's true, inner self) and thereby reaching a sense of wholeness of being. Kalff (1980) viewed Sandplay Therapy as an instinctive therapeutic process for intrapersonal and symbolic meaning making through offering a *"free and protected space"* and a delayed interpretation of the dual processes of 'regression into the preconscious' and unconscious material, to increase overall consciousness (Weinrib, 2004).

This chapter offers one case study example of applying Sandplay into an arson treatment programme in a low-secure unit. This follows from an external contract that I was invited to pilot, using individualised Sandplay Therapy to support engagement alongside an *"offence analysis* module" in a time-limited "fire-setting group" on a Learning Disability ward. This offered an additional space for offence disclosure and analysis through non-verbal, symbolic, and three-dimensional means of exploration. Providing individual Sandplay was thought to be of an additional assistance to those who had significant communication and expressive deficits, such as 'Reuben', who, due to his severe speech and language difficulties, was finding the group *hard-going* where he often felt like crying or getting angry due to *dreading talking* about his fire-setting.

This chapter also explores the 'conflict and resolution' held within the first image in the sand tray, its use for arson assessment, whilst also presenting some of the psychological concepts and themes that arise in arson work, particularly looking at themes of fantasy and elevation.

Reuben's First Tray; the 'Conflict & Resolution'

When I first met Reuben, aged 34, he told me that he was interested in trying Sandplay alongside the group as he had difficulties communicating his thoughts and feelings and considered that using imagery would help him to talk about his relationship with fire-setting and events from the past. Reuben not only had the diagnosis of a learning disability, with an extremely low range of cognitive functioning, but also psychotic illness. Reuben told me that he had been placed into foster care as a result of domestic and violent abuse in the home, with no idea where his mother and sister were also moved to, and was later convicted of arson after he ignited the flat he was living in whilst under the influence of drugs and hearing voices. Reuben was very concrete in his disclosures and explanations, telling me that "*I wish I didn't do it – wish I'd taken my medication – that's it*" and often referred to his fire-setting as being about "*it's the lighter that does it – it flicks on and off*" highlighting his lack of insight, responsibility, and perhaps more telling of his learning abilities too. I did wonder that on a symbolic level, he was actually describing his emotions that could be triggered impulsively.

Sandplay involves the creation of three-dimensional imagery or landscapes, using either one or two, wet or dry sand trays, or by adding a range of miniature figures that represent both reality and fantasy, thoughts and feelings, in order to create an 'inner world';

"a projection of the individual's experiential world and a representation of his/her worldview" (Dale & Wagner, 2003). The work allows a technique of 'following' personal symbols, examining their relationship to the patient, whilst noting any changes that occur. The idea was to offer an opportunity for someone like Reuben to reveal his inner relationship to fire through play where levels of fire interest and excitement may also be assessed through visual means. It seemed clear that this non-verbal approach would be an additional support to him when being expected to go into detail of his offence, and I was hopeful he would respond well to Sandplay.

During the first session, Reuben did not speak for some time, but began by rushing towards the miniatures and collecting as many as he could that related to fire and began to lay out his arson index offence; throwing items (a bed, a model of a fire, sink, cooker, toilet, money, bath, a bonfire on a lead (with a battery box to 'light up') into the wet tray to create a dangerous blaze of events, and dynamic scene that illustrated *"the fire in the flat"* (**Figure 1**). My first impression was that he had perhaps misunderstood what had been asked, but I also considered that this was significant in itself, considering his learning abilities, and his impulsive nature. Offering an outlet of emotional expression aimed to offer an extended sense of containment; important for the impulsive fire-setter like Reuben who also showed me through his physicality in the work that he was highly aroused by the sight and use of fire related objects. The process of the making of the tray is just as symbolic as the imagery completed, where Reuben seemed to be able to present more information for the assessment through symbols, rather than by talking. Reuben and I were able to comment on the process where he "chucked" items in the tray to then reconsider how they should be re-placed; we thought about what this meant and explored his struggle to feel cared for, and wanting others to think he doesn't care too. After we spoke about this, he then decided to re-place his items in the sand to consider he did actually care after all.

The first item to be placed into the sand is always significant; likely to be repeated or hold significant symbolic meaning. For Reuben, this was the bed; a bright red blanket, flame-like in its appearance, on a yellow bed. These predominant colours of red and yellow follow through the creation of the first tray and seem to demand attention in the same visual way that fire does. Jung (1964) considered that symbols always express the unknown and provide a language for the unconscious. The bed, from a collective symbolic perspective can often represent sexuality, or an internal need for reflection or psychic rest.

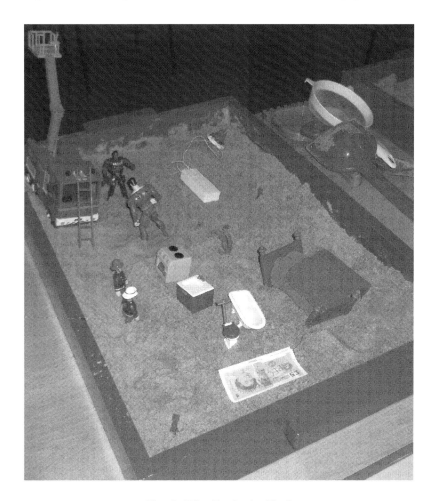

Fig. 1. "The Fire in the Flat"

As Reuben rushed to place all the fires and related fire imagery in the tray, he also seemed to rush though talking about his imagery and gave short descriptions of what had happened, sometimes muttering single words that were hard to understand and piece together – his speech felt just as chaotic as the making of the three-dimensional image. Associated with heat and fire, the dominance of red throughout the first tray links to red's visually empowering excitement and danger; a heightened sense of self, arousal, passion and aggression. Used in fire apparatus to alarm and warn a sense of danger, red calls for attention. The scene of red and yellow, and subject of fire makes the tray seem full of creative energy, danger and power; perhaps showing an active interest and excitement for fire. Yellow is a luminous colour that highlights and lights up areas of concern; a need for enlightenment. Fire-setting avoids direct verbal confrontation and communication through its non-verbal, abstract expression and there is thought to be a symbolic significance of fire and a displaced experience of fire in fire-setters with mild learning disabilities (Kelly et al, 2009) where there is a need to increase insight and understanding of *"self-defeating thoughts and behaviour"* whilst also *"developing more appropriate patterns of coping"* (p.70, Hall, Clayton, & Johnson, 2005). It seemed clear from the start that Reuben had a very active, chaotic, traumatic relationship to self and to fire, linked also to his ways of coping. Fire visually screams out for help and attention; screaming 'notice me', 'listen to me now,' 'see my pain'. I later found out that Reuben also had a history of sexual offending too, and possibly had been sexually abused, which may well have presented itself in the symbols of the burning bed for instance.

Reuben then quickly placed superman, a policeman, a large fire engine with a ladder propped up against it, two firemen figures, and some extinguishers placed in the top and bottom of the tray, telling me that the bank note represented his 'benefits' and that the cones represented *'fire – blocking it off*. Often there is a fascination and excitement to watch fires being put out, sometimes feeling rescued as a result, however, Reuben chose to walk away from his fire and not look behind, telling me he had *'walked past the fire engines and went to the supermarket to buy cigarettes'* whilst the fire in his flat was being put out by the firemen. When fire-setters leave their scene of destruction, it is often avoidant and lacking responsibility where they have not been able to face their issue head on but hope to communicate their distress and let it be seen. Fire screams out a visually bright exclamation for help and attention, it demands to be listened to and noticed and may provide the fire-setter, like Reuben, a sense of empowerment.

Fire setters with learning and intellectual difficulties may often feel that they have been able to create something powerful and effective through fire. Fire-setting can also be thought of as a reckless infliction of emotional pain and emotional processing. Burning buildings, for example, is symbolic of attacking a lack of protection and security where fire-setting can often be understood as a symptom of severe maternal deprivation and rejection, *'negative caregivers'* (Gannon et al, 2012), abandonment, abuse and neglect, painful and unresolved childhood experiences and anger at the 'absence or ineffectiveness of a father' (Lowenstein, 1989).

Fire-setting avoids direct verbal confrontation and communication through its non-verbal, abstract expression; expressing a desire, wish or need to 'attack the symbol' of perceived injustice (Williams, 2013) *"when there is no available safe object to express the rage towards"* (Delshadian, 2003). Reuben told me that *"no one was listening"* to him and lit the fire as a means of escape and a chance to be re-housed; communicating his distress at his inner and outer environment. I also thought that his attack on his own home felt even more deeply symbolic, and the tray was providing an opportunity to examine the scene and its symbolism. Those with a learning disability are sometimes known to have an inner need to exert some power over or revenge at society (Hall, Clayton, Johnson, 2005). Reuben felt his fire-setting was down to *"boredom and loneliness and having nasty thoughts about people – that's why I set a fire"*. He also said he *"wasn't with it"* describing the voices in his head, saying that *"it all got too much"*, but when he looked again at the contents of the tray, he told me *"it's haunted"*, relating more significantly to the past. Reuben's imagery evoked thinking about his past neglect in children's homes and foster care where he was beaten, and, considering the effect this had on his views of himself and others, particularly finding it difficult to speak the words 'dad', admitting that he really thought his fire-setting was a form of anger passed on by his father. I wondered if his fire-setting was perhaps an anger at Dad too but Reuben was very restricted on what he could explore with me verbally. Reuben had only managed to disclose fleeing from his early home, but had not stated that this was actually an escape from his father.

Not only held within the first tray, a series of sand trays can facilitate healing and transformation by bringing up conflicts from the unconscious, but also offering and suggesting ways to resolve the conflict (Kalff, Turner, 2005). By bringing internal conflicts towards consciousness, they can be disempowered and released (Pearson & Wilson, 2001). This process can also be compared to the psychological process and meaning of fire-setting. Sandplay offers a chance to explore the elements, where water can be added to extinguish fires. Both elements of fire and water help to illustrate Jung's ideas of alchemy, the removal of impurities and the manifestation of the self. Reuben's first tray seems to capture a psychological need to cleanse, transform and escape.

Both the firemen and the large fire engine, designed to fight fire, provide water, and an elevated platform provides all the necessary equipment for the task of rescue, and represent an internal need for rescue. If we think of this psychologically, and in terms of the psyche, the fire engine is a vehicle of regulating function (Kalff, 1980); there to regulate chaotic conditions, to put out the flames, and perhaps the ego. The ladder allows access or regress of fire-fighters and the fire victims at height, alluding to being 'high' at the time of the offence. In the safety of the tray, symbolic fire-setting can take place. Reuben's tray presents both the real and imaginary world; representing his conscious and unconscious emotional states. The tray evokes a sense of chaos and order; fire continuing to burn through scenes. It is a visual display and discharge of his emotion; similar to the act of fire-setting. His scene, full of fire, and his continued trays with fire in every scene during the assessment, showed me that fire was still a 'burning' issue for him. The kitchen and whole scene is within and outside 'the house', symbolically, the centre; *"the alchemical retort, the psyche's creative core"* (p.576, Ronnberg, 2010). The scene, although described on a conscious level by Reuben as being the fire in his flat, is more likely to be the internal fire in his unconscious, and presents both a 'fight and flight' response to his past experience of abuse and trauma.

The ladder provides an escape from Reuben's burning flat, an escape from his emotional self, the threat of engulfment, a mother-attachment or other unconscious contents (Ackroyd, 2015) where the escape may provide a greater state of being; the ladder hints that a form of resolution and coping for Reuben has been to elevate the self, or to 'flee' the scene of trauma. Reuben's way out of the tray may have also highlighted his fluctuating suicidal thoughts, where he often expressed wanting to die and retreat from all contact with others due to feeling uncared for. Ascending can be deeply symbolic of communicating with the true self and the ego, and there is an internal need for stability and containment, and an escape to a greater, internal state of height and illuminated state of awareness.

According to Ammann, the centre of the tray points towards the personality of the sandplayer (Ammann, 1991) which for Reuben is an uncontained, uncontrollable fire. The 'home' set alight illustrates his internal world and emotional states where this first tray (*Figure 1*) parallels the act of fire-setting; an emotional discharge and display of displaced anger, revenge and aggression that has been too overwhelming to understand. It also contains the 'conflict and resolution' which provides a snap shot of a subjective analysis of fire-setting where his perceived injustice about his 'home' needs to be lit up for us to see; his current feelings about being in secure care can also be examined. "*Emotional disturbances*" (such as fire-setting) "*can be dealt with by giving it visible shape*" (Jung, 1916/1952) through symbolic activity, 'free and protected' creative play, unconscious processes are made visible and three-dimensional in the sand.

Fire symbolism in the sand tray – hero or villain?

Superman and a policeman are in a battle, and Reuben said that they represented the computer game that he was playing at the time of the fire. This seems to suggest a psychic conflict for Reuben, where Superman doesn't usually fight the police, but works alongside the law. Here however, lawful behaviour needs to win over wanting to be a hero, and a sense of winning and overcoming authority needs to be felt, a battle for dominance and power perhaps. Many superheroes, such as Superman are marginalised men that lack a sense of home, identity and belonging; very similar to the fire-setter. The hero is an immature masculine archetype, an immature energy that fights battles for a self-serving purpose, but is required to evolve into a more mature and 'real' archetype. Superman, a symbol of strength, ability and perseverance, is in opposition to learning disabilities where superheroes potentially have the power to take away disability, or to hide it. They are crucial to the journey of heroism and an important archetype that represents the journey to individuation. Most superheroes have overcome a trauma and appear unaffected and stronger as a result; capable of resurrection. They are indestructible, immortal; they can be trusted as they do not ever change or mature, they get better and more powerful. They overcome trauma, and symbolise the success of order over chaos. Fires are indestructible too, where the fire-setter becomes all powerful; for the patient with a learning disability, a sense of empowerment is a rare opportunity and a dangerous enactment of fantasy.

The enticing attraction to superheroes and their stories may symbolise their need to find change over their static situation; feeling stuck, and incapable of making any changes for themselves. Fantasy, distinct from imagination, can be a compulsive form of self-soothing, an 'inner addiction' that could leave those who have been victim to early trauma, *'stay unembodied and away from the traumatic affect'* (p.206, Kalsched, 1996). Reuben's repetitive use of fantasy figures suggested an avoidance of looking at the real him and reminded me of the 'flight response' when feeling threatened or in danger.

The *'conflict and resolution'* for Reuben is all about fire; the need for alchemy and transformation. The superhero needs to transform into a more grounded, genuine, sense of self. The mastery of trauma held in the symbolism emerges in the use of the superhero. In order to carry out the symbolic attack through fire, the fire-setter needs to identify with their 'inner hero'. There is a revenge fantasy, a lack of empathy, and the need to transform. Fire burns, eradicates, cleanses and purifies; a way to extinguish and exterminate. To be rid of something is also a way to try to transform; it is fire that is the ultimate superhero for the fire-setter. Reuben's trays all undergo processes of chaos and order, merging and separation.

Reuben's superheroes may also help him to navigate his way through life, including his computer games and continual need for fantasy figures that may assume some of his energies of inner and outer villains such as *Dennis the Menace*, (a miniature used in all of his other sand trays seen in **Figure 2**) whom related to his personality and mischievous characteristics, and desire to 'play'. Often, fire-setters have experienced conflictual relationships, family instability and negative environmental experiences which then influence revenge fantasies in gaining control over their situation (Kolko, 2002). *Dennis the Menace* can be considered to be the shadow archetype of the hero, relating to the learning disability and with describing himself as a 'hooligan'; identifying his unlawful and disruptive behaviours. Having an intellectual disability can itself provide a motivation for fire-setting (Devapriam, et al, 2007).

Fig. 2. Fire Symbolism in the sand tray

Fire is thought to be viewed as either 'master or servant' to those with a learning disability (Hall, Clayton, & Johnson, 2005) but fire is always the hero. Here a sense of control and mastery recreates a positive internal efficacy and power, and is thought to even provide a sense of identity (Gannon et al, 2012). The ultimate superhero in the fantasy life of the fire-setter is fire itself that is able to conquer all, whatever the consequence.

Traumatised fire-setters such as Reuben could be thought about as having been affected by an intrapsychic arrest in the ego development; an inner struggle for dominance, fuelled by a fear of being subsumed (Neumann, 1973, Turner, 2005). Low self-esteem, depression and suicidal ideation is often managed by maintaining a rich fantasy life where fire-setters may sometimes seek a disguise, pretending to be someone else. His previous outlet for this was probably computer games and fire-setting. Sandplay, however, allows unknown unconscious processes to be seen, and for denied energies and insights to be re-integrated and acknowledged. Reuben would need to know how to integrate his hero or villain archetypes, where they may be psychologically stuck in an immature psychic state.

Elevation & descent to Self

Reuben talked about needing to "*bottle things up*", symbolically, alluding to the need for elevation. When figures are elevated, height symbolism represents an emergence, a hope for freedom of what weighs them down. Symbols of strength and perseverance like the statue of liberty provide important defiance in response to the abuse or neglect. The theme throughout all of Reuben's sand imagery was about 'lighting up'; the elevation of the platform of the fire engine, the fighting scene between superman and the police, the potential cooking process and uncontained fires surrounding the tray (**Figure 1**), all provided the message of emotions having some emergence and need to be lit up in his consciousness. There is a need to inflate the self and bolster up their sense of ego consciousness, to feel bigger and empowered over his trauma. Elevation, ascent and height symbolism all point towards an ascending to the '*excessive heights*' and losing touch with reality (De Vries, 2004). This is an example of how Sandplay animates collaboration between unconscious fantasy and conscious awareness (Ryce-Menuhin, 1991).

Reuben's battle scene between Superman and a policeman (**Figure 1**) suggests a hero turned into an outlaw; the fire-setter himself. The computer game he refers to at the time of the offence, and his 'addiction' or distraction to computer games on the unit, all hint at his need to ""*space out" into diffused undifferentiated states of melancholic self-soothing in order to stay unembodied and away from the traumatic effect*" (p.206, Kalsched, 1996). This battle hints at his aggressive energies. The hero archetype is subject to '*cycles of inflation and deflation*' (p.141, Papadopoulos, 2006) carrying shadow material;

'opposing personality' carries the shadow of the hero; an archetypal complex that is expressed though individual function attitudes of the personality (Beebe, Papadopoulos, 2006).

Analysis of archetypal interactions can take place through Sandplay where ego strength needs to be re-established in the patient. Dissociation from traumatic and painful experiences involves the process of repressing feelings, blocking emotion and losing touch with their real selves. Fire setters are known to have a low self-esteem and poor or distorted self-image, along with a perceived inability to affect social change, an external locus of control, have a low confidence in dealing with face-to-face conflict and avoidance of confrontation, interpersonal conflict or violence (Kelly et al, 2009). Sandplay aims to re-connect mind and body, asking the body to respond too; offering a deep way to reconnect to disembodied, dissociative states. From the repetitive use of the 'home' in all remaining sessions, (e.g. **Figure 3**) a strong imprint in the sand was left behind, marking a strong inner need for a sense of stability, grounding and security.

All used symbols such as the Statue of Liberty, and Superman evoke the fantasy of overcoming trauma and gaining a sense of empowerment. They are a manifestation of the fire-setter himself; the need to transform into a hero; to take flight, rise up and above the scene of trauma, defending against threat but also bringing justice and championing truth.

Prometheus, the most important myth and symbol associated with fire, teaches us that fire symbolises our need for creativity and a libido for life; a drive (Bachelard, 1987). This is the more positive symbolism of fire, which, having an internal relationship to fire can be motivating and creative, whilst having a lust for life; crucial for Reuben who often struggled with suicidal thoughts. Fire is often a means to escape, and a means to inflate the self. Reuben's trays often depicted a sense of wanting to escape on holiday to New York where his repeated use of the Statue of Liberty is also a superhero, one of autonomy, hope and the 'American Dream'. Like Prometheus, they are both bringers of justice and hope by raising their triumphant torches of flames. Prometheus is the ultimate fire-starter, the hero for giving man the gift of fire and the ability to be creative. Being creative can master trauma; the resolution here for Reuben.

Fig. 3. "The flat – a future relationship – settling down"

At the end of the assessment, Reuben thought that our sessions together had helped him to *"cool down"* before the fire-setting group and considered that *"people will only ever get 'half the story' about his fire-setting though talking"* but that through visual means, he would be able to show his story, his risk, where the *"full picture"* may be seen and understood. Reuben's repeated use of the house, Dennis the Menace, a female figure, and finally in the last session, a heart; expressing his need for love and to "settle down" emotionally where the fires had cooled off (***Figure 3***).

Central to all understanding of the process of Sandplay, is that there needs to be the core process of a descent into the unconscious to the self and a reintegration of the ego structure *"followed by a re-emergence into consciousness and a re-ordering of the ego to the Self. Towards a sense of wholeness and totality"* (p.53, Turner, 2005).

Conclusion

Sandplay offers visual empowerment and escapism from the engulfing fire of emotion. Symbolically repeating the pattern of trauma, fire-setters such as Reuben repeat the act of trauma of feeling burnt by their abuse. It is crucial that fires do not spread where fire-setters need to be offered safe containers for their emotional expressions. Sandplay Therapy, in its directly visual, symbolic approach can explore fire-setting, a visual symbolic crime, in a way that enables fire-setters to reveal and relieve their impulse for fire through a safer means. Sandplay seemed to help Reuben have a space for expressing suicidal feelings; the unspeakable was contained, secured and understood. Fire was a way to be seen and heard. Fire spontaneously emerged as symbolic, relating to his inner world; providing a glimpse of his emotional state. Fire symbolises our need for creativity, and through being creative, trauma can be burnt away.

The symbols and figures that are raised up in the sand tray present an elevated sense of self that is inflated and distant. Heat and fire rises above as if grandiose and ultra-powerful and magnificent, however, the fire-setter needs to descend into deeper work, whilst also needing to be grounded; exploring his sense of being, his sense of self. Just as fire rises, it is important for the fire-setter to raise his issue up; to metaphorically "light up" his issues for us to see and descend into the therapeutic process.

Through the observable manifestation of subliminal and symbolic material in Sandplay, the role of hero archetypes are a significant stage within the individuation process, and his role within psychic development for the fire-setter, highlighting the desire and inner need for mastery and control over past trauma and neglect. Fire provided Reuben a heroic sense of empowerment, escapism and mastery over trauma whilst symbolically inflating and elevating his sense of self, and ego consciousness. Reuben was provided with the symbolic opportunity to master his internal landscape of trauma, whilst also expressing and releasing his frustrations with communication and his learning disability. The sublimation of libidinal and aggressive impulses can take place though creative expression and *'provides means for escape'* (Gussak, 2004), but a chance to express and communicate distress and need for change.

Sandplay helps illuminate, "lighting up" the fire-setter's internal symbolic and fantasy world, archetypal defence systems, fire-setting characteristics, attitudes and beliefs, including fire excitement, creative energies; helping us to understand motives for fire-setting and offence analysis. This "different" approach provides the potential for the "different" side or state of the fire-setter's personality to be revealed and manifested through symbols; thus providing a different aspect to the overall psychological formulation and provides what Reuben described to be *"seeing the full picture"* of his emotions. This allows the therapist to work with both conscious and unconscious aspects, where, over time, a re-integration of dissociative states can take place through symbolisation. In turn this facilitates a reduction of risk as fire-setters become more aware of their behaviours and actions. Sandplay Therapy allows fire-setters to reveal and work through their inner conflicts and traumatic experiences, aiming to help make the connection between the behaviour of fire-setting and any feeling states that may fuel it, and may need to be put out by the sand.

REFERENCES

Ackroyd, E. (2015) *Ladder, Dreams-Myths-Symbols*, http://dreamssymbols.com/dsladder.html.

Ammann, R. (1991) *Healing and Transformation in Sandplay* (Translated from German) Open Court Press: La Salle.

Bachelard, G. (1987) *The Psychoanalysis of Fire*, Beacon Press.

Bradway, K. & McCoard, B. (1997) *Sandplay: Silent Workshop of the Psyche*, Routledge; London & New York.

Dale, M. & Wagner, W. (2003) *Sandplay: An Investigation into a Child's Meaning System Bia the Self-Confrontation Method for Children*. Journal of Constructivist Psychology, 16:17-36.

Dalton, R., Haslett, N. & Daul, G. (1986) *Alternative Therapy with a Recalcitrant Fire-setter*, Journal of the American Academy of Child Psychiatry, 25, 713-717.

DeVries (2004) *Elsevier's Dictionary of Symbols and Imagery, Second, Enlarged Edition, Elsevier Science.*

Delshadian, S. (2003) *Playing with Fire: Art Therapy in a Prison Setting, Psychoanalytic Psychotherapy, Volume 17, No.1, 68-84. Brunner Routledge, Taylor & Francis healthsciences.*

Devapriam, J., Lammata B.R., Singh, N., Collacott, R., Bhaumik, S. (2007) *Arson: Characteristics and Predisposing Factors in Offenders with Intellectual Disabilities*, The British Journal of Forensic Practice, Vol 9, Issue 4, December 2007.

Gannon, T.A., Ó Ciardha, C., Doley, R.M., & Alleyne, E. (2012) *The Multi-trajectory Theory of Adult Fire Setting*, Aggression and Violent Behaviour, *17*, 107-121.

Gussak, D. (2004) A Pilot Research Study on the efficacy of art therapy with prison inmates. Arts in Psychotherapy, 31-245-259.

Hall, I., Clayton, P. & Johnson, P. (2005) The Handbook of Forensic Learning Disabilities, Chapter 4 Arson and Learning Disability, p.51-72.

Jung, C. G. (1964) *Man and his Symbols*, Dell Publishing.

Jung, C. G. *Memories, Dreams, Reflections* (London 1983) Fontana Press; New Edition (1995).

Jung, C.G. (1933) *Modern Man in Search of a Soul*, 1933, Harvest Book, Harcourt, Brace & World, Inc., New York.

Jung, C. G. (1934–1954) *The Archetypes and the Collective Unconscious*, (1981 2nd ed. Collected Works Vol.9 Part 1), Princeton, N.J: Bollingen.

Kalff, D. (2003/1980) *Sandplay, A Psychotherapeutic Approach to the Psyche*, Temenos Press, California.

Kelly, J., Goodwill, A., Keene, N. and Thrift, S. (2009) A
retrospective study of historical risk factors for pathological
arson by adults with mild learning disabilities, British Journal of
Forensic Practice, 11 (2): 17-23.

Kalsched, D. (1996) *The Inner World of Trauma, Archetypal
Defenses of the Personal Spirit*, Routledge: London.

Kolko, D. ed. (2002) *Handbook on Fire-setting in Children &
Youth*, Academic Press: London & New York.

Lowenfeld, M. (1960) *The World Technique. Topical Problems
in Psychotherapy*, 3. 248-63.

Lowenstein, L. (1989) *The etiology, diagnosis, and treatment
of the fire-setting behaviour of children*. Child Psychiatry and
Human Development 19:186-194.

Papadopoulos (2006) *The Handbook of Jungian Psychology:
Theory, Practice and Applications*, Routledge.

Pearson, M., & Wilson, H. (2001) *Sandplay and symbol
work: Emotional healing with children, adolescents and adults*.
Melbourne: Australian Council for Educational Research.

Ronnberg, M. (2010) *The Book of Symbols: Reflections on
Archetypal Images (The Archive for Research in Archetypal
Symbolism)* Taschen.

Ryce-Menuhin, J. (1991) *Jungian Sandplay: The Wonderful
Therapy*, Routledge.

Steinhardt, L. (2000) *Foundation and Form in Jungian Sandplay:
An Art Therapy Approach*, Jessica Kingsley, London.

Turner, B. (2005) *The Handbook of Sandplay Therapy*, Temenos
Press, USA.

Weinrib, E. L (2004) *Images of the Self, The Sandplay Therapy
Process*, Temenos Press, California.

Williams, D. L. (2013) *Understanding the Arsonist: From
Assessment to Confession*, Second Edition, Lawyers & Judges
Publishing Company, Inc.

CHAPTER 8

Art Psychotherapy with an adult with autistic spectrum disorder and sexually deviant dreams: A single-case study including the client's responses to treatment.

DR SIMON S. HACKETT

Introduction

This chapter describes art psychotherapy undertaken with "Adam", a man with autistic spectrum disorder who experienced vivid dreams that included violent and sexual content against young girls. This single-case study was conducted as part of a larger research project that had been granted ethical approval by the UK National Research Ethics Service. The participating client gave his full consent to take part in the study.

This single-case study draws from the work of Elliott (2002) and has a number of additional features not commonly reported in art psychotherapy studies. The aim of the case-study was to provide a plausible explanation for therapeutic change by including the following features.

1. The content of therapy sessions were audio recorded so that the client's words can be quoted in the reporting of the therapy process. The client was also asked by the therapist to identify and rate the severity of their personal problems at the start and end of therapy.

2. Three months following art psychotherapy the client's responses to the therapy were sought during a recorded interview that was conducted by a research

assistant. The interview included questions about
how helpful or unhelpful the client had found art
psychotherapy.

3. Specific therapeutic changes reported by the client
were identified from the combined audio recordings
of art psychotherapy sessions and the client's
recorded post-therapy interview.

4. The client's report of therapeutic change is explored
by looking at related literature in the field and then
it is considered alongside a range of alternative
explanations for change.

Background

Adam was a twenty-three year old man who had a diagnosis of
mild learning disability, autistic spectrum disorder and Klinefelter's
syndrome. Adam had been in hospital for two years and three months
before participating in this study. He had been transferred from the
hospital medium-secure unit to the low-secure unit just prior to having
art psychotherapy. A comprehensive risk assessment completed when
he was in the medium-secure unit stated "Adam presents as a young
man who is rigid and inflexible in his approach to life. Any diversion
from set routines has the potential to induce anxiety and irritability
and lead to confrontation". During his treatment in the medium-secure
unit Adam's verbally and physically aggressive behaviour towards staff
had reduced. On a day-to-day basis he presented no difficulties to
the nursing staff and would appear to be amicable and compliant.
Some minor incidents of self-harm were reported but this was very
infrequent. Adam had developed positive relationships with nursing
staff after moving to the low-secure unit and said that he could trust
them. His interactions with staff would mainly revolve around seeking
assurance and "getting advice". Adam was able to speak clearly although
his manner of speech could appear monotonous and repetitive with
little use of facial expression. He did have some interaction with other
patients and his conversations were generally friendly. His response

Art Psychotherapy with an adult with autistic spectrum disorder
and sexually deviant dreams: A single-case study including the
client's responses to treatment.

147

time in conversation was delayed with some word-finding difficulties. He also needed longer processing time when thinking about new information. Misunderstandings could be the cause of his increased anxiety and, in turn, states of anxiety could impair his understanding. He was also reported as having become concerned about his physical health which raised his anxiety.

Adam did not have any contact with relatives and his requests to have contact with both his birth mother and a foster carer were not reciprocated. Adam was taken into care weeks after he was born. His foster home was not a stable placement and the placement was terminated due to one of the foster carer's misuse of alcohol. Further disruption continued in foster care. During Adam's school years he showed evidence of early developmental delay alongside increasing behavioural disturbance. He was suspended for threatening behaviour and then arrested and excluded from school after being suspected of rape.

During his early adulthood Adam was convicted of possession of child pornography. There are also reports that Adam was threatened in the community for his offence and taunted as a "paedophile". His admission to the Young Offenders Institute (YOI) followed being charged with and later convicted of fourteen counts of downloading child pornography. His sexual deviance had also been noted in reports with his predatory interest in pre-pubescent girls demonstrated in his history of trying to associate with young children at a horse-riding stable. He was also suspected of committing rape at age eighteen years but he did not hold a conviction for this. Adam had a serious history of violence which included hiding and using weapons, hostage-taking and making threats to kill whilst in possession of a knife. Adam had initially been transferred to the medium-secure unit from the YOI after writing down deviant fantasies about taking a female member of staff hostage.

During his admission to hospital Adam continued to show an interest in pre-pubescent girls and was found with pictures of young girls horse-riding. He would also report and write down vivid dreams and fantasies about stalking, raping and murdering young girls.

Art psychotherapy treatment

Adam completed 20 individual sessions of art psychotherapy over a six month period. The therapy sessions were provided by a female art psychotherapist with a staff escort seated outside the room. Typically his sessions lasted 45 minutes and took place in the art and craft room in the low-secure unit. Adam told the therapist that he was a quiet person and that he found it difficult to get to know people. He said that this had bothered him a little bit and that he also had an issue around girls. The three main personal problems he identified at the start of therapy were that (1) he found it difficult to think and talk about relationships; (2) he did feel low sometimes; (3) he was bothered by having nightmares that caused him a degree of distress at different times. Adam's 'nightmares' were mainly related to his sexual offences, both in terms of dreams with violent and sexual content and his fears about being threatened by people in the community who might know about his offences.

Adam responded well in early therapy sessions and told the therapist that he found that making artwork helped him feel "peaceful". Adam drew an image of a battleship, and described how he could become "submerged" in the artwork. Within the fourth therapy session Adam reported that he was feeling a lot more settled and related this to attending therapy.

Adam also spoke about his nightmares and told the therapist, "I might speak it out, yesterday night, I had a bad dream. If I'm living in my own place or with staff, some people were knocking on the door and make threats to me...because of my index offence." Adam had started to draw a picture of a horse in stable, a picture associated with his interest in pre-pubescent girls at a riding stable (Figure 1). This image appeared to encapsulate both aspects of his nightmares. Adam continued to speak about his disturbing nightmares related to the image of the horse. "Most dreams are very dangerous for me, to going...one dream I had, probably last week or this week - probably last week now - a farmer slaughtered a horse. We were getting that horse better, and he slaughtered me not the horse...I saved the...Before the horse had been slaughtered...I saved the horse. The farmer was not looking and he slaughtered me." Adam also drew images of the dreams that included fantasies about abducting young girls. He described

Art Psychotherapy with an adult with autistic spectrum disorder
and sexually deviant dreams: A single-case study including the
client's responses to treatment.

149

these images to the therapist, "Those are people on the street and two families. One at WH Smiths and one at the bus stop (Figure 2). That is me there, looking for an underage girl (Figure 3). I followed her around off on that road there, and kidnapped her."

Fig. 1. Horse in the Riding Stable

Fig. 2. Looking for an underage girl

Adam continued to discuss his dreams with the therapist and brought his written dream records to the therapy session. He also spoke about being attracted to a female patient he had seen in the hospital. His attraction to her was not reciprocated and the content of his dream record included a fantasy account of carrying out a violent sexual assault on the female. Adam stared to link pictures he made in therapy with his dreams and commented to the therapist that some of the places in his dreams and nightmares were in his pictures, he said that this felt "weird".

Toward the end of therapy Adam started to speak to his therapist about feeling more relaxed, "I think I have achieved something, working with art", "I think I have enjoyed session's last couple of months". Adam related his enjoyment to "painting as being relaxing" and "thinking about pictures, what to do". Adam identified one of his pictures as resembling a "dream catcher" (Figure 4). At this time Adam told the therapist that he was not having any more bad dreams and that he thought it was probably to do with his art therapy sessions.

The client's response to art psychotherapy

In the final therapy session the personal problems Adam identified at the start of therapy were revisited and he was asked to re-rate the severity of each problem again (Table 1). The biggest improvement at the end of therapy was for 'having nightmares' which Adam re-rated as having changed to being "the best it can be".

Problem Statement	First Therapy Session	Last Therapy Session
Thinking and talking about relationships	3	4
Feeling low sometimes	2	2
Having nightmares	3	5

Note. 1= the worst it can be; 5= the best it can be.

Table 1. Personal Problem Scale

Art Psychotherapy with an adult with autistic spectrum disorder and sexually deviant dreams: A single-case study including the client's responses to treatment.

151

The client's post-therapy interview responses

In a post-therapy interview three months after ending art psychotherapy Adam reported that he had continued to have fewer nightmares with violent and sexual content. Adam also reported "feeling more settled" as a result of art psychotherapy.

- *What changed?* "Probably I can't say something about it… I'm having less dreams about young girls."
- *What helped?* "Aye, telling [therapist's name] about my dreams."
- *What else changed?* "And I feel a lot more settled."
- *What helped?* "Probably doing that art therapy, talking out my problems with [therapist's name]. She's given me some advice, what to do. Speaking to her about what's happening, I feel more settled."

At the interview, when asked what the art therapy was like for him Adam replied, "It was quite interesting". Adam spoke about early sessions: "the first time I started I was quite nervous". When asked what he was nervous about Adam replied, "probably talking about my dreams". When asked how much he thought things had changed since doing art therapy Adam said, "probably quite a bit". Helpful things within the sessions described by Adam were, "probably writing things down, probably drawing things, painting it". Adam said that the things that helped were "…talking, drawing…feeling sad, feeling happy. All different things". He found talking to be the most useful part of therapy.

Adam also gave some mixed statements about his therapy when he was asked what was unhelpful. He said that he thought six months of therapy was "too long" and that art therapy would be useful for other patients in the hospital, but with fewer sessions. One difficult area was that he did find it hard to explain the pictures he had made in the session. "A little bit difficult for me to do with explaining what's happening in the picture." Adam later clarified this in the interview and said that he had some difficulties "expressing my feeling".

Fig. 3. "Dream catcher"

Helpful aspects of art psychotherapy

Adam's responses to questions in the post-therapy interview provide helpful information about key areas in the therapy that proceeded therapeutic change.

1. Adam said that he was a bit nervous at the start of therapy. His nervous feelings were also related to opening up to the therapist. "The first time I started I was quite nervous, probably talking about my dreams."

2. Adam described being involved in therapy sessions. "It was quite interesting." "Painting, drawing, talking."

3. Adam identified that speaking and explaining himself to the therapist was difficult for him. "Going over the pictures and talking about it." "A little bit difficult for me to do with explaining what's happening in the picture."

4. Adam reported that he was able to speak to the therapists and that this helped. "...doing that art

Art Psychotherapy with an adult with autistic spectrum disorder and sexually deviant dreams: A single-case study including the client's responses to treatment.

153

therapy, talking out my problems with [therapist]. She's given me some advice, what to do. Speaking to her [about] what's happening and I feel a lot more settled."

5. Adam was able to be open with the therapist about his feelings and said that he found therapy relaxing. Adam associated experiencing reduced nightmares to having art psychotherapy.

Exploration of the literature associated with Adam's clinical presentation

A number of complexities are presented in Adam's case, such as his diagnosis of Klinefelter's syndrome (XXY condition), a diagnosis of autistic spectrum disorder (ASD), and his deviant sexual fantasies and nightmares.

Klinefelter's syndrome

Klinefelter's syndrome is considered a sex chromosome variation (SCV), also referred to as XXY condition due to an extra X chromosome. The condition is the most common genetic cause of male infertility and it can occur as frequently as 1 in 500 in male births, although not all develop features associated with Klinefelter's syndrome. Insufficient testosterone is produced, commonly treated with hormone replacement therapy. Typically XXY males can present as being socially quiet and shy when they are children with associated literacy problems, language difficulties, problems with verbal processing speed, auditory processing, and deficits in verbal memory which can persist into adulthood (Boone, et al., 2001; Geschwind, Boone, Miller, & Swerdloff, 2000). This can adversely affect the ability of some men with this syndrome to express their thoughts and put emotions into words. Behavioural abnormalities also seen in this population include poor judgment, impulsivity, failure to consider consequences of one's behaviour and deficits in social skills (Boone, et al., 2001). Examples of detailed case reports relating to the psychosexual development and sexually deviant behaviours of XXY males can be seen in the literature dating back to 1953

(Hoaken, Clarke, & Breslin, 1964). Early studies in sex chromosomal abnormalities were commonly based in secure hospitals and penal units (Craft, 1984). Money and Lamacz (1989) described seven different cases with "sexological disorders" and paraphilia, including sadomasochism and paedophilia. Epps (1996) reports on the sexual preferences, behaviour, and fantasies of an adolescent boy with the 48-XXYY syndrome. Some authors have sought to establish a link between Klinefelter's syndrome and sexual offending (Hummel, Aschoff, Blessmann, & Anders, 1993; Lachmann, et al., 1991; Raboch, Cerna, & Zemek, 1987). Other studies provide counter-evidence supporting the hypothesis that Klinefelter's syndrome is associated with lower levels of sexual activity in comparison with peers (Raboch, Mellan, & Starka, 1979; Sorenson, 1992). Griffiths and Fedoroff (2009) cite Langevin's (1992) findings that endocrine disorders were apparent in 10% of sexual assault cases and evident in cases involving paedophilia. Whilst there is a range of historic case reports and studies of offender populations with chromosome and endocrine conditions, there is no known correlation with paraphilia (Gooren & Kruijver, 2002).

Autistic Spectrum Disorder (ASD)

Hare, Gould, Mills, and Wing (2000) reported an over-representation of individuals with autistic spectrum disorders in English high-secure special hospitals. O'Brien et al. (2010) found rates of ASD at 10% in a study covering three health regions in the UK, which included 477 people with intellectual and developmental disabilities. Offending behaviour was not found to be over-represented among individuals on the autism spectrum. Tantam (1988) identified 46 people with ASD in a sample of 60 patients with "lifelong eccentricity and social isolation". Nearly a quarter of the subjects had committed a criminal offence with two of the subjects detained in a special hospital. Antisocial behaviour is also reported in the sample with six subjects being identified with "morbid fascination for violence" of which three went on to act upon their interests and carry out violent assaults. Two of the men had violent sexual fantasies which included designing sadistic experiments on women, and violent fantasies. Both men carried out attacks on girls after writing explicitly about their aggressive feelings (Tantam, 1988). Berney (2004) suggested that some forensic

Art Psychotherapy with an adult with autistic spectrum disorder and sexually deviant dreams: A single-case study including the client's responses to treatment.

155

presentations in ASD, in particular Asperger syndrome, can include obsessive harassment (stalking), inexplicable violence, computer crime, and offences arising out of misjudged social relationships. In a brief commentary on offenders with autism spectrum disorders Murphy (2010) highlights the presence of dysfunctional and restricted coping strategies: "many people with autism include a profound alienation from other adults and maladaptive coping strategies (such as developing vivid and controlling daydream worlds) for dealing with emotional regulation and interpersonal anxiety" (Murphy, 2010, p. 45). There is also a clinical view that individuals with autism can find the experience of inpatient treatment and offence-related interventions anxiety-provoking. Symptoms of anxiety may be seen to worsen for some patients with autism during treatment, and close monitoring is recommended (Taylor, Lindsay, & O'Brien, 2011).

Deviant sexual fantasies and offending

The role of fantasy in leading to an offence has generated a wide range of theory, and differing opinion. Daleiden, Kaufman, Hilliker, & O'Neil (1998) consider that it might be the absence of normal sexual fantasies in sex offenders rather than the presence of deviant ones that stimulates offending. Howitt (2004) proposes that offenders' fantasies are more reflective of themes associated with their own history. The role of deviant sexual fantasies and internet pornography leading to contact offences has also been considered. In a study comparing the psychological profile of contact sexual offenders with internet sexual offenders, under-assertiveness was found to be predictive of internet offences (Elliott, Beech, Madeville-Norden, & Hayes, 2009). A conclusion from this study was that child pornography was used due to its lack of face-to-face contact. General rates of offenders reported to go on to commit contact offences after using pornography vary from 40% (Wolak, Finkelhor, & Mitchell, 2005) to 86% (Wilcox, Sosnowski, Warberg, & Beech, 2005).

Treatment of nightmares in psychotherapy

There is a small amount of literature relating to the reduction of nightmares in psychotherapeutic work, for example, reductions in "highly disturbing nightmares" are demonstrated as an outcome in psychodynamic-interpersonal psychotherapy (Kellett & Beail, 1997).

Willner (2004) reports a case study of a man with mild to moderate intellectual disabilities experiencing two recurrent nightmares, one of which was accompanied by congruent post-traumatic daytime ruminations. The 29-year-old man had committed a sexual offence and disclosed that he had been sexually assaulted. He also reported urges to re-offend which were associated with periods of personal distress. The recurring nightmares were addressed in a single therapy session including use of a relaxation technique, telling the story of the dream and then changing the ending of the story from a negative to positive outcome. This revised dream story was then rehearsed several times in the session and support staff were asked to monitor the man's dreams for a week. Reduction in nightmares and daytime ruminations were also linked to a reduction in the man's urges to offend and an increase in victim empathy. At six and 12 month follow-up only one repeat of a nightmare had taken place with no resurgence of urges to offend. Kroese and Thomas (2006) report two case studies describing the treatment of chronic nightmares for sexual assault survivors with an intellectual disability. The technique of imagery rehearsal therapy (Krakow, Kellner, Oathak, & Lambert, 1995) was applied in both cases with the addition of using drawing to help both client and therapist to illustrate the dream sequence. Both cases were reported to have had reduced frequency in nightmares which was maintained at six-month follow-up.

Reduction in nightmares reported by Adam during and following art psychotherapy

Adam reported that nightmares were a personal problem for him at the start of therapy which were improved at the end of therapy (Table 1). In a three month post-therapy client interview Adam stated that events taking place within art psychotherapy had led to a sustained reduction in his specific nightmares about stalking and kidnapping young girls and being attacked in the community because of his index offence.

Components of art psychotherapy (present in audio recordings) involved Adam in retelling dream scenarios, drawing imagery from recurring dreams and reflecting upon the content of these pictures with the therapist. In session 11 Adam drew a "dream catcher" (Figure 4) which he associated with a reduction in his nightmares.

Art Psychotherapy with an adult with autistic spectrum disorder
and sexually deviant dreams: A single-case study including the
client's responses to treatment.

157

Alternative explanations for therapeutic change

Is Adam's report of therapeutic change still plausible when considered alongside possible alternative explanations?

Possible alternative explanations for Adam's account that he had experienced a reduction in nightmares due to having art therapy could include an attempt to please the therapist after six months of working together; a hormonal changes associated with Klinefelter's syndrome; a generalised reduction in stress or anxiety un-related to therapy; or using 'self-help' techniques alongside art psychotherapy.

1. Was the reported therapeutic change due to superficial attempts to please the therapist?

Adam expressed some dissatisfaction during session 10 to the therapist, albeit reluctantly, indicating that he was able to raise specific concerns with the therapist. At post-therapy interview Adam said that he would have preferred a shorter duration of therapy and many of his responses to questions were, at best, measured. Adam continued to report therapeutic change at his post-therapy interview (when the therapist was not present) indicating no clear evidence that he reported therapeutic changes in attempt to please the therapist.

2. Was the reported therapeutic change due to hormonal fluctuation?

An alternative explanation for the improvement Adam reported could include hormonal fluctuation. Some studies have identified positive outcomes of testosterone treatment for men with Klinefelter's syndrome (Nielsen, Pelsen, & Sorensen, 1988). Whilst testosterone can influence the threshold of occurrence of erotosexual imagery and sexual activity it does not appear to change the content of imagery (Gijs & Gooren, 1996; Gooren & Kruijver, 2002; Money, 1986). Hormonal influences may offer an alternative explanation for change but as hormone levels were not measured in this study the potential for and/or full extent of this hypothesis remains unclear in Adam's case

3. Was the reported therapeutic change due to a generalised reduction in anxiety?

Adam related his nightmares to periods of increased stress. There is evidence that periods of stress increased during the treatment as a result of a number negative events taking place outside of therapy sessions including the rejection by his birth mother of Adam's attempts to make contact with her. Increased levels of Adam's self-reported anxiety would suggest that there might have been an increase rather than a decrease in the frequency of the nightmares he reported. A contributory rather than alternative explanation could be linked to Adam experiencing art-making as a form of relaxation within therapy which may have also supported a reduction in night-time distress during the treatment.

4. Was the reporting of therapeutic change due to self-help?

Adam kept a diary of dreams which he said helped him not to think about the nightmares during the day. However, Adam did bring the diary to the therapist for discussion. If left unchecked, Adam's written fantasies could be associated with heightened risk. It is not possible to assess if use of a dream diary on its own would have had a positive therapeutic influence. The additional influence of drawing and discussing the dreams and fantasies with the therapist appears to provide a plausible explanation for change which is supported by Adam's own account of events taking place in art psychotherapy.

Art Psychotherapy with an adult with autistic spectrum disorder and sexually deviant dreams: A single-case study including the client's responses to treatment.

159

A plausible explanation for therapeutic change in Adam's case.

It remains plausible that Adam's report of his experience of depicting and discussing his nightmares and deviant sexual fantasies in art psychotherapy supported a reduction in their frequency and severity. At the end of therapy Adam rated an improvement in severity score for "having nightmares" as "the best it could be". This improvement was reported by Adam to have been sustained for three months following art psychotherapy. The elements of Adam drawing explicit and deviant sexual dreams within therapy and discussing this with his therapist may have contributed to change. Adam's post-therapy reports, that specific events in therapy supported a reduction in the frequency of his nightmares appear to provide a plausible explanation to change when considered against possible alternatives.

Conclusion

Despite the limited and idiographic nature of the therapeutic change reported in Adam's case it has been possible to identify very specific links between processes taking place in art psychotherapy that were helpful for the client. This case is interesting given the range of complex factors in Adam's clinical presentation including his associated forensic risks. Within this study art psychotherapy does appear to have supported a reduction in the frequency of Adam's nightmares which included sexual and violent content.

REFERENCES

Berney, T. (2004). Asperger Syndrome from childhood to adulthood. *Advances in Psychiatric Treatment, 10*, 341-151. doi: 10.1192/apt.10.5.341

Boone, K. B., Swerdloff, R. S., Miller, B. L., Geschwind, D. H., Razani, J., Lee, A, ...Paul, L. (2001). Neuropsychological profiles of adults with Klinefelter syndrome. *Journal of the International Neuropsychological Society, 7*(4), 446-456.

Craft, M. (1984). Genetic endowment and XYY syndrome. In M. Craft & A. Craft (Eds.), *Mentally abnormal offenders* (pp. 116 -124). Eastbourne England: Bailliere Tindall.

Daleiden, E. L., Kaufman, K. L., Hilliker, D. R., & O'Neil, J. N. (1998). The sexual histories and fantasies of youthful males: A comparison of sexual offending, nonsexual offending, and nonoffending groups. *Sexual Abuse: A Journal of Research and Treatment, 10*(3), 195-209.

Elliott, I. A., Beech, A. R., Madeville-Norden, R., & Hayes, E. (2009). Psychological profiles of internet sexual offenders comparisons with contact sexual offenders. *Sexual Abuse: A Journal of Research and Treatment, 21*(1), 76-92.

Elliott, R. (2002). Hermeneutic single-case efficacy design *Psychotherapy Research 12*(1), 1-21.

Epps, K. J. (1996). Sexually abusive behaviour in an adolescent boy with the 48, XXYY syndrome: a case study. *Criminal Behaviour and Mental Health, 6*, 137-146.

Geschwind, D. H., Boone, K. B., Miller, B. L., & Swerdloff, R. S. (2000). Neurobehavioral phenotype of Klinefelters syndrome. *Mental Retardation and Developmental Disabilities Research Reviews, 6*(2), 107-116.

Gijs, L., & Gooren, L. J. G. (1996). Hormonal and psychopharmacological interventions in the treatment of paraphilias: An update. *Journal of Sex Research, 33*(4), 273-290.

Gooren, L. J. G., & Kruijver, F. P. M. (2002). Androgens and male behavior. *Molecular and Cellular Endocrinology, 198* (1-2), 31-40.

Griffiths, D., & Fedoroff, J. P. (2009). Persons with intellectual disabilities who sexually offend. In F. M. Saleh, A. J. Grudzinskas, J. M. Bradford & D. J. Brodsky (Eds.), *Sex offenders: Identification, risk assessment, treatment, and legal issues* (pp. 353-375). New York: Oxford University Press.

Hare, D. J., Gould, J., Mills, R., & Wing, L. A. (2000). A preliminary study of individual with autistic spectrum disorder in three special hospitals in England. London: National Autistic Society.

Art Psychotherapy with an adult with autistic spectrum disorder and sexually deviant dreams: A single-case study including the client's responses to treatment.

161

Hoaken, P. C. S., Clarke, M., & Breslin, M. (1964). Psychopathology in Klinefelter's syndrome. *Psychosomatic Medicine, 26*(3), 207-223.

Howitt, D. (2004). What is the role of fantasy in sex offending? *Criminal Behaviour and Mental Health, 14*(3), 182-188.

Hummel, P., Aschoff, W., Blessmann, F., & Anders, D. (1993). Sexually aggressive acts of an adolescent with Klinefelter Syndrome. *Uprax-Kinderpsychol-Kinderpsychiatr, 42*(4), 132-138.

Kellett, S., Beail, N., Newman, D. W., & Mosley, E. (1999). Indexing psychological distress in people with an intellectual disability: Use of the Symptom Checklist-90-R. *Journal of Applied Research in Intellectual Disabilities, 12*(4), 323-334.

Krakow, B., Kellner, R., Oathak, D., & Lambert, L. (1995). Imagery rehearsal treatment for chronic nightmares. *Behaviour Research and Therapy, 33*, 837-834.

Kroese, B. S., & Thomas, G. (2006). Treating chronic nightmares of sexual assault survivors with an intellectual disability - two descriptive case studies. *Journal of Applied Research in Intellectual Disabilities, 19*, 75-80.

Lachmann, M., Brzek, A., Mellan, J., Hampl, R., Starka, L., & Motlik, K. (1991).

Recidivous offence in sadistic homosexual paedophile with karyotype 48, XXXY after testicular pulpectomy. *Exp-Clin-Endocrind, 98*(2), 171-174.

Langevin, R. (1992). A comparison of neuroendocrine abnormalities and genetic factors in homosexuality and in pedophilia. *Annals of Sex Research, 6*(1), 67-76.

Money, J. (1986). *Lovemaps: Clinical concepts of sexual/erotic health and pathology, paraphilia and gender transposition in childhood, adolescence and maturity.* New York: Irvington.

Money, J., & Lamacz, M. (1989). *Vandalized lovemaps.* Buffalo NY: Prometheus Books.

Murphy, D. (2010). Understanding offenders with autism-spectrum disorders: what can forensic services do? Commentary on Asperger Syndrome and criminal behaviour. *Advances in Psychiatric Treatment 16*, 44-46.

Nielsen, J., Pelsen, B., & Sorensen, K. (1988). Follow-up of 30 Klinefelter males treated with testosterone. *Clinical Genetics, 33*, 262-269.

O'Brien, G., Taylor, J. L., Lindsay, W. R., Holland, A. J., Carson, D., Steptoe, L, ... Wheeler, J. (2010). A multi-centre study of adults with learning disabilities referred to services for antisocial or offending behaviour: Demographic, individual, offending and service characteristics. *Journal of Learning Disabilities and Offending Behaviour, 1*(2), 5-15.

Raboch, J., Cerna, H., & Zemek, P. (1987). Sexual aggressivity and androgens. *British Journal of Psychiatry, 151*, 398-400.

Raboch, J., Mellan, K., & Starka, L. (1979). Klinefelter's syndrome: Sexual development and activity. *Archives of Sexual Behaviour, 8*(4), 333-339.

Tantam, D. (1988). Lifelong eccentricity and social isolation. Psychiatric, social, and forensic aspects. *British Journal of Psychiatry, 153*(6), 777-782.

Taylor, J. L., Lindsay, W. R., & O'Brien, G. (2011). Offenders with intellectual disabilities. In J. Gunn & P. Taylor (Eds.), *Forensic psychiatry: Clinical, legal and ethical issues (in press)* (2nd ed.). Oxford: Butterworth-Heinemann.

Wilcox, D., Sosnowski, D., Warberg, B., & Beech, A. R. (2005). Sexual history disclosure using the polygraph in a sample of British sex offenders in treatment. *Polygraph, 34*(3), 171-183.

Willner, P. (2004). Brief cognitive therapy of nightmares and posttraumatic ruminations in a man with a learning disability. *British Journal of Clinical Psychology, 43*, 459-464.

Wolak, J., Finkelhor, D., & Mitchell, K. J. (2005). Child-pornography possessors arrested in internet-related crimes: Findings from the national juvenile online victimization study: National Centre for Missing and Exploited Children. United States.

Acknowledgements

I would like to thank Jillian Archibald Principal Art Psychotherapist for her participation in this study.

CHAPTER 9

Working with people who kill:
The role of the clinical specialist
in forensic art therapy

KARL TAMMINEN

Introduction

This chapter will discuss what makes forensic art therapists specialist, and what specialist skills we bring to the forensic clinical forum. It will argue that in this current political time of austerity, the loss of the role of art therapy generally, and specifically the forensic clinical specialist within it, will introduce a poverty of intervention and perspectives within forensic specialisms (Marian Fotaki/CHPI 2013). This paper does not argue for conformity of practice, but for effectiveness of practice. It does not argue for a manualised approach to standardised interventions, quite the contrary. It rejoices in the unique, an approach to clinical work that differs from one specialist to the next (Marcia Sue, Cohen Liebman), (Sarah, C. Slayton 2010).

This chapter recognises the everyday battle of the forensic art therapists within a complex set of ethics and morals (Gussak, D & Cohen, Liebman, MS. 2011). Starting from the position that, contrary to presently accepted wisdom, the efficaciousness of a clinical intervention is seldom to be found in the preordained path to some predetermined destination. The effectiveness is held within the unique journey and reaching the meaningful destination that makes change possible and desirable to the individuals themselves and safe for the society they live within. The journeying and arriving at a destination being about individually meaningful recovery, rather than a set of socially predetermined outcomes which make compliance necessary and difficult to resist without surrender of self and self-determination (Caddy. L. and "N" 2009).

This chapter does not argue for a comfortable practice as a clinical specialist's work should not be comfortable; it should be challenging and just a little bit scary. Clinical practice should stretch us to the limits of our experience, skills and endurance. It is that excess of effort I advocate, because that is what is needed to make the difference with people who experience extremes of distress and trauma and present with equal risk. The therapeutic encounter is not solely about being in the room, understanding the rules of engagement or having a thoroughness of understanding around theory, professional frameworks and the legislation, which governs practice. It is ultimately all of these things, whilst being none of them. Clinical specialists need to work on the edge of the known, the limit of the evidence and strive to nurture development and engender change through transition from a state of distress and disconnect, to a state that offers the possibility of self-determination. Specialists need to operate on the edge of the known psychiatric/ psychological/ sociological universe, quite simply because we know and understand so little about these states of extreme distress and deregulation. The challenge for all clinicians in mental health services is to use the little that we do understand about normal and abnormal psychology, and use it as a springboard for diving into the unknown that surrounds and vastly outweighs the little we do know.

The role of the forensic clinical specialist in art therapy is unresolved; it is an unfinished skeletal structure of a unique and specialist intervention. Art therapy is a vocation and calling with a quiet voice, which draws you into private, places and hidden worlds. Art therapy sometimes shows us things we would rather not see; it shows us worlds we would rather not know because not everyone lives in the same world as we do. Forensic art therapy is not a job from which you can easily clock on and off. The process of art therapy uses the therapists themselves as a catalyst for change, but also as a witness to a very personal holocaust. Art therapists working in forensic settings become the repositories for recording and witnessing the darker side of human nature. Their work is about casting light into those deep and dark places.

In many respects, clinical specialists in forensic therapy are still
seen as being different to their fellow art therapy registrants; they work
with people whose choices have been limited and whose liberty has
been curtailed. To survive in a forensic clinical setting, the art therapist
has to hold themselves and their practice to the highest of ethical
standards. If forensic art therapists are different from others of their
kind, it is something that happens along the journey. It is something
we learn from the people with whom we work, from the team which
we become a part, and even from the things we are legally obligated
to do, whether we agree with them or not.

Working within forensic settings as a clinical specialist teaches
you to treat people as individuals and to respect that individuality;
the context with its inherent risks makes the perspective critical. You
must explore each case in unique, singular and pioneering ways, but
you cannot be inconsistent. When working with people who have been
sectioned in accordance with the mental health act because they are a
danger to themselves or others, it is quite literally about life and death.
You must set high standards on your own practice, be rigorous in your
clinical endeavours, and be a good communicator. The environment,
the context, the client and the work all conspire to shape the newly
qualified art therapist and forge a clinician capable of practicing in
this setting. The profession can be chameleonic; we become the
therapists we are by what we are exposed to. Forensic art therapists are
exposed to extreme and unusual things. In order to survive that they
need to develop an intrinsic resilience which cannot be learned from
a book, acquired over a counter or copied from another. They need
to develop that semi permeable skin, a skin that allows the impact of
those images and those people to reach us, affect us, have meaning
for us, but not destroy us.

In my role, I am an archaeologist. Enabling the past to be
revealed, recording each revelation, insight and paragraph of the
individual's story, from their perspective and in their own words,
images and symbols. I apply my skills of critical analysis to the task.
I believe everything I see, hear, feel and know, and yet I believe none
of it. I see it as the total truth simultaneously with the confused,
multileveled attempt to communicate something that can never really
be communicated, and the experience of being alive and living in

this body, at this time and in this place. A medium-secure mental health unit in the UK is a place where serious business is conducted. A place, an intervention, a sanctuary that can offer life or death to the people who live and are compelled to exist within its narrowly defined borders. A place where I, as part of a team, am asked why a person did what they did and whether they are likely to do it again. I am also asked whether a person can change, evolve or develop skills or self-containment sufficiently to function again as part of a society. The one thing that has become apparent to me in my time as an art therapist is that people want to tell their own life story, from their own perspective, and where they do not, or are unable to tell it, then the story wants to tell itself and leaks out into their everyday life, not consciously summoned and not prepared for.

There are many levels of the therapeutic which art therapy engages with. There is the process itself, which can be therapeutic; the therapy can connect with our inherent healing processes, especially where they have become stuck. There is the intrinsic therapeutic effect of creativity. There is art as a communication, as when words fail to speak we need another language, a non-verbal language which art therapists are sensitive to. There is also art therapy as a clinical/psychotherapeutic tool for assessment and connection, which can build bridges with people that can have positive therapeutic outcomes.

I have no qualms about recognising that I continue to begin each workday with a vague nagging doubt and a sense of not knowing what my role will be today, and how it will be different to yesterday. There is no room in this clinical practice for passivity, unfounded certainty or arrogance of 'knowing' without learning.

Theoretical approaches

I am eclectic in the way I work, but that does not mean I randomly follow therapeutic models on a whim. I find, adapt, make or fit the tool to the person rather than the person to the tool. I see art therapy on an anthropological and historical level. I am working with people and their cultural, social and spiritual worlds, I am engaging with their ancestors and their children by connection. I see art therapy on a psychological level and altering and impacting upon the inner structure of the working of the human body at its most profound level. Where the thoughts change, the biology must follow. Art therapy is about change, both the profound and the seemingly inconsequential.

Forensic art therapists have to be open to alternative ways of understanding, to be alert and watchful for new ways in which to both conceive of and work with people's difficulties. I had to hold onto new and uncomfortable truths in order to hold a frame of reference that had meaning for me as an art therapist. I was to work with people who rape and kill, who assault and burn, who kidnap and torture and who have treated people as if they are not people. I was to work with those who hurt others as much as they have been hurt themselves. The reasons why they hurt others are complex, multifaceted and unknown even to the individuals themselves. They hurt others so they will not hurt them, but conversely they also hurt others so that others will understand how they feel, or hurt them in return. So the first step is to acknowledge that there is risk here, respect that risk, work with that risk but not be made impotent by it.

It is no easy task to write an account of one person's approach to working with people who kill. Each personal account is about the metaphysical, a plunging through layer upon layer of confusing and conflicting understandings. The work I do has to have meaning for the other members of the clinical team of which I am only part. It also has to be meaningful in its context to both the judiciary system and the health service in which I am employed. Ultimately it has to have meaning for the individuals with whom I work.

Case study

In my experience people who kill are not, as a collective, "bad people", but they are people who have done extreme things. To go from doing bad things to someone actually dying is the distance of a hair's breadth. Just because people have killed does not mean they will kill again; it all depends on the individual, the victim and the circumstances. People are unique; they each have a story to tell, some more fluently than others. This case study is a glimpse into the life and world of one individual amongst many. There is no way of telling this story that sanitises the event. When one individual kills another, it is shocking and abhorrent. I can only tell the story in the most sensitive way possible, without glamorising it or making it seem that I am in any way saying it is acceptable that one individual takes it upon himself or herself to kill another; it is not. Most importantly of all, I must maintain confidentiality. The identifying details will be sparse and just enough to tell the story, but not to identify the time, place, victim or perpetrator. This case study is a brief insight into the therapist's struggle to understand the process of change and put it into context. It is an attempt to recount the process of change that moves an individual from the position of a person who kills and is an active and on-going risk, to one who has killed, but is not likely to repeat the offence.

A man in his late twenties, whom we shall name Jonathon, killed an elderly relative. Confidentiality is crucial here as the UK is a comparatively small place and this death was big news, as all deaths connected with patients from mental health services are, even though the statistical evidence shows us that murders are more likely to be committed by people without a diagnosable mental illness (Philo 1996), by people we know, love and even trust. The relative lived with Jonathon and his partner, and was killed by Jonathon who drove a piece of household furniture into the victim's body whilst pinning the frail relative down. He then proceeded to break several of the victims' ribs post mortem before creating a shine around the corpse. He consistently stated that he killed the frail elderly relative out of fear and stated his belief that if he had not then the elderly relative would have killed him.

When I first met Jonathon I didn't know what to expect. The horror of his actions stimulated an expectation and a very human tendency to prejudgement. When someone kills another with their hands and weapons, you might expect to meet an animal or a vicious creature with no remorse or conscience. Rather than meeting a frightening and dangerous character however, I was greeted by an unassuming and quiet man who was desperate to be liked. Both of us being over six feet tall, we were similar in stature, but he moved a little too nimbly for the extra fifty pounds he was carrying. There seemed to be something cat-like about the way he interacted with the space around him. My heart pounded, my mind was full of the risk of working with this unpredictable man, but the professional training and experience within this setting brought about a reduce of physical and psychological signs of anxiety. I was aware that I was hyper vigilant in his presence, but found it to be a good survival bias as well as an acute clinical tool. My hyper vigilance enriched and heightened the therapeutic encounter, because I was alert to all levels of our interaction, listening to all levels of communication in all the ways it was to be spoken. This professional skillset was always held in a dynamic tension, my reaction time not quick enough and the alarm I carried hampered by a technology that was just too slow if help were required. I had been involved in a comprehensive risk assessment which is routinely undertaken before admission, utilising both the Sainsbury's risk assessment tool (Stein, W. 2005) and the assessment tools brought by each profession, I also had access to a full and complete history on this man before I first stepped into an enclosed space with him. I knew exactly who and how he had killed, but no one seemed to know the reason for this murder. On top of that, I also knew he had been trained in martial arts, which he had learned under the tutelage of leading martial arts experts in the UK, including advanced skills such as weapons training incorporating short and long sticks, numchucks, short and long knives and staff work. He had at some stage been involved in training health care professionals in the techniques of what was then known as control and restraint, which was the department of health's approved process for managing violent and aggressive individuals in the safest manner possible. In other words, he knew what mental health staff are trained in, to control violence, but also knew all the counter moves to render them impotent. This was not delusional or fanciful; it was evidenced, real and ultimately extremely disturbing for all the health professionals who worked with him.

Jonathon was one of the most difficult people I have ever had to work with in art therapy. What made him so difficult to work with, for an art therapist, was that he appeared to be totally lacking any creative mindedness and showed no signs whatsoever of possessing an active imagination. As I slowly and painstakingly got to know him and to unravel the complex conundrum of his personality, a creative light did eventually begin to shine as he talked to another person for the first time in his life. He talked about his dreams and fears, his hopes and aspirations and the tatters that were left of them. From moment to moment I was aware of his unique risks, the only tangible defence I had against this high risk was in the depths of the art therapy training, in communication, in making a connection and on being present in the space and safe in a way that offered a shared safety. In that dynamic can be found the essence of the role of the forensic clinical specialist in art therapy.

Whilst Jonathon sat opposite me working on whatever images he was tackling, the image, regardless of the title, story or ingredients would always look the same week after week. I could not let my mind wonder, nor would I let my (justified) paranoia and fear deskill me. As a constant reminder the scars down his forearms were not evidence of self-injurious behaviour in the way we generally know it, but the result of what is known in martial arts as sword work. After he had been taught how to fight with swords, sticks, chains and knives, as part of his martial arts training, he was also taught how an unarmed individual would take these weapons off an attacker. The scars on his arms were supposed to remind him of when he did not execute the moves correctly...and he had many scars, which had reinforced his learning until he became proficient.

Jonathon was one of those individuals who wanted to do well. He had experienced bullying and told stories which suggested he had existed in a state of hyper arousal, preparing himself for an attack he was certain would come, and he found his salvation in martial arts. He continually prepared himself for an attack and planned his course of action as he walked towards groups of children, youths and workmen. The process began in early childhood with children and continued as time progressed and was used to survive in a world as an adolescent and ultimately as an adult. Such an expectation became his normal template for dealing with others. The fact that the expected attack did not come seemed to increase his suspicions rather than alleviate them.

Jonathon was proud of his physical control. Our mental health service sought to begin his 'keep fit' programme again, given his history of physical exercise any engagement with physical activity was seen, very traditionally, as signs of and contributing to a positive shift in his mental health. Art therapy however, began to evidence that such an activity might be at the core of his difficulties which had led to his loss of control; resulting in someone's death. Once this insight was shared with the rest of the team it helped to reformulate the way we worked with him. Art therapy told us that he believed he could never be fit enough, strong enough or fast enough and that the attack would come when he was too exhausted to defend himself.

Jonathon's drawings were childlike and repetitive. For the first three years of our working together I was shocked by the rigid views he held which seemed to control his life. There appeared to be very little, if any, room for imagination or play, much less room for development. Jonathon wanted what most people wanted and had achieved most of them. Yet ultimately, he struggled to hold on to them and as they slipped between his fingers like fine sand, and he experienced terror and loss as only a child can. The public in trying to understand his capability of killing an elderly person with his own hands or with a weapon, held the assumption was that he was in some way inhuman. Nothing could be further from the truth. As incredulous as it may seem, fear seemed to be the reason out of many possibilities. Jonathon had been bullied as a child and had developed a belief that he was in constant danger. He began taking lessons in martial arts to boost his self-confidence and to improve his ability to keep himself safe. Unfortunately for him, a space was created in his mind between what he believed he needed to do and what he could actually do. The more proficient he became in martial arts, the more pronounced was his fear of the harm he believed others were planning to do to him. The stronger he got, the stronger his fears became, the more skilled he became, the more skilled he believed he needed to be. He would never be strong enough, fast enough or skilled enough, because the person he imagined to be pursuing him would always be faster, stronger and more skilled.

In order to put Jonathon's story into context, I later travelled hundreds of miles with Jonathon along with other members of the mental health team for a home visit. A concerned family had requested that he make a final visit to his ailing grandmother who was approaching the end of her life. Over the four years I worked with Jonathon I was left with a cupboard full of artistic artefacts, testament to the weekly therapeutic encounter, each carefully stored and conserved. From Jonathan's perspective, his partner had refused him permission to ever speak to his family again and we wondered whether his family shared this understanding. Expressions of love and support were given freely and without reserve. The home visit was a standard procedure conducted by the nursing team, I was able to sit back and observe Jonathon in his formative context, which as therapists we rarely have the opportunity to do. The meeting challenged aspects of my training and experience; I wanted to learn whether seeing Jonathon in his family context could enrich the art therapy encounter. I could now see the person with whom I had worked for so long within his own natural environment and his own people, as opposed to the representation of Jonathon I had known in the forensic service for four years. The difference had to be seen to be believed. Here he was someone's son, brother or uncle, a man who seemed to be unconditionally loved by his family.

Around the third year of our time together, we arrived at the index offence, the act of killing, which brought him into custody and ultimately into hospital. I had slowly built up a picture of this man's inner world as private, hidden and dark. Yet this was not a world full of anger, hatred or scheming to kill for pleasure, profit or reward. This was a world full of fear, sadness and loneliness. Back in the art therapy room when we finally reached the place where all roads lead, the death of the relative, he shared his recollection and perspective for the first time. "My …..("partner") had gone out and locked me in the flat with him (the relative he will ultimately kill), (partner) ….was worried about me and left me there for his protection whilst ….(they) went for help, I couldn't get away. He had something in his trousers, a weapon I think….or perhaps an erection….I just knew he was going to use it against me. I was afraid and thought he was going to kill me so I had to do something". We now had a more meaningful understanding of the "why" of the death.

This better understanding enriched the multidisciplinary treatment process. During our last year of working together, I made a determined effort to introduce playfulness into the art therapy process. My clinical instincts told me that play seemed the way forward. Jonathon however found it hard to play or make marks on paper, which were neither "right nor wrong". He struggled with doing something just for the sheer enjoyment of it. At first these playful drawings were regimented, but over time freedom and creativity started to develop. The effect of these sessions did not limit themselves to the art room. Jonathon's key nurse met with me and said, "Whatever you are doing keep doing it!" It appeared that there was a change in Jonathon being observed by others within the residential area. It seemed to staff that he was freer and was displaying a more relaxed approached to things. He was becoming less concerned with things being correct or incorrect in terms of fulfilling expectations. These changes were directly attributed to his art therapy sessions, because that was the only therapeutic approach he was actively engaging with.

Art therapy is not just a way of telling the story. It has the power to engage with the story, thereby initiating and supporting transformation. Initially the therapy had become stuck and lacked any spark that would indicate or translate into meaningful change for Jonathon. He was being a "good boy", of whom his family and staff members could be proud. He seemed afraid of the consequences that would befall him if he became a man, something that he seemingly struggled to come to terms with, but the act of creativity changed that. I am always stunned at how the simplest of things can have the most profound effect. Sometimes the hardest thing is to keep it simple.

Conclusion

There is absolutely no room for vagueness in forensic art therapy. It either tells the story or is an agent for transformation; it is not and should not be passive or disengaged. I begin from the client's view "as if", exploring the perspectives, assumptions and learning all the way. As a clinical specialist, I have to take myself, the work I do and the person with whom I am working seriously. My professional qualifications gave me the bedrock of my practice, but I have had to develop and evolve in peculiar and specialist ways.

The real art, in art therapy, is in the way people can articulate a whole new perspective for their lives. The art is in the articulating and conceptualising of themselves in time and space. The ultimate act of creativity is the transformation. In these times of austerity, when the arts are falling off the list of essential education, there is a real risk that this unique form of clinical practice is lost within secure units. Not only would this be a tragedy for the profession, but more importantly for the service users themselves. Ultimately the loss of art therapies in secure and forensic units would be felt in the community because there will always be people who kill and there will always be a need for a place of safety both for the perpetrators and society itself, but without this essential aspect of assessment and treatment we lose the only non-verbal approach which is recognised and employed by the NHS.

We have begun a conversation here, or perhaps brought it into a new forum. We have looked at how the role has developed for one clinical specialist and begun to highlight some of the aspects that seem to create distance between forensic art therapists and art therapists in other settings. Given that the core of forensic art therapy is about an approach that embraces creativity, both in act and thought, in individuality and also in self-control and determination, many find it hard to understand why the specialism thrives in a forensic setting which is the antithesis of creativity and which in essence is about restriction, conformity and imposed control. The answer is simple: words, or the lack of them. We do not process, live or experience life in words. We tell a story to others and ourselves with them and use them as a bridge to understanding with those around us. Words cannot encapsulate the moments we live; we remember those moments in a cacophony of images, smells, tastes, sounds and sensations. Words can and do often get in the way of processing and recalling those moments. The non-verbal aspects of arts therapies leave space for the memories and the feelings that make them, to surface and be re-experienced re-absorbed and re-newed.

The role of the clinical specialist in forensic art therapy is not solely about seeing the world in that visual/aural and spatial sense and working that way, it is about valuing that uniqueness, communicating that uniqueness and fighting for that silent voice to be seen and heard.

REFERENCES

Sandle, D. (1998), development and diversity: new applications in art therapy. London. Free Association Books

Tamminen, k. (2000) exploring the identity of the art therapist in health. Unpublished research

Fletcher, M (2011) assessing the value of specialist nurses. Nursing times: 107: 30/31, early online publication

Debbie Beirne (2012) httpo://clinfield.com/2012/06/research-
nurse-academic-clinical-specialist/).

Cathy Malchiodi (April 02, 2013) Art Therapy in the 21st
Century: seeking a picture of health for art therapy. Published
by Arts in Health. Psychology Today

Marian Fotaki/ chpi.2013. http:/chpi.orh.uk/wp-content/
up;oads/2013/CHPI-lessons-from-the-social-care-market-
october-2013.pdf

Marcia Sue Cohen-Liebman, M.S. (2014) investigation and
intervention forensic art therapy. https://www.psychologytoday.
com/blog/art-trial/201409/invesdtigatioin-and-intervention-
forensic-art-therapy

Gussak, D & Cohen- Liebman, MS. (2001) Investigation versus
intervention: forensic art therapy and art therapy in forensic
settings. The American Journal of Art Therapy, 40 (2),123- 135.

Sarah. C. Slayton et al (2010) Outcome Studies on the Efficacy
of Art Therapy: a review of findings: journal of American Art
Therapy Association, 27(3) pp. 108~11

Liz caddy and N. (2009) explorations: an e-journal of narrative
practice: more than we~ a story of identity. Number 1, 26-35.
Dulwich Centre Foundation.

Stein, W., (2005) Journal of psychiatry mental health Nursing.
Oct: 12(5): 620-33. Modified Sainsbury tool: an initial risk
assessment tool for primary care mental health and learning
disability services

Kerry. J.Pang. 2005 .The Behavioural Genetics of
Psychopathology: a clinical guide. Lawrence Earlbourne
Associates. London

Boyle, M. 2002. Schizophrenia a scientific delusion? Routledge
press. London

CHAPTER 10

Inside out: Art therapy with complex female offenders

SHAUN WASSALL[12] GRAHAME GREENER[13]

"The thing about art therapy is that it allows the women to shout without making a noise."

(Prison Officer 2012)

Introduction

The provision of art therapy was introduced in 2012 as an addition to an existing and specialist assessment and treatment service for women prisoners who are currently on the offender personality disorder pathway. The explicit goals of this service are to improve psychological well-being and to reduce risk of re-offending. In order to facilitate this, the service offers a range of interventions such as psychological treatments, art therapy, psychiatrist sessions, group and individual therapy along with other team building and motivational programmes.

The aim and purpose of the chapter is to highlight themes, which arise within art therapy, such as emotional masking and barriers to engagement and how to manage these. Thus, within the context of the chapter the themes will be explored in more depth, and strategies of management will be offered from both the clinical and

---

12   Art Psychotherapist

13   Prison Officer

discipline perspective. Furthermore, the chapter will aim to promote collaborative working where both professional identities support, inform and enhance the art therapy process. The chapter will conclude with a vignette of a prisoner who engaged in art therapy for 17 months. Images produced within therapy have been included with informed consent from the prisoner, who has chosen to name herself Tempest. Lastly, the art therapist's personal reflections, invoked by the work, will be interwoven throughout.

Collaboration and togetherness

Collaboration is about working together to achieve agreed goals. Throughout the process, we review and assess in order to improve and develop the service that we offer. Collaboration within the wider prison is also beneficial and necessary for the adequate and safe containment of both the prisoner and those working therein. Collaboration within the treatment programme includes multidisciplinary meetings, joint working and most importantly, the therapeutic alliance, which develops between the prisoner and clinicians/officers.

To further enhance the therapeutic relationship, prisoners and members of the team are encouraged to attend the monthly prisoner user group. Here, issues and ideas are put forward for discussion. These can then either be put into fruition, disagreed with an explanation or put on hold for further reflection. Within the meeting, one prisoner is allocated the job of chairperson or minute taker. Collaborative working also improves the consistency of care and aids outcomes. The sharing of knowledge and the strengthening of professional relationships has, in this instance, encouraged the development of a shared language. It is a language, which subsequently adds depth and richness to each piece of work. Collaborative consistency enables the prisoner's strengths and difficulties to be attended to, seen from all angles, and accepted within a safe environment. It is important to note however that nothing is ever perfect, and a collaborative approach can sometimes raise challenges. Difficulties can arise within the multidisciplinary relationship, and it is here where supervision and session debriefs are vital in discussing interpersonal dynamics and the unsaid which occurs in every session. Occasionally differing opinions and personality clashes can occur.

It is vital that these are handled with care and worked through correctly; if this is not adhered to, the therapy, purpose and rationale could lose focus. If not addressed at all, splitting could occur within the team dynamic, and consequently this could have a detrimental effect on the prisoner's progress and the success and strength of the team. Furthermore, differences in work styles and training backgrounds could also contribute to a damaging dynamic which would hinder both staff and prisoners. To avoid the possibility of splitting, mutual respect and an ability to listen is vital.

Identity

> 'The thing about identity is that everyone has one, but we are all different'
>
> **(Prisoner Officer, 2015).**

Like evolution, a species which has once struggled to exist and be successful within its own and sometimes unfamiliar environment, facing daily challenges within which to survive and progress, emerges and further develops. Within the adapting stages of collaboration, in particular that of multidisciplinary working as a whole, and again where several identities and personalities come together, a re-modelled way of working soon appears to become 'more capable' in that moment for the individual. We strive to continually adapt and be responsive and emotionally available to what can be presented within a session.

A lot like a recipe, many ingredients are needed to produce an end result. Initially the raw ingredients may be indigestible, sickly sweet or bitter, and yet when carefully measured and combined each ingredient achieves a product, which is palatable. By no means are we suggesting that we are 'making a product', but we do believe in the product of the service that we offer. Sometimes the recipe, or the interventions we provide, may not always be suited to an individual. In these cases a careful re-measuring and rethink of the basic ingredients is needed to enable successful outcomes. Like the ingredients, it is the successful therapeutic alliance and the most appropriate intervention, which provides the right balance. Each person brings a unique element into the mix.

Feeling like a dustbin

Within the traditional art therapy model, the dynamic, which we are used to as art therapists, is that of the triangular relationship. This consists of the prisoner, the art object as the mediator, and the art therapist. However, within our service we have constructed a triad with the addition of another, and an officer is usually present and involved in an art therapy session. The main purpose of this is to ensure the safety and security of everyone involved. Reflecting on the development of art therapy and the construction of this triad, everything appeared to be going quite smoothly on a superficial level. Whilst both disciplines had a specific role, as time went, certain roles were never identified or discussed. I just presumed that an officer being present throughout was just the way it was and always had been facilitated. Yet within this space, both professional identities became blurred and difficulty arose in the way a session would progress. With this in mind, I would often feel a lot like an art educator as opposed to an art therapist, and this became frustrating. The officer present would also be adopting more of a therapeutic role and although this was facilitated with good intentions, clarification was needed in order to progress with future sessions successfully. Thus a specific role was required in order for art therapy to evolve successfully. There were also occasions where I began to feel pushed out and absent within the room. Interestingly, the officers have also since spoken of feeling invisible at times. Furthermore, it is of my opinion that this dynamic was not so invisible to the prisoners. It became clear that this dynamic allowed the prisoners an ideal opportunity to become avoidant or dismissive and allow distraction from the real purpose and focus of the art therapy. Both disciplines, through no conscious purpose of their own, were unfamiliar and naturally indifferent to each other, and although difficult, this provided an opportunity to clarify and define the differing roles in order to come together in harmony, whilst establishing clear boundaries. The intended outcome for this was about devising a new recipe and a newly tailored model of working. For this to be achieved, both disciplines came together to adapt their approach. A new element and role was created, a role, which included a therapeutic role for the officer as well as being complementary for the art therapy itself. The officer now takes on the role of opening and closing a session. More specifically this refers to the initial "check in", where a few minutes are spent asking how the prisoners have been in themselves over the past week, and this has proved to be beneficial in sometimes informing the direction and content of the session. At the end of the session, a similar space is used to allow the prisoner time to speak about how they had found the session. If concerns were raised, either by the prisoner or by us as art therapist and officer, then a safe transition of the prisoner would be facilitated, by engaging in effective communication between all parties. This multidisciplinary approach thus gives a prisoner a space in which the sensitive information can be raised and discussed; it also enables the prisoner to leave the therapeutic space safely following a release of any concerns. At the close of a session, a debrief will then take place in order to reflect on the session content, dynamics within the image, the relational dynamic, and to discuss any feelings which we are left with. With this in mind, reflective art making from both the officer and myself has proven beneficial in trying to decipher a dynamic, which may have occurred. It is the voice we listen to when it presents itself, providing the voice for the 'difficult to say'.

As an art therapist, I can often liken my purpose to that of a dustbin, which in effect is the container. It is a role, which has evolved over time. When jointly reflecting on an image with a prisoner, I often feel pulled into their world and am given the permission to see and feel what they experience. The prisoners often refer to this as "giving me their shit". Whilst witnessing and subsequently holding this material, I too can feel traumatised and dragged into its pungency. Due to the complexities of the prisoners' histories as well as the work, it is unrealistic to imagine that this could never happen (Remen 1996, p. 52).

How people address me within the prison setting also imposes on my identity. I can be referred to as 'Sir' one minute and 'Shaun' the next, whilst walking from one area of the prison to the other. Although difficult for me at the beginning, I respect their choice of how they wish to address me. Prison etiquette, regime and rules override, and it is our duty to offer the best service we can within the prison system and environment in which we work. When I first came into the post I found it extremely challenging as an art therapist to 'fit' into the regime.

I felt that I had to prove my validity and justify my worth. This may have been due to art therapy provision having not previously been a part of the prison regime. Some people were sceptical, and like many interventions within the prison, some initially thought it was another "flash in the pan". To cement an identity for myself and give voice to the therapy, I offered art therapy awareness sessions to my colleagues, and this proved beneficial. People realised it was not about drawing pretty pictures. Although not intended to be a therapy session, attendees of the awareness sessions, whom participated in image making, were moved to tears. Following their experience of the art therapy awareness session, my colleagues have been very supportive ever since.

Reflections from an officer's perspective

I often feel like I wear two hats, where balancing a therapy role with a discipline role has proven both challenging and rewarding. One minute I may find myself in a treatment session listening to a prisoner disclosing traumatic childhood experiences and memories, where being empathic and offering support is imperative to the outcome of the session. Ten minutes later I could find myself restraining the same prisoner to keep them and others safe.

To some prisoners this could be very confusing and feel like, in one instance, I am trying to help them, and in the next I am challenging them. This can often prove obstructive within the prisoner's perception of my role. Many of the prisoners seem to perceive that prison officers will always act in an aggressive manner towards them, and often expect a prison officer to revert to restraint in order to resolve a situation. Within my dual role, and very much like the prisoners, I often wear many masks for different purposes; but which one do I choose and for what situation? Do I wear one more than the other? Which one is my favourite? Which one do I dislike? I am in no doubt that the dual role is confusing for all concerned and this plays a big part in my identity to the prisoners. With this in mind, I sometimes question the authenticity of my own identity. I really think it is about being real. In my role, I have a duty of care, and I wear the appropriate mask for the appropriate purpose. I can laugh, joke, listen, facilitate, implement boundaries, empathise and promote pro-social modelling. As such,

I am aware that sometimes the women perceive me as the 'good enough parent'. However, I am not their parent and I continually feel it necessary to reiterate the boundaries. My role is to offer guidance and support when needed, whilst also allowing the prisoner to develop by themselves. Nevertheless, the prisoners often consciously and unconsciously project their feelings into me, which can at times be uncomfortable. Previously I was not aware of, or understood, transference and counter-transference and the effects that others' emotions and my emotional responses can have upon me. However I am now becoming more familiar with this. It is in situations like these where I further discuss these dynamics within my reflective supervision and occasional reflective art making with the art therapist.

Since being involved in therapeutic interventions, I have realised that some of the 'banter' we have previously used could be deemed as sarcasm, which is a form of aggression. This was never my intention, as I thought it was just the way that prison worked, and most prisoners did appear to respond well to it. I now know that this was not always the most appropriate form of communication, and my actions could have left them with feelings of negativity. I am not saying 'do not use' banter, but I have become more aware of when and how to use it. It is our aim as co-facilitators within therapeutic interventions to encourage the prisoners to live pro-social lives without aggression and violence.

At times throughout my career however, I have raised my voice when dealing with difficult situations and conflicts. I have sometimes felt angry and frustrated when thinking to myself: "how dare they speak to me like that?", especially if I have attempted to help a prisoner and yet, despite my intentions of being as positive and pro-social as I can within my professional capacity and ability, their needs appeared to have not been met. Subsequently this has often resulted in the prisoner becoming angry, thus projecting their frustration onto me. It is here where I wear my invisible armour, an impenetrable boundary which keeps me safe. Stemming from this, I am aware that their aggressive behaviour may link to their own past experiences of thinking that the only accessible way to express frustration is through the projection of anger. However, as mentioned previously, aggressive behaviour is not acceptable.

As an officer working on the programme, we my colleagues and myself look at any possible underlying reasons for this behaviour.

Our specific training has helped us to value the importance of making time to reflect, and I would encourage other staff to do so. It is a role that requires self discipline in differentiating between prison officer and therapeutic prison officer. For the majority of the time, these identities are kept apart. Both are seen as separate roles, especially by some of our peers, who for their own reasons either cannot or do not want to engage in therapeutic relationships with the prisoners we support.

Being aware of our own emotions is one of the most difficult skills necessary in the role of being a prison officer, but one I believe not many prison officers give consideration to. It is a huge responsibility keeping someone safe, and yet throughout the process you have to constantly adapt your role, similar to changing the mask I wear. How can a person change from one role to another quickly and yet still maintain professional boundaries? People outside of the service often ask what it's like being a prison officer. My reply is always the same. I feel that my role is that of offering guidance and support when needed, but also allowing at the same time for the prisoner/s to further develop and reflect on their developing sense of self by themselves. In some respects it's a good feeling that a prisoner views me as someone whom they can trust and relate to, albeit within the boundaries of the therapeutic relationship.

Prisoner

We often ask the prisoners: "What sort of person do you want to be in the future?" A general response we often receive is: "To be honest; I don't know what sort of person I am now". As such, a prisoner is often someone's mother, sister, wife or partner and is an individual who has likes and dislikes. Most importantly they are women with gender specific needs. However, due to the individual's often broken and unsafe childhood and/or past difficult lifestyle, either through choice or imposed by others, they can present themselves as women who long to be mended, fixed and maintained. It is this maintenance aspect, which is particularly challenging.

When reflecting on the therapy I provide, I often liken the process of art therapy to that of a solid building, which once served purpose, housed an interior and had the foundations to last for a substantial amount of time. However, due to turbulent weather conditions and years of neglect, decay can soon set in. Without rebuilding, only the foundations will remain, and sometimes the foundations lay on unstable ground. Nevertheless, the foundations are there and it is these foundations, which provide the starting point for us to help individuals rebuild themselves from the bottom upwards and also from their inside out. Through all of the interventions we provide, we are providing the tools for the building of the internal structure. Hopefully in time, the psychological interior of the individual gains the skills to seek assistance with the construction and placement of the inner and outer environments, the exposed bits that people see, a little like fitting in the windows into an almost complete structure. The roof of a building offers the shelter. The windows are there to also protect, and yet they allow the outside light in; they allow the interior to breathe. They can be opened and closed. When this is achieved, it is then that the scaffolding can be taken down or slowly removed. It is then left to the individual to utilise the tools and knowledge gained to maintain, delay and repair any sign of decay, which may start to re-emerge. It allows for forward planning and awareness. It keeps us well.

With regards to the creation of an image in a session, I often liken the image to a snapshot of a moment in time. It is like I have been given permission to peer into a porthole, which delves into someone's internal world. However this in itself holds difficulties, which I will further touch upon later on in the chapter. When reflecting on their sense of self, a prisoner often experiences a sense of emotional pain when investigating deeply into their sense of identity. This is mainly due to their lives being that of witness and victim within traumatic experience/s, and at the same time the prisoner is also the perpetrator of trauma, and sometimes of death onto others. Despite the pain this holds, I have heard many prisoners express concern over letting go of the feelings that trauma encapsulates. One particular prisoner once told me that she would rather keep hold of the trauma because without these feelings, however difficult they were for her to hold, she would feel like she would be "giving away the diary of her heart". She also said that this would leave her "feeling empty".

In society in general, people can choose to change their identity. For instance, a person can change their name, hair and face, and can also enhance parts of themselves, which they are not happy or comfortable with. Problem areas can also be removed. Psychologically however, it is not so easily done.

Barriers to engagement

More often than not, a prisoner can appear reluctant to express their true feelings onto the paper through fear of being judged. However, I often explain to prisoners that art therapy is not about judgement or artistic ability. Barriers are often displayed, a little like a warrior holding their shield towards the enemy so as to not be harmed. This feeling of danger, an almost dualistic and protective feeling of keeping people at arms length, a putting up of barriers, can be challenging. However, it is our role to figure out ways to overcome these barriers. Within our service, the barriers can be influenced by certain factors such as experiences of past trauma, therapeutic readiness, prison regime and rules, gender of the therapist, and trust/mistrust of not only the therapist but also of the therapy. To overcome this I reiterate that there are 'no rules' as such in art therapy, and once this has been accepted by the prisoner they soon appear to relax and look more comfortable in their presentation. It is only then that engagement occurs.

A prisoner's past trauma can sometimes be an obstacle to the development of trust, especially within the early stages of therapy and the therapeutic relationship. Within the art therapy setting, a prisoner may fear exploring and revisiting past traumatic events or experiences. Trusting male therapists can also be difficult for female prisoners, especially as many of the prisoners have experienced interpersonal difficulties and abuse at the hands of males, or conversely have abused males in their past. A prisoner once told me that: "Trust is earned and not freely given. Sometimes people believe in trusting other people. I find that difficult".

In art therapy, each prisoner is offered an initial six sessions, which form the assessment stage. Within these initial sessions, the trust between prisoner and staff begins to develop, although it will take considerable time to become fully established. With this in mind, the notion of trust for the prisoner is one, which needs to be proven from our part, especially from a professional perspective. It is a necessary and huge responsibility, and yet an integral part of our service. Without it, any service would struggle to grow and flourish.

Within the therapeutic triad we offer the prisoner a safe environment, and one the prisoner may never have experienced before. This too can initially become a barrier, especially if the prisoner's experience has been that of people in their lives having ulterior and dangerous motives, motives which may have been disguised amongst the promise of false hope and good intention. It is also important to consider that the prisoner may experience difficulty in trusting themselves, the art therapy process and the images.

With regards to the image, the prisoner is sometimes confused about what will become of it, often enquiring, with genuine concern, what will be done of what they have expressed. They may be concerned about where the content of the imagery will be discussed, and what further actions may come of it, if any. However, the content is not often disclosed, unless there is a risk to self or others or if there is a security issue. A wing officer once said: "Just because they've drawn it, it doesn't mean they're going to do it". However, the feelings within the image are, and must always be, worthy of consideration.

What happens if trust is broken? Can it be repaired? For the prisoners, the majority of trust in their relationships has been broken time and time again. Along with this, the prisoner has also experienced trauma either by role of victim or perpetrator, and his is likely to be a major factor when gaining trust in a new relationship with either staff or peers. Many of the prisoners suffer trauma of different kinds. For instance these can be emotional, physical and/or sexual. Many prisoners struggle with their emotions within and following the trauma, sometimes for many years to follow. Prisoners can initially blame themselves for what they have experienced, and hold the traumatic event as something, which was their fault. In many cases a prisoner can appear, or desire to be defined by it. Although it may be difficult to discuss trauma, exploration of it is necessary in order to escape its claustrophobic grasp. Patience is necessary and time should be taken in order for the prisoner to access the trauma at a pace which does not overwhelm and re-traumatise. Support should be offered without judgement within a relaxed and empathic space.

Self-maintenance

A colleague once told me that: "To do our jobs well…we must keep ourselves well". Within a prison environment, working with such complex individuals where dynamics can often become heavy, supervision is an integral part of being encouraged to reflect upon the complexity of the prisoners we support, as well as targeting and untangling our own emotional responses to the work when we can often feel engulfed. Furthermore it is important to note that supervision plays an integral role in the way we work, reflect, adjust and move forward. Stemming from this, we are all human and naturally have emotional responses which are often difficult to digest. We can also feel repulsed, and yet the feeling of repulsion can be extremely rich material by which to own and work through within a supervisory setting. Clinical and team supervision thus allows for the material to be diluted to the extent where it becomes more digestible and easier to hold in mind.

As professionals working with such intense material, it is important to make room for fun in one's own life. It is also unhealthy to take the work home with you in a psychological sense. If recognised early enough, potential burnout can be avoided. Stemming from this, it is also essential to recognise when a therapy break would be beneficial to the therapy. Often the challenging nature of the work can have a habit of getting "under the skin". To carry on as if everything is going well from a clinical perspective will only mirror the prisoner's past experiences of thinking that they do not matter. Therapeutic breaks are, in my opinion, vital in discouraging unsympathetic attitudes. It not only shows the prisoner that they can be survived, but it enables the prisoner to experience the importance of being valued in a world where they may have been only tolerated.

Boundaries and containment

Within the service, containment and sufficient holding environments are key elements in facilitating positive therapeutic relationships and promoting a prisoner's self belief, which encourages positive outcomes. Our own emotional availability as a staff team is also extremely important for the prisoners as it offers them the opportunity and encouragement to approach us and discuss anything, which may be of concern to them. However, this has had its problems. For some prisoners, what we offer can often appear to never be enough, and in all honesty it probably never will be. It is for this reason that an officer clinic was set up to capture any possible material, which had not been caught elsewhere. The clinic was also intended to be a space where a prisoner could 'check in' by method of making an appointment should they wish to. The officer clinic was originally derived from prisoner need and, by being emotionally responsive, the officers offer a space where a safety net has been provided. It also offers a place where the prisoners can offload. It is an open forum, and yet is also safely contained through boundary of time. When thinking about containment, there are several inner and outer parameters when thinking about the prison as a solid vessel of safety. Starting from the inside out, the therapy room is the core, the wing is the outer container, and the prison walls are the outer structure which holds everything together. As sad as it may seem, for some prisoners a prison is probably the only place where they have experienced containment, sufficient safety and stability. This may seem odd for someone on the outside looking in, especially as the environment is initially a place of imprisonment and separation. With this in mind, a prisoner once spoke of how she was "grateful and needed to be in prison as it offered an opportunity to sort her head and life out".

As an art therapist, I immediately inform a newly referred prisoner that art therapy provides them with the opportunity of appropriately pushing boundaries which would otherwise be a discipline matter if displayed or projected in an inappropriate manner, either onto self, environment, or others. This can prove extremely liberating for a prisoner, especially as their existence and reality of daily living is encased within an environment where boundary pushing can often lead to further feelings of incarceration. In short, allowance is made for boundary pushing in art therapy. Creatively, many prisoners often produce an image which explores outside boundaries, whether it is that of the outside community, or a world which is far beyond that of the prison walls. In some instances, this can offer a sense of hope. For others, it can only strengthen a sense of loss, especially if the prisoner is serving a long sentence.

Tempest

Mask (ma: sk) definition:

> *"A covering for all or part of the face, worn as a disguise…to conceal, or to amuse or frighten others…a protective covering"*
> **(Collins English Dictionary online 2015).**

A brief history

Tempest is a 30 year old woman currently serving a discretionary life sentence for arson with intent to endanger life. She has a diagnosis of borderline personality disorder and probable antisocial personality disorder with psychopathic traits. Early childhood experience included alleged sexual and emotional abuse from her birth father between the age of one and three years, by which time Tempest and her twin sister were removed from the family home and placed with foster parents. Tempest states she was further physically abused and emotionally neglected whilst in their care, and was then placed within a number of children' homes between the age of 13 and 17. Her sister however remained in the care of foster parents. Throughout her life, Tempest has had three names; birth name, adoptive name, and is currently known by another name.

The beginning

Originally referred to me in early 2014, Tempest undertook an art therapy assessment within a group setting. In session one, Tempest greeted me with what appeared to be fear and mistrust, which seemed to be blanketed amongst a need to please. Early on, Tempest informed me of her previous experience of art therapy as being "a bit rubbish, everyone spoke over each other and it was really chaotic…and it was in a group, and I don't do groups…but I will give it another go". I felt tested and I sensed a strong desire from her to prove that the therapy and I "were not rubbish". Polite as she presented in that first session, I sensed a woman who was hurt and mistrusting of professionals. With this in mind, Tempest would often speak of how she felt professionals had historically "failed her", and how she had become wary of the "supposed care system". Given her history, it was easy to see why she thought this way. Tempest would often speak of this with what appeared to be disdain, anger and genuine hurt, and with this in mind, so much rich material presented itself within the transference and the unspoken word. A real feeling of bitterness was often present within the room, which regularly left a bitter taste in my mouth. However, Tempest did openly express that she has always had "anger issues...I am like a volcano, I am afraid that I will just explode", and following this Tempest produced her first image, which is illustrated in figure 1. When reflecting on the image, Tempest stated words such as: "anger... danger...contained...safety...barriers", and I too sensed a woman who craved containment and safety. However, I also sensed dangerousness. My mind would also occasionally wander to her early experiences, and a strong paternal instinct would often overwhelm me.

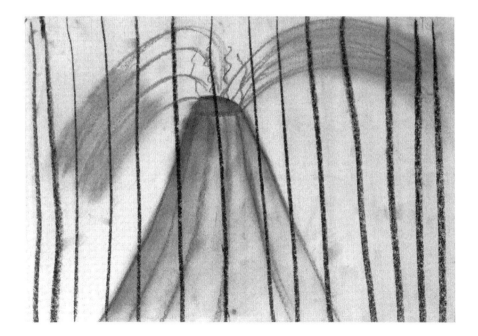

Fig1: Volcano

Within the group setting, Tempest would consistently present herself as closed, in both body language and also in her difficulty to verbalise her emotion in front of others. This presentation continued for the whole of the assessment period, and Tempest would often speak of how she "feared judgement and ridicule…and wouldn't be believed". Although aware of her preference for individual work, the team thought that this may elicit Tempest's unhelpful attachment behaviours. Following prolonged discussion however, the clinical team decided that Tempest should be given the opportunity to go ahead with individual work, and this is where the masks began to slip, and deep rooted and "suppressed" emotions surfaced.

Behind the mask

At around the same time as commencing with individual art therapy; Tempest also undertook a 12-week group programme, which focused on the emotion of anger, and most importantly its affects on womanhood. Within the programme, all participants were encouraged to reflect upon early experiences of anger, their witnessing of it, and lastly were encouraged to reflect upon and discuss any possible causes for their own anger and consequently, their offences. Initially, Tempest appeared to only be able to associate anger with the aggressive act. However, Tempest quickly became aware that it was 'ok' to accept anger as an emotion, which she could safely own. Interestingly, taking personal ownership of her anger appeared to be a liberating experience for her, as she did "not feel wrong for having it". It is important to note that the programme was co-facilitated by a female psychologist, a male prison officer and myself. What we found was very interesting; Tempest was able to openly discuss her experiences of anger, which historically had originally manifested from her negative experience of males. Stemming from this, at the end of the programme, Tempest stated that the work had allowed her to see that "not all men were the same after all".

For Tempest and us, undertaking art therapy and the anger programme at the same time proved beneficial in so many ways, as both appeared to promote and inform each other. The safe exploration of anger in the art therapy setting, through 'mask work' thus helped Tempest to become more accepting of her anger; by which time she became able to further engage in the anger programme without feeling "wrong or judged".

The shark and the octopus

Tempest would often describe herself as a "shark or an octopus". The shark being the "thing that people run away from", and the octopus being the role she often likens to her tendency to "reach out in all directions, to pull people in", so as to "not feel so alone". It is interesting that as clinicians we began to think about these roles as being a product of her diagnosis instead of facets of her identity. However, the facets were there, and Tempest became willing to unearth emotions, which had previously been hidden and disguised. With this in mind, it is important to note that Tempest was "always told to hide what was really going on at home from relatives and family friends…I had to pretend everything was good and that we were the perfect family…I was told to smile and not be heard". However, once Tempest had developed trust of the therapy and of me as the therapist, her early experiences began to be communicated through direct identification and projection onto physical masks through the use of paint. Reasons for suppression and disguise became evident, and the more the disguise was peeled away, the more apparent the pain of her early experiences became, and this was powerfully portrayed, as seen in figure 2.

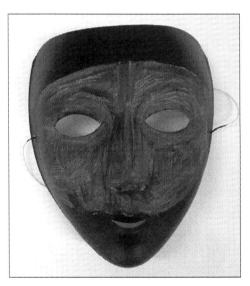

Fig. 2: "Youth and Hurt"
"This is to show you how shitty my life was and is"

Lifting the lid

As the barriers came down and the therapeutic relationship developed, Tempest would further engage me in conversation whilst mask making. For several weeks, Tempest would explore and create the masks she wore as protection, but appeared fearful of what lay behind them. However, through mutual reflection and "working it out together", Tempest began to touch upon her offending behaviour and her reasoning for it. This work happened to coincide with a 28 session fire-setting programme Tempest would attend in both a group and an individual support format. Within the group, she slowly began to open up and eventually admitted to her offence fully whilst speaking also of the underlying rational, something that she had never done before. Tempest stated that she "wanted to destroy the happy families in the B&B" and the thoughts driving this forward were "if I can't have it, they can't have it".

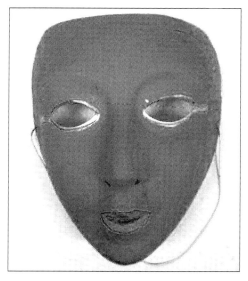

Fig. 3: Fun

At this time, Tempest often spoke of feeling "drained and exhausted", and requested to "do a nice mask…something to make me feel relaxed and chilled out". Tempest then produced a mask, which she named "fun", and whilst observing her creation of it, she appeared notably more relaxed in presentation and she too appeared to be having fun with the art materials. She also appeared playful. As shown in figure 3, the mask was notably different, and what struck me was the open appearance of the mouth. It was more prominent, and Tempest spoke of how "proud" she was to have "gained a voice and could now be heard".

At present, Tempest's time in art therapy has been drawn to a temporary close. I say temporary because Tempest, like any prisoner undertaking art therapy, can undertake art therapy at any one time along her pathway within our service. This has proved to be fruitful in many ways, especially if a prisoner experiences anxiety and worry around the content of upcoming intervention programmes. To prior express any anxiety and concerns within the art therapy setting allows the emotional content to be addressed in the intervention and with key professionals for the purpose of tailoring the piece of work if necessary.

Tempests reflections on the work

"When I was asked if I would contribute to this chapter, I was very concerned that my images would not be private or contained anymore. My reason for picking a fantasy name is because the images will be seen for real in public. Having a fantasy name allowed me to dissociate myself to some extent. My fantasy name allows me to be invisible, and yet still have a voice. It is my identity as much as the identity that I am trying to find. My masks have been a safety blanket for me for many years, but now I have begun to remove them".

Conclusion

In a report presented to Parliament (Ministry of Justice 2010), it was suggested that offenders tackle their underlying offending behaviour and criminal activity in order to improve public safety and to reduce the number of victims. Since being introduced into the service in 2012, art therapy has thus provided a space where this can be addressed in a pro-social, adaptive and reflective way within a contained environment. Interestingly, the prison regime and all it stands for has, in effect, evolved into becoming the "good enough parent". It is the environment, which has given many of the prisoner's sufficient safety, containment and emotional holding. With this in mind, many prisoners may not have experienced such emotional investment from another human being in their lives, and to some extent it is no surprise that the service, the therapies and interventions, which are contained within the prison walls, can be experienced as the idealised care as well as the identified parent. This is particularly interesting especially as the prison environment is initially a place designed to segregate and punish. Report writing does in itself have a place within this role and the language used within them is also something we need to hold in mind. Like tailoring the services we offer towards a prisoner's individual needs, I quickly realised that a no frills approach to the format of my report writing was also necessary to avoid confusion. If we really think about all of this as a whole, it really is a lot like facilitating the "alpha functioning" which occurs within the 'good enough' early developmental stages of someone's life experience and learning processes. Like some of her peers, Tempest herself has often spoke of "not doing attachments well…I don't do endings easily", and it is here where it is vital to remember to introduce the inevitability of an end within the early stages of the therapeutic relationship. The ending is in fact another trauma, and this is extremely traumatic to even think about for most of the prisoners when they are first accepted into our service.

Although difficult in the early development of art therapy, the collaborative approach is one that has proven to be successful after having been facilitated through several guises along its relatively short life to date. Within those early difficulties, roles needed to be clarified in order for collaboration and art therapy to succeed. Within the service, provision was and is continuously provided for identities to be explored, where trauma could and can be excavated and unearthed, and emotions held.

Some final words

"It's like I've sent an echo out
But the echo I sent out was louder
Than the one that has returned"

(Tempest 2015)

REFERENCES

Ministry of Justice (2010) Breaking the Cycle: *Effective Punishment, Rehabilitation and Sentencing of Offenders.* Available from: http://webarchive.nationalarchives.gov.uk [Accessed 11th August 2015].

Oxford English Dictionary [Online] Available from: http://www.collinsdictionary.com/dictionary/english [Accessed 13th August 2015].

Remen, R. (1996) *Kitchen Table Wisdom.* New York: Riverhead Books.

CHAPTER 11

Story to tell: Stories from animation projects in secure and psychiatric settings

TONY GAMMIDGE

"I haven't got the greatest story alive but I've got a story to tell"

(Ben 2010)[14]

Introduction

"So our stories go on and on, as they have since we humans first began sitting around fires, in caves, acquiring the language with which to tell our stories. For it is in telling stories that we originally acquired our humanness; and we are not so much rationale creatures, as Aristotle said, or tool making ones, as Benjamin Franklin put it, but first and foremost storytelling ones."

(Gilligan 2000, p. 4)

We all have stories, some linear and straightforward, others more complex and mysterious, ever changing and evolving. Some of our stories come from memories, some from our imaginations. Some are fantasies about what might happen in the future or what could have happened in the past. Our stories cross paths with others' stories, sometimes barely and at other times radically, and in doing so our stories change and alter course. Stories are universal and make us human (Gilligan 2000).

---

14 Evaluation ; Low Secure Unit

Stories lie at the heart of the animation projects I have run over the past seven years in secure and psychiatric settings. These settings give a particular importance and power to working with narrative. Of course, as I work with other people's stories, I consider my own and how they are part of this work, and also how they have led me to be doing this work in the first place.

Autoethnography

Autoethnography is a research methodology that connects "the autobiographical and personal to the cultural and social" (Ellis 2004, p. xix). It recognises that personal stories hold a wealth of information and meaning about the society we live in. It has been hugely influential for me in thinking and writing about the projects I describe in this chapter.

Autobiography: Part one

Monday morning 3.am:

> *"I can't sleep again, this is getting to be a habit, always the night before I go to the prison. Could be any number of reasons; no one might turn up this week and the whole project will be a failure, security might not let me in...again, the long drive...there might be traffic and I will be late. Perhaps because it is a prison rather than a secure unit?"*

I lie there restless and distressed, the clock ticking. My first night at boarding school when I was seven comes to mind, lying awake feeling lost, bewildered and grief stricken. Boarding school... prison... yes something of a link there. Perhaps this is what draws me into this work and frightens me.

Part two

Norton Grim, cartoon character, was (immaculately) conceived that first night in boarding school, a tortured and bitter alter-ego with his dome-shaped head, his shorts and thin legs. It was a long gestation period of about ten years before he was finally delivered onto a scrap of paper. He has since been the antihero of many 'comedic' stories about tortured love, masochism, dysfunctional families, family pets, death and spiritual questing, all born from the grief and loss of being sent to boarding school aged seven.

He has featured in books and films about the death of my father, my mother's Yorkshire Terrier, my sister's chickens and the death of my brother. He is currently involved in a project that brings him full circle: a film about my/his time in boarding school. He is, I believe, the precursor to the secure unit films and he has led/dragged me to this work.

Fig. 1

In the beginning

The first project I ran was on a rehabilitation ward for men at a medium-secure centre. I had been approached by the lead arts therapist at Oxleas NHS Foundation Trust who had heard of some arts in health opportunities at the Bracton Centre. I was looking to take my new, and at the time fledgling, animation skills into a clinical setting, so I jumped at the invitation to run an animation project there. The brief I was given initially by the clinical lead was to engage as many people as possible, to have fun, make a film with residents that could be shown within the public realm and *not* do therapy. The first project on a men's rehab ward ran for most of the day, once a week for three months. Participants could come and go as they pleased. Some people stayed for an hour or two, others popped in for just ten minutes at a time and a few would stay for most of the day.

Scene: At the first session.

Patrick:*"Can we make a film from one of my songs?"*

T.G.: *"Yes of course, can we hear it?*

(He plays it on a large ghetto blaster.)

"Fuck the judge, fuck the jury, fuck the police prosecution, fuck my attorney, fuck em all!"

(Patrick 2008)[15]

T.G.: *(Both delighted someone is interested but wondering where's the story within this angry rant)*

"That sounds great, I'm sure we can make something out of that."

We did; the narrative of 'Justice Gone Mad' emerged partly from Patrick's track and partly through the collaborative process with the group.

My brief did not specify a theme, so that participants could make a film about anything they wanted. This is the way that I prefer to work. I have found that if participants can choose what they make, their films about the projects are more successful. If a theme is imposed externally, participants can feel less invested. If I can say: "You can make a film about anything you want", then there is more of a likelihood that people will take part. Choice is limited in secure settings and it is powerful to offer potential collaborators this kind of freedom. The result is often stories that come from the heart. These are most often the stories that need to be told. With choice also comes greater safety, the freedom to leave bits out and to avoid difficult

---

15   The lyrics to 'Supreme Court'.

shameful bits. The storyteller should be in control, particularly in these settings.

Having been 'discouraged' from doing therapy, I considered my role as being part facilitator and part collaborator. I was facilitating the participants to tell their story and to make the film they wanted. I was also there as a collaborator, sharing skills, interests, influences and experiences. I was an artist and filmmaker working with other artists (even if my collaborators might not identify themselves as artists). I kept quietly in mind Beuys's saying, "every human being is an artist" (Beuys 1993, p. 22).

Every project is different though and I work in a way that is site-specific and tailored to the projects, according to the needs of the wards and participants. There is always a starting point from which the story begins to take off, like with Patrick's original track. Sometimes though, someone will write a screenplay or do a storyboard, other times it will be just a few vague ideas or a poem, and at others the narrative will emerge solely through the process.

"I get ideas in fragments, it is as if in the other room there is a puzzle, all the pieces are together but in my room they just flip one piece at a time into me and the first piece I get is just a fragment of the whole puzzle but I fall in love with this fragment... and it holds a promise for more and I keep it, write it down and then I say that having the fragment is more bait on the hook and it pulls in more and the more that come in, the faster the rest come in" (David Lynch 2014). It is always a gathering and emergent process.

Narrative

"We have this history of impossible solutions for insoluble problems"

(Eisner 2000).

Stories have long been used to navigate our way through life's difficult and perplexing experiences. We tell stories to try and make sense of things. *"And why did the world get Superman? Because a little boy named Jerry Siegel heard his father was murdered and, in grief, created a bulletproof man"* (Meltzer 2011). Superman was created by two sons of Jewish immigrants in the 1930s. There is a theory that one of the creators, Jerry Siegel, created Superman after his father died during a robbery at his store. In the first adventure, Superman rescues a shopkeeper bound and gagged by a gunman.

On the secure units many of the participants use these projects as a chance to tell a story, and most will tell their personal story or a version of it. These might be made up from fact, fiction, memory, fantasy or imagination. What makes it so powerful for participants, is that they can take full control (and responsibility) of their story in a way that they might not feel able to in their actual lives.

For everyone in a secure setting their story is encapsulated within their case notes. They are defined and documented by the institution, the criminal justice system and the psychiatric system. Case notes mostly focus on what has gone wrong and often miss out the good bits of someone's life, their interests, their loves, their kindnesses, their creativity and their humour.

> *"When we cannot find a way of telling our story, our story tells us"*
>
> **(Grosz 2014, p. 10).**

The films can become an alternative to case notes, in which the participant can choose what to include and what to leave out, what to make up and what to reveal. Some people tell stories straight from their lives, but leave out significant details; others make up the bulk of the story and then hide within it bits of truth; others recount their past and then rewrite parts they had no control of at the time or make up a different ending. Some even let the narrative emerge out of the animation process, and yet still manage to make something autobiographical.

One participant, Kerry, wrote a screenplay for her film which was largely fictional but contained within it some cleverly hidden truths. The name of the fictional abusive father is made up of the Christian names of the men who in real life abused her. Often participants will use the films to get back at the people they feel wronged by in a way that is metaphorical and safe.

*"It was kind of a way of venting my wishes after everything
that was done to me and how I would have liked to react, what
I would have wanted to do. The film helped me to release a
lot of anger towards a lots of people but as it came from my
imagination it was more about having fun and thinking that
what happened to me happens to a lot of people and realising
that I can get through anything. If plasticine characters can
get through things, I can too"*

(Kerry 2011).

People in secure units and prisons are amongst the most marginalised
and stigmatised people in our society, and their voices are rarely heard.
The 5.2 metre fence of a medium-secure unit and the endless locked
doors very effectively cut these people off from our society. The size
of the fence announces loudly that the people who inhabit this place
must be mad and dangerous.

The films however, tell a different story of people who are
vulnerable, creative, funny, passionate and caring but who are also
flawed. The audience gets, at least, a glimpse of the filmmakers lives,
experiences, imagination and creativity. Staff who work on the wards
see their patients in a new light. They might find out something that
they did not know. In the second project I did, Chester approached me
saying he had a story we could make a film out of. It was his story as a
boy soldier in Somalia and his travels across Africa. The clinical team
informed me they did not know Chester's story until he made his film.

The films have a punk, DIY, 'anyone can make a film' aesthetic.
They are made quickly and rarely use a second take (so the puppet
has to get it right first time). The aesthetics are not rooted in the
traditional ideas of form, colour and composition, but are instead to be
found within the heart of the narrative. Is it a good story? Does it ring
true? Is it interesting? *"John Cheever said the first canon of aesthetics
is interest"* (Barnes 2001).

The films aim to highlight the humanity of the makers so that they
become far more than statistics, diagnosis', offenders and outsiders.
Because stories are such a universal medium, the films reach out across
the fence and connections, instead of stigma, are forged.

Two scenes

1. In 'A Day In a Life', made in a category B prison, Neil shows the audience what his life in his cell looks like, the repetition, the boredom, the compulsions, the habits, the mundane things such as making a cup of tea, eating crisps, exercising, watching TV and going to the toilet. He then takes the cover off his budgie cage and gets out one of the baby budgies and sits it on his finger. *"Hello little baby... Are you going to learn to fly? Come on now birdie, up you go, up you go, flap your wings for Daddy, up you go, who's a pretty boy?"* (Neil 2015)[16] he coos, as he gently moves his arm up and down to encourage flight. It was a scene of extraordinary tenderness.

Fig. 2

---

16 From the film 'A Day in a Life'

2. On a medium-secure unit for men with a diagnosis of 'personality-disordered adult male offenders' Jim, who has the look of a man in a wanted poster, says to us in the midst of making the film 'Bear Faced Truth': *"You can use my little people if you want"*. We quickly agree not quite knowing who or what the little people are. He brings us three tiny delicate doll-like figures, a hippopotamus made of felt and some houses for them he has made out of polystyrene cups. *"They are fragile, so I don't want any swearing around them!"* (Jim 2013) [17], he says with a glint in his eye.

Stories elicit empathy and our imaginations because it is these qualities that are required in the forming of them and in their telling. What does he or she do now? What happens next? What does it look like? Where does it takes place? All of these questions are a constant in telling a story and in making a film. *"Imagination is subversive, because it puts the possible against the real. That's why you should always use your wildest imagination. Imagination is the biggest gift humanity has received. Imagination makes people human, not work"* (Svankmajer 2008, p. 141). My participants are being asked to exercise their imaginative muscle throughout the process and to consider their sense of empathy; how does she feel when that happens, how might they react?

> *"I didn't realise at the time, but I think at this point I started to see myself as someone I want to look after, not fight against. I slowly started to feel empathy for myself - something I've struggled to feel before"*
>
> **(Lauren 2013)**[18].

The filmmakers direct the puppets in their stories, anticipating their every move and emotion using their own experiences, emotions and imaginations. However the characters can also start to take on a life of their own. As the story takes shape the momentum gathers pace and the narrative twists and turns, perhaps away from the original idea

17   A half remembered conversation during the filming of Bear Faced Truth.

18   Written Evaluation; Adult Personality Disorder Unit

and into new and undiscovered paths. The characters can do anything, they can turn back the clock, but also can shape the future and not be bound by reality, probability, low prognosis, diagnosis or lock and key. *"It is a law too which allows your forms (characters) to spin away, take off, as if they have their own lives to lead – unexpected too – as if you cannot completely control it all... the only problem is how to keep away from the minds that close in and itch (God knows why) to define it"* (Guston 2003, p. 37). The participants discover the freedom of their imagination that is not constricted by the factual 'truths' of their lives.

I encourage the filmmakers to fictionalise their story, embellish it, change it. There is so much more freedom in this approach, and perhaps this is easier to do when it is not formal insight orientated therapy. People in secure settings are not often invited to make things up or embellish them. Despite the fiction/fact interplay, the films that emerge often have profound levels of emotional honesty and psychological awareness.

Animation

The animation process is magical, it can make things move that don't and gives life to inanimate objects. All is possible when using animation. This can be a powerful force in settings where so little seems possible.

As a sequential time based process, it is a perfect medium in which to tell stories. You can animate anything (security allowing) from puppets made of plasticine, clay, cardboard or cloth. Some of the materials I often use such as dolls, puppets and toys have a strong association with childhood. In the film 'Bear Faced Truth', we animated teddy bears I had adapted for the purpose. These bears were all in group therapy recounting their violent and drug fuelled pasts. Somehow reenacting scenes of bears beating each other, bullying, smoking huge spliffs or snorting cocaine was both powerful and poignant but also surreal and ridiculous. This provides the filmmakers a safe distance (Klugman 2015)[19] in which to explore and express their past traumatic experiences.

Several participants have commented that there is an irony in the use of these childhood materials where the subject matter, violence,

---

19 Supervision conversation.

abuse and suicide very much belongs in the adult world. Clearly the tragedy though, is that these subject matters are also part of the experience of childhood for many of the participants.

Scene

In the midst of the animation process in a category B prison, Gary asks TG a question:

"Does your Mrs mind you playing with dolls for a living?"

(Gary 2015)[20]

As well as the childhood connotations of the materials, there is a strong element of play in animation; play in terms of trying things out, making things up, experimenting and being imaginative. As Winnicott (1982) has emphasised, play is a vital part of a child's development and of making sense of themselves and the world. However, for a child to play effectively he needs safety and containment. Many people in secure settings have had chaotic, abusive or deprived childhoods and will not have had a chance to play as much as they need. These projects offer people the chance to connect with more playful and exploratory experiences in a safe environment and in a way that is not infantilising.

Participants have a chance to tackle extremely sensitive and distressing subjects. However the step by step, frame by frame process of animation seems to provide a safe distance (Klugman 2015) from the emotional intensity that is often being expressed and explored. The process is slow, repetitive and methodical. This offers scope for processing material that could otherwise be chaotic and deregulating. At the beginning of each session the participants watch the progress of their film before they go on to make the next scene. *"With the film you are constantly adding more and more to it and you could see it coming to life in front of you..."* (Kerry 2010)[21]. I wonder if this embeds into the process, not only a familiarity but also a sense of agency.

Some of the subjects that have been expressed in the films include

---

20 Conversation during filming on Category B prison

21 Evaluation; Medium Secure Unit

mental illness, suicide, self harm, abuse, loss, violence, bullying and addiction. Although the films are rarely just about these issues, it does highlight the need for due care in running the projects, particularly as they fall outside of an art therapy contract.

Springham (2008) alerts us to the potential dangers of arts in health interventions, the things that can go wrong and the consequent serious damage. In his analysis of art based risk, he identifies three key elements of arts in health interventions that cross over into 'art as therapy' (Springham 2008, p. 65). *"A participant who is vulnerable... an art activity, and some kind of linkage between the art and the participant's personal material"* (Springham 2008, p. 65).

Springham argues: *"The optimum state of art therapy play is where the art is felt to be real but known not to be"* (Springham 2008, p. 71). Thus, there is a need to emphasise the metaphorical nature of the work... 'these characters might be based on your experiences but they are not you'. By adding a 'what if...' into the mix, a sense of distance from the 'heat' of the material is created. This is why I encourage people to fictionalise their story, at least to some extent.

Shame, though, is another issue that haunts secure settings. This might date back to early years of abuse, neglect, disadvantage and poverty. For Gilligan (2001), shame is one of the main underlying factors that causes violence. *"The basic psychological motive, or cause, of violent behaviour is the wish to ward off or eliminate the feeling of shame and humiliation"* (Gilligan 2001 p. 29). For people on secure units and in prison, many of whom will have committed violent acts, shame can be an unbearable yet ever present emotion. However, it can also be a well kept secret, rarely named or acknowledged, particularly with men who might hide it under a wall of bravado, banter, nonchalance, ambivalence or lethargy.

So whilst it is important that this work does not trigger further shame, there is actual evidence that it can provide the antidote. *"I thought that making films was a big thing but it seems we can do it too"* (Ben 2010)[22]. Participants often feel a huge sense of achievement and pride at the work they have produced; *"a goal achieved, yes I do feel proud of it"* (Mr. 'J')[23]

---

22 Evaluation; Low Secure Unit

23 Evaluation; Low Secure Unit

"I felt proud" (Ian)[24] *"That's good, I'm happy with that"* (Gary 2015)[25].

Whilst the films frequently contain difficult and unpalatable 'truths', they are always about much more than those things; most consistently the films are about the spirit of survival.

> *"It is personal to me, especially the images of self harm, it was really good to be able to do it in a controlled way, in a creative way, turning something destructive and horrible into something creative and rather beautiful, if I may say so"*
>
> **(Jenny)[26].**

Although we have worked on some extremely disturbing scenes including a suicide, self harm and a young girl shooting her father dead, it was never a less than a joyful experience to help tell these stories. When participants express themselves in the films, it does not feel like that they are merely evacuating something they want to get rid of. It is more this: *"I didn't find it cathartic, but more to do with engagement with parts of myself"* (Clare 2013)[27]. So whatever is being expressed, there is a sense of integration rather than an outpouring. There is no expectation for me to 'fix' anything.

Humour has been a constant companion with these projects. There is something inherently clumsy and funny about animating things. Puppets are forever falling over, losing their limbs or heads. In the most poignant of scenes, the puppets will 'come over' all slapstick and behave like Laurel and Hardy. This can add a level of pathos that could never be planned. Often though, it is the humour that the participants themselves bring. In Irene's heart rending 'Just Like a Rag Doll' (2013) about the abuse she suffered at the hands of her father, there were comments from staff at the centre that all they could hear coming from the room where the film was being made was hoots of laughter. Humour can have a 'therapeutic function' (Kopytin & Lebedev 2015 p. 40) that helps participants tackle a particularly difficult scene.

---

24 Evaluation; Medium Secure Unit

25 Evaluation; Category B Prison

26 Evaluation; Adult Personality Disorder Service

27 Evaluation; Adult Personality Disorder Service

Scene

T.G.: *"When we did the scene of you finding your mum dead, that was very powerful, was that difficult?"*

Gary: *"Yes.....that's why I tried to avoid it for a few weeks"*

T.G: *"Is there any way I could have handled that better?"*

Gary: *"No......I think the best way is to have a sense of humour....if it is too serious I probably wouldn't have come."*[28]

Outcomes and impacts

I have delivered ten animation projects in secure units, prisons and psychiatric units and have been involved in the making of 25 films of 2-15 minutes in length, eight of which have won Koestler arts awards.

The films have a life beyond the actual projects; I have screened the films in galleries, conferences, in educational settings, in prisons and on secure units. Wherever possible, I organise or encourage the filmmakers to attend the screenings so that they can witness the response from the audience.

"Extremely moving and very intense. I felt privileged to be in the company of some of the filmmakers" (Audience member 2011)[29]. In one screening the filmmakers received a standing ovation for their work and received feedback such as: *"The patients' work was a lesson to all artists in willingness to tell a story from the heart"* (Audience Member 2011)[30].

Chester has since used his film to show clinical staff his story, instead of having to tell them. It was also used in a session with another Somali boy soldier at Broadmoor: *"I showed 'Chester' to my Somali patient, and he was very moved and very talkative... result!"* (Adshead, G 2011)[31]. Tezza said he plans to show his film to his children as it would tell them about his life. Gary wants his foster mother to see his film as he has never been able to talk to her about his experience of losing his Mum

28 Evaluation; Category B Prison

29 Evaluation of 'Voice From Behind the Fence' screening

30 Evaluation of 'Voice From Behind the Fence' screening

31 Personal email

when he was young: *"Without sounding soppy and shit, it probably just expresses what it was I went through"* (Gary 2015)[32].

A number of participants have dared to think beyond the projects and what they might do next. *"Jonathan is a good example of how it really has inspired him to take his lyric writing forward…it has spurred him into wanting to achieve things outside of here and thinking to the future and the long term"* (Whitfield 2010)[33]. Pat started to exhibit his work, eventually at the Tate Modern and Selfridges as part of the Museum of Everything, *"It changed my whole life, man because I knew I was a good artist but not this good"* (Pat 2010)[34]. A number of people have gone onto further education, *"I am now studying technical theatre at college which combines bits of film making with a lot of artistic creation"* (Kerry 2011)[35]. Lauren has been accepted onto an animation course and Kate has just received a distinction from her foundation course for her latest animation film. None of them had ever done animation before our project.

Fig.4

32   Evaluation; Category B Prison

33   Evaluation with OT on Low Secure Unit

34   Evaluation; Medium Secure Unit

35   Evaluation; Medium Secure Unit

Part of this work is about a telling a story, making a film and gaining a voice, but for some people it is also about a shift in their identity: *"I wanted to make this film because at the end of the day I knew I would feel better about myself. By handing back all the scars I gave myself over the 40 years, I could give them back to my parents....I have achieved something special since then, I have become an artist."* (Irene 2013)[36]. The public platform for this work is important as it takes the work out of the institution in which it was made, over the fence and into an arena which is not just about mental illness but also about art. Ideally participants can, as a result of making a film, see themselves more as artists, filmmakers or storytellers than just service users or offenders.

Conclusion

Despite the benefits, these animation based collaborations remain rare within forensic and psychiatric settings and are largely undeveloped within art therapy practice. Animation is a dynamic process that enables both aesthetic and psychological exploration, as well as producing an engaging, high quality end product. These films bear testimony to the participant's courage and generosity in bringing their stories to life. My own practice as an artist has in part shaped these films, but it has also been hugely inspired and influenced by them. It is these films that have given me the confidence to start telling my own stories. Norton Grim, who for so long was consigned to obscurity, has now been coaxed out of the shadows and into the limelight.

Thanks goes to Joanna Stevens, Mario Guarnieri, Kate Rothwell, Neil Springham, Olivia Laing, Sydney Klugman, Jane Wildgoose and all of my collaborators in this work.

BIBLIOGRAPHY

BARNES, J. (2001) *Breaking the Mould.* The Telegraph [Online]. 15th December. Available from http://www.telegraph.co.uk/culture/4727015/Breaking-the-mould.html [Accessed 25th July 2015]

36 Evaluation; Adult Personality Disorder Service

BEUYS, J. (1993) I Am Searching For Field Character 1973. In : KUONI, C. (ed.) *Energy Plan for the Western Man, Joseph Beuys in America*. New York: Four Walls Eight Windows.

EISNER, W. (2000) Preface. In : CHABON, M. Kavalier and Clay. 23rd Edition. London: Fourth Estate.

ELLIS, C. (2004) *The Ethnographic 1: A methodological novel about teaching and doing autoethnography*. Walnut Creek, CA: Altamira.

GILLIGAN, J. (2000) *Violence, Reflections on Our Deadliest Epidemic*. Forensic Focus 18. 2nd Ed. London: Jessica Kingsley Publishers Ltd.

GILLIGAN, J. (2001) Preventing Violence. London: Thames and Hudson.

KOPYTIN, A. & LEBEDEV, A. (2015) Therapeutic Functions of Humour in Group Art Therapy with War Veterans. *Inscape: International Journal of Art Therapy*. 20 (2). p. 40-53

LYNCH, D. (2014) Patti Smith and David Lynch talk Twin Peaks, Blue Velvet and Pussy Riot. In Newsnight Encounter Series [Online]. Available from http://www.bbc.co.uk/programmes/p02bwzrp [Accessed 15th June, 2015].

GROSZ, S. (2014) *The Examined Life*. 2nd Edition. London: Vintage.

GUSTON, P. (2003) Letter. In FELD, R. *Guston In Time*. New York: Counterpoint.

MELTZER, B. (2011) The Book of Lies [Online]. Available from: http://bradmeltzer.com/book/the-book-of-lies/ [Accessed 25th July 2015]

SPRINGHAM, N. (2008) Through the Eyes of the Law: What is it about art that can harm people?. *Inscape: International Journal of Art Therapy*. 13 (2). p. 65-73

SVANKMAJER, J. (2008) Decalogue. In HAMES, P. (ed.). *Dark Alchemy*. 2nd Edition. London: Wallflower Press.

WINNICOTT, D. (1996) *Playing and Reality*. 7th Edition. London: Routledge.

www.tonygammidge.com

CHAPTER 12

Violent imagery in art therapy
LYNN AULICH

The artwork discussed in this chapter was made in art therapy by young people attending an adolescent forensic mental health service.

The service provides assessment and treatment for young people aged between 10 and 19 who are emotionally and behaviourally disturbed, or who have a mental illness or an emerging personality disorder. They can also have learning difficulties or be on the autistic spectrum.

Most have a history of serious offending such as murder, attempted murder, assaults, arson, child abduction, rape and inappropriate sexual behaviour. They endanger their own life through self-harm and reckless behaviour, or threaten the lives and well-being of others.

Typically they have grown up in socially, culturally, educationally and financially deprived circumstances. Many have not experienced a secure stable family life, have lived in care, often with a succession of failed placements. The majority have suffered neglect and combinations of physical, sexual and emotional abuse. The consequences are problems with attachment, leading to difficulties in forming and maintaining relationships with others and a vulnerability to mental illness.

In a content analysis of the artwork made in art therapy by 20 young people, the number of images containing morbid imagery and images about violence was significant.

In this context, images depicting damage or threat of injury to people or animals, images of weapons and art works that can be used as weapons are described as violent. Morbid images are those about death, decay, injury, madness, cruelty, illness and pain. These images arouse strong feelings in the viewer such as fear, disgust, repulsion and anxiety.

Young people make images about violence and death in contexts other than art therapy. It should not be surprising to see references to violence in young people's art work; violence and aggression is ubiquitous on television, in films and video games, designed and produced by adults and legitimised through production and exhibition. Violent behaviour perpetrated by individuals, institutions, extremist religious groups and governments are relayed to us on a daily basis through global news.

Being responsible for making continual assessment and evaluation of the risks individuals pose to themselves and to others has an impact on the culture formed within institutions providing care. (Menzies Lyth 1988, Main 1957). Adolescent Forensic Psychiatry can have a defensive, intrusive and controlling culture within it, born from the accumulated painful experiences of working with people in this predicament.

Clinicians working on the secure unit often feel under stress through working in an emotionally charged atmosphere. Anxiety about risk and dangerousness leads to a tendency to overreact to the young people's behaviour. This includes people taking too literal a view about the contents of young people's artwork.

The service works towards helping young people to understand and change their dangerous behaviour to fit in with societal expectations, allowing them to live freer and more fulfilled lives. We have to make judgements about the risks that these troubled young people pose to others and be able to manage and reduce those risks.

This responsibility causes staff to become anxious when they see pictures with violent morbid contents and to fear that the images might be literally equivalent to a state of mind, signalling an intention to commit a violent act. It is difficult to persuade colleagues that images are frequently metaphorical and symbolic, a form of expression of and containment for violent feelings, not signalling an intention to act on them.

Images about violence can be an alert or a warning, a signal for us to pay attention. Some images are intended to repel people as a way to maintain defences against forming relationships. Some violent and morbid images are aggressive, deliberately or unconsciously attacking the viewer. Images can be made to instil fear, repel and upset people spreading rather than containing trauma and distress. Images with idiomatic reference to Gothic imagery are a sign of identification with a transgressive subculture as a need to assert dissatisfaction with the dominant culture in mainstream society. An example of this is drawing the Nazi swastika as a signal of affiliation to extreme right wing ideas.

Violent imagery as the expression of angry hateful feelings in art therapy

Colin was a 15 year old boy who put himself into care. In the chaotic milieu of the children's home he ran riot, set fires in his bedroom and behaved in a sexually exploitative manner towards other residents. Colin held a female staff member hostage for over an hour. Colin and his carers asked for help before his behaviour escalated into further criminality. Once he was settled in a specialist foster placement, art therapy was offered to address his psychological distress.

Colin called one of his early images 'letting the genie out of the bottle'. This image shows a young man squashed into a tiny bottle exploding forth popping the cork out. A psychiatrist in a supervision group who saw this image was worried that art therapy had unleashed Colin's rage and made him more dangerous to others rather than providing him with a safe contained way to explore it.

Subsequent images revealed feelings of contempt for and anger towards women. He made collages of women cut out of magazines without heads and arms with slashes cut into their bodies. Colin had already been acting out anger through his behaviour at the children's home, but in the art therapy his picture allowed him see and reflect on his feelings. Colin was difficult to be with in the sessions. In my counter-transference I felt as if I were complicit in a sadomasochistic relationship. It did not feel right to allow these nasty images but wrong to censor them. All I felt able to do was to voice my observations tactfully and comment on this conflict.

Colin made an image about his wish to harm himself in response to his curiosity about young people at the children's home who cut themselves. We talked about self – harm and how he could be testing my response to his image. Colin hadn't harmed himself, but he wanted to express and contain his fear that he might harm himself.

A later image is about a film Colin watched on television about a 'psychopath' who murdered his female therapist. It was a frightening story and a horrible sketch of a woman with no arms or legs. I understood this to be an expression of his ambivalence about art therapy. I wondered if he was afraid of his thoughts about doing this to me. Such was the power of the warning in this image that I double-checked that I was safe and could summon help if required.

Later in the therapy Colin drew a stunning picture of a knight wearing impenetrable body armour with the visor slightly lifted and a chink of soft pink light glowing through the gap. The armour was black and solid. Colin said that he needed armour to survive his life and told me what he needed protecting from at home. I thought that Colin felt safe enough in art therapy to metaphorically lift the visor on his helmet to talk about himself.

In the next session Colin made a picture of a boy's face in profile with a gun being forced into his mouth. The person holding the gun is not in the picture. Colin disclosed that he was raped by one of his mother's 'boyfriends', he'd never been able to speak about this before. He hated this man but he also hated his mum for exposing him to danger, ignoring him when he told her and doing nothing to protect him. This is an alarming unambiguous and painful image about sexual aggression. It is about Colin's experience of rape, being forced and threatened into sex, and also about how Colin's own sexuality had been developing in response to the trauma. This was a clear example of a victim identifying himself with the abuser, because it is so shameful and distressing for a young man to see himself as a victim. Colin was very afraid of his own anger and potential to harm others.

Colin's mother neglected her son in favour of using men who liked to engage in sadomasochistic relationships. An ongoing theme in Colin's art was his wish to punish all women. As therapy progressed, Colin articulated his amazement at being 'looked after' when he came to his sessions, being provided with a lift by his social worker, having a cup of tea, having art materials, being listened to and being spoken to like a worthwhile person. After the disclosure and a few sessions exploring this, Colin wanted to end the work. I was concerned that he should continue because of his hateful feelings about women, but trusted that he felt he had done enough for the time being.

In this case I often fell into the defensive position of 'seduction of the aggressor' by being overly kind, attentive and considerate in response to feeling anxious to avoid confronting the contents of the images (Blackman 2004). Supervision was very important in maintaining my ability to work with Colin.

I continue to find the images portraying violence to women disturbing. I worry that Colin continues to have relationships that are abusive to women. The consultant's scepticism, and his accusation that I had made someone more dangerous to other people rather than less, has contributed to me never taking the containment provided by image making for granted, but to question the role of any violent and morbid subject matter in images very carefully.

Case of pictures used as police evidence

Art therapists in forensic services are sometimes asked to comment on images made outside the context of art therapy.

At the scene of a murder, the police picked up scribbles and doodles on pieces of paper and a sketchbook from the perpetrators bedroom floor and placed them in evidence bags alongside video games known for violent content and DVDs of mainstream horror films.

Among the images there were drawings of scenes from a violent but readily available video game, some depicting the star ghoul from a commercial horror film marketed at teenagers. Two of the pictures could have related to the death but were ambiguous. A police officer felt that these two pictures indicated that the murder was premeditated. It was true that the modus operandi of the death was similar to an event in the film referred to in the pictures. The film may have suggested the means but was not the motivation or an incitement.

The family history revealed that Tony had witnessed the frequent and prolonged abuse of his mother by male relatives and their friends. Education, social and health services compounded his problems by institutional neglect and inaction to the extent that his considerable learning and developmental difficulties had not been acknowledged.

The police feared that Tony had used the drawings to feed his fantasies and arouse himself to kill. His pictures were not about what he would do but were a response to what happened to him and what he witnessed, represented through the imagery available to him in his environment, that is, films he saw and the video games he played. In the drawings Tony identified with the hero or protagonist in an attempt to combat feeling utterly powerless by creating a world in which he had the power to fight back. His drawings were an effort to contain his fantasies and feelings but sadly his anger and distress were too great to be contained by his drawings alone.

This tragedy reactivated the debate about links between violent behaviour and violence in the media marketed at young people. The evidence is inconclusive. What the studies have in common is the view that people who suffer from a mental disorder are vulnerable and more likely to be influenced by violence in the media (Springhall 1998). It is the trauma of witnessing and experiencing real violence in family and environment rather than fictional or mediated violence that contributes to the development of dangerous behaviour and mental disorders. It is possible that fictional violence might cause a flashback, reminding a young person of the real violence they experience and witness at home.

A case of sympathetic magic

Sharon, aged 17, broke into her teacher's house while he and his fiancé were sleeping. Sharon was armed with a hammer, a chisel and a screwdriver. Fortunately the man awoke and restrained her until the police arrived. Sharon had a crush on her teacher that she imagined was reciprocated. This was thought to be a delusion, but in therapy Sharon said that they had kissed in the storeroom after school and at lunchtime. Sharon became distressed and furious when the teacher introduced her to his fiancé when she saw them by chance, out shopping in town one Saturday. The teacher denied that he had behaved inappropriately towards Sharon, exacerbating her rage against him. Sharon undertook art therapy for two years as a condition of the court.

Outside the art therapy sessions, in secret, Sharon made a wedding gift for the man and his girlfriend. Sharon's mother found it hidden in her bedroom, suspected that the gift was something unpleasant and passed it on to her social worker who opened it. The social worker was alarmed and immediately passed it on to the psychiatrist who, excited and fascinated by it, passed it on to me. I had a good look at it and then hid it in a locked cupboard while I thought through what to do with it.

The 'wedding gift' was enclosed in a shoebox beautifully wrapped in pretty decorative paper. Inside, the box was lined with shiny black plastic. On a bed of black tissue she had laid two plastic dolls, 'Ken' and a 'Barbie' side by side. Both dolls were horribly mutilated with cuts punctures and burns in the plastic where their sexual organs would have been, smeared in red nail varnish, stuck with pins, needles and drawing pins. The dolls were also covered in little labelled samples of every possible substance from her own body, pubic hair, nail clippings, menstrual blood, ear wax, snot, saliva, scabs and sweat and vaginal secretions. Inside the box she had written a detailed description of what she felt about them, how she wanted to hurt them and bad wishes for the future. It also revealed the depth of her rage towards him.

Sharon understood the power this terrible gift would have had on the couple's wedding day and had been prepared to take her revenge on them both.

I told her that I had the box locked in the cupboard and that I felt very strongly that we should bring the box into the art therapy session. It was unorthodox as it was not made in therapy and had not been brought by her voluntarily. Bringing the wedding gift into the art therapy session would be a sensitive matter in an already antagonistic therapeutic relationship. It was important that the professionals involved in the case did not collude any further with the secret keeping and 'talking behind the back' that characterised the systemic issues in Sharon's family network. I felt angry that I was given the toxic responsibility of explaining the theft of the gift and asking her to explore her intention to give it to the couple on their wedding day. Sharon was absolutely furious that her mother and social worker had given the 'wedding gift' to me without her knowledge. The gift was cathartic for Sharon, at least she could inflict on dolls the harm she might have inflicted had she succeed in attacking the couple in their bed.

The 'wedding gift' had a malign presence. It wreaked its power on everyone who opened it to the extent that no one could bear to touch it or hold on to it, passing from hand to hand until I locked it up in a cupboard. Towards the end of her therapy and after discussions with colleagues, I gave the box back to Sharon to dispose of as she saw fit. She told me that she had burned it. Fire seemed to me an appropriate form of disposal, a purification ritual that matched its psychologically potency redolent of ancient sympathetic magic. I was never sure that she did burn it.

The 'wedding gift' provoked a primitive fear of contamination in everyone who handled it, as if the intense feelings contained in the gift would bring bad luck to those who handled it. The photograph I took reluctantly is completely out of focus.

The agency of art objects

The anthropology of art considers the network of relationships and social interactions which take place in the vicinity of an artwork in specific interactive settings; it 'focuses on the social context of art production, circulation and reception, rather than the evaluation of particular works of art' (Gell 1997 p. 3).

In Gell's theory, visual artworks are treated *as if* they were living persons with the ability to act or cause an effect on other people. The artwork gives us access to another mind. He is saying that the art object is an agent in relational terms, it mediates between itself, that is the subject or content of the artwork, the artist, the viewer, in some cases the commissioner or patron and the context or where the artwork is placed and seen. All of these relationships operate with each other in a nexus.

Agency is invested in artworks by people and can emanate from them towards others. The artwork is an objective embodiment of the artist's power or capacity to will a response.

Gell suggests that when we look at art works we make abductions or informed guesses about them. There is no one precise meaning because meaning depends on how the relationships in the nexus of art objects and people are configured. The abductions that we use to comprehend the meaning in artworks are very similar, if not identical, to those we use to understand and respond to other people.

The concept of artwork possessing agency is congruent with the art therapist's experience of looking at and responding to an artwork as an active not a passive object. The communicative function of the art object and its means of transferring meaning from the maker to the viewer, which can only be partially articulated, is accepted as being fundamental to art therapy. Art therapy is about a network of social, psychological and emotional relationships embodied within art objects. Things change when an artwork is brought into existence, not just as a product of a persons mind but also as a material 'being' able to affect the world around it. Art therapy situated in mental health services is a very specific context for art making. The artworks are considered private and not generally exhibited publicly. The art is thought and written about in a personal psycho-dynamic discourse rather than that of visual culture. Art therapy is written about through reports in a health-care record system and not through critical art journals. Art in anthropology, described by Gell, is an agent of social and psychological relationships with equal status to people.

How disturbing images carry agency in therapeutic relationships: an example of repulsion and fascination

Lisa, aged 14, embodied her feelings of murderous rage in hundreds of pictures, made in school, on the ward and in art therapy. Lisa used extreme self harm such as cutting, burning, inserting sharp objects into her orifices and wounds and trying as a way to symbolise and relieve her emotional pain. When prevented from doing this she was distraught. Lisa inhabited an imaginary world that bore very little resemblance to life on the unit. Lisa talked about horror, torture and her wish for death constantly discordant with her everyday activities. Her psychosis was understood to be a symptom of PTSD as the result of repeated trauma, and was leading towards a diagnosis of emerging borderline personality disorder or a schizophrenic illness.

One picture titled 'Killer Dolls' showed a row of four exquisitely drawn dolls, one with talons, another with a spiked ball and chain and two with daggers. Each doll is advancing out of the picture towards the viewer with a menacing expression and a speech bubble saying

'We are coming to get you'. The image evokes memories of childhood fears embodied in fairy tales about dolls coming to life after they have been put away at night. Lisa having suffered sexual and emotional abuse throughout her childhood may have wished that her dolls had really been able to come to life and kill off her abuser.

Lisa experienced staff who tried to get to know her as intrusive and potentially abusive; she could not tolerate closeness of any kind. Her strategy for self-defence was to make hostile, gory pictures. Lisa's images succeeded in repelling and frightening us but they also fascinated us and maintained our interest in her. The images and the relationships they generated around them embodied dysfunctional attachments.

Although the violence portrayed in the pictures is not physically harmful, the images affected everyone who saw them. The figures in her pictures seemed to posses an agency of their own, mediating Lisa's rage. Functionally, violent images in therapy are a very effective means of generating anxiety, thus making sure that professionals remain concerned with and attached to the individual who made them. Conversely, scary images can serve as protection from therapy, which is experienced as intrusive and threatening. Altogether the images bind us to people through the anxiety they generate; they create an impasse through not allowing therapy to happen. The intense anger in the pictures was disabling. Psychodynamically the process is a form of projective identification.

Communication through projective identification, repetition and re-enactment of trauma through metaphor

Bion's concept of projective identification, where the person in therapy has feelings that are beyond words arising from unspeakable experiences or from pre-verbal experiences, is useful in understanding the impact of violence in images. Unmanageable feelings may be unconsciously projected into the viewer of violent imagery. Where the young person as in the previous example is psychotic, the therapist feels overwhelmed by the fear and anxiety, but it can prevent the therapist from being able to work with the image. A process of projective identification between the patient and the art therapist is taking place through the image (Mann 1989). Eventually the therapist can understand, and contain these feelings in order to help the person in therapy to manage the feelings themselves (Casement 1990).

Projective identification is also at work when young people identify with the aggressor. Most of the young people I am talking about have been victims of abuse and have dealt with their, possibly unacknowledged distress by abusing other people. As a victim, they have experienced feelings such as loss of control, fear and helplessness that are so unbearable that they are turned around and replaced by omnipotence, the belief that you can control everything. Exerting control over others and causing them pain is an attempt to assuage rather than to accept their own experience and is doomed to be repeated (Van Der Kolk 1989, De Zulueta 2006).

With these two concepts in mind, young people who make violent images can be re-enacting aspects of their own experience of trauma through images, to scare everyone else from the position of the aggressor rather than the victim. Main (1957) identifies people using their distress as aggression towards caregivers with the unconscious aim of preventing therapeutic work.

Authors writing about the effects of trauma in childhood discuss repetition and the compulsions to repeat or re-enact unprocessed trauma through self-harm and violence throughout adolescence and into adulthood (Van Der Kolk 1989). Young people are frequently further traumatised by their own crime, their violence and abuse of others (Bailey 1997).

In art therapy, young people sometimes make artwork representing a reconstruction or re-enactment of their offence through metaphor. This is not requested or sought by the therapist, but arises unconsciously from the young person's need to do this when they are ready to explore what occurred. The re-enactment is contained by the process of making and embodied in the finished artwork. Re-enactment that is imposed or undertaken without the containment of the art could be re-traumatising.

Gothic and abject art in contemporary art practice

Violence, abjection, morbidity and trauma as subject matters in contemporary art discourse are not usually personalised back to the artists' processing of their own traumatic experiences, but are understood within the historical, sociological and political context the artists' work is positioned in.

A number of artists working since the 1960s who engage in self-mutilation, self torture, socially taboo sexually explicit acts, and defamation of religious symbols, and whose work is particularly challenging are legitimised through exhibition and inclusion in critical cultural discourse. Politzki (1995) uses the term 'dark art' to describe the ritualistic degrading performances of Paul McCarthy and Chris Burden and feminist artists Sue Williams and Jo Spence from a Jungian perspective. Others include photographer Cindy Sherman, the Chapman brothers, Mathew Barney, Stelarc, Robert Mapplethorpe, Andres Serrano and many others. These works can be understood as an expression of the concealed dark side of western culture, an exposition of religious symbols that have become defunct, tired and meaningless. They are about political protest, forcing the complacent to pay attention to injustice. Politski suggests that these artists take on the role of shaman and become scapegoats for the ills of society. 'Dark art' takes on and portrays the elements neglected by the collective unconscious and take on a healing and restorative function for society as a whole'.

The implications of art such as this for art therapy is the need for us to be aware of collective psychic trauma and to be open to the possibility that psychological problems can belong both to the individual and to society. This means remembering the everyday horrors of war and injustice that we are faced with through living in the world.

Art as transgression and the opportunity to explore forbidden subjects

Young people are often fascinated by imagery in the 'Gothic horror' genre: gravestones, ghouls, zombies, cannibals, sharp weapons such as daggers and knives dripping blood, scarred blackened hearts, swastikas and devils. Dracula and Frankenstein and other versions of the 'living dead' make frequent appearances in the art therapy room. The colours echo injuries, bruises, or dead decaying bodies - purple, black, red, grey and yellow. These images and characters can be understood as idiomatic sentimental images about fear, fear of living, sickness and dying.

Barry Richards defines the term 'sentimental' as 'the use of an expressive idiom which short circuits the tolerance and expression of feelings by offering a stylised and closed way of apprehending them' (Richards 1994). In therapy, Gothic images can be the precursors of more personal expressions.

Death, injury, illness, madness, misery, ageing, decay, cruelty and failure are aspects of life with few outlets for expression for young people. Most appear to be dealt with in examples of popular culture, many of which are subject to adult moral disapproval. A whole industry is aimed at young people in 'Indie', 'Death Metal', 'Emo', Mosh' or 'Goth' alternative scenes, marketed to appeal to the adolescent fascination with the combination of sexuality, eroticism, the macabre and the occult.

There is subversive pleasure and delight in horror and macabre fantasy; these forms of expression transgress cultured ideas about taste, decency and about what is suitable for the moral development of young minds. Being provocative, challenging and opposing the rules of adults is a way of separating from parents and becoming an individual. It is an essential part of adolescent development. Play is primarily about children testing the limits of safety within a safe relationship. Transgression of and rebellion against perceived norms is part of the process of learning social interaction, developing the capacity to differentiate between what is acceptable and what is not (Bateson 1979). Gory bloodthirsty images about cannibalism, murder and torture can be understood in the context of development.

Cultural historian Marina Warner (1998) writes about the human capacity to invent grotesque monsters, beasts and ghosts and to tell rude, disgusting, offensive jokes and stories that 'continually challenge and transgress the struggle to be fair, rational and enlightened.' In earlier times, the struggle was couched in terms of the struggle for good over evil happening in the world through the agency of outside forces; in contemporary times the struggle between light and darkness takes place within us and in our interactions with others. The 'bogey-man' of today is not from a mythological hell, but one of us. Images about violence and horror refer not to the murderous nature of children and young people, but the reverse, the reality of adult perversion, exploitation cruelty and neglect of the young (Warner 1998 p.158).

In art therapy, the young people experience power, agency and control in art making. Part of this power is in taking the opportunity to mock, tease, terrify and test the reactions of the therapist, who in turn is required to provide constraints and limits, not by forbidding such imagery, but by engaging with its intentions.

As Gell also suggests in his work on sympathetic magic, trauma is catching; you do not have to be traumatised yourself to feel it and it is easy to transmit it to others, especially through the arts. In a sense, those who look at disturbing images feel this trauma and pass it on, much like those who give me all the scary gory pictures young people have made. To bring these images into art therapy is to offer a chance to think about and understand the communication of the images and to work towards reducing the damaging effects of trauma.

Despite the proliferation of violence and death in imagery in the entertainment industry and culture, the use of this subject matter by young people in their everyday lives may be an indication that help is needed. Art therapy is the context for that help.

REFERENCES

Bailey, S 1997 'Sadistic and Violent acts in the young.' Child Psychology and Psychiatry Review 2:92-103

Bateson. G. 1970. 'Mind and Nature: A Necessary Unity'. Hamilton Press Inc.

Blackman J.S. 2004 '101 Defences: How the Mind Shields Itself' Brunner -Routledge

Casement P 1990 'Further Learning from the Patient' Brunner Routledge

De Zulueta F, 2006 'From Pain to Violence: The traumatic roots of destructiveness' Routledge

Gell. A. 1997 'Art and Agency: An Anthropological Theory' Oxford University Press.

Menzies Lyth. 1988 'Containing anxiety in Institutions: selected essays Volume One' Free Association Books.

Main .T. 1957 'The Ailment' in 'Personality Disorder: The Definitive Reader' 2009 Edit. Gwen Adshead and Caroline Jacob. Jessica Kingsley Publishers.

Mann. D. 1989. 'The Talisman or Projective Identification'. Inscape' The Journal of the British Association of Art Therapists,.Autumn

Politsky R 'Acts of Last Resort: the Analysis of Offensive and Controversial Art in an Age of Cultural Transition' The Arts and Psychotherapy' 1995.

Richards B, 1994 'Disciplines of Delight: the Psychoanalysis of Popular Culture' Free Association Books.

Springhall J 'Youth Popular culture and Moral Panics: Penny Gaffs to Gangsta Rap1830-1996' 1998

Van der Kolk BA. 1989. The Compulsion to Repeat the Trauma: re-enactment: re-victimisation and masochism. Psychiatric clinics of North America 12,398-411

Warner, M 1998 'No Go the Bogeyman: Scaring Lulling and Making Mock'. London. Chatto and Windus.

CHAPTER 13

Disobedient objects: Group art therapy for male patients with mild learning disabilities in a locked environment

KATE ROTHWELL

A version of this paper was first written for the Group Analytic Society International Journal' 'Contexts'. March 2015. Issue N0 67

W orking with people with intellectual disabilities in a locked setting is like working in the dark. It can stretch the skills, flexibility and imagination of therapists facing barriers with learning disability offence related work, and can limit the use of traditional techniques and ideologies. The work feels very different to my experience with patients with disordered personalities who find ways of communicating: "I take control by doing something so you can't do anything because I'm making you do something because of what I'm doing". Here, it was different; the patients with learning disabilities were communicating: "I take control by doing nothing so you can't do anything". This can be totally disempowering. Working with patients with learning disabilities has been the bread and butter for art therapists since the birth of the profession in the 1940s. Therapists have had to develop novel approaches to meet the needs of clients. It's been a natural path for non-verbal creative treatment, as art therapists have never faced the obstacles faced by verbal therapies: the assumption that people with learning disabilities are not 'normal' enough to be given treatment and not recognised as needing a valid treatment option. Arts therapies are the treatment option, maybe by default?

In my approach, I found I had to develop a means of working flexibly, creatively and playfully, taking on many roles in becoming a companion, authoritarian, teacher, confidant and deviant. Yet I found myself alone with my ideas. It seemed vital to combine others' thinking with my own for validation. There was no template to follow; I was discovering a way of working for myself by using my thinking and drawing skills, humour and art materials in an unconventional way. I had to be willing to form an alliance by feeling helpless, disempowered and dependent in order to let the patient take control and experience their own conflicts.

Rather than exploit the situation, it is important to be there as a boundaried container, listening to how they feel and taking on different roles, as if 'partners in crime'. To this end, I had to acknowledge my own disabilities, to become subversive and to own my disgust after building up enough trust to ensure the patient knows they won't be rejected. Sinason (2011) describes the disgust response as infantile and innate; it's the flip side of fascination and suggests we have to look into it to find something that moves us. We need not judge the deviance but understand it. I found it vital in forming therapeutic alliances, to be warm, approachable, accessible, funny, serious, empathetic, open, alive, real and authentic to the experience.

Wolfenberger (Manners 2005, p. 7) discusses the way in which individuals are perceived as deviant due to their differentness and lack of real emotional feelings (Kuczaj 1990). McKenzie, Chisholm and Murray describe how they were met with an institutionalised resistance to work psychodynamically with clients who had learning disabilities. They stated: "people with learning disabilities often find themselves disempowered when in a relationship with a helping professional, they are often required to perform difficult tasks for the psychologist or teacher etc" (2000 p. 5). From my own experience, teamwork is the best model for using a person centered approach in a systemic process, integrating recommendations of bespoke treatment from the 2008 'Valuing People Now' report. This seems a vast move from just 10 years ago, and Kuczaj states, "perhaps the structure that clients and staff find themselves in helps perpetuate this denial of feelings, along with staff inadequacies in ward situations which have prevailed until quite recently. The denial has a historical background, but is also linked with the prevalent assumption that a more limited cognitive capacity indicates a more limited emotional capacity" (1990 p. 117).

Yet, I discover surprise from patients when I ask how they are feeling. These patients have an emotional life that reaches beyond their acting out behaviour.

There is a great breadth of uncertainty and a need to question one's motives for this area of work. Given there is little sympathy for the offenders, most of whom are also victims of gross abuse, early separation, trauma and violence, there are also the projections carried by offender with learning disabilities that evoke a primitive fear in others. This fear either stimulates a response that the internal child must be protected, or a need to be protected from these over-sexualised beings. This perpetuates terror and anxiety and perverts the grief and mourning process of the "life unlived" (Corbett 2014). This is a direct indicator for deep work, rather than a sticking plaster approach linked to infantalisation of the patient. Keeping them childlike denies the importance of separation in a caring, thoughtful and reparative way.

There is a lack of willingness to tolerate this part of society. Societal stigmatisation leads to self-stigmatisation and increases the difficulty to integrate offender patients with learning disabilities back into the community. With the drive to implement the Recovery Model, there is also a drive for patients to return to the world outside. In some ways this can help reduce institutionalisation if people can be returned sooner into society, but does society want them back?

The members of the art therapy group are all too aware that they are very low down the pecking list, and some feel an ambivalent safety in the hospital. It can create confusion when they are told they are better off in the community. The images made by patients in the group project their anxieties about 'moving on' and usually depict solitary tropical islands surrounded by sea, blissful isolation or previous homes in high security where they were kept well away from society, but also as symbols of care, and paradoxically of abuse.

I worked with a patient who spent many months building a house from ice-lolly sticks to create a symbol of self, in the form of a psychic space and a place to move from. This represented increased flexibility and acted like a shell that provided a holding protective layer and an osmotic function with movement – in and out. He needed to do this work before he felt safe enough to join the group, but also to have a place to speak about his damaging experiences in his community where he was treated as an outcast. He feared similar retribution from the group who he saw as a hostile mob. He needed to build up the confidence to be with other people in the safe and familiar space of the art therapy room.

I experience many challenges in this work, which are well described and documented in the literature. Authors describe experiences with patients who resist any form of therapy, who don't identify themselves as having a problem and who suffer poor memory retention and a fear of rejection if their offences are exposed to others (Aulich 1994). There is another theme of patients gaining the ability to articulate their distorted thinking through therapy to increase avoidance and control. Added difficulties are that without therapy, sexual fantasies may spiral out of control, and that facilitating thinking through interpretation may be too painful for both patient and therapist, and is therefore avoided. It is equally difficult to understand emotional difficulties and needs as their emotional needs have been, until recently, ignored (Hagood 1994 p. 67, Tipple 1994, Stott and Males 1984, Kuczaj 1990). Patients may also be reluctant to use art materials, either due to physical difficulties to perform everyday tasks or because the experience makes them feel childish or increases their feelings of shame (Hagood 1994, Stott and Males 1984, Kuczaj 1990, Aulich 1994, Manners 2005). Authors also discuss the element of control and the patient's need to control their world or to have control over something, perhaps by doing nothing (Rothwell & Hutchinson 2011). This is a defence frequently used by patients in my work. The image and space is used to maintain control by making diagrammatic images that distance the therapist, keeping control over the artwork, one another, the session and the therapist, largely as a means of experiencing potency. Confrontation can cause feelings of helplessness and humiliation and tactics used to defend against this may include deskilling and humiliating the therapist. By having overwhelming needs and persistently negative experiences of relationships can cause the therapist to feel loss and failure (Hagood 1994, Kuczaj 1990, Willoughby-Booth & Pearce 1998, Aulich 1994). However, Manners argues that the psychodynamic model reinforces the power struggle of the therapist's knowingness and the client's not-knowingness (2005, p. 67). Corbett describes this as 'mind envy'; the therapist has the beautiful mind the patient was denied from birth (Corbett 2014).

Forensic patients with a learning disability are often exposed to 'trauma work', with little understanding of the impact of trauma or what it is to be the object or perpetrator of abuse. This can be equally traumatising, and those linking thoughts and memories can lead the patient back to trauma and pain. Sinason (2011) identifies trauma at the root of pain and hurt, and acknowledges the importance of creating a space where it will be heard and where something can be built and constructed to help something happen. She describes the development of a new constituted family where there are opportunities to learn, to be fascinated, to be respected and to care. The challenge is how to bear the pain and not pass it onto others, for example, through heightened sexuality as a defence against trauma or through enact[ing] the pain of early trauma on those children who are viewed as perfect, unflawed and non-disabled. Suppressed sexuality can be explosive when patients enact the worse elements of their experience and their abuse, causing a valiant desire for hurting the damaged, dependent and traumatised unconsciously, and are therefore vulnerable to be re-traumatised and exploited (Corbett 1996, Hopper 2011, Sinason 2011). This can make group work very slow paced and creates a need for safe boundaries to hold and acknowledge the emotions imbued in trauma work, holding the victim and offence in mind simultaneously.

Group vignette

It is an ordinary day and there are five patients waiting to go to the art therapy group. A psychology trainee asks if she can join us, and a social therapist is given the duty of co-escort. The trainee asks for a brief overview from the therapist, who then attempts to summarise a process and a historical context of the life of the group that is in fact beyond a pithy explanation, and tells the trainee all will be revealed once she has experienced the group. A collection of eight people make their way through the buildings, unlocking and locking doors, on a journey repeated many times before to the art therapy room. Some comments are exchanged to pass the time but generally everyone knows the routine. Once in the room, the therapist opens the cupboard to the art materials and patients retrieve their folders or select paper to work on. Everyone in the group instigates their own activity and finds somewhere to sit at a large table.

Initially there is silence as people settle down to focus on their work. At either end of the table, two patients sit side by side. On one side the trainee psychologist and the social therapist sit, on the other a patient and the art therapist sit. No one asks what to do. They have already begun.

One patient draws a green monster and asks the therapist what it is. A big lizard, comes the reply. No, it's a dinosaur comes the answer. This patient often draws scary things with large teeth. He shows the trainee who gives some positive regard. He then draws a flying dinosaur he knows the therapist will recognise from their trip to the Natural History Museum. Unfortunately she's forgotten what it's called, but he reminds her, given his incredible catalogue of dinosaur information. He then starts complaining that the staff are stingy and won't give him coke or chocolate and pretends to cry. The therapist has been through this routine many times previously and knows not to mention the word 'diabetes' (this word he will depict as 'killer bees', who have to be killed by a man with a big flame thrower). Instead she goes into a repertoire of reasons why superheroes don't eat chocolate, fizzy drinks and crisps. The patient knows the answer but asks why. Because they won't be able to fly off the ground, they'll be too heavy, they can have a bit of cake though. This pacifies the patient who returns to his drawings and produces a 'ghost with shoulders and a round face'. The therapist reminds him of the ghost family he drew recently. He looks pleased to have the image remembered, and begins muttering 'ghost family' under his breath and then looks through his bulging folder.

The patient sitting nearest the social therapist can't concentrate on his own work and takes delight in the social therapist's image by naming the characters rapidly. "It's a man, who is it? A dog, it's funny, who is it? A bird. What have you drawn?" The social therapist benignly replies that he doesn't know and it doesn't have a name. The patient beside him is very carefully drawing a flag and has a neat little palette of watercolours. He says he is drawing the flag of his country but can't remember the colours. Another patient from the same country reminds

him it is black, gold and green. This patient is new to the ward and to the
group. It has been noted that new members often start with a drawing of
the flag of their country, possibly to help their orientation and give them
a place to start. It also identifies their difference and, on occasions, has
been the inspiration for very rich discussions on people's racial origin
and heritage. This can lead into discussions on belonging and identity.

The patients are sitting together quietly drawing and painting,
but one of them chooses to show his image, stating it's a truck, a
jumper and an aeroplane. The therapist struggles to hear what he is
saying and thinks he is saying "shark". The patient is very tolerant
and repeats "truck"; the social therapist helps out as the therapist is
confused and says it looks like a vehicle not a shark. She is then told
that's because it's a truck. The patient makes no explanation for what
he has drawn. He has been attending the group for a couple of years
and has made good progress since before where he would attend the
group but would refuse to return to the ward, and emergency nursing
assistance would be called to carry him back if he refused to walk. He
would also lock himself in the toilet or just run off to the other end
of the corridor. Now he sits and draws with no need to run. He also
takes in everything being said, despite saying very little. The responsive
environment of the ward has enabled him to become 'human' and
socialised. He can be provocative to other patients, but in his artwork
he has matured developmentally from latency to adolescence. This
is visible in his imagery, as his sense of self takes form having moved
from painting very unformed shapes that cover the paper to creating
highly individualised figurative work.

An even quieter patient has been drawing competently and
colours in his depictions of his 'lucky numbers'. Each week he reveals
a little bit more about himself, becomes a little less withdrawn and
a little more self-exploratory. The therapist has to be mindful to hold
him in mind as he can easily drop off the radar. He wants to share
his work but would never initiate this action. He is encouraged and
willingly shows what he has drawn. Others start naming their lucky
numbers. In the middle of this, the curious patient asks to use the
toilet. This is facilitated by the social therapist. Whilst he is out, the
dinosaur-drawing patient begins a familiar game with the therapist
called 'what's the colour of…?' This is where he repeatedly asks the

colour of something and colours are named. This time the question is 'what's the colour of the desert', now asked to the trainee. The trainee goes into therapist mode again by returning the question on him. He looks a bit bewildered and dissatisfied.

The therapist knows the game so begins naming colours. At the end of the list he triumphantly points out her stupidity for leaving out the colour black and gives her a sideways look with a grin, his eyebrows shooting up in amusement. He then starts asking the trainee about her picture, and again she starts putting the questions back to him. This gets him nowhere, but as he tends to enjoy the company of the new young female trainees that have filed through the service over the years, he perseveres by drawing a 'troll monster'. He then asks her to write 'troll monster' and she begins to oblige until the therapist points out he is perfectly capable of writing this himself. He agrees then starts a new game of 'where do troll monsters live?' The trainee looks bewildered and states she doesn't know. This goes on for a bit until the resounding 'PECKHAM' sails through the air from the curious patient who has returned from the toilet. The group falls about laughing, much to the curious patient's delight; it is then agreed that's where Troll Monsters come from. The patient asks the trainee the same question and she confidently replies with: "Peckham". Everyone feels at ease and the group ends.

Discussion

Patient experience is paramount to gaining a view of what it is to be someone with a learning disability, to see how the learning disabled are viewed in society and to further appreciate how patients come to express themselves and communicate in the group. Change can be very slow, and there is much to be said about the need for a learning disabled person to protect themselves from the judgment of others and the lack of early stimulation or bonding. There is also a lot of dialogue about a resistance to relinquish familiar habits brought about through a core complex of being born with a learning disability (Kuczaj 1990, Hawtin 2009, Corbett 1996). Corbett describes this well stating: "Our clients tell us of the deep, inner pain when [that] attunement is misaligned, when [that] mirroring is distorted by a primary fear and rage at the disability itself. Certainly for the offenders with whom we work, some chaotic attachment patterns may produce mirroring of the core complex!" (Corbett 1996a).

I wondered if this is akin to an experience of 'being born deviant' in the eyes of society, when I found myself waiting and waiting for patients to make use of the art therapy group. It put in my mind a sense of my having to 'do' something deviant for something to happen, and also to consider the meaning of the action of doing something, anything?

Is it to be noticed, to evacuate frustration or to get help? Perhaps the act of deviance is defiant in causing something to happen? From my experience with violent offender patients, including those with a learning disability, it seems when trusted and respected, they do not behave violently. Sinason puts an interesting slant on this. She says patients become, or create in themselves, the person they fear, and that trauma-based work allows for a different way of being (Sinason 2011).

The role of art therapy in group work and the therapist's skills feature predominantly in relation to the therapist's skills as an artist and the weight of keeping an idea or thought alive against feelings of deadening boredom. Likewise, that drawing 'alongside' with or for the patient is an essential aide, as is the use of a more concrete approach to enable patients to internalise and think about what's been happening whilst feeling held and contained.

Tustin (1990 p. 47) states: "Such patients need to feel that there is a nurturing person who cares deeply whether they live or die and who affirms their existence by talking to them as if they exist" (Stack 1996 p. 11). There appears to be elements of the therapist's role that are specific to working with learning disabled people. For instance, the use of symbolisation is rarely contrived, attention seeking or second hand. The client's ability to cope with discussion of the artwork must be considered. Work can be both directive and non-directive and neither approach will detract from the individual's worth or capabilities. But, in one case example it was shown how drawing was the only way to pacify one client's difficult moods (Gray 1985, Stott and Males 1984). The art therapist is also described as the 'enabler' or 'witness', whose role it is to play, the experience of being utilised by another distinguishes this work (Willoughby-Booth and Pearce 1998). Other views see the therapist as the auxiliary ego whose role it is to stay in touch with aspects of the self one would prefer to detach from, and additionally to establish empathy to become curious, affectionate and open to the need for 'ordinariness', rather than searching to become 'normal'. It is to tolerate the unbearable imprint from childhood, and yet to provide friendliness, compassion, encouragement and positive reinforcement; to work at the person's pace and help them reflect on the content of the artwork to gain insight and overcome difficulties (Hopper 2011, Sinason 2011, Stott and Males 1984). There may even be a crossover of the therapist's role to be actively involved in social inclusion activities, going for a walk or an outing. Such is the case on the ward I work on where, regardless of the staff's banding, hierarchy and job description, it's all hands on deck, so to speak. Manners (2005) sees the role of the therapist is to act as a conduit between internal and external worlds by considering the patient's social context and the countertransference phenomena, as does Sinason, who points to the social and cultural context of violence for patients (2011). The shift of focus away from unconscious drives and past relationships are now described by therapists as a focus on 'immediate exchanges' in the here and now between the client and therapist (Tipple 2003 in Manners 2005 p. 69). This is reiterated by McKenzie, Chisholm and Murray (1997) who, in referring to Tipple (1994) see more of an interpretive and directive stance taken by the therapist than in other forms of art therapy, facilitating emotional expression to ameliorate psychological distress (p. 63).

The task of the therapist is to encourage self-esteem and self-development, to help individuals achieve in accordance with their individual development, and to have a gentle approach and low expectations of space, time, attention and continuity (Kuczaj 1990). Hawtin (2009) describes the art therapist as offering a different way of thinking. The art therapist wants to understand how the person views the world and how they feel, their role in providing a non-verbal expressive space.

The focus of the therapy and the approaches used appear very broad and incorporate group work ranging from a closed group using emergent themes and dry materials (Manners 2005), to a themed group focusing on positive aspects of self, as with my own work with sex offenders. Many authors point to the structured nature of their approach to provide the holding environment for the safe expression of anger, rage, frustration and fear potentially (Kuczaj 1990, Willoughby-

Booth 2009, Aulich 1994).

The image as a containing vessel for destructive emotions and thoughts is picked up by Pearce (2004), Willoughby-Booth and Pearce (1998), and Stott and Males (1994). The existing research provides positive rehabilitative indicators in the reduction in recidivist activity for the use of art therapy with offender learning disabled patients. It suggests group work and reflection are the most effective elements in treatment.

There is a change in direction in the work of art therapists in the new millennium. Psychotherapeutic approaches are combined with a debate on the role of the art therapist, the therapeutic space and the development of group work. Manners (2005 p. 67) describes this using an art therapy approach with a group of learning disabled men detained under the Mental Health Act (1983). He develops a view that the psychodynamic model can reinforce power struggles connected to the patient's sense of disempowerment and helplessness through lack of choice and staff responses to challenging behaviour. This he links to the patient's experience of being removed from society into institutions. He strongly argues that the role of the therapist is to act as a conduit between internal and external worlds by considering the patient's social context and the countertransference phenomena.

McKenzie, Chisholm and Murray (2000) describe running a group for learning disabled offenders with the goal to prevent further offending through the facilitation of emotional expression by using an approach not dependent on verbal communication. Evaluation throughout treatment confirmed results that none of the participants were charged with re-offending during the course of the group.

They state that "the skills of the art therapy profession clearly lie in the facilitation of emotional expression and amelioration of psychological distress by means which do not rely solely on the verbal abilities of the client" (p 63), and identify the ultimate goal of treatment as being preventative of re-offending; the patient's understanding of the 'why' they offended is secondary (p 63). McKenzie, Chisholm and Murray discuss the particular susceptibility of people with learning disabilities becoming victims of sexual abuse, and point out the overrepresentation of this population becoming perpetrators compared to the general population, citing McCarthy and Thompson (1997). Largely the authors' research identifies the need to adapt the group work for learning disabled offenders in order for them to engage in treatment by using multi-modal interventions, including cognitive behavioural therapy (O'Connor 1997). This was the only specific research published relevant to my own area of interest, until Manners took up the mantel for art therapy with learning disabled sex offenders in a secure setting in 2005. Manners states that his research highlighted power imbalances faced between patient and therapist and an important consideration of the social context of the work (p 69), reflecting on whether the psychodynamic model reinforces the power structure of therapists' knowingness and clients' not knowingness (p 67).

Pearce (2006) researched the link between personality disorder and learning disabled patients who have committed sexual offences. Using a focus group to explore the experience of art therapists working with dual diagnosed patients to inform the effectiveness of art therapy with this client group, she concluded that art-making materials enabled reflection to become possible.

The most recent research comes from Hackett who researched art psychotherapy with adult offenders who have intellectual and developmental disabilities (2012). This study showed qualitative results for service users with learning disabilities, and found that the artwork helped patients to process thinking, personal reflection and the ability to mentalise, thereby evidencing a reduction in the patients' levels of aggression.

The weekly group

This last piece of unpublished research mirrors the work of my art therapy group the closest, and puts an emphasis on valuing what the patient *can* do rather than what they can't. The group members can discover new talents and can learn how to appreciate one another's work whilst having their own work admired, appreciated or explored further through discussion. The use of images in a group can be gentle yet powerful; meanings need handling with care to avoid fragmentation or provocation of negative responses from the patient. This is not to say that there is an avoidance of negative transference, but to prematurely reawaken the fragile emotions contained in the artwork from a warded off or defensive position needs thoughtful handling to reduce the risk of an offence re-enactment (Beail 1998, 2003, 2004, 2005, 2007).

The most important attributes of the group are to offer choice through art materials and art-making with no restrictions. However, it is also the chance to be themselves, to find a place to explore their identity, to experiment with reasoning to renegotiate their developmental progress and to risk attachment to another human being. It's a chance to learn how to relate to others, which is first encountered through their relationship with their own images and sensory tactile experiences when using the mediums provided by the art psychotherapist. The artwork is kept safely in individual folders in the art therapy room to symbolise a healthy nurturing model mirrored through the art therapy group work. The art therapy group I now run has become a recognised and a well-held feature of the ward timetable. It often feels like a chance in the busy week to be with others in silence, to become a new (weirdly unconventional) constituted family, to learn from one another and to see a different way of looking at each other's lives through art.

REFERENCES

Aulich, L. (1994). Fear and Loathing. Art Therapy, Sex Offenders and Gender. In: Liebmann.M (ed) *Art Therapy with Offenders*. Jessica Kingsley Publishers. London. England.

Beail, N. (1998). Psychoanalytic psychotherapy with men with intellectual disabilities: A preliminary outcome study. *British Journal of Medical Psychology, 71*(1), 1-11.

Beail, N. (2001). Recidivism following psychodynamic psychotherapy amongst offenders with intellectual disabilities. *The British Journal of Forensic Practice, 3*(1), 33-37.

Beail, N. (2003). What works for people with mental retardation? Critical commentary on cognitive behavioural and psychodynamic psychotherapy research. *Mental Retardation, 41,* 468-472.

Beail, N. (2004). Methodology, design, and evaluation in psychotherapy research with people with intellectual disabilities. In E. Emerson, C. Hatton, T. Thompson & T. R. Parmenter (Eds.), *The international handbook of applied research in intellectual disabilities* (pp. 531-548): John Wiley & Sons. Ltd.

Beail, N. (2005). Evidence base for behavioural interventions: Critical commentary. *Mental Retardation, 43*(6), 442-445.

Beail, N., Kellett, S., Newman, D. W. & Warden, S. (2007). The dose-effect relationship in psychodynamic psychotherapy with people with intellectual disabilities. *Journal of Applied Research in Intellectual Disabilities, 20*(5), 448-454.

Corbett, A. (1996a). The Learning Disabled paedophile and paedophile rings. Clinical Open Evening.

Corbett, A., Cottis, T. & Morris, S. (1996b). *Witnessing, Nurturing, Protesting. Therapeutic responses to sexual abuse of people with learning disabilities.* David Fulton. London.

Corbett. A (2014) Disabling Perversions: Forensic Psychotherapy with people with Intellectual Disabilities. Forensic Psychotherapy Monograph series. Karna. London

Department of Health. (2001). Valuing people: A new strategy for learning disability for the 21st Century. London: Department of Health.

Department of Health (2004). Green light for mental health. How good are your services for people with Learning Disabilities? A Service Improvement Toolkit. http://www.valuing people.gov.uk/documents/mental health

Gray, J. The conscious and Unconscious processes. Parrallel Aspects of art therapy in mental handicap. *Inscape.* 1985. Pp3-8

Hackett, S (2012). Art psychotherapy with Adult Offenders who have Intellectual and Developmental Disabilities. PhD. Unpublished.

Hargood, M. (1992). states of child sexual abuse in the UK & Implications for British Art Therapists. *Inscape,* Spring, Pp27-33

Hagood, M (1998). Group Art Therapy with Adolescent Sex Offenders. An American experience pp197-219 In: Liebmann, M. (ed.) *Art Therapy with Offenders.* Jessica Kingsley Publishers. London.

Hawtin, A. (2009). Considering Clinical Issues in Learning
Disabilities and Art Therapy. MA Art Therapy programme
Lecture. University of Hertfordshire.

Hawton, K. et al. (1998). Deliberate self-harm: Systematic
review of psychosocial and pharmacological treatments in
preventing repetition. *British Medical Journal*, 317: 441-446

Hollins, S. & Sinason, V. (2000). Psychotherapy, Learning
Disabilities and trauma. *British Journal of psychiatry. New
Perspectives,* 176, pp22-36

Hopper, E. (11/02/2011). Supervision and Consultation in
forensic settings.

RESPOND/International Association of Forensic
Psychotherapies. Lecture. Directory of Social Change. London.

Kuczaj, E. (1990). Art Therapy with people with Learning
Difficulties. Ch 7. In: Leibmann, M. *Art Therapy in Practice.*
Jessica Kingsley Publishers. London.

Manners, R (2005). "It must be an honor to drive" Issues of
difference, loss of normality, power and disempowerment
in group art psychotherapy with men who have learning
disabilities who are detained under the mental health act.
Masters' Degree Dissertation. Goldsmiths College.
University of London.

Marshall, K. & Willoughby-Booth, S. (2007). Modifying the
clinical outcomes in routine evaluation measures with people
who have a learning disability. *British Journal of Learning
disabilities.* 35 (2): pp107-112

McCarthy, J. & Thompson (1997). A prevalence study of sexual
abuse of adults with intellectual disabilities referred for sex
education. *Journal of Applied research in Intellectual Disabilities.*
10,2 pp105-124

McKenzie, K. Chisholm, D. & Miller, L. (1997). Up the
slippery slope. Group work with sex offenders with a Learning
disability. *Journal of sexual Aggression.* 3 91) pp35-52

Pearce, J. (2006). Art therapy, learning disabilities and personality disorder: An exploration of attitudes, practice and theory. Masters' degree (MAACP) Goldsmiths College. University of London.

Rothwell, K. & Hutchinson, L. (2011). Hiding & Being Seen: The story of one womans' development through Art Therapy and Dialectical Behavioural therapy in a forensic context. *Art therapy Online Journal*. Vol. 2, Issue 1.

Stack, M. (1996).Humpty Dumpty had a great fall. *Inscape,* Vol: One. No 1. 1996

Stott, J. & Males, B. (1998). Art Therapy for people who are Mentally Handicapped. (pp111-126) In: Dalley, T. (Ed.) (1998) *Art as Therapy: An Introduction to the use of art as a therapeutic technique.* London. Tavistock Publications.

Sinason, V. (1996). From abused to abuser. In: Cordess, C. & Cox, M. (eds) *Forensic Psychotherapy: Crime, psychodynamics and the offender patient.* Jessica Kingsley. London.

Sinason, V. (2010). *Mental Handicap and the Human Condition:2nd Edition..* London: Free Associations.

Sinason, V. (11/02/11). How to be a Forensic Disabilities Therapist. RESPOND/International association of Forensic Psychotherapies. Lecture. Directory of Social Change. London.

Tipple, R. (1994). Communication and Interpretation in Art Therapy with People who have a Learning Disability. *Inscape*. Vol:2

Tipple, R. (2003). The importance of transference processes in work with people with learning disabilities. *Inscape*. Summer. Pp2-9

Tipple, R. (2003). The Interpretation of Children's artwork in a Paediatric Disability setting. *Inscape*. Vol.8 No.: 2.

Tustin, F. (1990). *The protective shell in children and adults.* Karnac Books. London.

Willougby-Booth, S. & Pearce, J. (1998). Ch 4. On the Edge. Art Therapy for people with Learning Difficulties and Disordered personalities. Reese.M. (Ed) (1998) Art Therapy with People who have Learning Disabilities. Routledge. London.

CHAPTER 14

Hide my face. Hear my voice: Speaking the unspeakable through characters and metaphor in dramatherapy films

LORNA DOWNING

> *"It is the paradox of the mask that it both conceals and reveals…"*

(Jennings 1990, p. 109).

Most of us find it difficult to speak about our difficult experiences. Forensic patients with mental illnesses also struggle to find their true voice: to speak about past trauma and abuse, committed by them and to them, without feeling exposed and intruded upon. Forensic units, secure hospitals and prisons are notoriously challenging places to work. Despite the shared mission of rehabilitation and the opportunity to 'talk', they are often not places conducive to therapy. They are unintentionally prone to be shrouded in collective persecutory feelings where perpetrators must be separated from society, locked up and punished. Stressed staff may unconsciously reenact abusive relationships and insecure attachments, finding themselves busy managing behavioural problems rather than trying to unravel what may be behind them. Whilst offenders are encouraged to voice remorse for what they have done, the details of the transgression may actually be "forgotten" by staff (Ruszcynski 2008) as a means to distance and protect themselves.

In the medium-secure unit in the East End of London, where this work took place, the unspoken offence can get 'acted out' in one form or another by patients whose needs get communicated through mental and physical attacks. Without clear boundaries and team support, the environment can become toxic, mirroring the patient's suppressed rage and hopelessness. Dramatherapy offers a safe way to allow the unspeakable to be spoken.

In any kind of drama we are invited to collude with a fiction; to experience and witness the paths and processes of the characters and allow ourselves to collaborate in a kind of deception where the imagined world is 'like me, but not me.' Stories have a reassuring structure where a beginning, middle and end are already decided in the narrative. Role and metaphor can have a "supportive, containing function", because the patient can "say how he feels, or what he did, without really saying it" (Cox, Thielgaard 1987, p. 111). Working through the metaphor and from a distance, we may then be able to say what is difficult to say; to unlock the hidden thing and glimpse beneath the mask. In the Greek myth, Perseus is unable to confront the snake-haired Medusa as he will be turned to stone by her gaze. By watching her reflection in his polished shield, he can safely confront the monster. In the same way, forensic patients may feel petrified of facing their monsters. When concealed behind a literal mask or character, there is an opportunity to approach what is terrifying. Once experienced, witnessed or spoken, there can be self-realisation and change. For example, a patient, who had always idealised his abusive father, was able to say in his character: "I don't understand father, why you don't love me". Two weeks later, in the group check-in, he offered: "You know, I don't think my father was very nice to me".

The use of a camera can add another dimension to an enactment, allowing the character's words to be witnessed, and mirrored back. Where chosen, the patient and therapist can review what has been recorded and can speak about what they witness through a lens. The footage can be edited for a wider audience, enabling his voice to be heard outside the therapy room, with consent and security clearance, outside the hospital to the world. But, with cuts, filters and effects, the editor has the power to make the finished result look slicker and sharper than it really is. This adds a further dilemma. Whose voice are we really hearing?

The camera as a mirror

*"Psychotherapy, is not making clever and apt interpretations;
by and large it is a long-term giving the patient back what
the patient brings. It is a complex derivative of the face that
reflects what is there to be seen"*

(Donald Winnicott, 'Playing and Reality' 1971).

Prior to Winnicott's theory of emotional development and the role of
the mother's face reflecting back to the baby its separate emotional
state, the rather controversial psychoanalyst Jacques Lacan refers to
'Le Stade du Miroir' ('The Mirror Stage' 1936) which describes when
a child first becomes aware of itself in the mirror. Lacan identifies this
moment as potentially unsettling. The reflection may initially appear
alien to the child's emotional state, causing a tension between how he is
feeling and how others see him. Lacan suggests this tension stays with
us into adult life. Modern day access to cameras on phones and the rise
of the 'selfie' may indicate we are more accustomed to having our image
seen by a wider audience. The 'tension' Lacan refers to, may however,
still be very present. We might be selective in promoting a particular
version of ourselves we are happy to share. We may choose to enhance
the image we portray to the world, so that the finished image may not
really be a true reflection. Once released into the ether, these images
may attract abuse and bullying rather than appreciation or admiration.

Older service users, detained for many years, often have no
experience of the Internet or social networking. Because of risk factors,
there is no access to phones and computers, and even glass mirrors
on the ward. This patient community has restricted their opportunity
to see their own reflection.

Considering this, it was with some trepidation that I first thought
about taking a camera into the therapy room. I was aware that it
might be the first time a patient has seen themselves since admission,
during which time their image may appear distorted with weight gain,
age or medication. They may have been mentally unwell prior to
the offence that brought them to hospital. There is also a risk of an
overwhelming ordinariness in their appearance in sharp contrast to
what their perception had been when unwell. Like Lacan's 'Stade du

Mirroir', the patient may feel distanced from the image he sees in the film and disconnected from how he feels or what he sees on the screen.

My role as a dramatherapist is to work with these fears and ease the path for the patient to find their voice through the role of 'another'. My role as film editor was less defined. I had the tools to trim all the mistakes: the delays, dribblings and fumblings, and make a more palatable, but perhaps less truthful, product to present to the outside world.

The Wizard of Oz

"A journey of a thousand miles begins with a single step"

(Lao Tse).

The performing arts group on the long stay ward had seen the 'The Wizard of Oz' on the television at Christmas, and had already begun creating masks and selecting roles. Although my first thought was to carefully explain the difference between directing and dramatherapy and gently decline. Once I had met the patients, seen the spectacular array of papier mache masks and seen how much enthusiasm and support there was for the production, it seemed a good place to start. 'The Wizard of Oz' is a modern day myth, laden with archetypal struggles and journeys. Rehearsals began using dramatherapy games and exercises as a 'way in' to get to know the group and the characters they would play. The archetypes did not need to be identified or analysed, but were allowed to work on an unconscious level for staff and patients on their own journeys 'down the yellow brick road'.

Joseph Campbell, mythologist and writer says "…through our dreams and through a study of myths, we can learn to know and come to terms with the greater horizon of our own deeper and wiser, inward self". He notes that we don't need to be able to intellectualise or make direct links to our own experiences for the myth to have a transformative effect, and "even if the mental message is not understood in so many words, the teaching is realised by the soul, beyond words." (Campbell 1989, p. 243)

Dorothy and Toto in the opening scene are able to express their difficult, real life feelings of boredom and purposelessness through their characters and their desire to be somewhere else; 'over the rainbow'. In a 'careful what you wish for' moment, a tornado turns their lives upside down and dumps them into the Technicolor Land of Oz, where Dorothy begins her heroic journey to individuation. Hopes and fears, good and evil, broken promises and authoritative figures who don't keep their word are all aspects of the story, mirroring patients' experiences in a secure unit.

The patient playing Dorothy wails "I just wanna go home" with such passion; he genuinely does want to go home. He later confides in me, "I've never studied acting…it just comes naturally". The Wicked Witch's words, "I'll get you my pretty!" take on a more sinister tone when the person saying them is really an offender, but there is an opportunity for the words to be witnessed by the group, and the narrative dictates that the evil is 'killed off' when the Wicked witch melts. The Tinman, Lion and Scarecrow are all searching for something they already have, but need a trip down the yellow brick road to discover this, and have an opportunity to vent their frustrations at their Consultant via the Wizard, who they loudly proclaim is 'a fake' and 'a liar'.

Fig. 1: 'I'm bored Toto' The Wizard of Oz

It was after some tricky rehearsals, where the reality of sticking to a rehearsal schedule in a secure hospital became apparent. Group members were often too unwell or deemed too risky to be allowed to attend. Discussing how best to proceed, we discovered that one member of staff had some film making experience. We decided making a film rather than a theatre performance would be our best route, thus allaying fears of failure or unexpected incidents that might interfere with a live performance. This also meant that we could alter our schedules at the last minute to allow for when individuals were unwilling or unable to attend the filming. Also, if we weren't too fussy about continuity, we could use whoever was available on the day, as the masks concealed the faces. This was a useful lesson in adapting to the needs of a forensic environment that has stayed with me.

So, using a camera really came about by accident, and along with it all the fears of what that might entail. The process of creating the film was something of a journey for the whole group. As in most good travel tales, there were moments when, a bit like our protagonists, we felt we would never reach our destination and times there were different routes needing to be chosen. I had no filmmaking experience and had never done any editing. The staff member who was the film expert had long since moved on, and there were all kinds of security restrictions about what could and couldn't be shown. We attempted to get the group members interested in the editing but it felt quite laborious, particularly as we were such editing novices, and there was very little interest. We tried simplifying, offering choices of this version or that scene, which worked, but then we ran out of time and realised bits were missing or unusable. By the time the film was finally completed, nearly a year later, there was a sense of satisfaction and also of great relief. Patients and staff reflecting back, rather like a traveller regaling their story, spoke fondly of the experience, remembering the good aspects and seemingly forgetting the obstacles they had to overcome. They all said they would "definitely do it again". 'The Wizard of Oz' is still discussed with affection and pride, when meeting with patients in the low-secure unit who were part of it. One of them speaks about the film as if it was of a happier past, and uses it to talk about other group members who are sadly no longer alive. He also shows it to his family when they visit, because "it gives us something to talk about".

So, the film has left something of a legacy, not only for patients, but also for dramatherapy and has prompted me to recognise how useful that might be as evidence of our work.

The king, the beast and their mum

"Voice hearers may have over distanced themselves from overwhelming feeling. Dramatherapy enables people to play with distance: to find the aesthetic or middle distance where feelings can be felt, observed and processed without overwhelming the person"

**(Casson, Drama, Psychotherapy and
Psychosis 2004, p. 244)**

Sanjay, 42, is hospitalised under section 37/41 of the 1983 Mental Health Act for sexual offences against his children. He has a diagnosis of treatment resistant Paranoid Schizophrenia and experiences auditory hallucinations, thought insertion and paranoid delusions on a daily basis. Like many forensic patients, he is both perpetrator and victim, and as a child, endured years of physical, mental and sexual abuse. Home was overcrowded and without privacy, boundaries or sanctuary. Consequently, all fear became split off and all attachments became sexualised. Sanjay was referred to dramatherapy after his involvement and enjoyment of 'The Wizard of Oz', but was more able to work individually than in a group, as he had a tendency to over share his past offences and paranoid feelings. This often led to scapegoating. He attended his individual sessions every week. Sanjay enjoyed stories, and over a period of three years, slowly developed an ability to engage mainly through movement. Sanjay required firm boundaries and consistency in the 1:1 sessions, as he was prone to make sexual comments and be over familiar. He found it difficult to identify his true feelings and tended to repeat 'pseudo' phrases about his paranoia and mental illness that had lost their true meaning. Remembering our previous work, he requested we did some filming and after careful thought and supervision, I agreed to take the camera into the therapy room. I invited Sanjay to choose some props to create some characters that I could interview from behind the camera. He chose 'The King', saying, "I am the King. I rule the world" and "The Beast", "I am the Beast. I am the Evil one" and the nagging mother from the story of "Lazy Jack" we had worked on previously.

It was apparent that the mother portrayed was based on his experience of 'a mother'. I kept the footage for several years after it was made, and only watched it again recently with Sanjay. It is a film for use in the therapy, never intending to be shown. It is the least edited of any of the films and possibly the most raw and accurate portrayal of what happens in the dramatherapy room as both the patient and therapist's voices are audible.

The film clearly shows Sanjay's fragmentation and changeable mood in three different guises. Watching the film together, Sanjay recognised these as three of his voices that he hears and it felt quite surreal to have given them form and permanence on screen. I am still undecided whether to show it outside the therapy room.

This was difficult to work as Sanjay often left his feelings of confusion, stuck-ness and damage with the therapist. With very little hope of recovery, staff and other patients get frustrated with him as he seemingly carries the hopelessness for the whole institution. In a climate of government directives of recovery and 'moving on', Sanjay's apparent inability to progress exasperates staff, who perhaps secretly feel they have failed him. Despite the paucity of his creative imagination, he was able to enter into the drama to have a voice and has continued with his individual dramatherapy sessions with another dramatherapist, now in the low-secure unit.

Inside out

> *"I'm not really a talk about my problems kind of guy"*
>
> **(Service user in film 'Inside Out',**
> **(Reflections on life inside a secure hospital 2011).**

A year later, still working as a dramatherapist in the same secure hospital, facilitating several group and individual sessions, I'd packed away the camera to the back of my mind. However, staff and patients who had seen 'The Wizard of Oz' often asked what films I was going to do next. I realised that somewhere along the line, the film had brought an awareness of dramatherapy to the unit.

I was approached about making a patient-led, staff training film
with the aim of educating and informing staff about how treatment
in hospital is experienced from the patient's point of view. The idea
came about through a discussion where a service user complained that
new staff have very little concept of what it's like to be a patient. This
seemed an ideal time to make another film to give the patients a voice.

> *The National Service Frameworks for Mental Health .... set
> out the vision for service delivery and user involvement. The
> vision is to move away from an outdated system of patients
> being on the outside, towards a new model where the voices of
> patients .... are heard through every level of the service, acting
> as a powerful lever for change and improvement.*
>
> **Framework for User Involvement Board version
> 11 September 2010**

This filmmaking project was kept separate from the dramatherapy
sessions and, although an exciting venture, I was aware that there
was no archetypal story to contain the narrative; I was unsure what
might happen. We asked a group of interested participants who voted
to devise a questionnaire asking how patients felt when they first
came to hospital and their experience of diagnosis and medication.
Patients interviewed each other and others recorded the audio. The
same questions were asked of everyone and a framework of themes
began to develop. Careful monitoring was needed for when people
were unable or unwilling to answer, though most service users were
keen to get their points across.

It felt as if I needed to collude with their victim as a point of
contact, so that they could have their say.

"I am a man more sinned against than sinning" (Service user
quoting Shakespeare's King Lear Act 3 Scene 2).

We filmed some mask improvisations using dramatherapy
methods. These were edited in to complement and enhance the
interviews. This worked on several levels: the creative work was more
interesting to view; it allowed for some distancing imaginative work
and people could remain anonymous, which allowed them to speak
more freely and complied with security restrictions.

Fig. 2: Inside Out

It was a vast project and once again I was learning on the job. It seemed like an impossible task. I had no structured beginning, middle and end. There were gaps and I was running out of time and money. 'Inside Out' was the first film that I really began to experiment with the editing software. As my passion and excitement grew with the discovery of how to use certain special effects, I began to try and make some cohesive sense of the hours of footage. Working late into the night day after day, whilst still doing my usual work, I became aware of my feelings of ownership of the film. It had started to become *my* creative project and *my* piece of art. I worried if I'd contradicted the initial aims of the film.

My fears were abated when the first screening to an audience in the hospital was well received and one of the participants stood up and said: "You weren't afraid to show how it really is". Looking back, I am not sure how true that statement is as, like most films, it might seem quite bland and mundane without the music and effects. Some older patients preferred 'The Wizard of Oz' than the hard-hitting reality of 'Inside Out', but the wider audience outside the hospital seemed intrigued. Interestingly, complaints about unmet needs were reported to be particularly low during that period, so perhaps 'Inside Out' gave the patients a voice, even if it was temporary.

Theseus and the Minotaur

"Everyone's got a bit of monster in them…"

(Service user after playing the Minotaur).

Exhausted and slightly confused about my feelings towards film with dramatherapy, I stayed away from the camera for a couple of years. Staff and patients would still ask in passing about the next film and a shortened version of 'Inside Out' had begun to be used in the staff forensic induction.

I reflected on my previous experiences and wondered if perhaps now, I had a proper grasp on how to use film in dramatherapy. At the time, probably in response to services threatened with cuts, nearly every arts therapies conference or email seemed concerned with evidencing our work. An upcoming presentation in Venice seemed an opportunity to create a new film that showcased forensic dramatherapy in the Trust Forensic Directorate.

The myth of Theseus and the Minotaur seemed an obvious choice for a forensic unit. We have a prison/ labyrinth, a violent half-human 'monster' contained within its walls and a brave hero, Theseus, whose job is to slay the beast and return safely home. In power, the old King Aegeus and the entrepreneurial young King Minos, each with their own familial issues, try to avoid military conflict and maintain a "superficial veneer of civilisation" (Cox and Thielgaard 1997, p. 95) whilst behind the scenes the 'monster's' demand for flesh is placated with human sacrifices. Ariadne, Minos's daughter, longs for independence and has the golden thread that enables the safe path to be found. Overseeing all this, we have the ancient gods themselves causing turbulence and upheaval for all that goes against the path of fate.

Phew! Sounds like average day in a forensic unit!

Working with the myth in both group and individual dramatherapy sessions was both powerful and unexpected. Having listened to me telling the story, participants were invited to choose their roles and the story was enacted improvising their own lines in each scene. The structure of the myth contained the story and also dictated the outcome, so that someone drawn to play a high status king would find himself facing loss and betrayal, the hero makes tragic mistakes and the beautiful princess gets abandoned. There is no happy ending and all the characters are flawed, which for patients in denial of their 'shadow side', was going to be a challenge.

I didn't want to take a camera into the actual dramatherapy session as I felt it would interfere with the process, but having enacted the story in session with consent from the participants, I arranged separate individual filming sessions to explore the characters further on film. I was transparent that I would be using the film to raise awareness of dramatherapy, and offered them an opportunity to either participate or decline attending the extracurricular filming.

Here are some quotes from patients improvising in character in the film:

> **King Minos:** *"I don't wanna talk about it... My wife, the thing she done, erm, I'm very ashamed of it and ... is my wife's problem... I am dealing with it, but I don't want it to be involve ..coz I want my kingdom to be respect...especially the King who deserves some respect."*

> **Ariadne:** *"... my dad can be quite a brute at times and I don't like the way he talks to my other siblings an' that....I wouldn't mind you know, going away with him (Theseus). I just don't really wanna be around my father...."*

Later when he discovers his daughter has run away with his enemy's son, Theseus.

> **King Minos:** *(angrily)* *"What are you doing Ariadne? I am your father and I have a very big reputation in this country. Why are you leaving?...(softer voice) I just want you back."*

In the myth, the Minotaur is depicted as not quite human, with the head and animal instincts of a bull. The 'monster' and his offences have been imprisoned in the dark damp isolation of the labyrinth, out of sight.

Ariadne: *"Oh him. He lives far away. We don't really like talking about him……He hasn't got a life. He can't live out in the community. He needs to be killed. I don't care if he's flesh and blood..he needs to go. My family need to be rid of him…"*

Interestingly, when improvising, the patients use 'forensic' language that is familiar to them, and are also able to express their own reticence about talking about their past or their family.

> *"Ariadne I don't really wanna talk about my family. I like it to be a bit hush hush.."*

Family reunion and subsequent loss are explored through the narrative. Theseus, reunited with his father, King Aegeus, spoke of it as "a joyful moment", and unprompted related it to meeting his own father after many years in care. The reunion gives Aegeus an opportunity in his role to be 'joyful', and reminded me that this patient has a son whom he hasn't seen for more than 20 years. Watching this moment back on film, he also spoke about his daughter, who used to visit, but has recently stopped.

In order to enter the labyrinth, confront the Minotaur and get back safely, Theseus must seduce his instinctive and intuitive anima (Stevens 1990, p. 206), here in the form of Ariadne, who offers the clew (clue) of golden thread. Ariadne also needs Theseus to get away from home. In the dramatherapy enactment, this courtship was improvised freely and developed a style more appropriate to the streets of East London than Ancient Greece.

Ariadne : *"I thought he was gorgeous, I really did…..He says he's gonna take me out. He wants me to run away wiv him an' marry him (sighs)"*

Theseus: *"You are so beautiful. Your hair is as fine as silk. Now, how am I going to get to this Minotaur. Do you think you can help?"*

In the individual session there was an opportunity to play both the protecting hero Theseus and the half human Minotaur; roles were interchanged with the therapist. On the ward, the patient's internal victim and perpetrator appeared to coexist, but were usually expressed separately. At times, he appeared to idealise himself and other offenders for having the power and then other times denigrate himself and others as being victims or passively compliant. In dramatherapy, he recognised his own chaotic and disinhibited monster, *"My monster..can be very rude, very violent, very obnoxious and it can upset people. It can be frightening…especially for me.."* but also his 'ideal' hero, *"Theseus is very good looking…big muscles..and he likes to help the elderly…"*

There was a tendency to minimise the violence of his offending, as if he was a naughty child.

> *"I've been called a monster to my face many a time,*
> *especially when I was a kid".*

In this version of the myth, Theseus used Ariadne to find his way, and then abandons her on an island. Ariadne was able to express her feelings of rage at being used sexually and then abandoned, without losing face.

> **Ariadne:** *"Theseus! You bastard! I can't believe you've done this to me!..I feel cheap. Absolutely cheap!"*

Later, in his rush to get home and receive a hero's welcome, Theseus forgets his promise to change the funereal black sails to white on the journey home. King Aegeus, white haired and waiting, sees the black sails and believes his son Theseus to be dead.

> **Aegeus:** *"Oh..what have I done".*

Through this role, the patient playing Aegeus was able to access feelings of despair that he can identify with his own mental health breakdown, offence and long incarceration. There was a gravitas to his role as he acted falling to his death on the beanbags in the dramatherapy room. He lay on a cushion for a moment before he was assisted to his feet marking the end of the enactment. The group applauded each other. The patient playing Aegeus looked different somehow, as if something heavy had shifted. He has since moved to the low-secure unit.

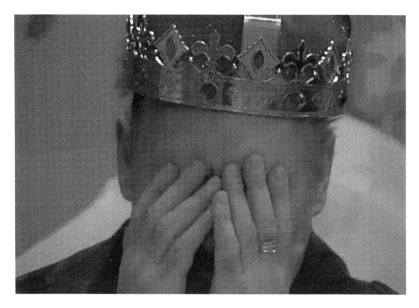

Fig. 3: What have I done?

*"Roles do not emerge from the self, but the self
may emerge from roles"*

(Moreno 1993, p. 13)

When asked about their experience of dramatherapy, the patients said:

*"It has helped me, I must admit. It's got me to talk about my
offences openly", "It's helped me to use characters to explore
how I'm feeling and to really get a deeper understanding of
myself...having a chance to act out that character and ...gain
knowledge about another person and apply it to yourself"*

*"I started to have a bit more confidence in myself and it just
made me feel more happier.......It made me in touch with
different emotions, I didn't think I could come out with
them things. I didn't think it was possible to have them
emotions myself...but acting them made me realise that,
yes, I do have them emotions"*

"What have I done.. I suppose"

Enactments of stories and myths in dramatherapy sessions can offer an experience to explore life's journeys and upheavals from a distance. Even if our patients are unable or unwilling to verbally express their processes during dramatherapy, the work with the unconscious continues through the metaphor in the hope that eventually this will be internalised by the patient.

Watching a film of the enactment can offer a larger symbolic frame where the threads of old memories can be stirred, new meanings can emerge. Once the unspeakable has been spoken and witnessed, it must be taken good care of by the therapist/editor. Then, there is the potential to weave a new transformative tale.

"The worst is not. So long as we can say, "This is the worst.""

(Edgar, King Lear, Act 4 Scene 1)

REFERENCES

Madeleine Anderson-Warren and Robert Grainger (2000) 'Self Disclosure and Disguise' Practical Approaches to Dramatherapy. The Shield of Perseus. London Jessica Kingsley Publishers.

Aiyegbusi A. (2009) The Nurse-Patient Relationship with Offenders: Containing the Unthinkable to Promote Recovery. Chapter 1 Therapeutic relationships with offenders. An Introduction to the Psychodynamics of Forensic Mental Health Nursing. Ed. Anne Aiyebusi and Jennifer Clarke-Moore. London. Jessica Kingsley Publishers.

Campbell Joseph (1989) The Power of Myth. Bantam Doubleday Dell Publishing Group.

Casson J (2004) Drama, Psychotherapy and Psychosis. Dramatherapy and Psychodrama with people who hear voices. Hove and New York. Brunner-Routledge.

Craig H and Brannon KH (2002) Superheroes, monsters, and babies: roles of strength, destruction and vulnerability for emotionally disturbed boys. The Arts in Psychotherapy 29. Elsevier.

Cox,M and Thielgaard A. (1987)_Mutative metaphors in psychotherapy: the Aeolian mode: London: Tavistock.

Jim Henson's 'The Storyteller': Greek Myths-season 1 www.tv.com/storyteller-greekmyths/theseus-and-the-minotaur10210

Jennings. S (1990) Dramatherapy with Families,Groups and Individuals. Waiting in the Wings. London Jessica Kingsley Publishers.

Ruszcynski. S. (2008)Thoughts from consulting in secure settings: do forensic institutions need psychotherapy Chapter 5. Gordon.J. & Kirtchuk.G. (Eds) **Psychic Assaults and Frightened Clinicians: Countertransference in Forensic settings**. Karnac Books. London.

Shakespeare W. King Lear Arden Edition 1997 London Metheun.

Moreno J. (1993) Practical Applications of psychodramatic methods. ASGPP ed Adam Blatner

Winnicott. D.W. 1971 'Playing and Reality' Routledge. Taylor and Francis Group.

CHAPTER 15

Acceptance dance: An inquiry into the process of dance movement psychotherapy sessions with young people in custody

ANGELES FIALLO MONTERO

"Well, I'd say it's different coz in jail is a different experience, coz you do usual stuff like Math and English...so to do something like that with such a small group and with new people as well, it's something quite good.... It's a place where you can let out your expression and a lot of energy.... It can help share how you feel and stuff like that as well".

(Thomas)

This chapter draws from a research study completed in September 2011 on the experience of Dance Movement Psychotherapy (DMP) in a Young Offenders Institution (YOI). This project was part of a Master's degree in DMP accredited by Canterbury Christ Church University (CCCU) and Dance Voice, and was presented at FATAG conference in November 2011._Pam Fisher, RDMP and research supervisor, has collaborated in writing this chapter.

I first set foot in the young offenders' institution in my 2nd year DMP placement. After a few sessions I was struck by the level engagement of the young people and the fact that DMP was, in my eyes, 'working' in a prison setting. After witnessing significant positive changes and DMP benefits in individuals - and finding very little literature on this subject - I realised that my own perceptions were not enough to validate this. This inspired me to immerse in a study in this setting. My determination, inspiration and passion for the work helped overcome the lengthy obstacles surrounding ethics and gaining consent. The YOI was very supportive and I was grateful for the opportunity practice again there.

The research participants were four males in custody aged sixteen to eighteen, with life sentences. Their wing was chosen by the YOI for practical reasons. Individuals with life sentence are in the institution on a long-term basis, thus, promoting attendance, continuity and easing the consent process, as the YOI have more regular contact with legal guardians. The young people attended voluntarily 1.5 hour weekly DMP group sessions, for fourteen weeks. The actual DMP group consisted of seven clients, but only four had consent granted for inclusion in the study. The DMP sessions were co-facilitated by two dance movement psychotherapists and supported by a Learning Support Assistant (LSA).

The therapeutic model within my practice is based on Carl Rogers' Person-Centred Approach, in addition to a variety of DMP interventions. Rogers' (1951;1961) believed that people have the inherent ability to reach their own potential. The therapist facilitates the process of growth through a non-directive approach. DMP interventions are adapted to individuals' needs, and sessions evolve as a creative process. The Person-Centred Approach is acknowledged as valuable for adolescents, offering acceptance, enabling sense of self (McFerran 2010), encouraging healthy relationships (Prever 2010), and in young offenders, reducing reoffending by enhancing "self-perception" and interpersonal skills (Hopwood 2007).

The research

The study design was qualitative, aligning with my therapeutic approach: an ethnographic perspective was taken, observing the DMP group in context of a prison setting and focusing on participants' experience.

Data collection methods included clinical observations, a reflective journal, client feedback, and interviews with integration of creative interventions to support individuals' feedback and engagement, offering alternative mediums to express themselves. I co-facilitated the DMP sessions, having the dual role of practitioner-researcher.

Subjectivity and biases of my dual role were considered through the reflective journal.

Being a high risk environment, security measures included the therapists undertaking specialised training, an LSA present at all times, corridors being constantly patrolled, an itemised list of props on entering the establishment, risk assessments, provision of a safe environment and clinical/research supervisions. In the first DMP session, confidentiality and the group's welfare were discussed.

As participants were in custody and mostly underage, gaining consent required very specific procedures to protect their interests, including going through an Ethics Committee and parental/legal guardian's consent. Throughout this chapter, confidentiality is maintained, withdrawing personal-identifiable information.

Finally, although the participants were under a life sentence, their sentence or causes of offending were not the focus or remit of this study, and thus are not considered.

The group

Session attendance averaged four/six clients. Group dynamics and participation varied from session to session. Especially at the beginning, there was a general sense of chaos, not listening, testing boundaries and issues of trust. Individuals seemed to take turns "to be disruptive". This peaked at session five; suddenly from then onwards, behaviours de-escalated, moving towards a sense of group cohesion.

Different influential factors were perceived: clients teasing or testing boundaries versus therapists trying to 'impose' session rules, lack of trust in peers and facilitators, lack of understanding or being uncomfortable with the process, not listening, boredom, attention-seeking and the room being too small for the group. (The sessions took place in a small First Aid classroom not purpose-built for therapy).

Another frequent theme, especially initially, was clients' assertion that sessions were "boring" and repetitive, thus questioning their purpose. Originally, my colleague and I responded to this by offering a variety of interventions, but soon after, this was taken back to the clients encouraging them to have ownership and responsibility of the session's content.

Movement observation is an important aspect of DMP practice. Some key observations were that clients were mostly against the edges or walls, "as if needing the solidness to support them". Each individual stayed throughout the session mostly in one place, coming back after moving around, and returning to it the following session, almost like a designated "school desk". There was little travelling around, unless this was instructed or in order to choose props/music, however, clients would leave their spot to sit next to another peer.

At times, clients found it difficult to stand, often sitting on chairs or floor, especially during the warm-up. It was "as if their bodies were weighted or something was pulling them down. I wondered if this was tiredness, or feeling emotional?" Also they seemed to struggle with stillness or quietness, especially when lying down in relaxation.

The clients engaged more in dance/movement within structure: for instance, the warm-up, which was led by a therapist, and 'pass-the-move' where everyone contributed movements. However, some individuals followed the warm-up with very little effort or used their own movements. At times, from an extreme of not wanting to dance clients shifted to dancing alone as if unaware of doing so. For instance, Thomas wiggling his hips at the edge of the room, Edward dancing on the chair to Grease, or the whole group moving in a travelling warm-up.

Choreographed dance also enabled engagement in movement and creation of steps, involving group and peer work, cognitive skills and use of touch with partners, e.g. clapping hand, interlocking arms to spin. The music/props, mostly chosen by them, also encouraged dancing.

Session 9:

> *People were in partners mirroring each other, wearing masks. Thomas was doing mime-like moves using his hands and body. Sebastian was completely still and was only moving his eyes, rolling them sideways and using different eye gestures. Edward was leading and following movement, really going for it. From the corner of my eye, I witnessed Alan and another client working together in unison as identical mirror-images.*

In this instance they moved without structure. A change in movement range was noticed, especially in Alan and his partner who often presented themselves as self-conscious.

DMP being a creative process, the content was different each week. Despite not sharing in depth or refusing to work on specific shared emotions (anger, for example), emotional meaning behind the story-telling, role-play, sculptures and games was noticed.

Examples of 'puppets stories' were:

- A crocodile sad and without money, robbing from the cow, the judge-lion being

- concerned about crocodile's offending future, so he is sent to an island for life.

- A lonely duck, without love.

- Around Christmas, a story had a Christmas wish for freedom.

- Towards the end, two different groups brought stories involving characters being killed and betrayed.

Mostly, they articulated, shared and created more when practising in a small group than when performing stories to the whole group. From my interpretation, the stories narrated their path to prison (crocodile), loneliness, lack of affection/love/physical contact (duck) and desire for freedom (Christmas wish). The last stories brought not only their past, but thoughts about death and betrayal.

Body sculptures, created by individuals putting the group into body-shapes, involved group work, engagement, creativity, humour, touch, verbal/non-verbal domains and empowerment to create something. It included a variety of themes, for example 'anger', 'happy' and 'horny'. Sexual innuendo emerged in clients' movement, suggestions and role-play/stories, i.e. *"Thomas asking to act horny when naming emotions for statues"*. The therapists saw a hidden message of lack of physical contact/affection, further evidenced by Edward's suggestion of *"hugs and kisses"* as a theme. Possibly this was due to the fact that the therapists were young women and the clients were locked-in without any contact. The therapists' clinical supervision identified this as a channel for clients' transference but also them being 'childlike'. In early sessions it was difficult to respond to this, but over time the therapists incorporated it into the process, making adjustments and generally responding with humour.

At points, individuals would take a hat/fabric/wig and randomly dress up, becoming something else. One session, as suggested by a client, the group role-played 'Take me out' (TV dating programme). Roles were reversed, my co- therapist role-played the man and *'suddenly'* three clients volunteered to play female roles, dressing-up, adopting female-like posture and voice:

> *They seemed to be having fun, and everyone was involved, even those watching. It actually felt safer and more appropriate to reverse roles.*

(Session-9)

Young people's interviews

The interviews were done towards the end of the 14 weeks. These were individual, audio-recorded, led by myself, and with the LSA present taking a non-participatory role. The interviews were semi-structured to enable flexibility and were guided by a set of questions (slightly different for staff). I had previously noticed short concentration spans and literacy difficulties in young offenders. Hence, in addition to the interview questions, I asked participants to express their experience of DMP through drawing and movement.

Edward

In the session, Edward was particularly drawn to dressing up and music, becoming "MR DJ". Edward described his DMP experience as *"good"*, *"interesting"*, *"different/unusual"* in comparison to prison activities and *"taking his mind off things"*. He felt *"more in-tune, chilled out and ready to take on the day"* after each session and overall: *"changed his attitude. In the way I go about things you know, overall behaviour, more relaxed when I go back to the wing"*.

Edward believed sessions were "easy" because he could choose to take part or watch and mentioned statues, dancing and games as engaging without thinking about it. I witnessed Edward sitting out, then suddenly joining in:

> Edward told us on arrival that he wouldn't do any dancing today but watch. Suddenly, he is dancing in his own space, dressed-up in a fabric. He fed-back: 'I couldn't help it, I needed to join in'
>
> **(Session-2)**

This was also pinpointed by Jacqui (LSA) and Helen (co-therapist) in their interviews. During Edward's interview I asked him about withdrawing from the warm-up:

> Were you finding that part difficult or was it that you needed some space?
> "I wanted to chill to be honest... last lesson of the day, you know, I just wanted to relax".

On reflection, Helen and I witnessed him needing to find his own space within a 'safe container' and participate in his own time, thus self-regulating. One occasion, "Edward was curled up in the chair, as a cocoon, eyes closed". (Session-10).

Edward saw DMP as fitting well in prison, bringing a routine change, being different from other YOI activities:

> "It's good to do something different, something fresher, creative, relaxed, chilled, maybe, you know, do some moves, and talk about things as well....about what you want to do in the session as well."

Edward took from sessions "a lot of love and warmth", noticing a change in the group, bonding together and expressing themselves:

> "You can notice the change from when I first came in... now, you know, everyone is doing what they are doing, suddenly dressing up like women. That wouldn't have happened on

the first session, you know what I mean? ...No one is going to laugh at them."

This illustrated my perception of Edward as being observant and aware of others; during one session in which everyone engaged throughout, he commented, *"Everyone was participating, no one was sitting out at one point."* (Session-11)

Edward defined DMP as *"a course to express yourself, relate to other people, how they feel, how emotions and music connected"*, *"probably I will bore you to death by talking too much about it."*

Then Edward asked about the funding situation, seeming interested in DMP's future. He advised to *"try other prisons"* too as *"different people will react different"*, and justified that *"it was a good course"*:

> *"Obviously, you might have some people sitting, you are not going to change them, they are criminals it makes no difference, but honestly it works, will help you with it."*

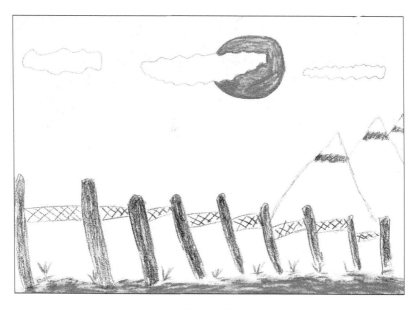

Image 1

Lastly, Edward drew a detailed landscape with mountains/countryside and the sun shining *"at noon"* (see Image 1). When asked, he said the drawing did not represent sessions. Yet the effort and focus witnessed in his drawing and the picture's peacefulness and warmth reflected his meditative and participatory states in sessions.

Alan

DMP was something new to Alan, *"a different way to get stress"*, *"unique"* and *"great"*. He took away skills learnt in sessions, which helped him to relax. He told me he played his own music back in his cell. In sessions, he engaged well with the relaxation:

> *Lying down with his head against the ball, with a sense of relaxation/contentment in his facial expression.*

> **(Session-3)**

Alan identified feeling calmer and explained that he had had *"Panic Attacks"* and *"bad images in his head"* for instance, worry that something would happen to his family. DMP enabled him to *"get rid of the images"* and *"feel more positive"*. Alan seemed to be in search of self-management, acknowledging that he talked to someone or engaged in leisure activities when stressed.

Alan found drama, role-play and props accessible, helping him get into role,

> *When we use the props for the acting, you don't think about the acting…or the props and the statues, like when I was pretending to be a pregnant lady.*

He added that games and fancy-dress helped by involving and amusing the group, *"The wigs were a laugh. It helps to have a bit of a joke… looking at everyone having fun, that was good."*

Alan was the only interviewee who identified something challenging:*"It's difficult to get involved when no one was getting involved."* He felt when people sat back he didn't want to take part by himself, thus holding him back. He also saw this as disrespectful towards the therapist and the research itself. Generally he was the one joining in most, yet seemingly self-conscious when moving, e.g. during 'Strictly Come Dancing' role-play:

Alan had volunteered to dance but after decided he wouldn't as "he can't dance". I wonder if he realised what he had signed up for and felt self-conscious. He was the only boy standing, maybe he decided to copy the others.

(Session-10)

Alan expressed struggling with *"getting an honest answer out of people"*, specifying the *"check in"* where people were not sharing how they really felt and he could see this in their body language, thus could not express himself. He perceived the session's effectiveness to be dependent on group cooperation, participation and honesty.

Alan was observed by Helen and Jacqui as absorbed in thoughts, introverted, *"self-conscious"* in his movement, yet creative, bringing ideas, always having a go, *"cooperative"*, *"wanting to be a good-boy"*, and engaging mostly with games, balls and drawing.

DMP fitted well with his prison life. *"It gets the courtroom out of my head"* and *"makes a difference"* feeling treated as *"a person not a prisoner"*, thus restoring his *"self-esteem"* and *"confidence"*. Alan struggled to focus in Gym training but believed DMP *"helped"*. *"The dance gets through that subject that is in my head blocking me off to do anything, it helps a lot"* overall, to get by and prepare for life/future.

He took and used from DMP "relaxing", "listening to music" and "stretching out to loosen up own body". He also mentioned the bouncy ball and creating statues with themes about "what people liked". He describes DMP as:

"....you don't really have to share what that problem is, you do random things to take the problem away like when I started I thought we're going to talk about why I'm upset and what I think about my situation. It was completely different. It was fun and really good to do and it does help you a lot to bond with people."

He mentioned two group members in his wing and gym, previously not getting along with them, *"taking the piss out of him"*, being competitive and having arguments/disagreements. Gradually, through the sessions their relationship improved, enhancing communication and "*working together*", noticing this outside sessions too and becoming less distrustful.

Alan made a disclosure during the interview (details were withdrawn to maintain confidentiality). This disclosure was made when the LSA had to leave the room, briefly. Alan's disclosure was not relevant to the DMP session, or part of the interview questions, yet he shared it with me. From this, and also observed in the sessions, there seems to be a longing for one-to-one interaction in these boys.

Alan considered therapists being "*good*":

> "*Coz they don't tell you what to do, they are there to help you on what you wanna do. They don't say 'we are going to do this', they get you involved, doing some stretches, 'do you have any stretches or moves you want to do?' It's not like you lot plan the session, we do it. It's a good way to cooperate.*"

Alan explained that in contrast with lessons where the teacher gives instructions, in DMP "*We do the work, we say what we want and you listen in a way that can help us.*" He summarised this with "*it takes two to tango, like we both work together*".

Alan drew the process from a bad day a "*dark night*", a bare tree and person crying "*to a good day*", "*sunny, clouds are out, birds on the tree, apples growing*" and a person smiling (*see Image 2*). He named it "*Motivation*", "*most days are like the bad day, but after the session it's good*", DMP "*is the sun*". He finished with laughter and clapping sounds and showing a stretch representing relief gain from DMP.

Overall, the interview process mirrored the therapy sessions, clients shared more as interviews progressed, needing time to access; some engaged or talked more during the creative task. For instance, when Sebastian's interview finished, the LSA asked him about the session and he began sharing more, making sentences rather than monosyllables.

I noticed interviews having an impact on subsequent sessions, I felt more empathic towards the clients, understanding their needs better and communication eased. Overall, I felt moved witnessing from their eyes, not just mine, what they had gained from the DMP sessions.

Image 2

Staff interviews

Jacqui's (LSA) experience was *"completely different"* from her work in prison and a change for her, as she usually supports lessons rather than physical activities. She had assisted the previous DMP group I ran in the YOI, thus was familiar with the process. She expressed DMP being *"brilliant"*, *"inspiring and thought provoking"*, saying how it was *"good"* supporting something that promoted *"feeling more like themselves"*, and seeing clients change and enjoy the sessions.

Helen (co-therapist) expressed that it took six weeks to get into the sessions and *"build rapport/relationship"* with clients. *"I became more with it and I think they did as well"*. Helen viewed the first seven weeks *"to get to know"* clients and the next seven *"to ground them"*, suggesting seven further weeks *"to shift patterns/apply interventions"*. Her experience was *"with the young people and the process"*, noticing shifts and the therapy beginning to flow. However, also she felt *"drained"* and a sense of *"stuckness"* working in that setting, which I identify with. She experienced *"warmth"*, *"enjoying"* working with the clients and *"a sense of nurture"* towards them.

Jacqui identified clients' reluctance to join in but *"as the group went on, people got into it". "They were given the choice"* to participate, at their own pace, but *"there was never anyone…sitting out for the whole session"*, even if they were tired. Neither were there behavioural problems, *"they were not disrespectful", "managed themselves and the environment"*. Jacqui observed a mood and attitude change, seemingly *"happier/cheered up", "relaxed"*, and *"a lot better people"*. They both witnessed humour and enjoyment, Jacqui in *"their body language and facial expression"* and Helen in *"laughing"*, and willingness to attend sessions, returning each week.

Helen perceived DMP for clients as *"a space to let go, be held, socially connect, learn trust", "explore transference/different relationships"* and *"be in the moment"*. She noticed *"the effect that they had on each other"* and the change from competing and teasing each other to a state of trust and group cohesion, similarly Jacqui mentioned clients' "embarrassment" to bring ideas/moves but it *"became a mutual respect/ understanding that they are in the same group/situation"*.

Jacqui believed clients found it easier to access relaxation (with fabrics/feathers/bubbles), whereas Helen witnessed it not fully accessed, *"chatting"* and *"dissociating"*; Jacqui considered the chatting as *"excitement"*. Helen acknowledged occasional intimacy/ engagement when introducing props. For Helen the session's middle part was easier, as clients made choices, becoming empowered, and perceived the story-telling, sculptures and games *"more grounding"* than when dancing/moving. Jacqui added they enjoyed "dancing together", dressing- up and masks, becoming *"a different character"* other than an offender, *"made them feel and act differently"*.

The 'check in' was *"alien to them, difficult to bring deep meaning (Helen)"* and *"unsure of what to say (Jacqui)"*. Yet often it was the time when they shared most emotions, occasionally going in-depth, i.e. Thomas expressing feeling lost like 'Nemo', and after the session *"not feeling lost anymore"*. Dancing alone was identified as embarrassing for them and the clients. Yet, Jacqui believed nothing was *"beyond people's capabilities"* and Helen that the group had grown *"comfortable to say no"*.

Both described DMP in prison as fitting well and *"different"*, as sessions were held by external people, the *"boys"* seemed particularly drawn to these being women. Jacqui mentioned various programmes available at the YOI as part of their sentence. Whereas those programmes are mandatory to address their crimes, in DMP they chose what they shared, attending voluntarily, giving them *"an identity"* other *"than being a prisoner, a number or a green uniform"*. She saw DMP for a lifer as *"a Bonus"*, *"help them cope"* and *"interact with others"*. Jacqui's views came from a non DMP or psychotherapy background, yet she understood its value in prison.

Helen believed fourteen weeks too short for a lifer, having *"deep wounds"* and unmet needs, thus needing *"a stable/ongoing therapeutic relationship"*. She represented DMP in prison in her drawing (*see Image 3*), titled: *"Inside I'm dancing"*, illustrating a house with an unfinished door *"not being able to get out"*, *"being inside body/head"*, green uniform and bars representing being in prison and blue elastic representing the session.

Image 3

Findings

The initial research question was: How does the experience of Dance Movement Psychotherapy affect young people in custody?

However, further questions emerged for me:

How DMP was accessed in prison; DMP benefits to young offenders; clients' perception of DMP; supporting staff's views on sessions and clients; difficulties/accessibility or likes/dislikes in session content; how DMP and person-centred approach fitted within a custodial setting and whether this approach met the clients' needs.

The findings answered some of these questions as follows:

1. Person-centred approach fundamentals were acknowledged: individuals being met as person "not prisoner" (acceptance), having opportunities to choose (client-led), "warmth and love" (empathy), the therapists' roles/interventions constantly shifting to meet clients' needs (unconditional-positive regard).

2. The clients benefited from DMP sessions, gaining: Individually: self-expression, changes in self, mood/ behaviour enhancement, release of tensions, self-management/regulation, empowerment, self-esteem/ confidence, self-worth, sense of self, in addition to addressing particular issues (i.e. panic attacks). As a group: group cohesion, teamwork, bonding, social learning, awareness of others, enhanced healthy relationship with each other and trust.

Encapsulating these, DMP enabled personal growth and well-being.

3. A variety of group dynamics: individuals affecting each other, an ever-changing process, going from testing boundaries, chaos to group cohesion, bonding and trust; from reluctance to joining in, to sudden participation; lack of ideas versus vast creativity; not using the space/ dancing versus dancing alone or in group.

Often individuals struggled with participation, dancing alone, in-depth sharing, working directly on issues/emotions and quiet/stillness in relaxation. However, dancing together within a structure or group, role-play, storytelling, games, thematic sculptures, and the use of props were accessed well and there was willingness to attend sessions.

4. Art/dance/movement/drama were used as alternative means of communication and metaphor/symbolism.

5. The research evidenced that clients needed to unwind/disconnect from prison life, explore projection/transference, relate to other people, enjoy/play, experience affection, be witnessed/accepted, have one-to-one interaction, experience group/peers container, have ongoing/long term therapy and complementary support.

6. Within a custodial setting, DMP in prison offers innovation, creativity and focuses on the person rather than the crime thus differing from other prison's activities/programmes. DMP offers individuals a routine change, a break from being prisoners, support with managing prison life and their sentence which for a 'lifer can be long, preparing them for the future, yet it may not be suitable for all individuals.

I cannot deny that there is a need to address crime and offending behaviour, yet I believe that first we must look at the individual as a whole, including emotional, physical, cognitive and social aspects in order to establish trust and enable changes. Smeijsters et al. (2011) identify that arts psychotherapists access a "deeper personal level" by focusing on arts process and products instead of offending behaviours. For Alan, being accepted as person not a prisoner gave him self-esteem and confidence; this correlates with Smeijsters et al.'s (2011: 42) beliefs that "self-esteem increases learning ability, empowerment, and the competence to change life" and that "focusing only on changing criminal behaviour is not successful if self-esteem is not addressed".

7. In general, DMP was perceived as unusual, different,
a place to share feelings, let go, make choices, use
a variety of themes, ideas, props, use energy, fun/
humour, creativity, play and imagination, as a space
to let go/unwind, disconnect from prison life, explore
projection/transference and socially interact.

Limitation, implications and conclusion

This study was prone to influence by the researcher's bias, which was
acknowledged throughout. However, I was as transparent as possible,
not imposing answers and taking a neutral role in interviews.

Regarding limitations, the study's time scale allowed only fourteen
weeks of DMP sessions, limiting observations and findings in research
context and the growth process in therapy. Thus, it is recommended
both for future research and DMP practise in YOI to assign at least
twelve weeks, in order to establish rapport with clients/participants
and observe changes. Secondly, more data/themes emerged than the
dissertation scope. I recognized six interviews being too ambitious.

The evidence showed the potential value of ongoing therapy,
especially with 'lifers', in addition the interview process recognized
the value of one-to-one interactions, thus one-to-one sessions
alongside group or occasionally meeting clients individually to talk
about the process or issues is recommended. Furthermore, this study
acknowledges the need for further DMP research in specified sectors,
life sentence vs. short sentence, pre/post-imprisonment work, female
YOI, focusing on reduction of offending/re-offending and mental
health/learning difficulties.

For me the highlight of the findings was participants valuing
and being aware of the person-centred approach. Illustrating this, in
a supervision session, my clinical supervisor asked me whether the
clients understood the person-centred model. I believe the answer to
this is yes. From the findings, it is evident that the clients, although
not naming the approach as such, viewed the process as client-led,
because of sessions not being planned, having opportunities to make
choices and experience the conditions of empathy, acceptance and
unconditional regard, thus acknowledging their benefits. This approach

corroborates with the HMP statement of purpose: "Our duty is to look after them with humanity" (Teasdale 2002, section 3).

Within the psychotherapy context, although deep emotions were not directly explored or articulated, non-verbal meanings emerged in the use of dance, movement, art, drama, props, music and creative process, as symbolism and metaphor. The process identified individuals' needs for affection, being witnessed/accepted, one-to-one interaction, group/peers container, ongoing/long-term therapy and complementary support. Group dynamics, process, participation and engagement were constantly shifting, each session being unique, as illustrated by both Payne (1988) and Seibel (2008).

The evidence also verifies my ontology of human capacity to change, demonstrating changes in the client-participants; the influence of 'inner' realities, environment and other participants to affect a change process as illustrated in individual, group processes and therapeutic relationship. The uniqueness of individuals was highlighted, each interviewee bringing different perspectives, for instance DMP helped Alan's expressed difficulties in getting involved, Edward noticed group changes.

In conclusion, this inquiry has shared insights of the DMP process in a male YOI, demonstrating its efficacy, identifying therapeutic benefits and values for young offenders, additionally giving them an opportunity to experience DMP and a voice to express their views. I hope this study can inform, inspire and benefit DMP practitioners, arts psychotherapists and other professionals working in this setting. On a personal level, I undertook this research with great passion and commitment, thus I feel highly rewarded by the participants' willingness and perceptions of DMP.

"It does make a difference coz you are treated as a person not a prisoner. Therapy made something good out of bad days, into a good day, motivation to keep it a good day, so I think it's good."

(**Alan**)

REFERENCES

Hopwood, B., 2007. Locked in. *Therapy Today*, 18(3).

McFerran, K., 2010. *Adolescents, music and music therapy.*
London & Philadelphia: Jessica Kingsley.

Payne, H., 1988. The Practice of Dance Movement Therapy
with Male Adolescents labelled delinquent. In I.K. Glaister,
ed. *Young people dancing : an international perspective / fourth
international conference of Dance and the Child International.
Vol.2, Dance in special education and dance as therapy.* London:
Roehampton Institute.

Prever, M., 2010. *Counselling and supporting children and
young people: a person-centred approach.* London: Sage.

Rogers, C., 1951. *Client-Centered Therapy.* 2003rd ed.
Constable & Robinson.

Rogers, C., 1961. *On becoming a Person: The therapist's view of
psychotherapy.* New York; Boston: Houghton Mifflin Company.

Seibel, J., 2008. Behind the gates: Dance/movement therapy
in a women's prison. *American journal of dance therapy*, 30(2),
pp.106-09.

Smeijsters, H. et al., 2011. Arts therapies for young offenders
in a secure setting: apractice-based research. *The Arts in
Psychotherapy, Vol.* 38, pp.41-51.

Teasdale, C., ed., 2002. *Guidelines for arts therapists working
in prison.* Reprinted and Updated ed. Prisoner's Learning and
skills unit, Department for Education and Skills.

FURTHER READING

Davis, R., 2008. Stage set for performers with a past.
Community Care, (1751), pp.16-17.

Dunphy, K., 1999. A creative arts performance program for
incarcerated women. *The Arts in Psychotherapy*, 26(1), pp.35-43.

Goodison, L. & Schafer, H., 1999. Drug addiction therapy:
A dance to the music of time. *The Health service journal*,
109(5677), pp.28-29.

Ling, F., 1983. In touch with self - in touch with others. *Prison Services Journal*, (51), pp.18-20.

Milliken, R., 2002. Dance/movement therapy as a creative arts therapy approach in prison to the treatment of violence. *The Arts in Psychotherapy*, 29.

Payne, H., 1999. The Use of Dance Movement Therapy with Troubled Youth. In C. Schaefer, ed. *Innovative psychotherapy techniques in child and adolescent therapy*. 2nd ed. New York & Chichester: Wiley.

Silberman, L., 1973. A dance movement therapist's experience working with disturbed adolescent boys in a city prison hospital. In *Dance therapist in dimension: depth diversity. Proceedings of the eigth annual conference ADTA*. Kansas, 1973. American Dance Therapy Association.

Winnicott, D., 1984. *Deprivation and delinquency*. London & New York: Tavistock.

CHAPTER 16

Rage, resistance and repulsion; grappling to find hope

JENNY WOOD AND REBECCA JOHNS

n this chapter we demonstrate, through three case examples, how traumatised service users' have impacted upon our personal and professional selves, drawing on attachment theory and a systemic view that everything is connected and interdependent and 'a change in one part has an effect on another part' (Rivett and Street 2009, p. 7). We show how our personal narratives, family scripts and attachment relationships shaped who we are, and how this influences the relationship with service users, both consciously and unconsciously, and how influences on our behaviour continue beyond the therapy room. Exposure to emotional projections from service users who have internalised rage, who resist our intervention and who repulse and challenge our inner belief systems and core identity beg us to question why we choose to work with another's pain, and where does our resilience come from to sustain us in the role?

There has been an influx of literature advocating the value of attachment theory in forensic settings in the last decade. It has been used as a useful tool in understanding difficulties associated with long-term dependency relationships involving both care and control (Adshead 2004); to understand the interpersonal dynamic that occurs between staff and mentally disordered offenders, highlighting how service users' early attachment relationships shape expectations of current caregivers, which has implications as behaviours often enact familiar abusive attachment patterns (Aiyegbusi 2004); and to support the supervision and management of staff affected by the projections of services users, sometimes triggering staff's unresolved trauma, possibly even connecting with their personal narrative of abuse (Aiyegbusi and Tuck 2006). Aiyegbusi and Tuck (2006) highlight deficits in preparing staff to work with the emotional demands of forensic service users who employ the primary defences of splitting and projection, and communicate their distress through physical impact (Casement 1985) They advocate exploring attachment relationships within recruitment processes and supervision structures to identify and support staff narratives.

Art psychotherapists are generically prepared to work in different settings with individuals acutely disturbed by their inner turmoil, but is enough done to explore would-be therapist's attachment narratives and, in particular, examining what draws us to the profession? Personal therapy and self-reflexivity is common practice in many psychological training programmes. However, I (Wood) found a feature of systemic family therapy training particularly helpful, which demands personal examination of trans-generational attachment relationships, cultural genograms and family scripts. Implicit to our functional role is an awareness of who we are and where we come from in order for us to be able to effectively use transference and counter-transference within the therapeutic encounter, and also to work empathically with service users. It is also important that we are aware of our own vulnerabilities, capabilities, prejudices and biases, and acknowledge that we, like our service users, continue to be challenged in the here-and-now by everyday relationships and stresses (Rivett and Street 2009).

Working with service users who have a violent background challenges the psyche of therapists and to think about it in any detail can generate unease. We encountered a dilemma as we began writing of how much to reveal of ourselves and of our service users in this very public forum. We became aware of the extent at which service users get under our skin and of the strategies we employ to blank out and protect ourselves from the unspeakable and unthinkable. Our clinical practice has evolved over the last 20 years, with changes in the National Health Service (UK) and legislation, in family and occupational structures and systems, and advances in information technology, the sciences and clinical research. This has inevitably impacted upon both our personal and professional selves, and we necessarily have adapted our clinical practice to meet service demands and current trends. Within our role as art psychotherapists, we have supported service users equally affected by changes such as the closure of low-secure units in favour of community-based therapeutic programmes. We have necessarily adjusted to an economic decline, which has seen job cuts, and service redesigns, whereby psychological therapies posts have been merged under different roles and guises. In order to survive these processes we have necessarily adapted our skill set to work within multi-agencies. Consequence to this is that we are privileged to work across a broad age spectrum, but with this, we are challenged by knowledge and a degree of fear for our younger service users who have the predisposition of risk factors pertaining to acts of violence and offending behaviours.

Adshead (2004) reports research findings suggesting that developmental consequences of early childhood trauma may contribute to identifying the psychopathology of violence in individuals. Insecure attachments in the early years influence the child's development of theory of mind (Fonagy and Target 1997). Violent individuals have also been shown to demonstrate inadequate capacity to mentalise, with deficits in recognising "that their own and others' reactions are driven by thoughts, feelings, beliefs and desires" (Fonagy 2004 p. 15). It is such individuals that we find ourselves working with in children's and adult learning disability services. Our case examples' narratives are commonly linked by experiences of insecure early attachment, having witnessed violence in their early lives, absent fathers, and having followed a path of criminality; they are challenged by internal struggles with strong emotions such as anger and shame.

Intense emotions projected by service users will make connections with our own attachment representations, and may even generate a trauma response if the experience so overwhelms our adaptive coping capacities or connects with unprocessed trauma. It is for this reason that we must be aware of our own family scripts, our gendered roles within our own family systems and other childhood experiences that have created our adult held view, so that we remain congruent with ourselves in the therapy room (Rivett and Street 2009).

Working with rage

Peter was in his early 50s, with a long history of institutionalised care and locked environments, when I (Johns) began work with him. His rage in his 30s was so great that he caused serious physical harm to staff, often hospitalising them. He was initially detained under Section 47 (Mental Health Act 1983) in a medium, then low-secure unit. He has recently stepped down into a rehabilitation unit with a view to move him on into the community, which has compromised the psychological and physical security that he experienced from the psychic structure of containment of locked doors and high fences (Adshead 2004). When I began work with him, he was placed under "long term segregation" (Chapter 15.63, Code of Practice) and we were separated by a boundary of a counter worktop, which spanned the room. Most interactions with staff were via this divide, and there were occasions when he would cross this boundary and attack staff. His unpredictability created an anxiety in staff, which could be sensed in their manner of approach with him. As the recovery process commenced, the boundaries, which had psychologically contained him, began to reduce. This troubled him as he continued to distrust the rage within himself. I had heard of, but not witnessed his rage directly, but was aware of his capacity to break limbs and rip off heavy duty fire doors from their hinges. Peter highly respected and valued our relationship through the mutual interest and pleasure in art, and there was a sense that he did his utmost to hide his shameful rage, not wishing for it to spill out and contaminate our relationship. He was extremely talented in drawing and in capturing his subject entirely from his imagination, with tremendous detail and astonishing accuracy. His creative resources came from his love of popular culture of the 60s, pop stars, cartoon characters, historical events and films, and were depicted on canvas boards using a black biro, gripped tightly and applied with pressure, like an engraver would do when dry pointing onto his plate. Peter distrusted himself to apply paint to his drawings, owing to self inflicted damage to his arms, which restricted movement and dexterity to hold a paintbrush. Not wishing to "mess up" his skilfully drawn images, he would ask me to apply paint under his direction, which generated a sense of being controlled by Peter.

We progressed to work across a table in his lounge, with an open door and staff near to hand, when one day, out of the blue, I was to witness an outburst of his rage. It was a direct physical assault, with a blow to the head from his fist and verbal abuse, which left us both at a complete loss after five years working together. I had believed I was attuned to tell tale signs of change in his mental states, such as rapid flickering in his eyes, and felt angry and ashamed that I had failed to notice on this occasion. It left me shocked to suddenly find myself at the sharp end of Peter's rage, undermining a long and enduring relationship. I felt overwhelmed by my emotions, as the experience shattered my illusion of safety and triggered an influx of existential dread (Mollon 2002). Trauma is a Greek word for 'wound', and there are many levels of trauma, often misunderstood to only relate to experiences such as abuse or global disaster. I certainly felt wounded and fearful as I suddenly came face to face with my own vulnerability. Trauma is experienced subject to an individual's lived experience, our internal working models of the world and our narratives, which informs a response to dangerous situations. Peter's attack evoked an attachment injury, as my expectations of trust were betrayed and I felt immense anger. I punished myself with questions and criticism, and felt exposed to my weaknesses of wanting to be liked as a therapist and to feel valued. In the moment, despite having the intelligence to predict danger, we can become overwhelmed and dismiss the cues presented of potential risks, as we reject the notion of feeling shame. I was driven by an overwhelming wish to be a good enough therapist, influenced externally by organisational dynamics and job insecurities, and internally by personal narratives and family scripts.

Strong emotions and feelings can erupt in any one of us at any time, often without any apparent warning and when we least expect them, unleashing extreme sides to our personality. Fonagy reminds us that we are constantly wishing to avoid "that which is potentially a part of us all" (2004 p. 13). We must be mindful and attentive to those strong emotions that hide deep within us and have some sense of their roots of origin in case they appear within the therapeutic relational dynamic. Beliefs and assumptions about emotions have been both supported and challenged in the last decade with advances in clinical neuroscience research. These have informed greater understandings of emotional affect and empathy, identifying the different areas of the brain, which influence behaviour and emotional response and affirming that a truly holistic view must be taken in order to understand human nature. It is no longer viable to hold a linear position of purely 'cause and effect', as research has revealed that other contributing drivers behind behaviour must also be considered. Researchers at Britain's University of Cambridge reveal how fluctuating serotonin levels in the brain, which can commonly occur when an individual is stressed or hasn't eaten, affect regulating behaviour. Reduction in serotonin levels has demonstrated that it may be more difficult for the prefrontal cortex to control emotional responses to anger, which may suggest why some individuals may be prone to aggression (Passamonti et al 2012). Renowned authors (such as Allan Schore and Daniel Siegel) in recent decades have influenced progressive psychotherapy by integrating growing knowledge of brain science with attachment principles. The quality of early attachment relationships can significantly impact brain and emotional maturation, and social relationships are acknowledged as fundamental in shaping how the brain develops and the way the mind constructs reality, which is significant in understanding the emotions and behaviours presented by our service users. It is through emotion that attachment experiences organise the brain (Siegel 2012). Warner refers to emotion as "a condition provoked or aroused in us" (1986 p. 136) by another, which for the context of this chapter sufficiently serves as a broad description. Human beings are all of the time in communication with one and other, even when we think we are at rest and not communicating, our body language is always projecting onto our external world and the external world is always projecting back. In turn, our responses, which are either conscious or unconscious, are based upon both verbal and non-verbal communications of sensory cues and are informed by our many layers of attachment representations. Rivett and Street suggest we are inclined to forget that "we are always part of something else" (2009 p. 11) and how the self formed in the therapist is equally valid to the self of the service user. Each of these come together for a brief moment in time and are influenced by both here-and-now experiences, such as a conversation held moments before the session with a nurse, and by past experiences and stories lived. Behaviour is a visual representation of communication, expressed by an individual, which is received by others. It is human nature to be inclined to "experience our communications solely as expressions of self" (Rivett and Street 2009 p. 11). Bedford (1986) suggests an inference of emotion being 'inner forces', which may or may not be outwardly represented in behaviours that have become associated with a descriptive word, such as 'anger', but identifies a flaw in using word association which may lead to "a misconception of function" (1986 p. 14). A descriptive word given to an emotion requires a common level of language skill and presupposes everyone holds a similar understanding. In our clinical practice, working with learning disabled adults and young people, we cannot afford the assumption that the service user has the same level of understanding or attributes the same meaning to words associated with different feelings. There is also likely to be a huge disparity in meaning to the experience of the emotion familiarly named as 'rage', between the individual in who rage unfurls and the person onto whom the emotion is expulsed.

It is interesting how we protect ourselves from trauma and so easily forget it. I (Johns) still find it difficult to recall events of Peter's session. Maybe it was my own denial that this could happen between us, especially when there seemed too much at stake (in my mind) to lose. My resilience and desperation to find hope was shaken, and I had to dig deep within my own resources to be able to find the compassion and energy to continue to work with Peter.

Resilience is closely linked with the internal working model (Bowlby 1969), which is individually experienced and generated through early attachment experiences, and provides the basis for adaptive or maladaptive responses to life experiences and events and constructs a perceiving and interpreting self. Central to establishing resilience is having developed insight, the capacity to reflect on our own sensation and make sense of it, and having successfully increased independence, whereby developing the capacity to negotiate separation from others and the ability to create a sense of personal security and space (Cairns 2002). Peter often found it unbearable when he experienced several good days or even weeks in succession, which reinforced the pending separation from our relationship, and indeed the security of what he had come to know as home as his discharge into the community loomed. I remember from my own childhood a saying that I repeated to myself when things were getting tough, which resonated as I reflected on the notion of returning to work with Peter: "If at first you don't succeed try and try again". It is these hidden personal constructs that shape our capacity to respond at such times that we are challenged. My own survival, to endure the emotional and physical pain of the attack, was built upon the quality of our attachment relationship, and the script to "try and try again" was the driver behind my return to work with Peter. In turn, my own resilience demonstrated a tolerance of the shameful side of Peter, which, at some level, modelled capacity to trust, and created opportunity for him to internalise some hope for change.

In order to understand where our own behaviour originates from, we must look to our roots of origin. Systems theory refers to intergenerational family scripts, which are shaped during our development, creating a blueprint that informs us how to behave and respond to different emotional and social contexts throughout our lives (Rivett and Street 2009). It is within this automated process that our resilience is formed, which is comparable to John Bowlby's theory of the internal working model, which is explained in the context of attachment theory and the formation of an individual's relationship to the self, the other and the self and other. Bowlby's (1969, 1973) theory defines the role of relationship with the primary caregiver and explains how experiences are stored in memory and how they begin to map the experiences of relationships for a lifetime. The experiences of the caregiver, their own beliefs, values, needs and their whole ways of being are infused with and become a part of the child's self. As the child develops their own autonomy, influenced by increased exposure to different relationships and experiences, the child learns different ways of regulating emotion and recognising the relevant responses to given situations.

Psychoanalysis, attachment and neuroscience are now finally all on the same page, after dramatic differences in views in the past, with advances in neuro-imaging techniques used in clinical neuroscience research producing evidences significantly influencing psychotherapy practice. Attachment theory is very much in vogue with extensive multi-professional literature now available on the subject. John

Bowlby combined ideas from object relations theory, evolution biology, cognitive neuroscience and systems theory to bring us an integrative model of attachment theory. His contribution to attachment provides a framework to understand emotion regulation in social contexts. It is a human condition to employ attachment strategies, consciously and unconsciously, as a means to survive relational and social experience. Taking a very systemic view, we value a trans-generational perspective of attachment and recognise that human beings naturally organise their experience by narratives. We are who we are today based upon where we come from (lived experiences), and our relational experiences in the here-and-now are influenced by the narratives we have lived. Our internal working model is shaped in attachment representations held in procedural memory (how we do things), sensory memory (sensory modalities e.g. smell, sound etc.), semantic memory (cognition, beliefs, attitudes), and integrative memory (meta-cognition). It seems easier to keep the spotlight on the service user, but we can be inclined to forget that therapists are also driven by personal narratives, beliefs and expectations about behaviour, our own and others, and hold a view of our self. Unconscious processes, self-questioning - "how loveable am I?" - and resistances against failing, all drive a persistence to keep trying again and again. Family scripts "provide the framework on which a person will construct a self-image" (Rivett and Street 2009 p. 24) and will be constructed through memories and everyday communications in the here-and-now, evoking emotional connections with our blueprint and informing how we respond. The notion of feeling valued and accepted by others is further shaken when we find ourselves facing service cut backs, which challenge our resilience and capacity to create a secure base for service users to engage in therapy and to progress and change. Organisational systems often fail to recognise the circular affect that this creates as we are asked to meet targets and outcomes, and yet with little thought or consideration for how fit the therapist actually is to undertake their role - an interesting faux pas. We must be mindful that we are transparent when we enter the therapy space, and just as we become attuned to service user's non-verbal communications, so too will they to ours. We may kid ourselves that we do not show any deflation or low mood, but it is inevitable that at some level we are transmitting communications all of the time which may impact with an adverse emotional response from the service user, for example evoking an anxiety within them.

In our role, we attend to the communication behind a behaviour, gesture, spoken word or mark on paper (or any other expressive form). Art and play embodies powerful feelings and the feelings evoked within the therapist must be separated and identified with rightful ownership between therapist and service user, which as a matter of course is what becomes discussed in clinical supervision. Supervision however has its limitations; it is only as effective as the communication between supervisor and supervisee. The supervisee presents a representation of a moment in time, that is a particular art image or a word spoken by the service user. Inevitably not all of the communications, said and unsaid, are relayed in supervision, and often missed entirely is the effect upon the therapist's internal working model and relational connections with the narratives that *are* the therapists.

Working with resistance

Some contributing factors often found in violent criminals, for example childhood exposure to domestic violence and to media violence, ineffective parenting and academic failure (Fonagy 2004), are sadly familiar backgrounds with the youngsters with whom I (Wood) work. Many young people coming into the specialist care and education provision are Looked after Children on a full care order (Section 30, The Children's Act 1989), with narratives commonly associated with those mentioned above, plus exposure to drugs and alcohol, various forms of abuse, parental separation and numerous service placements. Such individuals are well within their rights to resist risking engaging with and trusting in another adult in the therapist. When a child has been exposed to generally positive experiences, they are more likely to develop a more positive mental schema. However, when a child's experience has been mostly negative and has not successfully internalised necessary emotional processes required to function within societal norms and has also not developed the autonomy of independence; they may become the subject of maladaptive, anti-social behaviours. Adolescence involves conflicts of identity and self-expression, and defence mechanisms are rife which may be mistaken as resistance. As art psychotherapists we may find ourselves grappling to find hope; it is soul destroying to work with youngsters who see no hope for their future.

> *The adolescent is faced with an enormous task, one that can be accomplished only with the experimentation and rebelliousness that have come to be typical of teenage youngsters in our society. When the difficult process of self-definition is understood, the adolescents testing of self and others can be seen as productive and useful.*
>
> **(Greenspoon Linesch 1988, p. 5)**

The term *resistance* should be used with caution, described as the "therapist's error" by De Shazer (1982) who asks us to reframe resistance and to "go along with it". Resistance is commonly used to define the 'difficult to engage' individuals and can serve to justify why a service target has not been achieved, or to validate getting sucked into a premature discharge. It is challenging to stay with resistance as it may challenge professional integrity - "am I a good enough therapist?"- or may challenge the therapist's family script of being the child who did not live up to family expectations (personally or professionally). This can connect with insecure attachment strategies employed to protect from feeling emotions associated with a sense of shame. To resist, for the service user, is to self-preserve and deserves respect.

During an opening assessment session I was met by a short stature of a child, whose physical presentation with head stooped low, did not marry with the violent description I was privy to. Inviting him to tell me a little about himself and how he came to be in therapy he replied: "That's for me to know and for you to find out!" It was true that I entered the session with my own remit, a wish to see this youngster turn his life around, and I hoped that he would let me be a part of sharing that experience. I introduced him to sandplay, which is a useful introductory technique to distance individuals sufficiently from automated resistant dialogue, and can reveal a connection with the inner self through metaphor. It was successful on this occasion. A few sessions later he set out to make a drawing of a bear for a favoured attachment figure (a teacher), and I witnessed his struggles to 'get it right' as he clumsily went about creating his image. As he continued, he became frustrated by his struggles and turned the paper over and started again. He was heavy handed in applying pressure, making individual scratch marks with the pencil on paper and digging into the surface with his fingernails, using his fingers to smudge and drag the pastels. He asked me to help hold the paper down in place, which was the first open invitation to "help me, I'm out of control". A power struggle ensued and I felt I was being tested for my strength and resilience to contain him on the one hand, but also he was exerting and demonstrating power over me on the other. There was also a sense of an internal drive to resist and destroy something, which had potential – i.e. an attachment relationship with me was now forming, which heightened his anxiety. As the pressure became so intense and the paper buckled, I had to make a decision – to let go or not; should I let him destroy his creativity (self destruct) or should I come to the rescue?

Robinson et al (2006) explore Fonagy et al's (2002) notion of an 'alien self', whereby when trauma has been on the body, such as occurs in sexual abuse, a resulting fear and anger becomes trapped within the individual and constitutes an alien self. They further cite Straker's (2003) argument that trauma can create a variety of selves, as she refers to an 'uncanny self' which can only find expression through an enactment. The image of the bear represented the child's internal dynamics, both within the struggles in the process of making the image and in its visual representation. The bear was positioned behind bars, representing a self-portraiture expression of his experience of an uncanny self that had imprisoned himself in the care system as a Looked after Child, as his acts of violence had broken down numerous placements. A red pastel stabs the bear in the back representing an unconscious attack on the uncanny self trapped within his body.

I find myself resisting the description of 'having given in to him' as I let the paper go, which connects with my own attachment representations, memories of power struggles with my father in my younger years and a default position to back down in conflict. This poses an interesting question: was I acting subconsciously in response to my own avoidant attachment pattern? Rivett and Street (2009) suggest that difficulties taken to supervision, and once deconstructed, often echo the therapists' own experiences. My letting go may have been a response as a means of self-preservation against feeling overwhelmed, perhaps connecting with my own attachment separation anxieties. Or, was it a counter-transference response to his experience of feeling overwhelmed by intense emotions, overpowered and out of control, and vulnerable? Such dilemmas necessarily need to be untangled in clinical supervision through reflexive processes, so that feelings and responses can be appropriately placed with the rightful owner.

Feeling repulsed

Repulsion may connect with our internal working model, our core beliefs and our values through the service users' narrative of their early years' experiences, their criminal offense or behaviour, or through enactments or violation of the therapist's psyche within the session. The emotional impact upon professionals working with traumatised abusers in forensic settings cannot be underestimated (Aiyegbusi and Tuck 2006).

Sam attended art psychotherapy for three years in a low-secure unit, placed under a hospital treatment order following an index offence of rape and indecent assault. He was raised by his mother, grandmother and aunt in, what was essentially, a brothel, and witnessed adult sexual deviances and was subject to sexual exploitation from a very young age. On the ward, he often made sexualised innuendoes towards female staff, and towards me (Wood) in his art psychotherapy sessions, reflecting an interjection of his perpetrators, which served to re-enact his trauma and project his experiences onto others, asserting control over what he perceived as authoritarian figures.

Sam's upbringing was far removed from my own, having attended a Catholic boarding school. My eyes were opened to an underworld of violence and I learnt coarse, sexually explicit vocabulary. His blueprint internal working model of the world was created within a female dominant environment, and with failings in maternal attunement (the mother's ability to attune to the baby's experiences and needs and respond to them effectively). The primary care-giver's affective attunement limits a baby's exposure to traumatic events and facilitates the child's developing capacity to mentalise, that is to say, to develop a theory of mind (Fonagy 2004), and influences the child's capacity to regulate affect. The absent father brings further challenges to the developing self, which prevents the transfer of identification from the mother-child dyad to the triad of identification with mother–father–child, and thus creates a black hole "filled with resentment, guilt, idealizations and mistrust" (Corneau 1991 p. 16). The father helps create the child's internal structure. Sam hadn't experienced the sense of being 'held in mind' (being considered by another person). He had only himself to rely upon to meet his needs, which was driven by an innate need for survival, and he never learnt the process of empathising and forming relationship to others.

Art promotes bilateral stimulation, allowing sensory memory to transfer to verbal memory. His images graphically reflected childhood memories, represented in a style comparable to the developmental age of when he lived through the trauma, as if he had become frozen in time. Intermittently he projected intense anger for his mother, then expressed compassion and forgiveness for her. He expressed an internalised shame and guilt in response to having been such a bad child, as if somehow justifying his mother's neglect. As therapy progressed, we began to explore the index offence and the perpetrator within Sam which he found challenging. He climaxed with a painting depicting a rape of a woman, which he described to be me. I found myself momentarily frozen and feeling sickened by what had just occurred, but was able to compose myself. I recognised the need to conclude the session, but to not necessarily end therapy, which would have compromised all of the work achieved in the last two years and would only reinforce his past experiences of rejection for his badness. My own sense of shame set off connections with my representational systems and an emotional response that challenged my personal scripts centred within gender, sexuality, spirituality, culture and religion, compromising my self-identity.

Like the example presented earlier by Johns, my own resilience enabled me to continue to work with Sam for another year, which created opportunity to work with empathy and shame, whereby using my 'self' with mindful and purposeful intent to enable him to develop capacity to mentalise. Our continued working relationship enabled co-creation of risk management strategies. The psychodynamic-attachment based approach of art psychotherapy, which is supported by accessing non-verbal communications, was complemented by Sam's attendance on a cognitive behavioural approach sex offender treatment programme. He was discharged into the community, where he has continued to successfully build more meaningful relationships with women.

Grappling to find hope

Why do we work with some of the most challenging individuals when research shows that the stress on therapists comes at high "human cost" (Rivett and Street 2009)? Rivett and Street note findings which suggest that identity types of individuals who are 'naturally attracted' to the profession (speaking of family therapists, but equally applicable, we would suggest, to art psychotherapists) as those who have experienced childhood in an observer role; who may have been a confidant to parents; who are the youngest child; and/or whom by adolescence have already established an identity with the therapy role. Analysis of my (Wood) family scripts and cultural genogram during systemic training affirms this premise. There is literature (Miller and Baldwin 2000) that suggests therapists enter the profession in connection with the Jungian notion of the 'wounded healer', to take up a role in part to heal their own psychic trauma, and "paradoxically, it will help the healer stay in touch with the pain of suffering" (Rivett and Street 2009, p. 229).

Peter's use of colour and simple forms, his narrative of incarceration and feeling trapped within his own emotional identity with shame driven rage, continued to influence my (Johns) own processing and integration of meaning beyond the therapy relationship. Several months after the attack, while standing in front of a painting by Kandinsky, I was drawn to the way Kandinsky worked through many processes in order to control both colour and rhythm. He experienced an artistic block and found himself unable to continue when his assistant suggested he focus on the musicality of the word "uberflut" (flood or deluge) rather than the meaning. He completed the painting in a matter of days later. Attending a sandtray group a week later, I produced a tray I entitled 'Homage to Kandinsky'. I set out deliberately to collect objects for their colour rather than their symbolic representation, with a purposeful need to create a deliberate balance between the hard and softness of the colours. I used a bicycle reflector, casting an orange path of light across the tray to the opposite, complementary colours placed in the sand. I had seen this echoed in Kandinsky's painting, with a universal dancing of colour and rhythm, and I now understood the many processes to achieve this extraordinary balance between control and harmony - familiar versus the unfamiliar. The tray, so I thought, was *my* tray, a representation of my own need to control and balance my own sense of colour and rhythm. However, during the process of reflective narrative within the group, my colleagues shed further insight into my internal processing, which found connections with Peter via the red object, the inner workings of a door lock. I found myself talking about the experience of attack from Peter and the sandtray objects and Kandinsky's painting in relation to Peter; with no key to unlock his external and inner world's; his bold use of colour; and his control in orchestrating how he wanted his paintings finished. I began to consider the other objects, which, in their juxtaposition, perhaps reflected hope and light (see figure 1). The plastic green treasure chest, positioned against the shiny red bauble and the yellow circus tent, with its opening against the blue rubber ring, signified the opening up and continuity of mine and Peter's relationship.

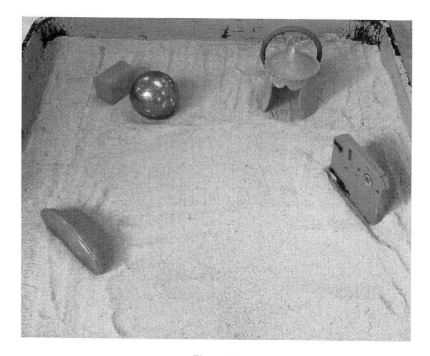

Figure 1

Two years after Sam's discharge from therapy and subsequently hospital, my (Wood) self-analysis was to influence me increasing my skill set, introducing me to and leading to qualification in clinical hypnotherapy. In turn, this introduced me to the work of Milton Erickson who has been influential in systemic family therapy and evoked an interest in advancing my career still further. In the true spirit of circularity, this introduced me to child and family work and reconnected me with attachment theory, which is my current area of practice as I continue to work with young adolescents whose future narrative is yet to be mapped.

To conclude

Self-reflexivity facilitated in good quality supervision enables the opportunity to identify influences rooted in therapist's (and indeed any professionals working with traumatised individuals and offenders) personal narratives. Therapists' resistances and prejudices can be toxic to the therapeutic relationship if not acknowledged, and our grappling to find hope can be nurtured and hypotheses-generated within the supervisory framework. All of us have an attachment narrative, which heavily influences our resilience, our internal working model and capacity to mentalise, formed during our early years of development. It is this that enables our ability to stay with the job. Family scripts, such as John's 'try and try again', have influenced a resistance not to give up on hope. Strategies have evolved, built on evidence-based experience that confirms one's capacity to survive, learnt through overcoming trauma-induced anxieties provoked by life experiences and founded on a secure attachment base. Systemic theory provides a contextual framework to understand how everything is connected and gives meaning to the notion of service users 'getting under our skin'. At some level, it is true that something about the relationship with service users will extend beyond direct interactions with them, as they make connections with our own narratives, our lived experiences, and our whole self-identity.

There is approximately a 20 year generation gap between each of the three service users we have presented, and each has experienced comparable early year's trauma and insecure attachments. Interestingly, and coincidentally, there are also similarities between the two authors' early attachment relationships, cultural, economic and educational identity. There has been some purposeful resistance, guarding the extent of self-disclosure as self-preservation. However, writing this chapter has prompted a curiosity to further reflect about its content, and we hope to have generated a similar interest in our reader to examine the narratives that have influenced you and led you into your professional role.

Note: All names have been changed and some information altered or omitted to protect individual's identity. We are indebted to the service users with whom we have worked who have taught us all that we know.

BIBLIOGRAPHY

Adshead, G. (2004) Three Degrees of Security: Attachment and Forensic Institutions. Chapter 5. In Pfäfflin, F. and Adshead, G. (Eds) 'A Matter of Security: The Application of Attachment Theory to Forensic Psychiatry and Psychotherapy'. London and New York Jessica Kingsley Publishers

Aiyegbusi, A. (2004) Forensic Mental Health Nursing: Care with Security in Mind. Chapter 6. In Pfäfflin, F. and Adshead, G. (Eds) 'A Matter of Security: The Application of Attachment Theory to Forensic Psychiatry and Psychotherapy'. London and New York: Jessica Kingsley Publishers

Aiyegbusi, A., and Tuck, G. (2006) Too Close for Comfort -Traumatic Experience and Forensic Nursing. *Forensische Psychiatrie und Psychotherapie*, Werkstattsschriften.13. Jahrgang 2006 - Supplement II. Pabst Publishers (pp51-59)

Bedford, E. (1986) Emotion and Statements about them. Chapter 2.In Harré, R.(Ed) in 'The Social Construction of Emotions' Oxford: Basil Blackwell Ltd.

Bowlby, J. (1969) Attachment: Attachment and Loss, Vol.1 London: Hogarth Press

Bowlby, J. (1973) Attachment and Loss: Volume 2. Separation: Anxiety and Anger. New York: Basic Books

Casement, P. (1985) On Learning from the Patient. London: Tavistock Publications Ltd.

Cairns, K. (2002) Attachment, trauma and resilience: Therapeutic caring for children. London: British Association for Adoption and Fostering (BAAF)

Corneau, G. (1991) Absent Fathers: Lost Sons. Boston Massachusetts and London: Shambhala Publications, Inc.

De Shazer, S. (1982) Patterns of brief family therapy. New York: Guildford Press

Fonagy, P., and Target, M. (1997) Attachment and reflective function: their role in self-regulation. *Development and Psychology,* 9, pp.670-700

Fonagy, P. Gergely, G., Jurist, E., and Target, M. (2002) Affect regulation, Mentalization and the Development of the Self. New York: Other Press

Fonagy, P. (2004) The Development of Violence in the Failure of Mentalization. Chapter 1 In Pfäfflin, F. and Adshead, G. (Eds) 'A Matter of Security: The Application of Attachment Theory to Forensic Psychiatry and Psychotherapy'. London and New York: Jessica Kingsley Publishers

Greenspoon-Linesch, D. (1988) Adolescent Art Therapy. New York and Abingdon, Oxon, Great Britain: Routledge

Miller, W., and Baldwin, D. (2000) Implications of the wounded healer paradigm for the use of self in therapy. In Baldwin, M. (Ed) The Use of Self in Therapy (2nd edn) New York: Haworth Press

Mollon, P. (2002, 2nd edn) Cracking the shell of illusion: a brief theory of trauma and dread. Chapter 1 in P. Mollon 'Remembering Trauma'. London: Whurr

Passamonti, L., Crockett, M.J., Apergis-Schoute, A.M., Clark,L. Rowe, J.B., Calder, A. J., and Robbins, T. W. (2012) Effects of Acute Tryptophan Depletion on Prefrontal Amygdala-Connectivity While Viewing Facial Sign of Aggression. *Biological Psychiatry,* 2012 Jan 1; 71(1): 36–43. Copyright: Elsevier Inc. Sourced on April 4th, 2015 http://www.ncbi.nlm.nih.gov/pmc/articles/PMC3368260/http://www.ncbi.nlm.nih.gov/pmc/articles/PMC3368260/

Rivett, M., and Street, E. (2009) Family Therapy: 100 key points and techniques. Hove, East Sussex: Routledge

Robinson, T., Taylor, G., O'Connor, F., and Scoda, M. (2006) When the Trauma Becomes Sexualized: A Case Study of a Priest Who Sexually Abused his Nieces. *Forensische Psychiatrie und Psychotherapie*, Werkstattsschriften.13. Jahrgang 2006 - Supplement II. Pabst Publishers (pp101-119)

Siegel, D.J. (2012, 2nd edn) The Developing Mind: How Relationships and the Brain Interact to Shape Who We Are. New York: Mind Your Brain Inc.; The Guildford Press

Straker, G. (2003) Enroute to Paedophilia: ravishment in another scene. Paper presented at Institute for Psychoanalysis International Conference Melbourne.

Warner, C.T. (1986) Anger and Similar Delusions. Chapter 8. In Harré, R. (Ed) 'The Social Construction of Emotions' Oxford: Basil Blackwell Ltd.

Department of Education. Children's Act, 1989
Department of Health. Mental Health Act, 1983
Department of Health (2008) Code of Practice, Mental Health Act 1983. TSO (The Stationery Office)

C H A P T E R   1 7

'… for just a little while today I forgot I was in prison …'
Expression on the inside; finding a place of freedom in a young offenders institution
LISA SHEPHERD

Abstract

Within the bars and locked doors of this prison, flower beds flourish and laughter rings out.

Despite living in a community where reputation is everything and weakness cannot be tolerated, a group of young men create a place where they can play, regress and express themselves. Inspired by the quote above, spoken by an inmate in one of the sessions, this case study will explore how dramatherapy created a space of freedom for self-expression in an environment of danger, restriction and control.

Set in a young offenders training prison, the dramatherapist sets up creative expressive dramatherapy groups with young men who have been convicted of various criminal offences.

This was the first time any arts therapies had been available to inmates and provided a space in their week where they could "let their guard down" and do "things you can't be seen doing by the others (inmates)". Sharing the participants' voices throughout, the author will explore the nature of the space created, how the participants engaged with and made use of this space and the impact of the dramatherapy provision amongst the participants.

In this chapter, I will be using pseudonyms and generalising locations to maintain confidentiality and to protect the identity of individuals. Throughout the chapter I will share the participants' voices through statements made in sessions, language used, lyrics written and answers given on participant feedback forms. When quotation marks are used and no citation follows, the participants' voices are used to provide data, deeper understanding and will take the reader on a journey into this fascinating piece of work.

Introduction

"To be or not to be, that is the question.
  Should I follow the violence of wealth and power
  Or should I look at my troubles and try to end them?"
  (Eli)

Have you ever been inside a prison? It is never a pleasurable experience; air locks, keys, locked doors, locked doors behind locked doors, high fences, barred windows, stern faces, a need to be constantly on alert for anything outside of the normal routine and an unrelenting feeling of being observed are all part of the experience. Freedom is not a feeling readily experienced within a place designed for observation and control. Yet, just as the well kept flower beds bring moments of colour into the otherwise angular and dull landscape of the prison, dramatherapy offers offenders a space of freedom where, for a moment, you might even forget you are locked in.

Data for this study is drawn from the author's experience of facilitating short-term group dramatherapy interventions within a category C training prison in greater London. The prison population is made up of males aged between 18 and 25 years who have been convicted of a range of offences including; acts of violence, theft and drug dealing. The prison offers offenders the opportunity to engage in a range of academic and vocational activities including; art, radio production and barbering. Offenders are encouraged to gain qualifications whilst they are resident in the prison and can enroll on a variety of courses including open university study.

A dramatherapist was employed to further enrich the varied programme aimed at reducing reoffending. The dramatherapist soon found out that: "Prison work is not straightforward. One's flexibility is tried to the limit" (King 2000:3). Times shift, things are delayed

'... for just a little while today I forgot I was in prison ...'
Expression on the inside; finding a place of freedom in a
young offenders institution

309

and sessions are cancelled at short notice. Given the short and intensive period of delivery, ten 2.5 hour sessions over 10 weeks, the dramatherapist took a creative expressive "community dramatherapy" (King 2000) approach to the work. The young men engaged in; drama games, enactment, mask and role-play activities, improvisation, script work and relaxation. The opportunity to "play games" and "learn about theatre stuff" was generally well received. Each of the groups engaged with a similar range of activities, however each group took a different journey through their 10 week programme. From purely engaging in play, to engaging with script, rewriting Shakespeare, 'spitting rhymes' about the prison environment and crafting an original performance exploring the experience of leaving prison, the creative content of the sessions was vast.

The participants in the groups ranged in experience, academic ability, ethnicity and religious belief, and sentence length ranged from less than six months to two and a half years or more to serve. On the outside the first question we may ask someone after meeting them would be: 'What do you do?'. In the groups, this question was: "What are you in for?" and the answer was generally "food" or drug related offences. The truth of the reasons given amongst group members is subject to many variables, including maintenance of reputation, which is of high importance in the life of an inmate. Hearing of the participants' histories and offences involved the signing of the official secrets act, so the dramatherapist chose to not obtain any information pertaining to the participants' histories or convictions unless they personally volunteered the information. The prison carries out a rigorous assessment for risk for each activity; ratio of staff to offender, sex of facilitator, offence history and known gang affiliations are all taken into consideration when putting a group together.

During the interventions some participants revealed information about their lives prior to being resident in the setting. This involved; previous imprisonment, gang life (although all were very careful not to discuss open cases), childhood and on occasion family life. From the disclosures made in the sessions, we are able to identify some shared experiences in the lives of the young men including; being witness to violence, growing up in single parent families and being suspended and/or excluded from school. A few of the young men involved had experiences of being in care and many of the participants had children of their own.

Relationships were often a focus of discussion within the groups and there is potential that some of the young men may have experienced insecure attachment in infancy. There is evidence to suggest an infant who is deprived in early infancy is much more likely to develop internal structures embracing primitive defensive methods, which may lead to destructive or criminal behaviour (De Zulueta 1993).

The hierarchical structure of 'rep' or reputation existing within the population of the prison was also echoed within the groups; "Respect is crucial amongst gang members and to be feared is to be respected" (The Centre for Social Justice 2009:25). Strong characters with a lot of 'rep' would often dominate sessions, be it with a strong sense of calm and high levels of respect for the facilitators, a joyful energy and appetite for play or an imperious presence seeking to make others uncomfortable. Group dynamics would often shift significantly depending upon who was in attendance each week. The atmosphere of the sessions ranged from joyful elation and playfulness to tension and frustration. A majority of the young men participating in the groups had been in another prison or young offenders' institution previously and many had been in and out of different institutions for many years. The participants in the groups grew close whilst working together; new relationships and alliances were formed. Those who had more experience of being inside offered support to the new arrivals and the more mature participants offered guidance. Things happened in the sessions, which could not happen anywhere else in the setting; nothing outside the boundaries of the institution but things outside of the unwritten code of conduct drawn up amongst the prison population. In the groups, participants felt safe enough to play, creatively express themselves and take risks by doing things they could not be seen doing outside of the space the dramatherapist and group members created.

The participants mastered games quickly and particular games became firm favourites; chair football, "the wolfy game" and clap ping pong were popular in all the groups. Competitive games, sometimes involving an element of deception, were particularly well received and played often. Participants also enjoyed engaging in enactment activities and playing improvisation games. Drama equipment successfully

'... for just a little while today I forgot I was in prison ...'
Expression on the inside; finding a place of freedom in a
young offenders institution

311

cleared with security, and masks and small costume items were welcomed into the sessions, prompting playful exploration of a variety of different roles and scenarios. Scenes took place in a range of places away from the prison; classrooms, courtrooms, community centres, movie sets, and "on road" or out on the streets, anywhere but in prison. One group expressed an interest in writing a sitcom about prison life but could never quite bring themselves to begin it, perhaps indicating that exploration of current circumstances was not something, which could be engaged with by all or with ease. Another group crafted a touching scene about an offender leaving prison in which they used physical theatre techniques to represent the "big door" or vehicle entrance through which the young man exits. This group had bonded particularly well and been working together for eight weeks when, prompted by the departure of two members of the group in the weeks previous, they crafted the scene. All groups would discuss prison life and aspects of their prison experience, but creative expression around the same themes was resisted. The question arises: Why would you want to enact being in prison when you are in prison? Although the young men had lots to say about their experiences of incarceration they did not want to use theatre as a vehicle to share this. They wanted to use it to escape it, even if this was for just a little while.

Like something out of a movie ...

Life "on road" is tough for boys and young men growing up in areas proliferated with gang crime. Opportunities are limited, and as Leon states in the report 'Dying to Belong: An In-depth Review of Street Gangs in Britain', "No one wants to be in a gang, it's the only choice they've got. You don't see no progress. It's not how we feel, it's how it is" (The Centre for Social Justice 2009:100). Case studies presented in the report offer an insight into the histories of the young men and women who are part of gangs across the UK; broken homes, low levels of education, school exclusion and witnessing violence are all prevalent factors in a child as young as 10 becoming part of a gang (The Centre for Social Justice, 2009). This is inline with some of the past experiences disclosed by participants within the sessions. The report goes on to suggest territoriality is a strong factor in prompting gang violence. Indeed within the groups, participants discussed the existence of "postcodes" where they knew they could not been seen, even travelling through, for fear of attack by opposing gang members. It may be safe to assume that a significant number of the young men who took part in the dramatherapy sessions had been exposed to violent behaviour be it as witness, victim or perpetrator. Studies in the US suggest a link between exposure to gang related violence and Post Traumatic Stress Disorder (PTSD), particularly the areas of hypervigilence (Rich JA, Grey CM 2005;95(5):816824)and symptoms of emotional numbness (Richardson et al 2012).

The following vignette took place during week six of a 10 week intervention following a prompt to think about a description for the movie of your life:

Anton is telling the group a story about the time he was attacked outside a supermarket and stabbed. He opens with the line "It was like something out of a movie...". He takes us on an action packed tale of knowing he is somewhere he shouldn't be prior to the attack, being stabbed, his escape from further harm and his journey to the hospital to receive medical care for his wounds. The story is reminiscent of a sequence from a tongue in cheek action movie.

It is very entertaining and nearly everyone is laughing. Anton's story prompts further discussion amongst the group of similar experiences.

In this vignette, traumatic experiences are shared as one may share the tale of a humorous occurrence with a friend, a series of unfortunate comical events relating to a life threatening experience. This is perhaps a stark demonstration of how common it is for these young men to have experienced violence on the streets; many of the group members expressed that they had a similar tale to tell and a few also shared them in the session. Anton defends against the trauma of events by using humour as a distancing technique (Chen & Martin 2007; Martin & Lefcourt 1983). In return, the other group members offer him understanding and acknowledgement by the sharing of their own stories. Through the reframing of a traumatic event as a comical anecdote, the group could talk openly about their experiences of witnessing violence. Amongst peers the temptation would be to adapt stories to avoid appearing weak, which could damage your "rep." However, when stories were told in the session above, there was a feeling of sincerity as participants spoke of feeling scared, being

'... for just a little while today I forgot I was in prison ...'
Expression on the inside; finding a place of freedom in a
young offenders institution

313

in pain and fearing for their lives. Although described as if on stage doing a stand up routine, the content of the stories appeared to be true. Only those who told them will know for sure but the sharing of traumatic experience may have offered the group some catharsis of difficult emotional content. In his post intervention feedback Marcus tells us "I have changed, I felt positive and happy after each session", indicating he felt an shift in mood both in each workshop and in the longer term. It may be that the sharing of traumatic experiences, through a creative expressive means, offered participants relief from the emotional stresses associated with their experiences of violence.

For just a little while today ...

Sue Jennings (1986) points out; "Drama not only helps us to come to terms with our everyday life and facilitates exploration of our inner life, but it also enables us to transcend ourselves and go beyond our everyday limits and boundaries"

(Jennings 1986:4). Bearing similarities to Moreno's (1977) 'surplus reality' (Blomkvist and Rützel, 1994:235), engagement in dramatic play is "a temporary leaving behind of the everyday way of being together...an arrival in a special space, where something new and creative can take place." (Chesner 1998:17). Working in the 'surplus reality' (Moreno, 1977) is particularly 'well suited to adolescent trauma survivors' (Cossa, 2002:142) such as the young men who took part in the groups.

During reflection on a session which primarily consisted of games and role play activities, Josh states that he has experienced the space in a significant way:

The session has been filled with laughter, as the group members were lost in the enjoyment of play. In the closing check in Josh says "Yeah today was good, it's strange...for just a little while today I forgot I was in prison."

In the above vignette Josh tell us that he has experienced the space created in the session as something outside of his prison experience thus far; a space in which he could forget where he was. Josh experienced the space of the dramatherapy session as a space of freedom, a space where he could escape, for a just moment, despite never leaving a locked room. As Colin notes of his experience of dramatherapy in Wormwood Scrubs, " you can be allowed without

being told you're doing wrong. I enjoyed the freedom of expression…
Sesame was a break from being in prison" (1996:138), recognising the
difference and value of the space created within the dramatherapy
sessions as something outside his previous experiences of being
"locked up."

Prison life is slow moving, repetitive and boring. Inmates live
in close quarters with one another and conditions are tense; a minor
disagreement between inmates can easily escalate to something more,
in some cases violence. The author can only imagine the myriad of
feelings inmates may feel during their incarceration; fear, shame,
anger, homesickness and hopelessness. There are few opportunities
for privacy and a need to avoid expressing emotional content for fear it
will be taken as a sign of weakness. Inmates need to keep up a front;
to be alert to danger at all times, to not let anyone know you're scared.
Within the dramatherapy sessions Josh and the other participants
were able to relax for a short while, to let go of the mask they must
wear day to day and simply enjoy playing together. In feedback Mark
commented: "I enjoyed the environment that they made for us",
indicating that he particularly valued having this space in his week.
Participants often made use of the space to "blow off steam" and get
some relief from the monotony of a prison existence. Several of the
participants agreed with Jon when he fed back: "I'm able to express
myself more now. They got me out of my shell", indicating that the
provision offered the inmates opportunities to build confidence in
expressing their thoughts and feelings with others.

Miss, you don't know …
"Is this a shank I see before me?
I like the handle, let me grab that
are you a shank in my mind?
Is all this coming from my burning brain?"
(Dan)

In this intervention, young men who may have traumatic
experiences of violence and potential symptoms of PTSD came
together in a special space where things outside of their normal prison
existence could occur. The question arises of what the dramatherapy
space offered to these young men? When your existence is one of
danger, mistrust and oppression, what does a space of freedom and

'... for just a little while today I forgot I was in prison ...'
Expression on the inside; finding a place of freedom in a
young offenders institution

315

self-expression offer you? In a world where routine and boundaries are paramount, the feeling of freedom can be seductive. What happens when too much is revealed?

The vignette below documents one of the groups discussing this very issue:

During an improvisation game, group members dare one another to do increasingly silly things. There is much laughter as the ante is upped each time. Samson is requested to dance, and after a little reluctance does so. On the next turn the request is point blank refused and a heated discussion erupts about those who hadn't participated fully in the game. Samson is at the forefront of the argument, targeting the individual who had refused the request following his dancing.

In this vignette we see the group members arguing over the very issue of how much you can express yourself in this space, in this prison; where is the line? Samson felt safe to do something he would never do outside of the session but later regrets his decision when others refuse to do the same. Perhaps he forgot where he was when others remained vigilant to the threat outside of the room. This brings up a question of safety; what would happen if others did find out Samson had danced? Had engagement in dramatherapy placed him in danger?

Things are now calm and reflections fall upon the event. The dramatherapist brings up the game and the subsequent argument in reflection. Samson tells her: "Miss you don't know what it's like in here, if the others out there saw that." Others mumble their agreement and looks are exchanged. Bob responds to Samson: "It's cool. We all did it, it's cool, it's cool."

Each group drew up a contract agreeing the rules of conduct within the sessions throughout the intervention. All contracts included a clause on confidentiality and each group discussed the need for discretion. Bob is well respected within the group and wider prison population, and his reassurance offers safety to the whole group; there is an unspoken understanding that the events of the game will not be shared with others in the prison. Never once did it appear that events from inside any of the sessions had been shared with inmates outside of the group, at least not in a malicious manner. There was much interest in the group amongst other inmates who would come to ask what we did in the sessions and if they could join the groups, although this may have been partially motivated by the fact all the facilitators for the groups were female. The group members were protective of their space, sending the inquisitive on their way and telling those who ask: "We play games and that, it's alright yeah."

A gang member will often refer to their gang as their 'fam' or family. Experiences of "family breakdown and in particular fatherlessness is a key driver of gang involvement" and "The gang, for a significant number of young people growing up in our most deprived communities, has become a substitute family" (The Centre for Social Justice,2009:27).

Within the groups, participants developed strong relationships, which extended beyond the weekly sessions. Being part of a group was important to the young men; in his feedback Ste tell us: "It was nice whilst it lasted. I just liked talking with the group", indicating that he valued the group experience highly. When reflecting on what they had learnt from taking part in the group, Tony identified that "it is challenging to work as a group and when you do it's a great experience and good fun", and Dan stated: "I can handle my anger in a group." Both responses indicated that they had overcome social situations which they found challenging during the intervention. Dramatherapy offered the participants a meaningful group experience within which they could safely express and manage their emotions, experience discord, recover from it and build positive relationships with their peers. Reminiscent of the experience of being part of a gang based 'fam', the young men who took part in the dramatherapy sessions had a new group experience which offered opportunities for the development of interpersonal skills, and may go some way to positively reframing their expectations and experiences of being part of a group.

Reflections

This small scale case study has dipped a toe into the exploration of dramatherapy provision with young male offenders in a young offenders prison, exploring participant experiences, the nature of the space created in the sessions and the benefits engagement offered participants. The participants' voices have been present throughout, offering the reader an insight into the author's experiences of working with the young men, so it seems only fitting that the final reflections also come from them.

'... for just a little while today I forgot I was in prison ...'
Expression on the inside; finding a place of freedom in a
young offenders institution

317

At the end of the intervention, participants completed feedback forms asking; what they have enjoyed and remember most vividly from the sessions, where they may like to see improvements, what they have learnt and if they feel they have changed from taking part.

The forms were completed retrospectively, and were distributed in envelopes for participants to complete and return to the regimes manager if they wished. Sixty percent of the total participants who attended four or more of the 10 session offered returned the forms, five participants did not receive the form due to changes in their circumstances, making a true return rate of 75%. Of the 15 participants who completed the forms; 47% said that they felt they had developed in confidence and learnt something about themselves through participation, 53% expressed that they valued the group experience and had developed their interpersonal skills and 20% identified the environment as being significant. The responses captured from the completed feedback forms offer further data to support the benefits of the provision, which have been outlined above.

Participants indicated that they had valued the therapeutic aspect to the group work: "I liked everything especially the therapy".

Participants also showed signs of having seen a positive change in themselves:"I do think I have changed, I have learned to communicate and cooperate with others and learnt to understand others." Dramatherapy provision meant a lot to those involved, indicating a clear need for further provision to be made available and research completed. One group member commented 'it is helping my sentence to pass quicker, coming here' giving clear evidence to the value to offering a space for creative expression in a prison environment. It may or may not be that this intervention will have a direct impact on reducing reoffending amongst the participants. From meeting the young men, it strikes the author that being resilient enough to turn your life around after prison is a tough and long process which is individual to each offender. It is hoped that the dramatherapy sessions offered those who participated development, which helped to build resilience and perhaps alleviate the some of the emotional discomfort associated with previous experiences of trauma.

The author hopes the reader has been able to gain an insight into an interesting and challenging field of work. This is a very small study of an isolated piece of work and thus cannot be used as strong evidence of any particular thesis or phenomenon. The intention of this study was to share the voices of those involved, to take the reader on a journey through the work and provide some evidence for the efficacy of offering dramatherapy as a means of self-expression with young offenders in a prison environment.

All that remains is to extend my deepest thanks to the young men who took part in the groups and who are part of this chapter. Your voices inspired me to write this piece, and I hope the work we did together will stay with you as you move forward in your journey to true freedom.

REFERENCES

BRITAIN, THE CENTRE FOR SOCIAL JUSTICE. (February 2009) Dying to Belong; An Indepth Review of Street Gangs in Britain. London:The Centre for Social Justice

Blomkvist, L.D. & T. Rützel (1994) 'Surplus reality and beyond' in P. Holmes, M. Karp & M. Watson (Eds) *Psychodrama since Moreno*, London: Routledge Chen, G.H., & Martin, R. A. (2007). A comparison of humor styles, coping humor, and mental health between Chinese and Canadian university students. *Humor*, 20, 215–234.

Chesner, A. (1998) *Groupwork with Learning Disabilities: Creative Drama* Oxon: Speechmark Publishing Ltd

Colin. (1996) The Drama Gave Me Inner Freedom In Wormwood Scrubs. In: Pearson, J (ed.) *Discovering the Self through Drama and Movement; The Sesame Approach*. London: Jessica Kingsley Publishers

Cossa, M. (2002) 'DRAGODRAMA: Archetypal sociodrama with adolescents' in Bannister, A. & A. Huntington (Eds) *Communicating with children and adolescents: action for change*, London: Jessica Kingsley Publisher Ltd

De Zulueta, F. (1993) *The Traumatic Roots of Destructiveness: From Pain to Violence*. London: Whurr Publishers

'... for just a little while today I forgot I was in prison ...'
Expression on the inside; finding a place of freedom in a
young offenders institution | 319

Jennings, S. (1986) *Creative Drama in Groupwork*. Oxon: Winslow Press

King 'Community Dramatherapy at HMP Magilligan' *Dramatherapy* Vol22 No 1 Spring 2000

Martin, R. A., & Lefcourt, H. M. (1983). Sense of humor as a moderator of the relation between stressors and moods. Journal of Personality and Social Psychology, 45, 1313–1324.

Moreno, J. L. (1977) *Psychodrama*, (Vol. 1), 5th edition, New York: Beacon House

Rich JA, Grey CM. *Pathways to recurrent trauma among young Black men: traumatic stress, substance use, and the "code of the street."* Am J Public Health. 2005;95(5):816824

Richardson et al. (2013) Pathways to Early Violent Death: The Voices of Serious Violent Youth Offenders. *American Journal of Public Health* Jul2013, Vol. 103 Issue 7, pe5 12p

Thanks to all those I worked with on this project. It was truly a pleasure and none of this would have been possible without you. This is not my paper, it is ours.

CHAPTER 18

'Key moments in training': A trainee's perspective of working in a forensic setting

ROANNA BOND, MAY MAUNG, LAURA SCOTT

"I knew that I was plunging into the unknown...I knew nothing; but I had taken the step into darkness"

(Jung 1995: 225)

Introduction

The experience of undertaking a training placement in a forensic environment, where the trainee therapist is constantly surrounded by and engaging with high levels of psychic disturbance, is a challenging one. Being a trainee requires you to grapple with the 'unknown', tolerating inexperience as a matter of course, but taking on this position in a setting in which you are the subject of intense projections and where patients require strong containment is rigorous, demanding and acutely consuming. It involves allowing yourself to inhabit a position of vulnerability amidst violence to maintain robustness alongside the capacity for openness in a situation in which you are still learning and developing. Perhaps, above all, it involves allowing yourself to remain alive and responsive to the experience of failure. This chapter will explore the complexities involved in living out these dichotomies, examining the dual and conflicting nature of working in a world which is chaotic and yet contained.

Over the course of this chapter we will consider three different perspectives, each focusing on particular moments from arts therapy trainees' engagement with service users in a medium-secure unit. The experiences shared here reflect the importance of boundaries and containment and recognise the systemic significance of power and authority. They also acknowledge the institutional dynamics that get played out in a forensic setting. Each contribution examines the difficulties trainees face in establishing a meaningful therapeutic relationship with patients, in both group and one to one contexts, while working within a variety of art and drama therapy interventions.

'Stuck on the threshold' by Laura Scott

My key turned in the lock and the door opened; four patients and an occupational therapist entered the room and sat down in a circle, I attempted to remove my key and join them, my key was stuck. I was stuck.

Everything about the session was different; it was at a different time; it was the first session that I was facilitating without the hospital's dramatherapist, and an occupational therapist was co-facilitating with me. A circle was created in the middle of the room; there were four patients waiting for their session to start, an occupational therapist who had never experienced any dramatherapy before, and an empty chair waiting for me.

My mind worked on overdrive as I thought about how to handle the situation. I drew upon the resources I had gained throughout my training and suggested that the group take the time to explain dramatherapy to the occupational therapist. Despite the numerous suggestions of conversation and activities that I made, the time seemed to drag and the amount of control I felt I had of the situation gradually reduced. I filled up with a range of emotions; disbelief, humiliation, vulnerability, but I also noted a moment where I realised that the session had been practically taken out of my hands, but with a calm and realistic frame of mind I could still provide containment and safety for the session and its participants. I also sensed the fear fade as humour crept in. It was an embarrassing and intimidating situation but as I realised how out of my hands it was and the level of support and safety that I felt, I was able to see the situation with some distance and found the humour in it, which in turn eased the atmosphere.

When reflecting on the situation in supervision at The Portman Clinic, we talked about why I did not pull my alarm, whether containment lies in the room or in the therapist and how I dealt with the situation. I was reassured that I dealt with the situation well, but of course there are always things that can be learnt, such as thinking about where my mind was at in that moment where I did not pull my alarm. I reflected that my reason for not doing so was that a member of staff came by just after my key had become stuck and she called security. In that moment I thought all was taken care of and I just had to wait and look after the session. However, on reflection I realised just how vulnerable I was and I should have drawn upon the help in the room (my alarm, the phone and the occupational therapist's radio). In discussing this, I wondered if I had in turn placed the containment of the session in the staff member who assisted me with security. Perhaps my resilient and calm presence was provided by this staff member's assistance, and in turn provided an element of containment and togetherness to the session.

A few days after the incident, I took the scenario to group supervision and with the help of my supervisor and peers the scenario was re-enacted. People took on the roles of the occupational therapist, the patients and also of the objects in the scenario. The re-enactment was paused and each person was asked to speak in role. This encouraged me to think further about how the incident was dealt with, to reflect on my actions and feelings and also to think deeper into the feelings and thoughts that may have been present for the patients.

The symbol of freedom, a set of keys, was the very thing that was trapping me. The door and lock were holding on to me, but was I also holding on to them? There could have been a part of me that did not want the session to start. I thought about whom the door and keys may represent, and about whether I was holding on to someone or whether I felt I was being held back. With this being my first session without the hospital's dramatherapist, I was nervous and perhaps was holding onto her. This concern, hesitation and lack of confidence could be where I got stuck, and in turn may have held me back had this situation not drawn my attention to it.

In the time that I was stuck and awaiting assistance, the patients expressed their concern for me but did not cause a fuss; they sat in their circle and waited as I waited. One of the patients brought humour to the situation and another came over to see if he could help; I began to feel a sense of being looked after by the patients. This was an encouraging feeling that reminded me of the humanity of the situation and the people in it.

With a door wide open, keys stuck, a lock taken apart, the session at a different time and a different staff member being present, the potential for risk due to vulnerability, unpredictability and uncertainty was huge. It is possible that my feelings about my position as a dramatherapist were being physically presented to me. I was uncertain of my ability, trying to establish a balance of involvement and relying on other people. On reflection I can see that I had the resources to handle the situation safely with containment and that is what happened. As much as this incident was scary and complex, I learnt a lot from it and it will always stay with me as a reminder that sessions are not predictable, but with flexibility and calmness they are full of enriching opportunities from which I can grow.

'Feeling the intolerable' by May Maung

While on my placement, I was actively aware of the plethora of terms being used within the hospital. It made me query what the terms learning disabilities and offender engender in people's minds and the preconceptions, which lead to a denial and avoidance of truly understanding the people, associated with them. Valerie Sinason (1992) describes the difficulties in comprehending and accepting people with learning disabilities. Sinason illustrates society's "death wish" for disabilities in our attempt to eradicate them through medical and nutritional development. It is also questioned how this translates to existing people with disabilities, to know that they were initially unwanted or abhorred and instilling an internal "death wish". Sinason explains that it is the encompassing "death wish" from the individual's internal and external worlds that lead to the "secondary handicap"; a cutting off of intelligence from "a hostile world" (Sinason 1992:32).

Neville Symington shares this view with Sinason when speaking about the unconscious contempt clinicians' carry when treating learning disabled patients. Symington recounts a workshop at the Tavistock for professionals in which they confronted their "shocking inner attitudes" to people with learning disabilities (Symington in Waitman and Conboy-Hill 1992:132).

Rothwell (2008) speaks about her work in a secure unit where the patients have committed violent, impulsive and destructive offences. The importance of psychological and physical safety is discussed from the potential overwhelming material that can be brought up in therapy with these clients. Disentangling the counter-transference and projections from the patients is illustrated as crucial for the survival of thought for the patients in a harsh environment.

My placement was based within a large medium-secure unit in East London. A medium-secure unit is a hospital for people who are in need of mental health treatment and have committed an offence. The medium-secure unit is set within tall metal fencing surrounding the site and tall brick walls, which make up the buildings. Each member of staff has a unique code, which is entered with their fingerprint for access to the building and carries a pinpoint alarm and a set of keys, which need to be attached to a belt. When starting my placement, I was immediately overwhelmed by the building itself, instilling anxiety and unease in me. The level of security informed me of the level of containment needed for these patients and this fed into my apprehension. Karban (1994) speaks about responding to fear and how fantasies about patients and their potential for violence can be amplified.

The art psychotherapist on the ward was my supervisor and is also the Head of Arts Therapies for the forensic service, supervising all arts therapists at the unit whilst practicing as a clinician. It was initially difficult to have supervision at regular weekly times due to her workload and the limited amount of days I was at placement. Without this consistent space to explore my experience of being in an intense, alien environment of a forensic setting, I did not feel held. Initially the setting created a disturbance in me, which was reflecting the patients' own internal tumult and was not being processed. Due to my lack of experience in mental health and a forensic setting this may have affected my ability to be aware of the patient's defences and my own. This can be seen in the first encounters in my clinical work.

Early on in my placement, my supervisor notified me that a patient had requested individual art psychotherapy with a trainee.

Amar had been attending the art therapy group since he had arrived on the ward the previous year. After further discussion with my supervisor, I approached Amar in regards to his interest in individual art therapy and set up an initial meeting. Amar's self-referral came as a surprise to most of the clinical team as he had not chosen any of his other treatments himself. In fact this referral was taken with some scepticism by the psychiatrist. It was queried in his Care Plan Approach meeting whether Amar had referred himself in a disingenuous attempt to show progress in order to be discharged from hospital quicker. I felt Amar's request for art therapy was almost laughed at instead of praised, for taking responsibility for his own treatment. I wondered whether Amar was frequently not taken seriously and if the team were re-enacting an attachment pattern of relating (Ashead 2004). Amar had been making progress and his transfer to the less restricted low-secure unit was also discussed. It was agreed that I would start individual art therapy with him at the medium-secure unit and would continue the work at the low-secure setting.

Amar was diagnosed with paranoid schizophrenia, mild learning disability and problematic polysubstance misuse. Amar was placed on Section 37/41 of the Mental Health Act (1983). This is a hospital order given by the crown court, which meant he was moved from prison to hospital with a restriction order stating he was a risk to public safety. Amar's index offence was arson, which resulted in minor damage to property and no harm to anyone. The index offence is the most recent offence committed before entering the secure unit. Amar's report of the incident was unclear and ambiguous; he stated that he had set papers alight because voices told him to but also described it as an accident.

The art therapy sessions felt consistently hollow, empty and inauthentic, with no playfulness or risk-taking from Amar or I. Amar was unable to stay in the room longer than twenty minutes, which he offered different excuses for at the end of each session. This fed into questioning my own ability again and into inadequacies of providing a good enough space, but I also wondered whether these were projections from Amar feelings. Within supervision, I also saw a parallel process occurring in which I felt inadequate, useless, worthless and incompetent. I found it difficult to verbalise my thoughts in supervision, as they came out fragmented and unformed.

With further thought outside of the setting and within confronting these feelings in supervision, I understood that this was to do with my counter-transference.

At the start of the relationship, I was too afraid of my own anxieties about failing and incompetence to consider whether these intolerable feelings belonged to Amar. The deadness I felt was projected from Amar onto me and the sessions. This prompted me to look at the defence mechanism of projective identification. This is when a person projects into another until the other experiences the projections as part of themselves (Aiyegbusi in Adlam et al 2012:39). Projective identification comes from the paranoid-schizoid position in infancy where good and bad parts of the individual are split and cannot be held together in the mind due to overwhelming anxiety. Good parts of the self are retained and the unacceptable bad parts are projected onto a suitable object. Another place for Amar's intolerable feelings was the artwork. It is through the projection of these feelings onto the artwork that they can be recognised and thought about.

Within the sessions, Amar and I began to collaborate on paintings, which seemed important in building our relationship. They allowed for an intimate way of communicating to each other without the need for words, and permitted a space for thought and reflection. It seemed that both our defences against the "deadness" in the sessions were diffused by the joint art making. Collaborating creatively allowed for witnessing and mirroring reflecting back my experience of Amar. When art-making with Amar, I was aware not to impinge on his creativity by taking over, and was actively sensitive and responsive to his mark making. It was the collaborative art making that allowed for an attunement to occur between us. For this emotional resonance to occur, there is a need for that initial mother-infant gaze. The artwork allowed for a shared emotional experience by the joint attention and mirroring in the art making.

The art making was a pivotal tool in changing mine and Amar's relationship. It diffused my defences fuelled by preconceptions and assumptions about working with offenders and learning disabilities. I was able to be present with Amar in the art, without pretence or fear. Confronting the social and cultural assumptions and judgements made towards offenders with learning disabilities, art therapists can examine their own feelings in relation to this client group. Once clinicians face these uncomfortable feelings, the client can then be helped to "approach their indescribable pain" (Symington 1992).

'Integrating Jekyll and Hyde' by Roanna Bond

I worked with T for about seven months, running hour long one-to-one dramatherapy sessions in an interview room on the ward with him, before the time felt right to move our weekly sessions off the ward. From the start, T had commented that he would much prefer to work off the ward, as he was very sensitive to noise and commotion occurring outside the therapy room, and was understandably paranoid about the attitudes and interest demonstrated by other patients. He was worried that they might peer through the paper concealing the window in the door and watch what was going on.

We moved the sessions off the ward in September 2013 and this seemed to mark a significant shift in the therapeutic process, our therapeutic relationship and the level of disclosure T felt comfortable with during sessions. However, the initial transition from facilitating sessions on the ward to facilitating them in a room off the ward with him was daunting. During the first session I ran with T off the ward, he presented as very elated and I suddenly felt acutely vulnerable. During our check in, I chose to offer an exercise in which we both acted out different emotions and asked the other to guess what the emotions being portrayed were. Instantly, when I did my check in to demonstrate how I was feeling, T responded that the emotion he thought he was seeing in me was 'fear' and he seemed to indicate a certain pleasure in thinking that I was feeling this. At the time, I immediately felt defensive; I suppose I didn't want to admit that I was afraid of him, nor convey that I was concerned about being fully alone with him for the first time, without swiftly accessible support systems. I remember articulating surprise that he felt this was what I was enacting and denying it, suggesting instead that I was actually aiming to convey interest and concern. Looking back, I recognise that T was entirely right and accurate in his assessment of how I was feeling, and I think it could have been more helpful to acknowledge the anxiety present on both our parts about the new setting and circumstances we found ourselves in. I was too aware of my own vulnerability to be able to use it in a helpful way. Instead it inhibited my interaction with T, and the work became less authentic and responsive.

This was not the only instance in which this dilemma reared its head during the course of the dramatherapy intervention I ran with T. I recall an ongoing desire whilst facilitating our sessions to communicate a sense of strength and capability in my therapeutic presence. I now realise that by projecting this image, I missed how useful the genuine feelings experienced in the counter-transference can be, in enabling me to understand vital parts of my client's internal world. This became especially clear during another session I ran with T a few weeks later, in which I became very aware that T was staring at my hands constantly and I couldn't work out what the meaning of this was. What I was sure of, however, was that it made me feel very uncomfortable. We had been working on a story, a fairy tale I had told to T. The story was about a poor woodcutter who finds three golden eggs, then loses them again. The woodcutter then has to cope with his disappointment and shame when he returns to his family to admit he has only managed to retain one of the eggs he found, the third of which is then stolen that night by their neighbour. T instantly related to the character of the neighbour and asked to re-enact the scene in which the neighbour creeps into the woodcutter's house and steals the last remaining egg. We recreated the scene, with me taking on the character of the woodcutter and T the neighbour. However, both during the re-enactment of the scene and throughout the rest of the session following it, T stared fixedly at my hands whenever I moved them or gestured. When I then invited T to draw his character using art materials, as a way of grounding out of the exercise, he drew the character of the neighbour as a figure without any hands. I wasn't confident enough to acknowledge that this was happening and be curious about it at the time, instead I essentially ignored what was occurring between us and pretended I hadn't noticed. The instance had disturbed me, though, so I took it to supervision later that week.

Whilst in supervision, my supervisor helped me to reflect further on what the potential meaning of T's fixation with my hands could have been. One thought was connected to the change in our relationship, now that our sessions had moved off the ward, and the idea that this change had potentially elevated the relationship into a more intensive interpersonal bond. Perhaps this could have led T to develop a wish to merge, particularly with what he might perceive to be a whole or intact object? Another observation, which was hugely helpful for my clinical work, centred on highlighting the lack of boundaries that T had experienced previously in his relationships. T's only other experiences of intimacy were of something abusive and attacking. He had never had another emotionally intimate relationship, which was non-threatening. Maybe the lack of hands was a signifier of this?

This experience demonstrated to me the importance of acknowledging our vulnerable aspects, both as client and clinician, in the therapeutic relationship. It also inspired me to feel more confident in encouraging my patients to engage with and integrate their more sensitive unguarded facets within their personality. This learning played out for T and I in our work in dramatherapy together, particularly through the art form, as next in our sessions we explored the theme of superheroes and persona. During one activity, I suggested that we did some spontaneous improvisation and created a character, based upon any image T chose from a series of images laid out on a table in the room. Following this, T chose to devise a character from a picture of Superman. When I asked T why he had chosen the image and character of Superman above any of the others, he stated that it was because he was drawn to his 'confident posture'.

Over a number of sessions we then worked on the duality represented in Superman's persona and alter ego; the contrast between Superman and the more humane part of him, Clark Kent. But try as I might, I couldn't get T to embody the Clark Kent side of Superman's personality. He physically couldn't, or wouldn't, do it, even as a still image or a 'tableau', so in the end; I had to model this for him. It would appear T was only drawn to Superman's powerful aspect; he couldn't bear to embody his vulnerability. By taking this dilemma to supervision, I began to realise that perhaps this could be due to overcompensation within T for his recurrent feelings of subjugation and powerlessness, and I wondered if the same attitude also applied to me?

At the end of our 1:1 intervention working together, T and I collectively chose to look at the story of Jekyll and Hyde. This tale

provided the perfect metaphor for integrating aggression and
vulnerability alongside one another and acknowledging the importance
of giving space to both. For each of us, I think delving into and
exploring the conflicting parts of our psyche which relate to both
shadow and ego aspects of ourselves allowed us to evolve and realise
a more authentic and integrated state of being.

Conclusion

Each of the three examples of burgeoning clinical practice explored
in this chapter encapsulate the essential conflict present in the
trainees' experience of being asked to take on a position of authority
in an environment where, just like the patients they are working with,
they feel they have none. Perhaps this experience, then, uniquely
places the trainee in a position to understand something particular
about the sense of powerlessness, lack of control and often at times
of hopelessness regularly lived out by clients in a forensic setting.
There is something very moving about feeling like you are failing
and readjusting to this rupture, without being defended against it,
in an environment where those around you are living out lives which
have also not always gone as planned or succeeded. Above all, the
core difficulty these examples seem to highlight, for both students
and patients, is the struggle involved for all of us in bridging the gap
between the secure and the insecure.

BIBLIOGRAPHY

Jung, C G. (1995) Memories, Dreams and Reflections. London,
Fontana Press

Sinason, V. (1992). Mental handicap and the human condition:
an analytical approach to intellectual disability. Free Association
Books, London

Symington, N (1992) Countertransference with Mentally
Handicapped Clients in Waitman, A., Conboy-Hill, S. (1992).
Psychotherapy and mental handicap. Sage Publications,
London; Newbury Park.

Rothwell. K (2008) What Anger? Working with Acting- out Behaviour in a Secure Setting in Liebmann, M., 2008. Art Therapy and Anger. Jessica Kingsley Publishers.

Karban. B (1994) Working as an Art Therapist in a Regional Secure Unit in Liebmann, M., 1994. Art therapy with Offenders J. Kingsley.

Aiyebusi. A (2012) The Dynamics of Difference in Adlam, J., Aiyegbusi, A., Kleinot, P. (2012) The Therapeutic Milieu Under Fire Security and Insecurity in Forensic Mental Health. Jessica Kingsley Publishers, London.

Ashead. G (2012) "Mirror Mirror": Parallel Processes in Forensic Institutions in Adlam, J., Aiyegbusi, A., Kleinot, P. (2012) The Therapeutic Milieu Under Fire Security and Insecurity in Forensic Mental Health. Jessica Kingsley Publishers, London.

CHAPTER 19

The *'good enough'* couple
The containment of conflict and the roots of creativity in a music and art therapy group for forensic patients with intellectual disabilities and mental illness

JAMES O'CONNELL AND TRISHA MONTAGUE

Introduction

This chapter will describe our experience of setting up and co-facilitating a music and art therapy group for patients with intellectual disabilities in a medium-secure unit.

The process of bringing together the two modalities of art and music provided us with opportunities to share our respective clinical skills experientially, and explore new ways of thinking about and working with our patients.

We inevitably encountered challenges, particularly in relation to differences in our clinical approaches and personalities, and it became necessary to examine the functioning of the co-therapy relationship. We looked at the significance of our gender differences and at our role as a therapeutic 'couple' in its capacity to contain the attacks made on the group, while at the same time offering its members a creative space and the potential for recovery and growth.

There were times when the existence and continuation of the group felt threatened, by patients who were disruptive or repeatedly absent, sometimes by our inexperience and keenness to get started, and also by the conflicts that emerged between the two of us.

Over time, it was the hours spent processing and making sense of the conflicts and difficulties that helped reassure us about the value of the work we were doing. We were also able to make useful links with our client group whose experiences of 'difference' are central to the problems they encounter in society.

The functioning and "… the real working out of the dynamic relations…" of the group (Barenboim and Said 2004, p. 53) will be illustrated with examples of artwork and descriptive session material in the form of vignettes.

Formation of the group and the therapeutic frame

When we began planning the group in 2010 we first identified what was fundamental to each of us as clinicians. We then worked on developing shared conceptual and therapeutic frameworks that were central for us both. These included working according to psychodynamic principles, and drawing on attachment theory, as well as the emerging use of mentalisation and neuroscience.

We wanted to offer the patients the experience of a long-term stable group that could 'hold' them throughout their journey in hospital until their eventual discharge to a low-secure setting and on into the community.

We were aware of potential difficulties finding patient referrals for the group who were interested in both music and art, and who would have the capacity to engage in psychological therapy.

In our experience, forensic patients with intellectual disabilities struggle to share thoughts and ideas in group settings. They often lack social skills and have problems identifying and connecting with emotions. They show an unfamiliarity with listening to and being thought about by others. In many cases they have difficulties coming to terms with feelings of shame and guilt related to their index offences.

Much of the therapeutic work with patients in this hospital is aimed at recovery from mental illness, reducing the risk of reoffending and helping patients make a transition back into the community. We incorporated these overall aims in a variety of ways when planning the group. We felt that it could help patients develop a capacity for listening to each other and thinking together, thereby reducing isolation. It would offer opportunities for self-expression, identifying emotional states and increasing self-awareness. This could include

The *'good enough'* couple. The containment of conflict and
the roots of creativity in a music and art therapy group for
forensic patients with intellectual disabilities and mental illness

335

gaining insight into their index offences by taking responsibility for their behaviours and being compliant with treatment in order to prevent relapse.

When formulating our therapeutic frame, we needed a containing structure that would 'hold' the patients as well as ourselves. The model of a 'slow-open' referred group meant that the patients could continue to attend throughout their time in hospital. We felt that the long-term nature of this form of treatment would be central to the group's stability and effectiveness.

The therapeutic frame needed to be constant but offer flexibility where appropriate. It was important that it would allow for, and be able to cope with, our differences including where disagreements and conflict might arise.

The 'constants' help to provide a setting and a way of working together that is predictable and reassuring. They include the following:

- The group only takes place when both therapists are present. We do not work individually or with substitutes.

- The setting is always the same; the same room, layout of instruments and art materials.

- The length of the session is one hour and 15 minutes, and we aim for the same start and finish times where possible.

- The way the group proceeds in terms of the order (initial discussion, playing music, making art) has been established. We experimented with changing the order but found it to be more containing to start in the opening circle with shared music-making.

The flexible aspects were generated over time by the needs and aims of the group process and the group members, giving them a sense of ownership and empowerment. They have come to include the following:

- Division of time between the discussion, playing the instruments and using the art materials will vary from week to week.

- The use of directive and non-directive approaches is different; the music-making tends to be more directive while the art-making allows more individual autonomy.

Room layout and procedure

The sessions take place in the art room. The patients initially sit in one half of the room on chairs placed in a circle around a large djembe drum (see fig 1). A range of other portable instruments is placed on tables outside the circle (shown as rectangles). These include a xylophone, two guitars, a violin and various other drums and small percussion instruments.

The other half of the room is set up with large tables on which is placed paper and a range of drawing and painting materials. Clay is also available.

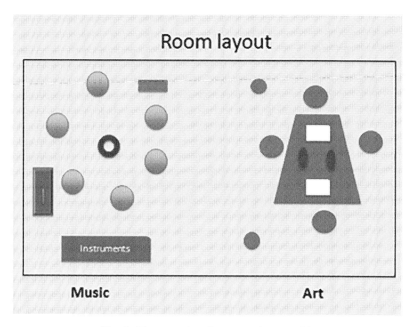

Fig. 1: Diagram showing room layout with musical instruments and art materials

The *'good enough'* couple. The containment of conflict and
the roots of creativity in a music and art therapy group for
forensic patients with intellectual disabilities and mental illness

337

At the beginning of every session there is a space for discussion when
the patients can speak about whatever is on their minds. This can
range in length from 10 minutes to the entire session.

After the discussion, the group begins improvising on the
instruments. There are opportunities for playing individually, in pairs
and as a whole group. The playing might include turn-taking, call
and response and mirroring. Changing their choice of instruments is
encouraged in order to help them move away from the 'safe' and familiar.
As well as playing the instruments, we sometimes use rhythmic hand
clapping and foot stomping as an alternative means of self-expression
and to encourage playfulness.

Another variation is when we turn our chairs round and face
outside the circle. The experience of not looking at each other while
playing the instruments encourages more careful listening. However it
also allows imaginations to wander: "I imagined I was playing in front
of a big audience" or "it felt like being in the Albert Hall".

The members are also given opportunities to conduct the rest
of the group by indicating speed and dynamic changes, starting and
finishing. This can give them a sense of empowerment when the whole
group responds to their signals, helping to develop confidence and
communication skills.

Comments on the experience of playing together are invited: a
discussion is developed in terms of their emotional responses to the
shared playing and the 'sounds' created by the group. This can include
the exchange of compliments and criticism. One word responses
such as 'good', 'invigorating', 'enjoyable' etc. are common, and yet the
expressions of satisfaction on their faces often say much more than
can be put into words.

Following this, the group moves across to the art tables where
they may continue with an on-going piece of artwork or start
something new. The character of this part of the session can vary
between concentrated silent working, humorous banter (which can be
inappropriate and provocative) and the sharing of ideas and interests.

In contrast to the music making, the art making is primarily non-
directive with regard to themes and use of materials. Consequently
the different personalities and needs of the patients come to the fore,
for example how independent they are or how much support they

require. The facilitators will sometimes offer to engage in a 'squiggle game'[37] with individuals when they are stuck for ideas and to bring them into the 'creative space of play' (Winnicott 1971).

We allow time in the last part of the session for each of the patients to display their art works for discussion. All members are encouraged to contribute their thoughts and responses to each other's work.

It is evident that the group offers space for many contrasting forms of expression, both verbal and nonverbal: quiet reflection, loud cathartic playing, interpersonal exchanges, questions and demands. Examples will be given in the vignettes that follow.

'The couple' and some of our thinking

The title of our chapter is a reference to Winnicott's idea of the 'good-enough mother'. He describes how the mother begins with an "almost complete adaptation to her infant's needs" but then gradually modifies her behaviour "according to the infant's growing ability to deal with her failure". This leads to frustration in the infant, however as this coping ability increases, the infant manages to mature and eventually separate (Winnicott 1953, p. 87).

As therapists, we are aware of our limitations, and our potential for 'failure' in the eyes of our patients.

The patients in our group have all experienced family breakdown and have significant histories of violence, neglect and abuse by parents, carers or family members. Early trauma in their lives has clearly led to problems with attachment and emotional development. They also have mental health diagnoses of paranoid schizophrenia, personality disorders, attention deficit hyperactivity disorder (ADHD), paraphilias and autistic spectrum disorder (ASD). They have committed offences including arson, sexual assault, abduction and burglary.

Our aim is to provide them with a model of a 'couple' that offers an alternative experience which could help repair some of the damage caused in the past. To achieve this it needs to be able to survive the attacks made on it for its perceived failings and inability to satisfy their needs in a consistent way.

---

37 The Squiggle game – a drawing technique used by Winnicott to communicate with children and elicit their thoughts and feelings in an unstructured way.

The *'good enough'* couple. The containment of conflict and
the roots of creativity in a music and art therapy group for
forensic patients with intellectual disabilities and mental illness

339

We do not see ourselves as representing a traditional 'parental couple' for the patients, but instead have recognised the potential for any 'pairing' to be sufficient to provide containment. The fact that we are male and female, potentially maternal and/or paternal figures, is not fixed according to our respective genders. Instead it fluctuates according to changes in our behaviour and how all group members perceive us at any given time.

The patients sometimes treat us in ways that reflect their personal histories and experiences. They may feel anger towards one or both of us when historical family issues are activated consciously or unconsciously. Examples might be memories of the 'abandoning mother' or the wish to preserve the relationship with the 'idealised father'. Inversely, there may be triggers which remind one of them of the ineffective or absent father, leading to overt attempts to please and seek proximity to the 'caring mother'.

The potential for disruption to, or even destruction of, the group is often present in our minds. The members of this group are unpredictable and impulsive. When one member tells another, "Don't hit that drum so hard or you'll break it", or asks: "Is it ok for me to play the violin?", we are reminded of their vulnerability as well as their potential for uncontainable aggression and the fear of their own anger. These contrasting interactions seem to reflect the patients' histories as both aggressors and victims.

David Morgan writes about "...the active desire to love and tolerate frustration [which] enables the child to allow the parents their creativity and to become creative himself". He refers to Kleinian thinking where "...the couple becomes an internal object, which develops partly from experiences with the real parents and partly through the complex interaction of love and hate, guilt, reparative feelings, towards not one parent or the other but the link between them." (Morgan 2001, p. 44).

As facilitators we regularly become targets for patients' projections. One moment they may feel angry and challenge us, and the next wish to protect us. The atmosphere can change and tensions can arise in seconds. We may feel ourselves being pushed into responding in particular ways, taking sides, reassuring or offering solutions. Alternatively we may be excluded, criticised or blamed.

During especially difficult sessions it can be hard for us to process in any useful way what is going on. The sense of despair and hopelessness that can arise is sometimes overwhelming for us. Alongside feelings of sadness and concern, we have both experienced shameful and even sadistic feelings of irritation and disgust.

Corbett speaks about the defence mechanism of splitting being activated by intellectually disabled patients to fend off feelings of depression, which they are not psychologically equipped to feel. He locates much of the content of their projections within the countertransference, which he describes as the container for the patient's "unfeelable feelings such as depression, sadness, love, hatred, arousal and numbness" (Corbett 2014, p. 78).

There are times when we have found ourselves overcome by such feelings leading to a mental 'shut-down'; however one of us usually manages to hold onto some thinking ability, allowing the other time to recover until we can start to think together again. This shared 'holding process' happens most effectively for us when functioning as a 'couple' that has spent time getting to know and trust each other. This has involved facing very uncomfortable experiences during our early attempts at building up a working relationship. By recognising and being open about our disappointment and anger towards each other, we have been able to work through our differences and use them to benefit the group.

Sessions: content and reflection

The following three vignettes illustrate the functioning of the 'couple' within the group, and give an account of our understanding of what is happening in the sessions.

We will call the patients Brian, Terry and Derek. The therapists will be referred to as MT (music therapist) and AT (art therapist). The music therapist is female and the art therapist is male.

1. 'JAMES, JAMES' and 'THE GLASS OF WATER'

An illustration of internal conflict in a patient (Brian) being projected into 'the couple' and causing a split.

The *'good enough'* couple. The containment of conflict and
the roots of creativity in a music and art therapy group for
forensic patients with intellectual disabilities and mental illness

341

Brian had recently joined the group. In the first month
it became clear he was giving little recognition to MT's
presence in the room. He kept forgetting her name and
she often felt invisible. His comments and demands were
repeatedly directed towards AT as though he was being
idealised, while she was being ignored.

We felt that Brian's history of insecure attachments and
neglect by his family were being re-enacted within the
group, leading to defensive and avoidant behaviours. This
was manifested in his need for control which resulted
in splitting between the couple. It eventually led to
projections of powerful feelings occurring within the group,
which needed to be thought about and processed in order
to reconcile and understand our conflicting experiences.

*Brian came into the room angrily stating he was "ready to break
jaws" following the suspension of his ground leave by his female
consultant psychiatrist in a recent ward round.*

*His playing of the large djembe drum was aggressive and loud,
and he was clearly irritating and alienating the other group
members with the deafening noise. Another patient warned
him that he would break the drum. Brian eventually refused
to play any more after MT commented that his loud playing
was showing the group how he was feeling.*

*MT attempted to engage Brian and the rest of the group in a
reflective discussion. The atmosphere became tense and it was
not clear whether Brian might need to be escorted back to the
ward. He suddenly turned to AT and asked him for a glass of
water, but as AT started to get him a cup, MT asked them to
wait until the discussion had finished. She felt momentarily
overwhelmed with anger towards both Brian and AT as she
wanted the group to stay together and think about what was
happening. However AT was feeling slightly humiliated and
began to feel some anger towards MT.*

*Following a short discussion the group members resumed
playing music together and settled down. They then moved
across to the art table without any further interruptions. It
was clear later that both therapists were still carrying strong
feelings about what had happened earlier.*

This was the first significant attack on our functioning as a therapeutic couple. It left us feeling uneasy with each other, and we even questioned our capacity to continue working together.

We needed to be open and honest about our responses to what had taken place. We had to identify what had caused us to feel so threatened and to disentangle our personal issues from those of the patients and the dynamics of the session. This included recognising that the toxic aspects of what had occurred needed to be understood in relation to the group members.

We were aware that Brian had experienced neglect and abandonment by his mother who had a history of substance misuse. As a result of her inability to look after him and family breakdown, Brian was taken into care. When his father remarried, Brian briefly went to live with him and his new family. However this arrangement also broke down and although his father maintained contact, Brian spent the rest of his early life in institutional care. The following piece of clay work was completed by Brian after he discovered that his father had moved permanently abroad with the rest of the family. Brian had not been informed and all contact between them ceased (see figure 2).

It seemed to us that the anger we had been feeling towards each other was a response to Brian's projections. On reflection we recognised how, in our role as therapists, we had in turn become the neglectful, rejecting mother and the available, conciliatory father in his mind.

The group had helped him start to process the devastating impact of his abandoning family, and this was later reflected in a drawing which contained the words: *"My Dad love me very much."* It showed a sense of wishful thinking and hope, linked to the idea of reparation.

The *'good enough'* couple. The containment of conflict and
the roots of creativity in a music and art therapy group for
forensic patients with intellectual disabilities and mental illness

343

Fig. 2: Brian's clay work:
Brian's clay work, understood to be a self-portrait
which he flattened by bashing with a rolling pin.

After this session Brian's relation to MT began to improve. The
therapists felt the patients were aware of the splitting nature of what
had taken place between the 'couple'; what they then experienced over
the following weeks was that some kind of recovery and reparation
had taken place, which allowed the 'couple' to continue to function
together and provide a containing space.

2. "HAVE YOU HAD A SEX CHANGE?"

An illustration of how the group members discovered
something about 'difference' with particular reference to
gender and sexuality.

It is not unusual for the group members to comment on
who sits where in the circle when they arrive in the room.
This is part of the transition into the clinical space and
provides an opening for discussion.

It is also a way to avoid the feelings associated with moving from being an individual (separate and potentially isolated), to becoming part of a group process.

After sitting down in the circle, Brian pointed out that Terry was eating chocolate and reminded him of the rules about not eating in the art room. Terry ignored these comments and turning to AT, asked him if he had had a sex change and started laughing. He then said: "you are sitting in MT's chair". There were surprised looks on everyone's faces.

AT commented that sex is not often discussed in this group and that he wondered if this is a difficult or taboo subject. Derek said sex was too embarrassing to talk about in a group and made sniggering noises. Brian was cautious about speaking his mind and asked for the group rules to be restated before he could feel comfortable talking. The others remained quiet.

MT made a statement about 'difference' – how each of us is different and how each of us thinks and reacts differently to each other and to situations. She pointed out that amongst us there are obvious differences, such as Derek has a beard but no one else has a beard. Derek seemed anxious and started making jokes. He was bringing attention to himself while at the same time shutting down the group discussion.

MT said there was one specific difference about her from the rest of the group. They went quiet for a few moments and then spoke almost in unison saying "she is a woman".

This 'momentous' discovery seemed to open up the patients' minds to 'something new'. It appeared to give them permission to be 'curious' without the defensive jokes.

We wondered whether they had now recognised us as being individuals (who are different and separate from each other), while at the same time making the link between us as a 'couple'.

The *'good enough'* couple. The containment of conflict and
the roots of creativity in a music and art therapy group for
forensic patients with intellectual disabilities and mental illness

345

We felt that the original question posed by Terry had brought about an opportunity to discuss sexual identity and difference that had previously been unacknowledged. This has been particularly important for him as he has a preoccupation with autoerotic asphyxiation and bondage.

Terry's difficulties with intimacy extend to all interpersonal relations and he finds being part of a group particularly challenging. His wish to get close to MT was highlighted by his comment on the seating arrangements. This is manifested in other ways – wanting to sit close, play duets and dance with MT and commenting on her clothing. His enmeshed relationship with his own mother is felt to be a source of deep resentment and anger, which appears in the form of passive-aggressive behaviour. It is likely that early developmental issues are at the root of his paraphilia and the isolation he is struggling with. This can be understood in terms of Mervyn Glasser's theory of the 'core complex' which explains how sexual perversion develops from a need to control the object with the aim of avoiding traumatic states associated with feeling either overwhelmed or isolated (Glasser 1964).

It was apparent to us that the patients' defences were being challenged by the discussions, which enabled them to think more openly about their relationships with each of the other group members. The themes of identification, gender and difference seemed to be emerging in Terry's mind and were brought to the group when he asked AT whether he'd had a sex change. The group had discovered that it was possible to experience and talk about intimacy in a safe way.

3. "THEY ARE WATCHING ALL OF US WANKING IN OUR ROOMS"

An illustration of the impact that breaks in therapy can have on patients and therapists: the fear of being 'forgotten about'.

The group members are clearly affected by breaks, however they can struggle to recognise and articulate the feelings that arise. A common reaction is a denial of any attachments and the loss of the 'secure base' (Ainsworth 1968 and Bowlby 1988).

We feel that in our role as the 'couple' we contribute to their sense of security and attachment based on us both being present every week.

When Derek says "breaks are good", we are reminded of his past. He has been setting fires ever since he witnessed the death of his young sister when he was only four years old. The trauma of this early loss, compounded with a breakdown in family structure, has continued to resonate with him. He has been unable to move out of secure hospitals for over 20 years.

The group members were aware that it was the final session before a two-week break. Some of them acknowledged the importance of the group, and there seemed to be an increase in their need to be 'seen' and 'heard' (and not forgotten about).

The group took a while to settle down that day.

Brian brought up the issue of on-going bullying on the ward. He often felt scared, and said he had now been moved to a new room where the nursing staff were able to keep an eye on him.

Terry joined in and gave his own examples of being picked on.

Derek confirmed what the other two had described, saying he had seen the bullying himself, adding that he sees everything on this ward. He said: "They don't come near me because I'm quiet and it's the quiet ones you have to be careful of".

Derek seemed keen to talk about the break, and said he thinks breaks are good as they offer a chance to relax.

Brian and Terry both said they would miss the group during the break.

The *'good enough'* couple. The containment of conflict and
the roots of creativity in a music and art therapy group for
forensic patients with intellectual disabilities and mental illness

347

*Derek said: "What if one of you got sick and was off for a
long time?" His comment prompted a long discussion where
they all began to question the issue of always having the
same two therapists present.*

*We avoided offering unrealistic assurances that we would
always be there to run the group, but held the focus on the
group's fear of loss and separation.*

*Terry started strumming the guitar and MT took his lead
and agreed that it was a good idea to play some music. After
playing the instruments together, the group moved over to
the art tables.*

*In the last 10 minutes of the session, the group moved
back to the circle to look at their artwork. Derek's artwork
provoked a discussion on the theme of watching and being
watched (see figure 4).*

*Brian started laughing at this idea of being watched on
the ward and said loudly: "Hey they are watching all of us
wanking in our rooms", and continued laughing.*

In this vignette we felt there was something in Brian's statement
that illustrates a particular paradox for this patient group, related to
'watching' and 'being watched'. There is being watched and feeling
intimidated, and then there is being watched over and feeling safe
and secure.

Brian's sexualised statement seemed to be implying an
exhibitionist aspect to imagining that he is being watched by the
(voyeuristic?) nursing staff. In contrast, he likes to tell everyone in
the group how much he enjoys watching a particular porn channel on
TV – he becomes the voyeur.

We interpreted Brian's comment as also being related to the
forthcoming break; it is painful to realise that we won't be there to
'watch' them in the group over the coming two weeks.

Terry shows a desire to be watched or seen when he rings the alarm alerting nursing staff to come and find him naked on his bed with various bondages around parts of his body. His desire to give others a strong sense of his disturbed inner world is also perhaps being enacted in his repetitive drawings of female figures (see figure 3).

Fig. 3: Terry's image of a row of female figures
One of many images depicting his fetish for women
dressed in boots and leather clothing.

Derek talks about being watched all the time and seeing everything that's happening on the ward. He often describes his colourful paintings as psychedelic and many contain the 'all seeing' eye. They cover the whole sheet of paper and can also feel suffocating, which we feel has a special meaning related to his obsession with fire-setting.

In the vignettes we have shown how the therapeutic 'couple' can experience damaging projections from patients which has an impact on the functioning of the group. As painful as these experiences can be, we feel they are an essential element in the group's development and survival.

The *'good enough'* couple. The containment of conflict and
the roots of creativity in a music and art therapy group for
forensic patients with intellectual disabilities and mental illness

349

Fig. 4: Derek's 'psychedelic' painting
The 'all-seeing eyes'

When splitting occurs we feel the group members unconsciously take note of what is happening between us. Our capacity to 'stay together' and continue thinking together allows them to feel 'held' and 'safe'.

We have focused on the central role played by 'the couple' in the functioning of the group and in promoting 'creativity' and 'symbolic thinking'. This has meant understanding our relationship and how to survive the attacks coming from within, from outside and from each other. The containing role of the 'couple' has helped provide a containing space which has encouraged the expression of intrapersonal and interpersonal conflicts which can be tolerated and thought about together.

Summary and conclusion

During the early stages of forming this group, there were times when we were unsure whether it would get off the ground and whether it could survive the uncertainties as well as the challenges. We were fully aware that we were working in a toxic and unpredictable environment, and we were all - therapists and patient members - working in the dark at times. However, we brought to the project our commitment and determination and we also knew that we had support from our team and managers.

Some of the positive outcomes that have been recognised are encouraging. The group members have become more spontaneous and playful during sessions. They have been learning how to take responsibility and tolerate frustration. They have started thinking together about the way they relate to each other (both within the group and outside it) and to us. They also show an increase in empathy towards others as well as to themselves, and are better at listening to other people's voices and views, and have begun discovering their own. Overall there is evidence of an increase in relatedness to the instruments, to the materials and their art imagery and to each other. Over time there has been a notable reduction in defensiveness, an increase in trust and a stronger sense of ownership of the group by its members.

Writing this chapter has provided us with an opportunity to look back as well as forward. Our earlier uncertainty and vulnerability has been replaced by a deeper understanding of what we are dealing with and what is possible.

The changes in our perspective throughout the development of this group have led to plans for a second group with 'hard to engage' patients. The new patients being assessed have watched their peers attend the existing group with regularity and commitment and are showing a healthy curiosity.

Since setting up the group over five years ago, we have seen some changes in the membership. One of the core members of the group we have been describing has very recently been discharged from hospital, and several members have moved into low-secure settings.

BIBLIOGRAPHY

Ainsworth, M (1968) *Object relations, dependency, and attachment: A theoretical review of the infant mother relationship.* Child Development, 40, 969-1025.

Barenboim, D and Said, EW (2004) Parallels and Paradoxes: Explorations in Music and Society. London, Bloomsbury.
Bowlby, J (1988) *A Secure Base*. London, Routledge.

The *'good enough'* couple. The containment of conflict and
the roots of creativity in a music and art therapy group for
forensic patients with intellectual disabilities and mental illness

351

Corbett, A (2014) Disabling Perversions: Forensic
Psychotherapy with People with Intellectual Disabilities (The
Forensic Psychotherapy Monograph Series). London, Karnac.

Glasser, M (1964) Aggression and Sadism in the Perversions. In
I. Rosen (Ed) *Sexual Deviation*. Oxford, OUP, pp. 279-300.

Klein, M (1946) 'Notes on some Schizoid Mechanisms' in M.
Klein, *Envy and Gratitude*. London, Vintage, pp. 1-24 (1997).

Morgan, D (2001) 'The internal couple and the Oedipus
complex in cases of perversion' in Morgan, D and Ruszczynski,
S (Eds), *Lectures on Violence, Perversion and Delinquency*. The
Portman Papers (2007) London, Karnac.

Winnicott, DW (1971) *Playing and Reality*. London, Tavistock.

CHAPTER 20

The internal bomb

MARIO GUARNIERI[38], ALEX MAGUIRE[39],
MARTINA MINDANG[40] & DERYK THOMAS[41]

Forward

The Internal Bomb was a performance-based arts therapies piece which the authors first showcased at the 2008 International Association for Forensic Psychotherapy conference in Venice. The piece was reprised at the 21st Forensic Arts Therapies Conference in London in November of the same year.

In contrast to the more typical approach of reading a prepared text, here the presentation took the form of a live multimedia performance intended to provoke a visceral response in the audience. In fact, from the outset we had an idea of playing with conference goers' expectations (in terms of what would most likely happen) as we attempted to show how we worked in our unique setting, rather than simply describing it. The vitality – and sometimes urgency - of our clinical environment was preserved by our insistence on an improvisatory approach to the material.

Writing from a perspective of revisiting this work several years later, the printed page now offers an opportunity to add some of our thoughts on presenting as a team, as well as our reflections on that

---

38 Dramatherapist

39 Music Therapist

40 Art Therapist

41 Art Therapist

most exacting of institutions: the high security hospital for mentally disordered offenders. Indeed, the live presentation of The Internal Bomb turned out to be as much a comment on our experiences of working in this particular NHS forensic setting as it was on our patients' often chaotically volatile material, and we hope that the additional material offered here serves to open a window - if ever so slightly - on an otherwise closed and fortified world.

Context

The Internal Bomb was developed during a time when persistent reorganisation of the institution had become a constant and disorientating backdrop to our daily work. The national picture suggested that we were not alone in this respect. We became aware of numerous long-established disciplines, including other arts therapies services within the same NHS Trust, being similarly instructed to undertake repeated reviews of their efficacy as part of greater organisational changes within the health service up and down the country.

Key therapeutic concepts that we held as valuable and 'worth something' – ideas of stillness, sanctuary, reflection, reverie, process and so forth - rapidly seemed anathema in the face of ever pressing drives to cost-improve year on year. Providing more with less became the mantra, as our own arts therapies service came under increasing scrutiny in terms of its value to the institution. On more than one occasion we were advised to 'get creative' when it came to finding ways of honouring the desired savings each year. In fact, precisely around the time of our presentation, two colleagues had recently left their posts, only for these positions to be frozen without any hint of a future thaw. As if to demonstrate this now cost-improved situation within the service, we watched in dismay as their recently re-fitted clinical space quickly simply became a storeroom for large items of discarded and obsolete equipment.

Whilst we felt generally valued by fellow Multi-Disciplinary Team[s] members, quite how we were viewed by the larger institution remained persistently unclear. In this respect, we shared a commonly felt tension: that of knowing the value of the work with our patients - because we saw it, heard it, wrote about it and presented it - but then struggling with the quantitative modes of evaluation by which we were being measured and judged. This balance between internal and external knowing is at the heart of both this chapter and of our continuing clinical work in an ongoing time of austerity.

Paradoxically, within the total institution of a high security hospital, there exists something of a predictable unpredictability, in that expecting the unexpected is all-pervasive, to the extent of becoming the accepted norm. When an incident alarm bell rings, for instance, it can be heard by everyone across the hospital site. Staff who may have only seconds before appeared composed and unhurried might suddenly be seen running from all directions towards the source of the alarm. Indeed it's this sense of alarm and response that is never too far from each and every, moment by moment, interpersonal exchange between staff and patients. When devising - and then evolving - a form for presenting The Internal Bomb, we looked to convey something of this sudden and unpredictable movement in the work. In this respect, we wished to connect with the inherent tensions involved in enabling the safe expression of a patient's explosive material in a highly risk-averse environment.

Setting the scenes

Prior to writing our presentation we met regularly as a team, both formally and informally. In retrospect, our professional relationships with each other were not only enriched by clinical discussions during work hours, but were also enlivened by our attending galleries, music/ literature events, theatre and films with each other. These shared experiences were drawn upon in preparation for our presentation making for lively, creative and mutually supportive discussions - reminding each other of who we were professionally, and why it was that we did what we did. Additionally, this was a way of keeping our media in our own, and each other's minds. Our work actively engaged with the strains and resistances in the patient and the hospital, both of which contain the lived experiences of extreme and destructive forces at play.

As we set about the task of showing the uniqueness of our work, we decided that our presentation should not necessarily follow the path of a written academic paper nor a PowerPoint slideshow to be read aloud to delegates. Rather, we wanted to use the collective whole of our vocabularies and incorporate something of our artist selves. The presentation, we decided, needed to have art, music and drama actively present, and after much experimentation we arrived at a piece of inclusive theatre as a form which we all felt best held these elements together.

A series of workshops were then planned into our timetable. Theatre director Jungian analyst and psychoanalytic psychotherapist Richard Wainwright were recruited as guide and director of the devising and rehearsal process, providing the all-important third position. Like any creative process, the workshops were enlivening as we played, improvised, experimented and tried out ideas. Eventually the piece took form and was shaped into what became a working script, which, even in performance, still left room for further improvisation.

What follows is an updated version of our working script, edited to facilitate reading from the printed page.

The performance

Throughout, the therapists/performers move fluidly in and out of character and role, each playing the therapist, the patient and the narrator in rotation. There are four scenes each representing one therapy/patient relationship. It is important to note that whilst we are representing our patients, we are not imitating them but using their words. To mark the end of each scene, all four therapists/performers move to stand with their backs to the audience, allowing a moment of stillness before moving to take up new roles in the next scene.

As the audience enters the space, the performance has already begun. The sound of a metronome ticking is heard, which remains constant throughout. The set is occupied by a number of objects situated on different visual planes. Projected onto a large screen at the back of the performance area is a series of changing images showing patients' artwork and quotations. In a corner there is a large hanging blank paper with inks and marker pens at the ready. This is called The Image of the Institution - throughout the performance, each presenter will contribute to what will become, by the end of the performance, a live group picture of the changing institution they work in. Scattered around the stage area, resting at various heights on tables, chairs and the floor, are hand-held musical instruments, masks and lots of other small objects that might typically be found in art, drama or music therapy rooms.

> ALEX, DERYK, MARIO *and* MARTINA *are in the performance area, each depicting an experience of their patients they are about to present.*

> MARTINA *is sitting on the floor, playing with paper (cutting, ripping, shaping…).*

> DERYK *is drawing/painting and playing with building blocks.*

> ALEX *also plays with building blocks, and tinkers with musical instruments.*

> MARIO *is moving from one place to another - stopping to look at the others, destructively criticising whatever he sees and hears, and knocking over the building blocks. Sporadically, he stands or sits still, looking at the projected images before moving again. He then starts playing with a co-oper band, (big elasticated band covered with fleecy material), slowly, accidentally, getting himself tangled up in it, getting more and more frustrated.*

> ALEX *starts to create more noise – using objects as percussion as well as other instruments. This gets gradually louder and louder, ending in… a CRASH!*

Silence.

In this piece ALEX. DERYK *and* MARTINA *rotate the role of* NARRATOR, *contribution to the 'Image Of The Institution' and rearrange the time-objects.* MARIO *represents* SIMON. *The performance area is suffused with movement.*

SIMON: *(Still entangled, can hardly move. Ranting) It's always stuffy in this hospital. (Finally, he untangles himself, opens the windows and continues roaming around the space, never still, except momentarily). They always have the heating on; breeds germs. Supposed to be a hospital! Still, who cares about us? The professionals know best!*

NARRATOR: *Mario worked with Simon in individual dramatherapy for six years. The way Simon moved through the space and his rageful ranting allowed Mario to see and hear more clearly the symbolic connection with his internal psychic space.*

A number of offences coloured Simon's forensic history, involving explosive devices, kidnapping, and sexual offence against a child.

SIMON: That's just a sick report from someone who works for the system - and the system is corrupt.

NARRATOR: *Simon never missed a session, and he always roamed the space, looking searchingly, suspiciously, reminiscent of a caged lion.*

SIMON: *I'm going round in circles. People don't care what I think. How can I trust people who don't care? People don't trust me. Nobody believes what I say. Nobody listens. They hear but they don't do anything. I tell the truth. I never tell lie. Professionals tell lies.*

NARRATOR: *Simon discharges his rage. It's a verbal onslaught. He cannot include the concept of otherness, and cannot enter into a dialogue that can explore the issues that underpin his enraged and encaged experience.*

Mario struggles to manoeuvre freely, to facilitate Simon out of his internal claustrophobia to where space can be safely tolerated. Mario questioned the validity of the sessions, but also felt a deep compassion for Simon and thought it essential to remain present, engaged and indestructible. For Simon, the space to think was perceived as threatening. Before any meaningful therapeutic engagement could occur, Mario needed to act as a container for Simon's destructive projections.

Simon is the middle child of five, all born roughly a year apart from each other. So, Simon was 'boxed in' from the beginning. As a child he was witness to, and a direct victim of, familial violence, sexual abuse and neglect. Simon recalls being rendered immobile, paralysed by fear of the violence within the household. He reported the abuse to the social agencies, but was apparently not believed and sent back home. He tried a number of times to commit suicide.

Simon re-enacts his painful past in the sessions, projecting into Mario all the feelings he cannot contain within himself - the sense of being stuck, overwhelming sadness and frustration, and of course, an all-consuming rage. Simon moves through space but without awareness of it. He is always looking for the danger zones. He is only concerned about controlling the space around him; refusing to see the possibilities that objects in the space can be of help to him - a good enough other. Mario wondered how Simon would experience a state of stillness and quietness - of letting space in.

SIMON: *Too much space is dangerous.*

NARRATOR: *Simon experienced stillness as abusive, linked to felt paralysis during familial abuse. He therefore must constantly be moving and filling silences with his ranting. Controlling his objects, immobilising them in order to feel safe himself. The impact of abuse and neglect, together with the authorities whom sent home, has dominated Simon's experience of professionals as dangerously bad objects. And, he uses the institution to show what it is like to be 'boxed-in'. His combative state, although frightening for Simon, is perhaps less frightening than the non-combative state. The latter would mean that his pain is really felt.*

In forensic arts psychotherapy practice, the idea of allowing a space where creativity is possible is all-important, even though much of the work concerns the containment and survival of the patient's need to destroy.

> **SIMON:** *It's hard to be creative in a place like this. How can I be normal in a place that isn't normal?*

> **NARRATOR:** *Simon's internal bomb was constantly threatening to explode, but together they managed to contain it to smaller, controlled explosions. As Simon left the dramatherapy space for the last time after six years, he said…*

> **SIMON:** *I don't know what I'm going to do now.*

> **ALL:** *Move upstage, one by one, stand in a line with backs to audience - momentary stillness – before moving into the next vignette.*

In this piece ALEX. DERYK and MARIO rotate the role of NARRATOR, contribution to the 'Image Of The Institution' and rearrange the time-objects. MARTINA represents MATT is sitting on the floor colouring a large piece of paper with a fine pen.

> **NARRATOR:** *Matt is a tall, burly man of 33 years with a baby face. His diagnosis is paranoid schizophrenia and mild learning disabilities. Historically, Matt has not been referred to psychotherapy - he presents no management problems, and apart from being suspected by staff of 'holding a grudge', he is generally pleasant.*

Matt came to art therapy for four years during which time he said very little and the action of the art therapy moved slowly despite the art therapist's effort to change the pace.

Tick Tock

It is obvious that Matt does not like to experience beginnings and endings. He never starts or ends an image within a session and a picture is always left in an unfinished state, he picks-up where he left off in the next session.

The sessions assume a monotonous, continuous, uneventful pace, which the art therapist often anticipates with dread. During sessions the art therapist's mind would wander to unrelated matters, experience time at an excruciating slow pace. She is angry, sleepy, bored and unable to change this.

Tick Tock

This patient material is brought to supervision often with the thought that this is not working-out and with the question: 'Should I bring this therapy to an end?'

At times they move in the space together to look at pictures but Matt walks around the table and chairs to avoid standing close by. In the image the figures and objects are as separated as he is in the room from the art therapist. He works seated at a table with image very close to his chest.

Tick Tock

NARRATOR: *Often the image is a repeated one. Matt discusses it in a fixed and predictable way: the same trees, the same number of trees, in the same shape and position. The therapist feels sleepy, angry, guilty, redundant and intrusive when she comments, "Is he filling in time?"*

During those sessions when the therapist's mind has drifted she is jolted awake by the thought that Matt stabbed to death an older man who had befriended him, believing the man to have sexually assaulted him whilst he slept. He retells this event as though it was carried out with the same amount of deliberation and preparation as his activities in the sessions.

Eventually a bed in a Regional Secure Unit is identified. Beginnings and endings are discussed in every session and he is warned that the unfinished image may not be completed next week.

Tick Tock

But the art-work is planned and predictable as usual, no room for improvisation or mistake. There is no mixing of colours. No spillage. No mess. Working from left to right with pulled up sleeves...

SUDDENLY MATT SNEEZES AND MAKES A MISTAKE ON THE PAGE!! He apologises, tidies up and begins to talk about the mess he has made. Over the remaining few sessions Matt makes a series of disclosures that ring alarm bells in the therapist's mind. She is now very much awake and paying attention to the messiness of his internal world as it is now being described.

NARRATOR: *His useless parents; neighbours who were* **PISSING** *against him through the walls; the victim a* **BAD APPLE** *- Matt describes a world which is full of hostility, loneliness and rejection, where people are out to* **GET** *him,* **TAKE***, or* **PUT** *into him something hateful. Matt considers himself to be the victim and in his world he is justified in killing another person.*

The art therapist heard all of this like a wake-up call - **like an exploding sneeze or mess!!**

Matt's wishes and fears of being alone could not be articulated but a relationship picture was made. When sessions came to an end, the therapist is left believing that she had not been asleep at her post, so much as surviving the onslaught of a projective identification of Matt's early history and on-going delusional state - an indirect communication of his terror of being a sleeping victim. At other times cast in many precarious roles by him: a careless parent, a nosy neighbour, and a judgemental observer. She had borne-with his image-making, daring to maintain a curious stance and finally arrived with him at this ending position. Matt's 'live' dangerousness could not be carried over to his new clinical team.

By delivering this disturbing material whilst ending the work, Matt again avoided an ending and on hearing that he had left the hospital, she was left with the feeling that this person is most definitely...still ticking.

ALL: *Move upstage, one by one, stand in a line with backs to audience - momentary stillness – before moving into the next vignette.*

In this piece MARTINA, DERYK and MARIO rotate the role of NARRATOR, contribution to the 'Image Of The Institution' and rearrange the time-objects. ALEX represents EDDIE. The performance area continues to be suffused with movement as Eddie screams

"Avoidant! Dependent! Schizoid! Histrionic! Sadistic! Borderline!"

Eddie punctuates his diagnoses with ear-splitting cracks on a drum

NARRATOR: *Eddie is a 24 year old man diagnosed with multiple personality disorders; he shouts these out between violent attacks on a drum. His brother is just a year younger. Eddie killed and then sexually abused a young woman in a bar.*

The metronome ticks on, inexorably unwinding its coiled spring.

Whilst his father carries out a campaign of excessive discipline against the two boys, and sexual violence against his wife, Eddie's mother becomes increasingly needy and reliant on others. Reckless overspending, an empty promise pursued in a fruitless search for an elusive feeling of well-being leads to frequent downsizing, and she shuttles the children between schools and homes as a relentless cycle of separation and reconciliation slowly takes its emotional toll.

And the metronome ticks on, oblivious to fearful eyes and ears.

Eddie wears his school trousers, the only pair he has, to go out to play. He's playing at playing; a game that's no fun. Eddie mucks up his homework. Eddie spills some food. Punishment rains down; punishment reigns. Wild, angry, sadistic fantasies rush in to fill the potential good and fertile space. Eddie feels ugly, a social misfit, a bit of a loser, as he can't help saying.

A sexually motivated burglary at aged 13, still wetting the bed a year later; a sexual assault on a family member. Regular sex is impossible for him; he's powerless, his impotence only assuaged by knife-wielding fantasies.

Tick tock, bash and crash, will it never stop?

Then things accelerate; the banging drum joins the robotic metronome; the see-sawing between high and low becomes distorted; feelings of humiliation, fear, anxiety, shame and disappointment become predominant. In therapy, Eddie probes the sand tray with his index finger and I recoil with memories of his offence. Since being in hospital, he's got into every possible space,

endlessly searching for home: one-to-one therapy, various
groups, every supervision space possible. The offence
is re-enacted with the relentless stabbing drumbeats,
the merciless banging. Then Eddie raises a motorcycle
magazine between us.

EDDIE: *You can't make me do therapy.*

NARRATOR: *He dreams of mean machines, the roar of*
the engine and the thrill of getting away from it,
away from the one-way street he's trapped in.

He imagines that I live in the building where therapy takes
place - that I'm 'on call'. His neediness is barely tolerable.
There is nothing inside which can meet these needs;
nothing inside him, nothing inside me. He bangs through
my thoughts and I admire the way his projections are so
clearly aimed, so true to their mark. He feels unskilled
in the therapy. He's a loser at snooker on the ward. He
wants to do therapy better. Eddie wants everything tidy;
he wants to sift through his stuff. He wants to get on, to
get out, get a job, get something. Anything to take the
place of all these raw, unresolved feelings, jangling and
banging together in the internal void, anything to soften
the blows, the undying tick and tock of the cursed clock. I
sit drained, invaded, perforated, empty.

The metronome swings its pendulum; it's won; we give up;
merciless, it smirks (in time) at our wretched attempts to
forge our own path, to evade the inevitable.

One word orbits the therapy room from week to week:
shame. Then two words: shame and punishment.

And then there's more punishment, and the more there
is (for Eddie surely knows how to punish, whether
himself or others), the more shame is heaped up until it

topples over into another punishing episode. And when Eddie feels like this, no-one will necessarily know. Eddie needs…something (anything)…to put in the emptiness.

"Wait until your father gets home" still rings in Eddies ears. The big black cloud of childhood that he's told me about still hangs over him. Petty infringements come back round the carousel, as always met by their familiar punishments and privations. In therapy, Eddie interprets the murder as an act of self-loathing, an attempt to end his life, to take himself out, which in effect, is what he's finally managed to do. He's taken himself out; he's taken control the only way he can; he's taken a life so as to give himself one.

The banging wears itself out, the drum marked with tell-tale scars; silence swirls like mist in the room and we breathe, as after a workout. Faintly yet firmly, the unforgiving tattoo emerges from the silence, and the metronome resumes its deadly march.

ALL: *Move upstage, one by one, stand in a line with backs to audience - momentary stillness – before moving into the next vignette.*

In this piece ALEX. MARTINA and MARIO rotate the role of NARRATOR, contribution to the 'Image of The Institution' and rearrange the time-objects. DERYK represents GRANT. He holds a mask to his face.

NARRATOR: *Grant is 27 with a history of assaults using weapons. When I first meet him, he's screaming obscenities from the far end of a long ward corridor. He's become "a management issue" - racially abusing staff and patients; throwing cups of urine; biting and spitting. I'm reliably told there's a queue of people "waiting to punch his lights out". I see Grant and*

*instinctively want to turn around… instead, I'm shown
a small interview room where Grant sits on the edge of a
chair and continues his tirade. I sense something awful
could easily happen if I say or do the wrong thing.*

Grant's been directed to high security having attacked
a member of staff at his MSU using a piece of metal
furniture. I'm told it's miraculous that the staff member
survived his injuries. The attack had taken place as Grant
was being transferred to an intensive care ward, having
previously run riot in a hospital canteen, smashing the
place up, sending everyone inside fleeing. Months before,
he'd ransacked his hostel placement, barricading other
residents into their rooms until the police eventually
rushed him with shields.

He stops, draws breath, and stares at me…

GRANT: *I'm public fucking enemy… number
fucking one…*

NARRATOR: *Blazing a trail through High Dependency
and Intensive Care – burning/fragmenting all the
while – Grant finally 're-enters the atmosphere' and
is deemed well-enough to be seen off-ward. He claims
he can't remember a thing; "my mind's just a blank".
Therapy might help, he concedes. But then he has
an expectation that I will ask him to look backward
into a past that he can't, or won't, acknowledge.
"The past is gone boss; it's over… no use to me…" his
repeated refrain…*

GRANT: *Just accept it… I'm no one… I've come from
nothing, out of nowhere.*

NARRATOR: *A small mountain of art materials in front
of him, Grant shouts to ask what each of them is
and/or does. It's difficult to get started. Eventually*

he grabs a pen and draws a leering, goofy face: no outline of a head; no sign of a body - just two painted dots for eyes and a sickly grin. The following week, he asks if he can paint one of the plain white masks. He paints the eye-balls black and the lips dark blue. The mask looks "creepy" he tells me, because it looks dead. In the next session, he attempts to give it life by approximating a skin of lurid pink poster paint. His results look raw… like torn flesh… He goes back to this mask, week after week, painting layer upon layer of colour. He discovers oil paints and is intrigued by the length of time they take to dry.

Grant's mother gave him up to social services when he was 5 months old. He spent his formative years in institutional care, with his mother returning unexpected from time to time, saying that she wanted to try again and give her baby a home. In one session, Grant paints a red 'London Bus' and jokes that he'll soon be on one of these, travelling "back to the real world". He then stops and tells me that his mother had visited him in a children's home one Christmas. She'd bought him a red toy bus and said she'd return the next day - maybe they could play with it together. Of course, she never did.

A fragment from his past: It lands in the room like something thrown out from a long dark tunnel.

Grant's attendance improves as he continues painting his masks. They become fleshed and colourful; each one more 'realised' with its own identity and form. Grant looks forward to amending/tending and caring for them. They become objects of good when the colours turn out right, or if the paint dries in time for the next session. They became something frustrating and altogether damnable if the work doesn't go according to plan. Grant settles in the space, exploring and discovering different approaches to painting his masks. Gradually - slowly/steadily - he starts to invest them with feeling… and we both notice this… We begin to talk more about this "weird" (new) process of thinking and caring about the things that he's making: playing and attaching meaning to this play…

"They look alright, don't they?" a new refrain…

MARIO, MARTINA, ALEX *and* DERYK *move upstage
one by one...
The ticking stops... Stillness...*

END OF PRESENTATION

Afterword

Those Arts Therapists who work in the forensic area will be familiar
with the difficulty of explaining what it is they do. Our intention with
The Internal Bomb was, as far as possible, to *do* what we do; to get
as close as possible to using our art to represent our art; we offered
no commentary and no conclusions. In keeping with our patients'
feelings of the endlessness of experience, the performance had no
real beginning or end - we could have started anywhere, and finished
anywhere. The anxiety of the unexpected was ubiquitous and the
improvisatory qualities inherent in our media were called to the fore.

The task of writing this chapter has also been a challenge. In
the original performance we found a way of presenting an experience
of the arts therapies whilst allowing the individual disciplines their
differences, permitting them to be seen and heard together. To try
and retain that aspect here in words is to inevitably lose something
of the immediacy of these similarities and differences; a mirroring of
our patients' move towards the depressive position.

The audience was complicit in this process, which was open to
the unexpected and encouraged improvisation from the presenters.
Using our media in a live performance setting helped to demystify the
feeling-thinking-being process as well as the setting; throughout the
patients' engagement with the media, the materials and the therapist,
the anxiety of engaging in the therapy was ever-present.

As arts therapists working in this environment with patients who
have, in their offending, been out of control, we looked to the creative
script that is our professional disciplines. This specialised alloy of the
arts and psychotherapy gave us the confidence to bear the unknown
and accompany the individual on the move towards material that has
previously been experienced as explosively volatile. Through a symbolic
re-enactment with the medium, a metabolisation of 'psychological

semtex' can be safely handled, and we may work with the patient towards a controlled explosion or a defusing of the violent psychic state which we have referred to in this chapter as: The Internal Bomb.

BIBLIOGRAPHY

Bailey, D. (1993) *Improvisation: its nature and practice in music*. Boston, Da Capo Press.

Boal, A. (1992) *Games For Actors And Non-Actors*, translated by Adrian Jackson. London, Routledge.

Brecht, B. (1964) *Brecht on Theatre*, ed. John Willett. New York, Hill and Wang.

Cox, M. and Theilgaard, A. (1997) *Mutative Metaphors in Psychotherapy: the Aeolian Mode*. London, Jessica Kingsley Publishers.

Grotowski, J. (1969) *Towards A Poor Theatre*. London, Methuen & Co. Ltd.

Nuttall, J. (1980) *Performance Art Volumes 1 and 2*. London, Calder Publications.

Schechner, R. (1985) *Between Anthropology and Theater*. Philadelphia, University of Pennsylvania Press.

Stern, D. (2004) *The Present Moment in Psychotherapy and Everyday Life*. New York, W.W. Norton and Company.

CHAPTER 21

An art-based exploration in forensic treatment in the Netherlands

THIJS DE MOOR

Introduction

Art therapy treatment in the forensic facility at the Pompekliniek in Nijmegen, the Netherlands, is where patients who have committed serious offences and suffer from psychotic and/ or personality disorders are treated. The art therapy studio at the Pompekliniek provides a holding and containing environment where both the patients and therapist can gain new insight into art therapeutic processes. The use of artistic material and the therapeutic process act as a vehicle for a better understanding of the forensic patient. I will describe how art-based interventions and art-based inquiry provide new possibilities and opportunities for art therapeutic treatment in forensic psychiatry.

Forensic treatment in the Pompekliniek, the Netherlands

The Pompekliniek in Nijmegen, the Netherlands, is a private clinic for forensic psychiatry. This institution treats male offenders who have committed an offence as a result of their mental health issues. The clinic contributes to a safer society by offering the patients opportunities to not reoffend. The central theme is safety, that is, to prevent new or repeated offences being committed both in the short and long term. In the short term, staff monitor and supervise patients so that, if necessary, immediate and adequate action is taken using the means available to us. To achieve long-term safety, patients are helped to develop a way of life in which there is no room for new offences. Successful treatment requires a safe environment, one in which patients are given sufficient time and space to develop what is necessary to live an offence-free life. Each of the 130 patients at the Pompekliniek has committed a serious offence, for which a judge has imposed a secure treatment order. Every second year, the judge can impose a new treatment order if he or she finds the defendant not fully accountable for his crime, due to a mental disorder, and fears that the offence may be repeated.

The frame of the inpatient offender treatment is largely the same everywhere in forensic treatment in the Netherlands. On his arrival the patient is confined to his cell at the unit and can only leave under strict supervision by a member of the staff. After this period, the patient attends the therapeutic places, occupational places and workplaces. In time he gains more freedom, extending from ground parole to escorted and unescorted walks and visits. The patient's participation in the treatment program aims at rehabilitating the offender to the extent where he is able to return safely into society. Treatment programmes vary from cognitive behavioural approaches to psychodynamic and psychotherapeutic programmes. The final goal in the treatment of offender patients is to prevent repeat offending. In the Netherlands, society believes that treatment is a better option for reaching that goal than a prison term.

For the therapists working in a multi-disciplinary way in the Pompekliniek, a safe environment is a prerequisite; they need safety in order to carry out their work properly. Security and treatment interlock in many ways.

Since the early months of the year 2000, the Pompekliniek has been working with 'treatment programming', a method applied in the general mental health care system. Such programming means that for the patients, the essential, state-of-the-art diagnostic and treatment elements are determined.

The clinical environment is organised to promote the treatment aims. An important rule is that the environment may not obstruct the treatment process, as a prison environment often does. Where possible, the clinical environment is organised so it facilitates the realization of the therapeutic aims, and is in a practical way representative for the 'outside' world in society so patients can experience 'normal' daily life situations. So the clinic is not only the holding environment, but also the space where the male patients live.

The life history of the majority of forensic patients is characterised by early physical abuse and affective and childhood neglect (disturbed home environments, paternal and/or physical or mental absence), with a family history of psychiatric problems, criminal histories and substance abuse. So far it seems that there is a repetition of intergenerational transmission of trauma. Fraiberg et al (1975) describe these phenomena as existing when a parent seems condemned to repeat the tragedy of his own childhood, re-enacting his/her experience with exact detail.

Patients in forensic psychiatry with personality disorders and/ or psychotic disorders may intimidate and offend others without remorse as a result of their disorganized attachment. In general they lack concern about the consequences of their actions.

Most common issues are: irresponsibility and disregard for normal social behaviour; difficulty in sustaining long term relationships, lack of ability to tolerate frustration and to control their anger, lack of guilt or not learning from their mistakes and blaming others for problems in their lives (NICE 2013).

Many patients in the Pompekliniek have a severe traumatised development background, and as a result of that, have problems with attention deficit problems and perception (Hinz 2009). One of the main characteristics is the low ability to change attention to oneself (initial stimulus) and their environment and back to the self (Ogden, Minton & Pain 2006).

These interactions make reflection, learning and development progress very difficult in art therapy treatment and often lead to therapy dropout. In general patients in the Pompekliniek have low coping scales in dealing with every life situations. The therapeutic environment in which the patients are confronted to work with treatment aims can be experienced as threatening for them.

Art therapy in forensic psychiatry

Art Therapy in the Netherland has developed into a huge collection of theoretical approaches such as psychoanalytic, humanistic, gestalt and cognitive behaviouristic approaches related to different separated or integrated art forms. Despite many differences, all arts therapists believe that the very act of creating is healing, and the majority of approaches aim at providing a safe non-verbal creative space that usually combines with a verbal psychotherapeutic use of the artwork (Lusebrink 1990; Smeijsters 2008).

In the Netherlands, the basic assumption of art therapy is art, and to a lesser extent psychoanalytical theory (Smeijsters 2008; Visser 2000). Theories on art therapy embody the basic 'image elements' of that particular art and the patient's presenting problems guide the art experience, whereas the therapist's task is to try enhance that experience (Baeten 2007). Within this approach, the patient and the therapist also play an essential and irreducible role in successful therapy. The Dutch orientation fully recognises the value of the art therapy triangle, that is, the dynamic relationship between patient, artistic medium and therapist (Smeijsters 2008).

Approaches in art therapy with offenders aims at providing a safe non-verbal creative space in which artwork can be used as a vehicle for communication and expression, further more than verbal expression.

The ideal art therapy triangle is one that is characterised by free verbal and physical communication and elaboration, voluntary participation of the patient and mutual agreement of the patient and therapist on the goals to be reached.

Language impairments and a personality disorder in the initial stages of development usually cannot engage in a free verbal communication.

They often lack the capacity to discuss and set the goals for therapy when they are expected to undergo therapeutic treatment (Rutten–Saris 2002).

Art therapy for patients with underdeveloped or disturbed interaction structures contain aspects that are valuable, provided the intervention is focused on healthy development of the interaction structures through the art therapeutic medium. Making art creates representations of movement and inner motivation. There is similarity between movement in lines and the internal motivation originated from this movement. These expressions include vitality, or the lack of vitality (Rutten-Saris 2002; Smeijsters 2008). A personal expression or signature has a particular quality, which Stern (2004) called vitality. These vitality effects become visible in the patient's movements towards other people, towards himself and towards the things in the world that surround him. Thus, the traces the patient leaves on the surface, irrespective of whether they were drawn intentionally or accidentally, also display a vitality affect.

Stern (1985) developed the term 'vitality affect' to describe aspects of mother-child interactions that could not be captured with regular categorical effects, and also applies the term to adult behaviour. All things appeal to our sense of movement and expression.

In terms of Arnheim (1974), the arts have a visual force; they reveal something of the artist who made the 'drawing'. Smeijsters (2008) defines the acting in the artistic medium and art therapy as the analogue-process model. The 'analogy' between the artistic medium and the psyche implies that psychological processes express themselves in the artistic product. So, art product and art process do not exclude each other; they complement each other.

Many of my patients with challenging behavioural problems often become aggressive as a result of experiencing failure during their art making process. This failure is due to their impulsive behaviour. Through the art therapy process, the patient can learn to attain clear art forms with personal structures and interactions. By making physical contact with the art materials, the patient learns to develop more healthy actions (Muijen & Marissing, 2011). Art materials provide new strategies in interacting and offer structure by means of their artistic possibilities. The process of making is a safe experience where the patient can learn to organise feelings and thoughts. The unique quality of art materials in the art making process demands a disciplined way of acting.

The art materials will act as a motor of dialogue, allowing access to both conscious and unconscious content in a holding environment, and would promote a reorganisation of attachment wounds and issues. This would trigger, starting with the curiosity of the nature of the object (sensory element of play), the capacity to create, imagine and produce an object, the capacity to use this creative act as a way to establish a relationship and finally usage of the space as a facilitator (Winnicott 1971).

Winnicott (1971) located a space between the baby and the mother, calling it the transitional space. The Pompekliniek can be visualised as a transitional space between the outside world and the inner world, realistically and symbolically speaking.

Material interaction, self-expression, and working through offence related behaviour are major themes throughout the art therapy processes. The engagement with art materials offers the patients opportunities to start 'doing' and to learn to explore in the momentum of the art making process. Daniel Stern (2004) highlights the value of energy or momentum in grounding the patient in the present moment by this principle of 'doing'.

Fig.1

By sharing with the therapist in the art process, patients learn to trust the clinical environment, myself as the therapist and themselves. The safety of the art therapy materials and the art therapy studio help patients to regain a grip on their own lives again. Having internal and external dialogue with the artwork during the whole art making process and to relate this to psychodynamic theory gives a deeper understanding in material interaction, communication levels, and the impact of early disorganised attachment on development possibilities.

Art Based Exploration

Visiting the Prinzhorn Collection in Heidelberg, I was totally struck by the work of Josef Forster. Forster was a psychiatric patient from whom some very interesting works survived during the Second World War. Forster was probably suffering from schizophrenia, and during his years in psychiatry he developed his own unique way to use art in a way to survive in life.

Looking at his work I saw a lot of similarities with the work my patients make in the forensic psychiatry. In particular, the search for frame and structure in constructing images is very similar.

Forster found a way to compose his ideas in a rhythmic way to express and to deal with his suffering in life. The use of this metaphor gave him the ability to develop his own creative skills and to express his need to cope with life. This way of expression is somehow the most ultimate form in art therapy in my opinion: the patient is capable, has learned to make new steps in art expression and to give new meaning to his art and life. The artwork of Josef Forster inspired me to start a small art-based research. The method of art-based research gave me new ways of reflection and creating artwork, and helped me to understand the work of my own patients in a new way.

Smeijsters (2008) argues that there is a unit of media and mind, and that the relationship between the two not only comes about through associations or verbal reflection, but also in interpretation. Therapeutic benefit is therefore in the medium already. Admittedly, what occurred during the medium activity level verbal play was also meaningful and used therapeutically, but this is not (always) necessary nor always possible or desirable.

Inside the therapeutic relationship the contact with the media and the use of the media can trigger mental process and sensory experiences that occur outside the clinical setting and throughout evoking these experiences the client could use the space and relationship to enact (replicate) as a parallel process of situations and/or dynamics.

By this analogy, Smeijsters had two things to say. First, along with mental processes, analogous processes occur in medium. Secondly, in the fictional state of the art therapy, real feelings occur, analogous to real situations' outside the therapeutic situation. Within media activities such as drumming or signs are mental processes, or feelings called analogous to psychological processes occurring in the everyday reality of the patient. Based on that, (double) analogy can be treated.

Visual expressions can give meaning to the art therapist as part of their reflective practice and insight into the process of their patients and interventions related to form, shape and symbolism.

The images and creations made by Forster, gave new meaning to my ideas about art therapy and forensic treatment: the metaphor of using artwork during the process gave me insight in a non-direct approach. Forster found his path to do that in a unique and very expressive way. His art making process gave him the structure and ability to cope with his mental issues in life.

In the forensic field, it is visible that patients have major problems with flexibility, learning and problem solving. Patients suffer from schizophrenia or have severe personality disorders. The cyclic method of art-based research can also be used to understand the patient:

By finding new possibilities *in* the art medium, new opportunities and insights may occur. Especially for the forensic population, it is very useful because of the focusing and learning *in* the art medium, and not by learning to verbalize. Patients might be more able to learn to make the analogy between the art process and daily life (Stern 2004). The therapeutic process is possible because the change of expression in the art form is experienced as a change of vitality affects. By experiencing vitality affects in art forms, forensic patients can work through unarticulated layers of experiences and gradually become conscious of cognitive schemes (Smeijsters & Cleven 2006).

One of my patients whom was in treatment for sexual related crimes and diagnosed with a personality disorder made symbolic paintings for 2 months in art therapy treatment. Within his painted images human figures are visible; shaped and expressed in an abstract way. The figures are without detailed faces or shaped with covered faces, and accents with black coloured strives. His handling of brushstrokes is very loose and the background is in only one colour. Every single image seems not well integrated as a whole. For over eight weeks these actions in the art material were repeated by my patient in his way of working. It is becoming clear and visible that my patient is not taking into account what his earlier actions are when setting up his painting. After nine sessions I take time with my patient for reflection and evaluation of his images and therapy process. Within this evaluation we concluded that he has always lived separated lives in a way, and that he lived emotionally and practically in two worlds, repressing his emotions and by that himself. We agreed that it could be helpful for him to change the way of painting, setting up, and expressing. This 'new start' gave my patient more insight in his actions and offered a new opportunity to see and learn how his (crime) behaviour and personal needs in daily life could be expressed and lead to new insights and learning. After this moment my patient also felt more in control of his actions which leads to more self confidence, and more responsibility of his artistic process. This is just a simple example of how art therapy contributes to working on the therapeutic aims.

Reflections

Shape, colour, content, subject and symbolism of the artwork are the assumptions and healing factors in art therapy treatment. Especially in forensic treatment art therapy contributes as a result of the learning component *in* the art medium. In the Pompekliniek many patients suffer from personality disorders and as a result of that they developed a low window of tolerance leading to aggressive verbalizing and acting out behavior. The way of working through the process gives insight into the possibilities for treatment with offenders in forensic psychiatry. Art therapy seems effective by its individual nature by giving patients space to explore conscious and unconscious processes. Visual expressions can give meaning and insight into the behavior of the patient and the accompanying thoughts and feelings.

The degree of progress is connected with many different factors. The developmental abilities of the patient especially determine the outcome of the therapy. A huge advantage of art therapy is that working with art materials is achievable by all patients. By working with simple patterns, materials and assignments and repeating these, it is possible to get unconscious processes in motion. The individual character of art therapy makes it possible for the therapist to offer customized materials, and exercises, or in other words to develop new models of intervention, adjusted to the specific requirements of the context.

Art therapy in forensic psychiatric treatment gives good results especially with patients who still have skills and possibilities for changing and developing because they benefit of the relation between their experiences in the art work, and daily life situations.

This is the group of patients whom will probably return to an independent life in society. These patients in general do not have a long history of crime, do not have the burden of severe psychiatric disorders and have a relatively high level of intelligence and education. Within this group of patients, where very often a traumatic experience is a cause of their mental issues, the new insights and experiences in coping with their mental issues helps them to sustain a offence free life.

For the group of patients with a long history of crime and offences, suffering from personality disorders in combination with addiction problems, the prospects are less hopeful. During treatment, it is extremely difficult to predict which patient does, and which patient does not, have development possibilities. Art therapy can contribute to diagnoses and, in the case of healthy development by the patient, to the treatment. Patients with severe psychiatric disorders can benefit from art therapy after they have had medication treatment because of the safe and more chanelled way art therapy can offer in working on the treatment aims in therapy.

Within the group of patients where the therapeutic aims and developmental possibilities are extremely low, art therapy can contribute to stabilization, dealing with tension and gaining self-confidence. This population of patients has to accept that a full independent return to society is not a possibility. The treatment program for this population is aiming to help these patients to have a life under protected custody.

Further Discussion

Forensic patients in art therapy treatment are encouraged to act differently and explore experiences in the present moment. This approach during the present moment in the art therapy process appeals on the vitality affects of the core self of the patient. Proceeding in the art process is analogous to experiencing vitality affects in the core self. In the art process, the patient can express the shifts of feelings in the core self and explore new ways of feeling and behaviour.

The challenge for art therapists is to rely (more) on the power of the art therapeutic medium. By following the general standards in methodology and research, art therapists are not true to the specific craft of the art therapeutic medium. In my opinion it demands from art therapists that they must have a broader view on the use of the artistic medium, and the way to use the art medium in research. In the forensic field, like in the general spectrum of art therapy treatment, there is always the need and pressure to prove that art therapeutic interventions work.

So in art therapy research it is necessary to participate and to unite as art therapists in large scale research studies to contribute to evidence based practice; in my opinion it is also useful to show what art based research specifically can add to the specific qualities gained *in* the art therapeutic medium, both in methodology and in research. For art therapists, the methodology of art-based inquiry is helpful to show in their own institution how relatively small research gives specific information about better understanding of the forensic patient. Results from art-based inquiry can give more knowledge about expressions in the artistic medium from patients, and for better insight in the related crime behavior of forensic patients, and in multidisciplinary treatment in forensic.

As an experienced art therapist in forensic psychiatry, I do not believe in single treatment programmed on disorders. In many cases it is necessary to customize treatment to the developmental possibilities of the patient and to work therapeutically in person centred way. The best outcome in art therapy treatment is where the forensic psychiatric patient can work on his therapeutic aims and art process in a way where he has as much autonomy, control and responsibility as possible in his art therapy treatment. However it is not possible to predict in advance what works and what does not in art therapy. There are too many facets in life influencing the behaviour of the patient. Some patients benefit mostly from medication, others by (art) psychotherapy. Some benefit the most from the non-verbal character of the artistic material, where others benefit the most from the personal contact with the therapist.

The most important interventions are, in my opinion, being clear and reliable and allow the client to heal attachment wounds when possible. As a therapist I take as much space as is necessary to make agreements with my patient. This is essential for building up trust and being a reliable 'other' to my patient. If a patient does not trust the situation and the contact, all other art therapeutic interventions will not work. In the beginning of the art therapy process, my aims and interventions are mainly focused on the patients' behavior with the material and on increasing the intensity of the art working process. Interventions relating to form, shape and symbolism, will be directed later on in the art therapy process. I strive to allow patients, within the safe environment, to have as much control as possible during their therapy process.

Conclusion

The main goal in the Pompekliniek, and in forensic art therapy in the Netherlands in general, is to strive to help the patient to a healthy return in society, this reflects in my therapeutic attitude in giving my patient as much autonomy and independence within the framing of the therapeutic aims and process.

Forensic psychiatric patients are difficult to treat in general. The main focus in treatment is to reduce the offensive behaviour, but it is difficult to get through the thoughts and emotions around these behaviours. Within this group of patients adapted behaviour is very common. They seek stability in structure and rules, and as a result they are capable of showing doubt and emotions. In expressing and working with art materials the patient is not only showing himself, the patient is also being himself. Art working is undisguised and it very often results, in the first instance, in many patients fearing this 'uncontrollable' medium, and showing a great deal of resistance.

The patient in forensic psychiatry knows he is not able to hide in the material and art process. At the same time, this is the power of the art therapeutic medium. If the art therapist is able to have the patient work through the materials, things can be visible, which otherwise would have stayed hidden. Even though the patient will take over control again during verbal evaluation and will try to explain his acts, the experiences during the art making process and the product of the process will remain as visible clues for his thoughts, feelings and behavior. The forensic patient, who is obliged to change his behavior, needs this contact with his thoughts, feelings and fantasies. Patients have to replace emotional effects ot the crime they commited in their past in their continuing life. This traumatic experience should be chanelled in such way that the patient is able carry this burden whereby he can stay in touch with his emotions *and* is able to change his behavior.

REFERENCES:

Baeten, N. 2007. *Art Therapy, in Forensic Practice.* Uitgave EFP: Amsterdam

Bogdorf, H. (2005). *Het debat over onderzoek in de kunsten* (Lezing).

Fraiberg S, Adelson E, Shapiro V (1975) 'Ghosts in the nursery. A psychoanalytic approach to the problems of impaired infant-mother relationships'. *Journal of the American Academy of Child & Adolescent Psychiatry 14,* 3, 387–421.

Kaplan, F.F. (2000). *Art, science, and art therapy: Repainting the picture.* Philadelphia, PA: Jessica Kingsley

Muijen, H., and Marissing, L., 2011. *'Iets' maken.* (making 'something'). Antwerpen: Garant.

National Institute for Health and Clinical Excellence (NICE). 77. March 2013 *Antisocial Personality Disorder: the NICE guideline on treatment, management, and prevention.* Great Britain: The British Psychological Society and The Royal College of Psychiatrists.

Odgen,, P., Minton, K., Pain, C., 2006. *Trauma and the body. A sensorimotor approach to psychotherapy*. New York: W.W. Norton & Company, Inc.

Rutten-Saris, M., 2002. *The RS-index: a diagnostic instrument for the assessment of interaction structures in drawings*. PhD dissertation. Publication University of Hertfordshire

Smeijsters, H. (ed.), 2005. *Praktijkonderzoek in vaktherapie*. Bussum: Couthino.

Smeijsters, H., 2007. *Agressieregulatie in de forensische psychiatrie*. Heerlen: KenVak

Smeijsters, H. (2008). *Handboek Creatieve Therapie*. Bussum. Couthino.

Smeijsters, H. & Cleven, G (2006). The treatment of aggression by means of arts therapies in forensic psychiatry. Results of a qualitative inquiry. *The Arts in Psychotherapy*. 33 (1), 37-38

Stern, D., 1985. *The interpersonal world of the infant*. NY: Basic Books.

Stern, D.N. (2004). *The present moment in psychotherapy and everyday life*. New York: W.W. Norton.

Visser, K., 2000. *Handboek basaal beeldend handelen*. Amsterdam: Thela/thesis.

Winnicott, D., 1971. *Playing and reality*. London: Tavistock Publications.

INDEX

Illustrations are noted by the prefix 'fig' alongside the page number. References to the bibliography are highlighted with the suffix 'bib'.